delectable harmony aromatic pungent flavoured spicy tasty orgasmic mouthwatering

palatable tempting appetising arousing condiment bite kick spiced rich strong evocative

complex gutsy full-bodied mellow savoury seasoned herby fragrant redolent refreshing

scented perfumed emotive sexy exciting stimulating intoxicating heady exhilarating

provocative piquant tantalising inspiring thrilling SPICE

S P I

CHRISTINE MANFIELD

PHOTOGRAPHY BY ASHLEY BARBER

VIKING

Excerpt from *The Mistress of Spices* by Chitra Banerjee Divakaruni reprinted with permission from Transworld Publishers Ltd

Viking
Penguin Books Australia Ltd
487 Maroondah Highway, PO Box 257
Ringwood, Victoria 3134, Australia
Penguin Books Ltd
Harmondsworth, Middlesex, England
Penguin Putnam Inc.
375 Hudson Street, New York, New York 10014, USA
Penguin Books Canada Limited
10 Alcorn Avenue, Toronto, Ontario, Canada M4V 3B2
Penguin Books (N.Z.) Ltd
Cnr Rosedale and Airborne Roads, Albany, Auckland
New Zealand
Penguin Books (South Africa) (Pty) Ltd
4 Pallinghurst Road, Parktown 2193, South Africa

First published by Penguin Books Australia Ltd 1999

10 9 8 7 6 5 4 3 2 1

Designed by Guy Mirabella
Photography by Ashley Barber
Glass plate on front cover handmade by Peter Crisp and supplied by The Bay Tree, Woollahra
New South Wales

Typeset in Times by Post Pre-press Group, Brisbane
Produced by the australian book connection

National Library of Australia
Cataloguing-in-Publication data:

Manfield, Christine.

  Spice.

  Bibliography.
  Includes index.
  0 670 87085 4.

  1. Cookery (Spices). I. Barber, Ashley. II. Title.

641.3383

Photographs

In addition to the photographs of dishes facing their relevant recipes throughout, the following photographs have been included in the book.

front cover   Salt-and-pepper Oyster Fritters with Shaved Fennel and Blackbean Dressing (recipe on page 141)
back cover   Chicken Laksa (recipe on page 104)
pages vi–vii   top: Chilli Jam (recipe on page 58); bottom: Harissa (recipe on page 58)
pages xiv–1   Bengali Panch Phoron (recipe on page 36)
page 5   ingredients for Paramount Laksa Paste (recipe on page 43)
page 9   Tandoori Masala (recipe on page 37)
pages 12–13   clockwise from top left: allspice, cardamom pods, cubeb, star anise
page 23   clockwise from top left: cloves, coriander seeds, amchoor powder, cardamom pods, dried Kashmiri chillies, ground turmeric, cinnamon sticks (centre)
pages 30–1   top: Green Masala Paste (recipe on page 41); bottom: Lemongrass Stir-fry Paste (recipe on page 44)
pages 48–9   assorted chilli oils (recipes on page 61)
page 63   Star Anise Broth (recipe on page 65)
pages 70–1   clockwise from top left: Hot Mango Chutney (recipe on page 55), Eggplant Pickle (recipe on page 52), Date and Lime Pickle (recipe on page 52), Spiced Tomato Chilli Pickle (recipe on page 52), Green Mango Pickle (recipe on page 53), Coriander Yoghurt Sauce (recipe on page 67)
page 94   galangal
page 112   right: fenugreek; left: black peppercorns
page 144   liquorice root
page 170   ñoras chillies (large version of Mexican cascabel chillies)
page 190   turmeric
page 208   cloves
page 242   left: mace; right: nutmeg
page 264   cinnamon sticks
page 282   vanilla beans
pages 334–5   fennel seeds in suribashi bowl

Countless thanks to Apicius and all those who followed him, for their writing, wisdom, shared knowledge and passion for spiced foods. And to the traders for opening up the world, and in doing so, opening our every sense to the pleasure of spices.

CONTENTS

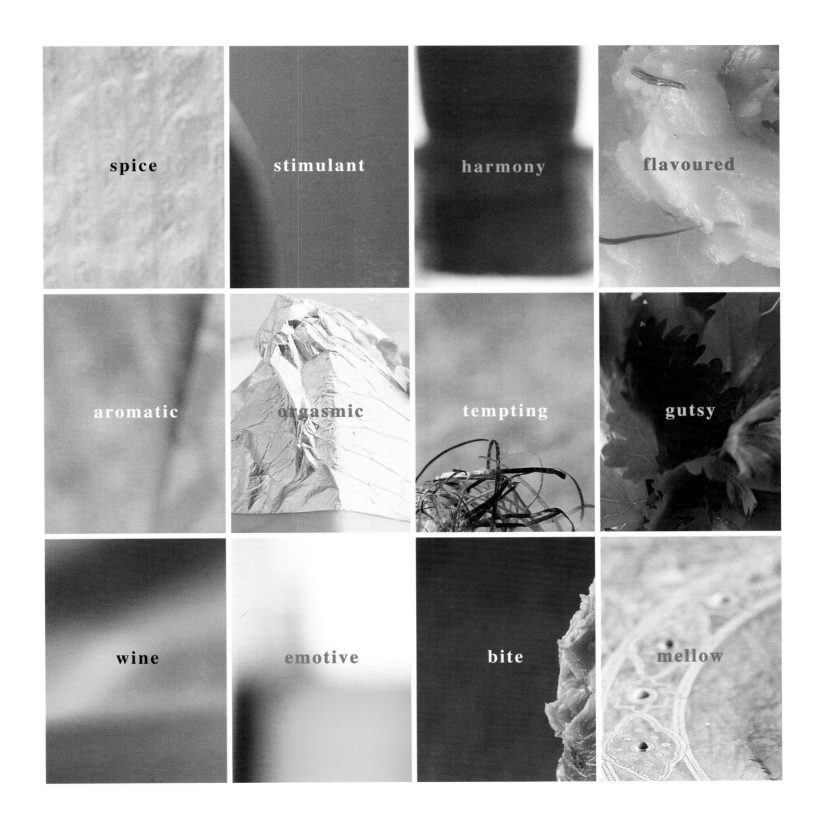

ACKNOWLEDGEMENTS

Spice is a compilation arising out of years of cooking, eating, reading and travelling. It is a statement of obsession with the food world. It celebrates the pleasures of taste, smell, touch and feeling, sight and hearing – all responsible for the seduction of the palate.

My passion is shared by:

✳ Margie Harris, my partner in life and work, who endured many long, solitary moments while I abandoned life's pleasures to write maniacally – without her support and care, such achievement would not be possible

✳ the entire dedicated team at Paramount

✳ Julie Gibbs, my publisher, who gently but persuasively forces me to reach for the sky – and then some

✳ photographer Ashley Barber, who has once again captured the very essence of my work through his lens

✳ Guy Mirabella, who is responsible for another stunningly original book design

✳ editors Caroline Pizzey and Katie Purvis, both of whom kept me honest and accountable.

Once again, this dedicated team has collaborated to understand the integrity and energy that drives me and to produce this outstanding work. Together, we believe the philosophy that life is too short to eat bad food – an ongoing mantra.

At Paramount we take great pride in our wine list, our collective wine knowledge and our enthusiasm for the matching of food and wine. It is an integral part of our focus and operation. Margie Harris and Paramount's wine man, Nigel Nickless, are responsible for purchasing and cellaring the wines we use at the restaurant and for putting together the constantly changing and evolving wine list. With every new menu we work together to taste the food and wine to get the right chemistry, and find the right balance, the perfect partnership. Without Margie and Nigel's formidable knowledge, and in particular Nigel's many hours spent poring over the 'Wine and Spice' chapter with me, finding the right words and making the challenging world of wine approachable and inviting, this invaluable part of the spice story would have remained untold.

My appreciation also goes to Ian and Liz Hemphill of Herbie's Spices for allowing me to use their beautiful spice box, which appears in the opening pages. It is like a magical chest, full of secret treasures.

Thanks to Con Nemitsas from Demcos Seafoods for providing helpful information on the possibilities for the fish recipes.

Special thanks to Alison Morath for discovering some special plates and silks for the glorious photographs. The following suppliers were generous in lending their wares for the photographs:

Accoutrement (Mosman, NSW) – small bowl (in foreground) on pages 70–1; small dipping bowl on page 124; hexagonal plate on page 197

The Bay Tree (Woollahra, NSW) – handmade glass plate, 'Ottoman' pattern, by Peter Crisp, on page 140

Country Road Homewares – plate on page 187

The Essential Ingredient (Camperdown, NSW) – dish on page 94; double square dipping bowl on page 112; dish on page 170

Inne (Woollahra, NSW) – 'Arabia' bowls on pages 129, 222 and 226; 'Arabia' plates on pages 153, 163, 201 and 234

Inyaka (Paddington, NSW) – wooden spoon on page 1

Made in Japan (Paddington, NSW) – green bowls on pages 70–1

Orson & Blake Collectables (Woollahra, NSW) – bowls on pages 108 and 117; plates on pages 75, 132 and 290; square plate on page 124

Papaya Studios (Double Bay, NSW) – coconut wood dishes on page 242; plate on page 282

Ruby Star Traders (Glebe, NSW) – marble bowls on page 5; napkins on page 290; tablecloth on page 297

I am a Mistress of Spices.

I can work the others too. Mineral, metal, earth and sand and stone. The gems with their cold clear light. The liquids that burn their hues into your eyes till you see nothing else. I learned them all on the island.

But the spices are my love.

I know their origins, and what their colours signify, and their smells. I can call each by the true-name it was given at the first, when earth split like skin and offered it up to the sky. Their heat runs in my blood. From *amchur* to *zafran*, they bow to my command. At a whisper they yield up to me their hidden properties, their magic powers.

Chitra Banerjee Divakaruni, *The Mistress of Spices*

INTRODUCTION

THE SENSUAL WORLD OF SPICES

I like food that enlivens the palate, that speaks of strength of flavour, of refined textures, of seductive and sensuous aromas that activate the tastebuds and tantalise the mind – essential food for body and soul. I believe that eating must be about enjoyment and health, and that gastronomic pleasure must be a part of everyday life. ❋ MY LOVE AFFAIR with all things edible began long before I started cooking professionally. Spices, herbs and aromatics have played a central role in that love affair, and have been an integral part of my everyday diet for many years. They determine what I like to eat, the sorts of flavours I seek in food and how I cook. ❋ FOR CENTURIES, spices have been used to flavour food and drinks. They have played a major role in food preparation and preservation, and their diversity and availability continue to make them an essential component of cooking practices. But spices, herbs and aromatics go beyond the pleasures of the palate. In early trade, spices often took the place of hard currency. They have played an important role in health, adding healing properties to medicines, and they have been used to give scent to perfumes. A study of Ayurvedic practices in India gives an understanding of how spices can work for the well-being of the body. Such beliefs and practices are becoming widely accepted in western society's search for a healthy diet and sense of wellness. SPICE IN AUSTRALIAN COOKING Food is synonymous with particular places, and certain foods cause immediate recognition of where they come from and how they determine social behaviour. When we think 'China', we might think 'dim sum'; similarly, we might think tandoori in India, bouillabaisse in France, cous cous in Morocco, a bowl of pho in Vietnam, a satay in Bali, tom yam in Thailand, sushi in Japan and pasta in Italy. Barbara Santich rightly claims in her book *Looking for Flavour* that a cuisine is an expression of the culture from which it comes: 'Cuisine is just as much a medium for expressing culture as is art, literature, newspapers, television, architecture or urban design'. In suggesting an Australian cultural language as determined by food, she uses the example of standing at a roadside cart eating a meat pie – an instantly recognisable feature of what we represent, as much as we might dislike or want to change it! Although I sympathise with and understand the example that Barbara uses, I am optimistic enough to think that this symbolism may change in the future. Food and culture reflect our quality of life to the point where, as Waverley Root suggests, 'every country possesses, it seems, the sort of cuisine it deserves, which is to say the sort of cuisine it is appreciative enough to want'. I like to think that current food practices in Australia are symbolic of what we have come to represent as a society – that our expanding culinary horizon reveals an intelligent understanding and appreciation of diversity. ❊

UNTIL RECENT TIMES, Australian cooking in general has had very little to do with spice. In the formative years of white settlement in this country, diet and eating habits were entirely inappropriate to resources, climate and lifestyle. Our forebears preached austerity, blandness and economical practicality at the expense of indulgence and taste. Reference books and cooking manuals used in Australia in the latter part of the nineteenth century and early twentieth century reveal that household storerooms stocked what we would call today a 'basic spice collection' – a mere twelve or so spices, among them nutmeg, cinnamon, caraway and black pepper. In contrast, the array we can now access and utilise is dazzling, an encouraging sign of gastronomic and epicurean maturity and confidence. ❊ MANY FINE CHEFS, cooks and writers in this country have made major contributions over the past couple of decades to changing the perception of Australian cuisine as just prawns on the barbie and meat pies. Thanks to them, as we move into the new millennium we are armed with a better, more exciting and more powerful culinary language than we have had in the past. I fully embrace the changing face of Australia and the radical, positive effect our immigration policies have had on our eating habits, our access to produce and everything that makes up and defines our food culture. We have adopted foodstuffs and methods previously deemed 'foreign' and adapted them to make them our own, integrated them into our cooking repertoire and made them part of our everyday lives. We have been exposed to the authenticity of many different cultural groups, where traditional practices and cooking methods have remained intact and given us the opportunity to educate, broaden and excite our palates. AN OBSESSION WITH SPICE From a personal viewpoint, travel has been a prime motivating force behind my interest in the world of food and wine. Travel allows and, sometimes, forces me to experience many things of a different nature, giving me a broader perspective and opening my mind to new interpretations. I maintain a keen curiosity about everything around me and find it challenging, not intimidating, to be surrounded by foreign languages, tastes, aromas, architecture and customs. They are invigorating and exciting, and can give added strength and valuable meaning to my own beliefs and practices. ✳ I HAVE a deep-seated fascination, passion and affinity for the spice world and its pervasive qualities. It permeates every aspect of my life and work. Personal taste has led me to exercise creative ingenuity, to be an artist of the palate. The foundation of my cooking is the use of spices and associated flavourings. Used with a deft hand, spices can be a statement of subtlety or one of complexity. ✳ I WILL ALWAYS remember the wise words of well-known Indian food writer and film star Madhur Jaffrey, who said that our palate

consists of two parts: taste and memory. When we taste something, it is important to remember it to develop a palate, an understanding and a feel for what we eat. Our palate is a store of taste experiences and we are continually building and strengthening our repertoire. ❋ S P I C E S R E V E A L the sensuality of food and, when used properly, create an intensity, harmony and complexity in food that cannot be found with any other combination of ingredients. Learning about the specifics of spices and food is like learning a new language: the more you practise and understand, the better your skills become. It is the knowledge of how to use spices and aromatics to unlock the secrets of their rich flavours and aromas that I dwell on and share in this book. ❋ T H E R E C I P E S I N T H I S C O L L E C T I O N generally serve six, but sometimes you may come across recipes that yield more (or less), depending on the appetites of those at the table. Do not worry! I tend to err on the side of generosity. The extra can always be used later to cover your tracks if something goes wrong or can be incorporated into another dish. As you become more comfortable with the recipes, you will find it easy to adjust and amend where you feel it is necessary. Madhur Jaffrey suggests that 'you start off with buying specific spices you need to cook a selected dish and then slowly increase your spice "wardrobe". It is a bit like being a painter, I suppose. If you have a palette glowing with magenta and cobalt blue and sap green and vermilion, it will give you the confidence – and the choice – to do anything you want. You could use one colour, if you desired, or ten. It is the same with spices.' ❋ *S P I C E* I S A P E R S O N A L odyssey of the discovery of flavour, of the seduction of the senses, of my quest for gastronomic information and subliminal pleasure and of my romance with the ingredients and tastes of foreign lands. This is what drives my work and gives me focus, tests my ambition and occupies my leisure time. In short, it is a total obsession!

THE ESSENTIAL SPICE CUPBOARD

For spices to achieve their full potential in cooking, it is of paramount importance to be aware of the practicalities of their proper management and use. Your first tentative steps into the wonderful, seductive world of spice will involve becoming familiar with specifics of taste and smell and how each spice variety works in the alchemy and art of cooking. This familiarisation is not difficult, nor is it a test. It is best approached with a passionate heart and an inquiring mind. Discover the unlimited and exciting world that awaits your palate – learn what spices are and where they come from, how to store them to their best advantage, how to deal with them, the specific techniques involved in their preparation and the sort of equipment you need to have on hand.

THE ELEMENTS OF SPICE Spices are best described as the dried parts of aromatic plants whose qualities are perceived through our sense of smell and taste. They have been used throughout history for their flavouring and medicinal properties. Spices have a profound effect on health, affecting many functional processes in the body. Because they act as anti-oxidants, they are essential in the preservation of food. ❋ SPICES AND AROMATICS fall into specific groups, consisting of ❋ flowers – capers, cloves ❋ berries – allspice, cubeb, juniper, pepper, sansho pepper, Sichuan pepper, sumac ❋ seeds – ajwain, anise, annatto, basil, caraway, celery, coriander, cumin, dill, fennel, fenugreek, grains of paradise, long pepper, lotus, mustard, nigella, papaya, pomegranate, poppyseeds, sesame ❋ fruits – amchoor powder, barberries, black dates, cardamom, cayenne pepper, chillies, dried citrus peel, kokum, paprika, pepperberries, star anise, tamarind, vanilla beans ❋ kernels – mahleb, nutmeg ❋ roots – horseradish, liquorice, wasabi ❋ rhizomes – galangal, ginger, turmeric, zedoary ❋ leaves – bay, coriander, curry, kaffir lime, lemon verbena, lemongrass, salam ✳ arils – mace, saffron ✳ bark – cinnamon, cassia ✳ sap – asafoetida, mastic.

Flavoursome and arousing, spices are addictive – and your best friend in the pantry!

HOW TO LOOK AFTER SPICES Whole spices retain their aroma and potency much longer than ground spices, so it is advisable to purchase them whole. Ground powders often give no indication of age or taste until it is too late. If a spice smells faint or musty, discard it immediately and buy a fresh amount, otherwise you will end up with a dusty, weak taste in your cooking. Purchase spices in small quantities for freshness and replace them as you use them. ✳

ALL SPICES ARE more aromatic when crushed or ground. To capture their fragrance and full flavour, it is best to crush or grind them as you need to use them. You can grind spices by hand with a mortar and pestle, or use an electric spice mill. A small electric coffee grinder is also useful, but make sure you use it for spices only – keep a separate grinder for coffee. ✳ WHEN MAKING PASTES where spices and aromatics are blended together, use a food processor or an electric blender. Of course, if you want to take the more traditional or 'primitive' approach (for good muscle development!), you can persevere with a pestle and mortar. ✳ WHEN BLENDING SPICES, it is extremely important that all the spices combine harmoniously without one overshadowing another. The blend should give a fullness of palate when tasted. Some spices are extremely pungent and overpowering, and should be used with caution so as not to upset the delicate balance created with blending. Learn to detect the specific qualities and characteristics of the spices you choose to flavour your food. ✳ SPICES CAN BE difficult to digest in raw form, which is why they are often dry-roasted, fried or cooked before eating. To maximise flavour, spices need to be either incorporated into the cooking of a dish or, if added at the end or to an uncooked dish, dry-roasted.

Dry-roasting is the practice whereby spices are placed in a wide, heavy-based pan over extremely gentle heat and roasted until they begin to change colour and smell fragrant. If you have the heat too high or try to roast the spices too quickly, they will burn on the outside, giving a bitter, nasty taste. Shake the pan frequently to ensure even roasting. Cool the spices before you grind them so that their essential oils aren't left stuck to the mortar or spice mill: you don't want to miss out on that flavour! SPICE EQUIPMENT Small glass, plastic or tin airtight containers are the best places to store your spices. Keep them in a dark, cool place, well away from any light, heat or moisture. This will prevent discoloration and bleaching, which reduce the flavour and aroma. Label and date each container and discard any old or stale spices. A spice box with a tight-fitting lid is a most useful addition to kitchen equipment, which you can also carry with you quite easily if need be. ❋ FOR GRINDING SPICES, you can use an electric spice or coffee grinder for easy convenience. It is always advisable to have a pestle and mortar on hand as well, especially for cracking open cardamom pods and the like. Grinding spices by hand is a therapeutic and rewarding exercise, if you have the time and desire to practise it. There are many different types of equipment available, including the rough granite bowls of Thailand and Malaysia, the smoother stone plates and grinding stones of India and the ceramic and marble ones of Europe, and the Japanese suribashi, a ceramic bowl with deep ridges in its sides which prevent the ingredients slopping around during grinding. It is up to you to decide which you prefer to use – just make sure you buy one that gives you room for generous arm movements. It is quite difficult to grind successfully by hand in something the size of a cup!

SPICE SUPPLIERS There are many places to purchase spice supplies in Australia. However, none seem as evocative as those in Asia, India, Africa or the Middle East, with their piles of coloured wares inviting you to plunge into the sensuousness of it all. Many of the fine cloths made in these countries and worn as clothing echo the colours of spice, making the visual landscape even more spectacular. Nevertheless, we have some terrific suppliers in this country whose untiring efforts have enabled us to obtain those exotic tastes and fragrances. ❋ IT IS POSSIBLE to purchase just about every known spice in Australia, albeit in a hygienic package. When you go shopping for spices, search out those that are fresh, that haven't been sitting in a back storeroom for a long time. Look for a reputable retail shop with a high turnover that doesn't display dusty-looking packets of faded, nondescript goods. Wherever possible, try to smell the freshness, look for good colour, and ask as many questions as you need to, to find out how something unfamiliar can be used and to access as much information as you can to make you better equipped to handle your precious goods. Some spice shops and suppliers are listed on pages 349–50.

SPICE INDEX

THE FOLLOWING IS A GUIDE to the spices that are used throughout this book. Many of

those listed are available widely (from supermarkets, delicatessens and gourmet food stores, for

example), while for others you may have to seek out ethnic outlets (Indian, Middle Eastern or Asian

food stores). Specialist suppliers are becoming established in some areas (see page 349); these are

the most likely of all outlets to stock a wide range of spices, including the less-common ones.

Wherever you shop, make sure you choose somewhere with a high turnover to ensure freshness. ❊

YOU WILL NOTE that some words in this Spice Index are printed in SMALL CAPITALS. These

indicate other relevant entries in the section.

ajwain seeds

These tiny seeds are produced by a herb related to cumin, caraway, parsley and dill. They have a similar fragrance to CUMIN with a more intense and assertive flavour that resembles thyme with liquorice overtones. Used whole to flavour breads, lentils and pulses in northern Indian cooking, where it is also known as carom or bishop's weed, ajwain aids digestion and has antiseptic properties (it is used in poultices and the manufacturing of toothpaste). *Available*: Indian food stores.

allspice

Whole allspice are the dried, unripened berries of a large evergreen tree, a member of the myrtle family. The tree is indigenous to the West Indies, and allspice is produced mostly in Jamaica (Jamaican allspice is regarded as being of the highest quality of all). Dark reddish brown and pungently aromatic with a clove-like fragrance, allspice combines the characteristic flavours of cloves, nutmeg, pepper and cinnamon. It is used in preserving and pickling, in French and Caribbean cooking, in northern Indian curries and for making pot-pourri. Allspice is also highly regarded for the pervasive scent it gives to soap and perfumes and some alcoholic beverages. The whole berries can be ground in a pepper mill or an electric spice grinder. *Available*: widely.

amchoor powder

Green mangoes are sun-dried and then ground to make amchoor powder. This spice acts as a souring agent that gives balance and provides acidity without adding moisture. It is used extensively in Indian pickles and vegetable cooking. If added to hot oil at the beginning of the cooking process, amchoor powder gives a deeper taste; added at the end, a more subtle flavour results. *Available*: Indian food stores.

anise

In use in 1500 BC, anise is one of the oldest known spices. These oval, aromatic seeds (also known as aniseed) come from a herb closely related to CUMIN and FENNEL that is native to the Middle East and the eastern Mediterranean. The spice is popular in German, Italian, Portuguese and Indian cooking and has a bittersweet, strong fruity flavour with a hint of liquorice. The seeds are used whole in soups, stews and curries and are ground for use in cakes, biscuits and sweets. An oil extracted from the seeds is used to flavour liqueurs and medicines. Anise is also known for its digestive and diuretic powers. *Available*: gourmet food stores and specialist spice suppliers.

annatto seeds

The brick-red seeds and their pods of the small evergreen annatto tree, native to tropical South America, are ground to a paste or powder and used as a dye and for colouring food without adding any discernible flavour (notably butter, margarine, Cheshire cheese and smoked fish). The seeds have a faint peppery, nutmeg flavour and are used as a spice in Latin American and Caribbean cooking; they were introduced to the Philippines by the Spanish, where they are used extensively to colour and flavour noodle dishes, meat stews and curries. *Available*: specialist spice suppliers.

asafoetida

Made from the resinous sap of a large fennel-like plant that grows in Iran, Afghanistan and the northern Indian state of Kashmir, asafoetida is sold in either powder form or as a resin that is ground as required. It has a characteristic pungent, sulphuric smell and an unappealing taste when raw, and is used as a flavour enhancer, predominantly to counterbalance acidity in Indian cooking. Asafoetida has been known since 4 BC, when it appeared in Ancient Roman cooking, and was an essential component of Persian food; it was introduced to India in the Mughal empire. Asafoetida is also used to counter flatulence and for respiratory problems. *Available*: Indian food stores.

barberry

The barberry is the red and sour fruit of a prickly bush that grows throughout Europe and Asia. Too acidic and not sweet enough to be eaten raw, it is cooked into rice, stews, syrups and preserves to give a refreshing tartness, particularly in Iran and Iraq, where it is known as 'zereshk'. The berries are also used in jams, preserves and candied foods, and are particularly good with quinces. The barberry bush used to be a common sight in England, from medieval times through to early this century when it was realised that it harboured wheat-mildew parasites. *Available*: Middle Eastern food stores.

basil seeds

The tiny black seeds from the herbaceous lemon basil plant (known as 'manglak' in Thailand) are used primarily in Asian sweet drinks and desserts as they have a cooling effect on the body and aid digestion. They are also often served with young, green coconut flesh. The seeds are odourless with an oily, slightly pungent flavour. They are usually soaked in water for 15 minutes before use, during which time they develop a gelatinous coating. *Available*: Asian food stores.

bay leaf

The aromatic, green elongated bay leaf comes from the evergreen sweet bay tree native to the Mediterranean. Used since Roman times, when it symbolised victory and greatness and was used to crown emperors, poets and writers, the bay leaf is a compulsory ingredient in all European and Mediterranean cooking for flavouring stocks, sauces, soups, pickles, preserves, meats and vegetables. It is also an essential part of a bouquet garni, the classic herb combination of bay leaf, thyme and parsley. Bay leaves should be used sparingly to avoid bitterness and should be removed before serving. Prefer fresh bay leaves to dried – once dried, they lose their colour, fragrance and flavour. Bay leaves are also regarded as an appetite stimulant with digestive qualities. *Available*: widely.

betel nut

Betel nuts, which grow in clusters at the top of tall, slender areca palms that are native to Malaysia, are harvested either when they are green and tender or when they ripen and become orange. Both types are sun-dried and then husked before use. In India the tender nuts are mixed with spices and sugar to aid digestion and act as a mouth freshener. Cracked, ripe betel nuts can be used in marinades to tenderise meat

as they help break down sinew and muscle tissue in tougher cuts. Chewed in quantities for its stimulating powers, the ripe betel nut is also known to produce a mild state of euphoria and for its aphrodisiac properties. It is used in some Chinese medicinal preparations because of this, and as an antidote to malaria and for expelling intestinal worms. Green betel leaves, eaten raw and used as a wrapping for food in India and Thailand particularly, are not from the same palm as the nut, but from a plant closely related to PEPPER. *Available*: Indian and Asian food stores.

black bean

The process of drying black soy beans and then fermenting them with salt was discovered in China some 2500 years ago. Black beans taste very pungent and salty and are used with garlic and often chilli to flavour meat and to subdue fishy flavours in Chinese cooking. Available in dried form or canned in brine, dried black beans must be soaked in cold water for 30 minutes before use to remove the excess salt; canned black beans need only be rinsed lightly under running cold water for a few minutes. *Available*: Asian food stores.

black date

The reddish 'dates' from the Chinese jujube tree are dried and then smoked until they are black and wrinkled. About the size of an olive, the black date has a pungent, slightly smoky, sweet flavour not dissimilar to that of a truffle. Used in Chinese cooking, black dates are used in savoury dishes that may include sticky rice, smoked sausage, lotus leaves or poultry. The stone must be removed before use.

Black dates should not be confused with red dates, which are not smoked and are used in sweet rather than savoury preparations. *Available*: Asian food stores.

black salt

Used in northern Indian cooking, particularly in the snacks, beverages and salads sold from street carts and stalls, black salt is sold in crystal or powder form, has a very mild but interesting flavour and smells more pungent than it tastes. It is not a SEA SALT, but rather is mined in quarries found on the fertile plains of central India. Sometimes sold as rock salt, the amber to dark-brown crystals become a smoky grey when ground. Black salt contains no sodium, so has no effect on blood pressure and is in fact considered an antidote to dehydration (it is even mixed into lemonade to counter the effect of the heat). *Available*: Indian food stores.

caper

The caper is the unopened flower-bud of the caper bush, a trailing shrub native to the warm, dry Mediterranean region. The flower-buds are picked by hand and then salted and/or pickled in brine or vinegar and used as a condiment. (I prefer the small salted capers as they are more flavoursome and less acidic than those in brine or vinegar.) While the tiny capers from the south of France are good, those from the Eolian Islands off Sicily are considered the finest in texture and flavour. Capers are used predominantly in western European cooking (particularly that of the Mediterranean) to provide piquancy in sauces and condiments, and to give a lift to bland food. Capers should be rinsed thoroughly in cold water before use to remove excess salt. *Available*: widely (particularly gourmet food stores).

caraway seeds

Although the Netherlands is the largest producer of caraway seeds in the world, the caraway plant, a member of the parsley family, is a native of Asia. The firm, brown seeds are similar in appearance to and often confused with CUMIN SEEDS. They have an astringent character with a warm, nutty flavour that has a hint of liquorice and have been used since medieval times to flavour vegetable and meat dishes, breads, cheese and cakes. Caraway seeds are popular in German, Indian and Jewish cooking, and are used to flavour kümmel, a German liqueur. The ancient Egyptians, Greeks and Romans used caraway seeds in love potions; they are also regarded as a spring cleaner for the body as they relieve flatulence, reduce nausea and activate the kidneys! *Available*: widely.

cardamom

The small green pods of the cardamom plant, a member of the GINGER family, house fragrant, sticky black seeds. The crushed seeds release a strong camphor-like aroma, are sweet on the palate and have a cooling effect on the body. Once ground, cardamom quickly loses its essential oils and flavour. For this reason, and because it is one of the most expensive spices, always purchase plump green pods that are closed, look fresh and are even in colour, then remove and crush the seeds as you require them. As cardamom pods age, the green fades to a pale khaki. Some producers also bleach the pods for aesthetic reasons and sell them as white cardamom. If you come across a recipe that calls for this, prefer the premium green pods where the seeds are at their best.

Black cardamom, sometimes referred to as 'greater' or 'brown' cardamom in Indian texts, has a larger pod and coarser seeds that have a more antiseptic flavour than those of green cardamom. Used only in savoury cooking, the seeds act as a tenderiser in meat marinades when lightly crushed and are also used in some garam masala mixes (see page 34) and to flavour rice biryanis.

It is generally regarded that the best green cardamom in the world is grown on the Malabar Coast in the south-western Indian state of Kerala. In fact, the Western Ghats, the dominant range, are referred to as the cardamom mountains. The spice is used extensively in India, Germany and Scandinavia, and also appears in the desserts of many countries, including Spain, Africa, Portugal, Holland, Britain, France, South-East Asia and India. Cardamom is also used as a digestive, a breath freshener and for the relief of stomach disorders and heartburn. *Available*: widely (Indian food stores, in particular).

cassia

The Indian name for the outer bark of the cassia tree is 'dalchini' or 'wood of China'. In fact, although cultivated in China and used in its cooking since 200 BC, cassia is from a camphor laurel native to Assam in north-eastern India and to Burma. Cassia appears most commonly in Chinese, Vietnamese and Indian savoury cooking. It is used in a similar fashion to CINNAMON, to which it is related, and is often confusingly referred to as Chinese cinnamon. Much harder and coarser than cinnamon, however, cassia has a more pronounced pungency and an intriguing but less-delicate flavour. It is an essential flavouring in many Chinese preparations, such as Chinese Five-spice Powder (see page 39), red-braising stocks (page 339) and tea-smoking. If a recipe asks for ground cassia, make an exception to the rule and purchase a small quantity of the spice already ground as the toughness of the bark will destroy any domestic grinding machine. The leaves of the cassia tree are also used in Indian cooking to flavour curries, rice and lentils in the same way a BAY LEAF is used in European dishes. *Available*: Asian food stores (look for dried cassia leaves in Indian food stores).

cayenne pepper

The capital of French Guiana on Cayenne Island gives its name to the spice that originated there. Usually sold in powdered form, cayenne pepper is the ground dried cayenne, arbol or guajillo CHILLI, which are all South American varieties. The cayenne chilli, which tastes acidic and tart, is closely related to the Asian bird's-eye chilli and has the same level of intense heat. A familiar ingredient in South American, Caribbean and some European cooking, cayenne pepper is used in curries, cheese dishes, and white sauces that include smoked fish, oysters and prawns. *Available*: widely.

celery seeds

These tiny, light-as-a-feather brown seeds are produced from the celery plant the season after the vegetable has been harvested. They have a strong, bitter flavour and are used predominantly in pickling and in the cooking of Russia and Scandinavia, where they are added to soups, vegetables, sauces and dressings for their warm and tangy flavour. In India, where it is believed that celery seeds are a tonic for asthma and rheumatism, the seeds are added to tomato-based curries. Wild celery, which is the precursor to the cultivated variety we know today, is native to Europe and Asia. *Available*: widely.

chilli

In her *History of Food*, Maguelonne Toussaint-Samat writes: 'the last spice to be revealed to the world at large, chilli has in a way become the superlative among spices'. Native to South America, the chilli was introduced to the western world by Christopher Colombus, who first mentioned it in his journal on 15 January 1493. It was introduced to Africa, Arabia and Asia by Spanish and Portuguese traders, and in less than two centuries it was in use worldwide.

Today the chilli is the world's most cultivated spice crop. The many varieties – at least 200 have been identified – range widely in size, shape and heat factor, and all are good sources of vitamins A and C. Part of the capsicum family, chillies are grown in all equatorial countries. They are essential to the cooking of South America, India, Africa, Mexico, Thailand and China, as well as all the countries of the South-East Asian region (including Australia), and make intermittent and modest appearances in most cuisines of western Europe and the Middle East.

The heat of the chilli, caused by the presence of the chemical capsaicin, has the effect of stimulating the palate and increasing blood circulation. This causes the body to sweat, which in turn has a cooling effect – this is why chillies are so dominant in tropical regions. The flavour and heat of chillies are quite addictive as endorphins are released to deal with the heat, and in time the regular chilli consumer needs a bigger dose than someone with an uninitiated palate.

The use of chillies in cooking should result in a delicate balance of heat, fragrance and flavour, the latter points often being overlooked. Selecting the appropriate chilli for a particular purpose is of gastronomic importance, regardless of region. Chillies work to stimulate the appetite by increasing the flow of saliva and gastric secretions, aiding digestion. And they provide flavour: they can be mild, smoky, bitter, nutty or intense and can add liquorice, citrus, tropical, toasty, sweet fruit or berry notes.

Green chillies, the unripe fruit, ripen to red, orange, yellow or purple. Green chillies are used for their colour, immature acidity and raw flavour. All chillies turn red when dried. It is probably safe to advise that the smaller the chilli, the hotter it will be. The seeds and membranes contain the most heat and some cooks prefer to remove these before cooking. The option is purely personal.

Asian chillies have been available in Australia for a long time now, and some of our better suppliers have been offering fresh Mexican varieties recently. Among the chillies available here is the small Thai bird's-eye chilli (red or green), which has a clean flavour and intense heat similar to that of the Mexican serrano. The slightly larger and fatter red Lombok chilli can be compared to the powerful red or yellow Tabasco chilli, while the larger and longer, red or green Chinese chilli is most like the milder, sweeter red Kashmiri, Dutch or New Mexican varieties. The squat Mexican habanero and African Scotch bonnet are considered the hottest chillies of all and have fruity overtones and thin skins and flesh. The closest Asian equivalent is a tiny version of the bird's-eye, dubbed the 'scud' by Darley Street Thai's David Thompson. But these are just a few of the varieties available, and space precludes me exploring the subject further. So much has been written about the chilli (I have several books devoted to just one variety) that I suggest you turn to the experts. For detailed information about Mexican and American varieties refer to Mark Miller's *The Great Chile Book*; to learn about the more commonly available Asian chillies, turn to Charmaine Solomon's *Encyclopedia of Asian Food*.

When buying fresh chillies, be sure that the skin is firm and crisp. Dried chillies are used when specific results are required as drying intensifies the flavours of the fresh chilli. Look for dried chillies that are of a good and even colour and that are not broken. Many other chilli products are available too – powdered or ground chilli, flaked chilli, and chilli pastes, oils and sauces. *Available*: fresh and dried Asian chillies can be found in good greengrocers, Asian food stores and most supermarkets; fresh and dried Mexican chillies are becoming increasingly available from good greengrocers, specialist spice suppliers, Spanish food stores and some supermarkets; chilli preparations – pastes, sauces and so on – can be found in Asian food stores and many supermarkets.

cinnamon

Cinnamon is the soft inner bark of the cinnamon tree, a camphor laurel indigenous to Sri Lanka. As the bark dries and contracts, it is rolled into tight quills and has an aroma reminiscent of a tropical jungle, with a warm, sweet and intense flavour. Sold as cinnamon sticks, the quills are relatively soft so are easy to grind. Powdered or ground cinnamon may be convenient but becomes stale quickly, losing its flavour. Whole cinnamon sticks should be removed from a dish and discarded after cooking. Incorporated into many cuisines, cinnamon is particularly favoured in the cooking of Morocco, India, Iran and Malaysia, where it is used in curries, desserts, rice and meat dishes. It is also an essential component in garam masala (see page 34) and the Indian tea, masala chai. Cinnamon should not be confused with CASSIA. *Available*: widely.

clove

One of the most prized and ancient spices of the Orient, the clove – the dried flower-bud of a member of the myrtle family – is considered the most fragrant of all. Cloves, indigenous to the Moluccas, are now produced commercially in Zanzibar, the West Indies and Madagascar. They have a powerful, intoxicating flavour that is slightly astringent and sweetly pungent. Cloves are used extensively in many cuisines for pickling and are also an essential ingredient in many spice mixtures, such as garam masala (see page 34), Quatre Épices (page 38) and Chinese Five-spice Powder (page 39). They should be used sparingly and whole cloves should be discarded after cooking. Cloves also contain an essential oil that is used in perfume, dental products, Indonesian cigarettes and food preservation. They are also regarded as being a powerful antiseptic and preservative. *Available*: widely.

coriander seeds

The seeds of the coriander plant, native to the Mediterranean region and related to parsley and the carrot, are the spice and the leaves and roots are the herb, and each tastes and smells completely different from the other. Coriander seeds have a clean, orange flavour and a sweet, woody and peppery aroma that is greatly enhanced by dry-roasting and grinding. The lemon-scented leaves, which are often described as smelling like insects, lose their flavour with cooking so are best eaten fresh, although the root, used as an aromatic, enjoys longer cooking in Thai curries and the like. Ground coriander seeds are used in many countries – particularly in the Middle East, India and Malaysia – as a staple or foundation spice, and the whole seeds are a necessary ingredient in pickling. One of the earliest known spices, coriander seeds have been used since Egyptian times in cooking and medicinally (for their digestive properties, primarily). The plant is referred to as Chinese parsley or cilantro in American texts. *Available*: widely.

cubeb

Slightly larger than a peppercorn and with a distinctive tail, the dried, dark-brown, unripe fruit of *Piper cubeba*, a climbing member of the PEPPER family, has a warm, aromatic and bitter taste that is probably closer to allspice than pepper. It is used in a similar way to pepper. A native of Java, cubeb was a popular flavouring in medieval Britain, is used in Indonesian cooking and is an essential component in the making of the North African spice mix Ras el Hanout (see page 37). Cubeb has long been used in Eastern medicine, where it is valued for treating respiratory complaints, cystitis and bronchitis and for its antiseptic properties. It is also regarded as a stimulant. Cubeb is often referred to as West African pepper in African texts. *Available*: specialist spice suppliers.

cumin seeds

Cumin, a member of the parsley family, is native to the southern Mediterranean region and has been known since ancient times and is mentioned in the Bible. The golden brown seeds are a staple in the spice world, particularly in India, Sri Lanka, Morocco, Tunisia, Lebanon, most Mediterranean countries, Indonesia, Malaysia and southern Thailand, and are essential in all Asian spice blends. Cumin seeds, which look similar to and are often confused with CARAWAY SEEDS, have a distinctive strong aroma and a slightly bittersweet, assertive and lingering warm, earthy flavour. Dry-roasting the seeds releases the flavour further. The seeds are used medicinally to treat biliousness, indigestion, colds and fever.

Black cumin seeds are slightly smaller and finer, dark-brown to black in colour and sweeter in flavour with no hint of bitterness. Used specifically in the cooking of Kashmir, Iran and Pakistan, black cumin is more expensive than regular cumin. Do not confuse NIGELLA, sometimes also called black cumin, with the true black cumin. *Available*: widely (look for black cumin in Indian food stores).

curry leaf

Murraya koenigii, a small, tropical shrub or tree native to India and Sri Lanka, provides the powerfully aromatic curry leaf, which is used with fervour in the cooking of those countries as well as that of Malaysia and Indonesia. Prefer the dark-green, long and slender fresh leaves to the dried leaves – the curry-like aroma and the pleasant, aromatic and yet slightly bitter flavour of the fresh leaf dissipates with drying. The plant grows quite successfully in gardens or pots in the warmer climates of Australia. In India curry leaves are used as a tonic and calmative, to aid digestion and to maintain eyesight, and, when crushed to a paste, to cure skin complaints and bites. *Available*: Asian food stores.

dill seeds

These small brown seeds are the dried fruit of the herb dill weed. They taste similar to the leaves but their liquorice flavour is more pungent. The seeds are used predominantly in pickling solutions, condiments and fish cookery, and initial dry-roasting brings out their flavour more fully. There are two varieties of dill seed – the European and the Indian, the latter being paler but longer and more slender. Although interchangeable, these varieties differ slightly in flavour: the warming, pungent European dill seeds resemble CARAWAY SEEDS; the Indian seeds are less sharp and cause a slight tingling on the tongue when eaten whole. A native of the eastern Mediterranean region and southern Russia, the plant and seeds were believed to have held magic powers during medieval times. *Available*: widely (look for Indian dill seeds in Indian food stores).

dried orange/mandarin/tangerine peel

Dried orange, mandarin or tangerine peel is used in many Chinese dishes – stocks, soups, sauces, congees and stir-fries – and especially those from the Sichuan and Hunan provinces. It adds a subtle citrus flavour that is more haunting and less obvious than that of the fresh zest, and the acidity of the peel cuts through the fat of pork or duck, with which it is sometimes cooked. The peel, often used in conjunction with STAR ANISE and SICHUAN PEPPER, needs to be reconstituted in warm water before use. *Available*: Asian food stores.

fennel seeds

Vibrant green in colour when fresh and drying to a dull greenish yellow–brown with age, fennel seeds have a warm, sweet and intense liquorice flavour that mellows with dry-roasting. They look similar to but are larger than CUMIN SEEDS. The fennel plant is indigenous to the Mediterranean region, where it grows wild, and the seeds are used extensively in Italian, Chinese, Middle Eastern and many Indian preparations, from pickles and chutneys to rich sauces, fish cooking, sausages and breads. The sweet character of the seeds also lends itself well to dessert cooking. Recorded in Greek mythology, fennel seeds have long been favoured for their medicinal properties, being reputed to aid digestion, menstruation, inflamed eyes, respiratory ailments and slimming. *Available*: widely.

fenugreek seeds

From the pods borne by a small perennial member of the pea family native to the eastern Mediterranean and in use since early Egyptian times, fenugreek seeds are small, smooth, hard and brownish yellow. The seeds have a pronounced aroma not dissimilar to curry or celery, and a lingering bitter and astringent flavour that mellows with dry-roasting. Used in many spice preparations – such as Indian masala pastes, sambars and condiments, and African Berbere (see page 37) – the seeds are often softened in vinegar before being added to other spices to make masala or curry. They are also used extensively in pickling solutions. The leaves of the plant are used as a vegetable in Indian cooking. Fenugreek seeds are eaten to relieve flatulence, diarrhoea, diabetes and high blood pressure; they are also reputed to promote lactation. *Available*: widely.

galangal

Two types of this rhizome, both members of the GINGER family, are available on the market and shouldn't be confused. Greater galangal, native to Java and Malaysia and resembling ginger in appearance, has pinkish red skin with creamy white flesh, a dense texture and a gingery lemon flavour. Lesser galangal, a smaller rhizome with a more pungent, peppery aroma and fibrous texture, originated in southern China and is used predominantly in that country for its medicinal properties. (Greater galangal is also used medicinally to cure nausea and stomach ailments and to fight bacteria.)

Greater galangal is valued as a seasoning in all South-East Asian cooking, particularly with fish and chicken, and is often pounded with other aromatics to make spice pastes – for example, Thai curry pastes (see pages 44 and 45), laksa pastes (pages 43 and 44) and other Nonya preparations, and Larp Paste (page 46).

Galangal is available fresh, dried (in slices, or ground and sold as laos powder) or as strips pickled in brine. Dried galangal needs to be soaked in water for 30 minutes before use. Prefer fresh galangal for improved flavour, unless otherwise instructed. *Available*: Asian food stores (look for fresh galangal in good greengrocers, too).

garlic

Although not a spice, garlic must be included here as its use with spices is mandatory and its flavour permeates the food of every country in the world. In particular, it is part of the holy trinity of flavours essential to Asian cooking: garlic, onion and ginger.

Garlic grows as a bulb or quorm of numerous cloves, each of which is encased in tissue-thin skin, which must be removed before use. Found in the tomb of Tutankhamun, garlic has been used since ancient times for its antibiotic powers and as a deterrent to cholesterol, as a blood purifier and as a digestive aid. Its strong and pervasive aroma diminishes with cooking, giving way to a gentler, sweet flavour. The flavour of the many garlic products available is inferior to that of fresh garlic, so it is compulsory for a good cook to chop, slice, crush and mince fresh cloves for the best results. *Available*: widely.

ginger

Ginger, thought to have originated in China or India, has a long culinary and medicinal history that dates back to the writings of the Chinese philosopher Confucius. By the thirteenth century it had

become the most commonly used spice in the world after pepper. Today ginger, a rhizome, is grown all over the world in suitably warm climates and is indispensable when cooking with spices. Fresh ginger has an unmistakable, pungent aroma, which is both sweet and woody, and a warm, penetrating flavour. Green or young ginger has smooth, papery skin that doesn't need peeling and soft, dense flesh that is very easy to cut and slice. Older ginger develops a more fibrous texture and the skin becomes thicker. Ginger can also be purchased in powdered form (good for cakes and confectionery work), preserved in syrup, candied, crystallised, dried in slices, or pickled. Ginger is highly regarded as a digestive aid, for improving blood circulation, as an antidote to gout and as a cure for travel sickness. *Available*: widely (look for young ginger in Asian food stores, in particular).

grains of paradise

Grains of paradise are the seeds of a reed-like herbaceous plant that is a member of the GINGER family and native to western Africa. These peppery, hot seeds resemble CARDAMOM seeds and make an appearance in the North African spice mix Ras el Hanout (see page 37), otherwise they remain exclusive to the cooking of western Africa, where they are highly prized and used to season meat and game and in herbal remedies. *Available*: specialist spice suppliers.

horseradish

A member of the MUSTARD family and native to eastern Europe, horseradish is prized for its large, white root that resem-

bles a small parsnip. When bought fresh (during the autumn and winter months), it needs to be peeled before being grated. It loses its pungency and freshness quickly once grated or minced, so only prepare the amount you need each time. Horseradish, used since classical times, is noted for its powerful aroma and biting, fiery flavour that instantly clear the sinuses. It is used to counter fatty foods and can be found in many European condiments, especially those of Russia, Germany and Scandinavia. Horseradish is also used in Jewish cooking. Creamed horseradish is widely available and can be used in place of freshly grated horseradish but it is milder and less sharp in flavour. *Available*: look for fresh horseradish in good greengrocers in the winter months.

juniper berry

A cypress native to the British Isles and commonly grown in northern Europe, the evergreen juniper tree produces small purplish blue berries that have a resinous flavour. Juniper berries are used quite specifically in the cuisine of northern Europe, in marinades and pâtés, with pork, game meats and poultry, and, notably, in German sauerkraut. But perhaps juniper berries are best known for the flavour and aroma they give to gin. To release their flavour, lightly crush juniper berries in a mortar and pestle or grind them in a mill. Juniper berries are believed to improve blood circulation. *Available*: widely.

kaffir lime

Native to South-East Asia, the kaffir lime tree produces distinctive double dark-green leaves and the fruit itself, both of which are used extensively in the cuisines of the region, in Thai cooking in particular. The limes give little juice – instead, their thick, lumpy rind is used for its clean, intense floral flavour and perfume, which cannot be replicated by any other ingredient. The zest of the lime is used in many preparations: it is added to curry pastes, Larp Paste (see page 46), Lemongrass Stir-fry Paste (page 44) and I add it to laksa pastes (pages 43 and 44). It is also an essential ingredient in Thai fish cakes. The leaves are extremely fragrant – but describing their perfume as being redolent of lemons and limes is as close as one can get. The leaves are added to soups whole or perhaps torn and are usually cut into very fine strips for adding to salads and curries. Fresh and frozen limes and fresh, frozen or dried leaves are available, but the frozen and dried options lack the tangy flavour of the fresh fruit and leaves. The rind of the kaffir lime is said to be good for the blood and the digestive system. *Available*: Asian food stores and some good greengrocers.

kokum

Kokum is the dried rind of the purple-fleshed fruit from the kokum tree, which is native to India, where it is used in the Gujarat, Maharashtra and Kerala regions on the west coast. Kokum is used as a flavouring for food and drinks – often in coconut-based sauces, with fish and in vegetable curries bound with a gram-flour (chickpea) sauce – and imparts a pinkish colouring to the food with which it is cooked. It is particularly known in the coconut curries of Kerala, where it is combined with potato, okra and lentils. Kokum is sour and acts as a cooling agent for the body. It needs to be rinsed, sliced and soaked in cold water before use. *Available*: Indian food stores.

lemongrass

Lemongrass is an important aromatic herb in the cooking of South-East Asia, and is easily grown in temperate zones, given enough water. In fact a tropical grass, it grows as a bushy clump of tightly furled, fibrous, tall stalks. The pale base of the stalk is used in various preparations – as an addition to curry pastes or for flavouring soups, for example – and the upper part (the 'leaves') makes a wonderfully refreshing tea. When fresh, lemongrass has a firm texture, a sour lemon fragrance and a clean citrus flavour. Lemongrass demands careful slicing with a sharp knife or cleaver. The dried variety is a poor substitute as it provides very little flavour. Lemongrass is used in Chinese medicine to cure coughs and colds. It also promotes good digestion and is valued as a diuretic, tonic and stimulant. Lemongrass encourages perspiration, which cools the body, and is valued as an essential oil because it improves circulation. *Available*: widely (from Asian food stores and good greengrocers, in particular).

lemon verbena

This fragrant, deciduous shrub, a native of Chile and only known to Europe since the late eighteenth century, enjoys prolific growth during late spring and summer in any sunny, warm climate. The long, slender green leaves have a potent lemon-like perfume and refreshing flavour and should be used sparingly. They are used predominantly in desserts but are also used to make a herbal tea or tisane that is said to aid digestion. As lemon verbena leaves are rarely seen for sale, the best option is to grow a plant yourself. The leaves can be dried and stored for use when the plant is out of season – use half the specified quantity when using dried lemon verbena. *Available*: fresh leaves are rare (plants are available from nurseries) and dried leaves can be found in health food stores.

liquorice root

The liquorice plant is a member of the pea family and native to the Middle East and south-west Asia. A concentrated extract made from the root is used as the well-known confectionery flavouring and in the making of the liquorice-flavoured sambuca, an Italian liqueur. In China the root is dried and sliced for culinary purposes – it becomes yellow in appearance and has a characteristic sweet liquorice smell. Liquorice has long been valued as a medicinal herb, particularly for its role in relieving constipation and as a Chinese or Indian treatment for gastric ulcers. Chewing on the root is also said to relieve a dry cough. *Available*: Asian food stores or Chinese herbalists.

long pepper

Indigenous to India, long pepper is related to the PEPPER plant but bears mild-flavoured, greyish black fruit about 2 cm long. It was traded as a valuable commodity and used as currency in Roman times long before the small, round black peppercorns were discovered. Long pepper is used whole as a pickling spice in South-East Asia and otherwise in Javanese and Indian cooking (where it is often combined with green chillies and garlic, or

with lentils). *Available*: rare (try specialist spice suppliers or Indian or Asian food stores).

lotus seeds

The lotus or water lily plant is indigenous to Asia – from Iran to China and Japan – and was introduced into Egypt and the Middle East in about 700 BC. The plant is very versatile: the roots are eaten as a vegetable and the leaves are used to wrap poultry or sticky rice. The small, creamy white and delicately flavoured seeds produced by the beautiful flower are commonly used in Chinese cooking, especially with duck and winter melon. The seeds are also cooked in oil in India in the same way that popcorn is, and in Vietnam they are used in sweet soups. Best purchased in their dried form and boiled until soft, lotus seeds give a gentle nutty flavour and texture to food. *Available*: Asian food stores.

mace

A large equatorial tree originating in the Moluccas produces an apricot-like fruit that in turn provides us with two spices – mace and NUTMEG. Mace is the aril or seed covering that encases the nutmeg seed inside the fruit. It looks like a red lacy glove, but the colour fades to a dusty orange–yellow when the aril is sun-dried after it has been removed from the nutmeg seed. Mace has a perfumed, sweet scent and a clean, bitter flavour, completely different from that of nutmeg. Mace is best purchased as whole arils (often referred to as blades) and ground as required as the flavour starts to diminish once the whole spice is ground. Mace is used in spice pastes and desserts in India, Malaysia and Indonesia. In French and European cooking it is used to flavour béchamel or onion sauces, cheese soufflés and cheesecakes. Long considered an aphrodisiac in Asia and the Middle East, mace is used to relieve rheumatism in Oriental medicine. *Available*: widely (look for blade mace in Indian or gourmet food stores).

mahleb

Mahleb is the dried kernel of the stone of a sour black cherry native to the Middle East and Turkey and is small and beige in appearance with a soft texture. Used specifically in Turkish cooking and the Arabic food of the Middle East, mahleb gives a delicious nutty flavour and vanilla aroma to breads, pastries and cakes, although tastes quite bitter when eaten on its own. Crush mahleb as you need to use it for the best flavour, as the powder form becomes stale very quickly. *Available*: Middle Eastern food stores.

mastic

Mastic is the sap or resin from an acacia native to the Mediterranean and comes in either crystal or powder form. The crystals need to be pounded in a mortar and pestle before use. Mastic provides a subtle liquorice flavour and is used in Greek and Middle Eastern cooking, particularly in ice-cream, bread and sweet biscuits. *Available*: Middle Eastern and Greek food stores.

mustard seeds

Pungent, hot and aromatic with an acrid taste, mustard seeds have been in culinary and medicinal use since at least the beginning of recorded history. Species of the mustard plant, a *Brassica*, provide the yellow (also referred to as white), brown and black mustard seeds we use today. The species that produces the yellow seeds grows freely across much of Europe and North America and is grown in most temperate countries; black mustard is native to southern Europe and temperate western Asia, and India is the home of the plant that produces brown mustard seeds. The most commonly available seeds are the yellow and the brown, with the more pungent black seeds only available in South-East Asia and India.

Yellow mustard seeds are used more in European cooking, and the smaller brown seeds are better suited to spice blends, for which they are usually tempered in hot oil to bring out their nutty flavour. Brown seeds are also used in many Indian spice preparations as a thickening agent. The slightly more pungent black mustard seeds are used in the same way as the brown seeds. A fiery, pungent essential oil is also expressed from the brown or black seeds for use in the cooking of Bengal and Kashmir. Mustard seeds make an excellent preservative, which is why they are a common ingredient in pickling solutions. Mustard seeds are also processed into a paste with other seasonings and vinegar to create the variety of mustard preparations readily available on the market. Mustard powder is made simply by grinding the seeds very finely. Mustard seeds are used medicinally to relieve arthritic pain and as a diuretic. *Available*: widely (look for black mustard seeds in Asian and Indian food stores).

nigella seeds

Nigella sativa or love-in-a-mist, which many cottage gardeners will recognise, is native to the Mediterranean region. The tiny, pungent, black seeds are nutty in flavour with a hint of pepper and poppyseed. They are a familiar ingredient in Persian and Indian cooking, where they are added to spice pastes and blends, breads, salads and rice pilafs. Breads of the Middle East and Turkey are also flavoured with nigella. The seeds are often mistaken for black CUMIN or onion seeds. Nigella seeds are believed to act as an insect repellent and as a diuretic; ground to a paste, they are used to cure scorpion stings. *Available*: Indian and Asian food stores.

nutmeg

Nutmeg is the kernel of an oval, brown seed produced by a large equatorial tree originating in the Moluccas. The seed is encased in a covering that, when sun-dried, becomes MACE. Nutmeg is far more aromatic and sweet than mace and has an established role in most of Europe's classic cuisines. It also appears in the food of India and Indonesia, and is used in Arabic food, particularly in meat and rice dishes. It is best to purchase whole nutmegs and grate them as required for the best results as ground nutmeg loses its flavour and aroma quickly. Although nutmeg has a long history (it has been found in Egyptian tombs), it was initially used in Europe for its intoxicating, soothing and hypnotic properties rather than for culinary purposes (it is a potent calmative drug – in fact, a narcotic, if taken in sufficient doses). The discovery of the Moluccas by Magellan in the sixteenth century changed all that, and the lucrative nutmeg market was opened up to the world. *Available*: widely.

papaya seeds

The fresh black seeds of the tropical papaya, native to Central and South America and taken to Europe by the Portuguese, have a peppery flavour similar to mustard cress. They include papain, an enzyme that breaks down meat fibres and activates digestion, and are used primarily in marinades as a meat tenderiser. The seeds can also be dried and ground, and are used in South America and Indonesia in the making of kebabs and koftas or in salad dressings. Papaya seeds are also used medicinally in India. *Available*: look for fresh papaya in greengrocers; dried seeds can be found in Asian food stores.

paprika/pimiento

Paprika is a fine reddish powder made by grinding dried, mild-flavoured members of the CHILLI family. It has a sweet and pungent flavour and is used to season savoury dishes specific to the food of Spain (where it is referred to as pimiento) and Hungary. The Spanish pimiento is available in two styles: sweet and hot/smoky. Both tend to be hotter and more earthy than the milder, sweeter Hungarian paprika, which is considered by some to be of superior quality. Because it is purchased already ground, buy paprika or pimiento in small quantities to ensure freshness. *Available*: widely.

pepper

Once the most highly prized spice on the trade routes, holding equal value to gold, pepper is native to the tropical coast of west India, where the prized Tellicherry pepper, named for the port in the state of Kerala, is grown. The peppercorns grow in clusters on long stems on a vine that is now grown throughout the equatorial regions of the world, including North Queensland.

Green or immature peppercorns are used predominantly in Thai cooking. They are available fresh, freeze-dried or pickled in a brine solution, but the latter two lack the pungent, zesty flavour of the fresh. Green peppercorns are softer in texture and milder than black or white peppercorns, hence their use as a fresh spice. Black peppercorns are simply green peppercorns that have been sun-dried until they harden and shrivel. Black pepper, the strongest-tasting pepper of all, has a hint of sweetness. It is also a stimulant and acts as a digestive. White peppercorns are allowed to ripen and turn red on the vine and are then soaked in running water for up to a week and then dried and milled to remove their tough outer husks. With a smooth, creamy appearance, white pepper is less aromatic and piquant than black pepper, but sharper in flavour. Both black and white peppercorns should be ground as required for maximum flavour. *Available*: widely (look for fresh green peppercorns from North Queensland in good greengrocers and Asian food stores). *See also* CAYENNE PEPPER, LONG PEPPER, SANSHO PEPPER, SICHUAN PEPPER.

pepperberry

An indigenous food source of Australia, the spicy pepperberry can be used fresh or dried in cooking, as can the leaves of the bush. The berries have a strong, peppery, chilli-hot flavour but the heat dissipates quickly once cooked. *Available*: gourmet food stores that stock bush foods.

pimiento *see* paprika

pomegranate seeds

Grown in the gardens of Babylon and seen to symbolise fertility, the pomegranate has been used for its seeds and juice in the food of the Middle East and western Asia for centuries. The fresh seeds are most often used in Middle Eastern and Mediterranean cooking, particularly spinkled over hoummus and in meat cookery in the Middle East, and in fruit salads. In their dried form, when they darken and become slightly sticky, the seeds are popular in the cooking of northern India, where they are used in chutneys, curries, rice stuffings, with lentils and chick peas and sprinkled over yoghurt raitas. Fresh or dried, the natural astringency of pomegranate seeds makes them an ideal souring agent. The seeds and their juice are also used to make the liqueur grenadine. Pomegranate molasses or syrup is used in salad dressings and sauces, particularly in Persian and Middle Eastern cooking. Pomegranate juice is used as a gargle to relieve fever and diarrhoea. *Available*: look for fresh pomegranates in autumn in good greengrocers and the dried seeds and molasses in Indian or Middle Eastern food stores.

poppyseeds

Poppyseeds are from the same plant that is native to Asia and produces opium, which is obtained from the juice of the unripe seed pods. Opium is not evident in the ripe seeds. Three varieties of poppyseed are available – the grey European seed, the brown seed of Turkey and the white seed of the Indian plant. The tiny seeds have a distinctive nutty flavour and provide texture when added to food. In Indian cooking the seeds are ground with other spices to act as a thickening agent for sauces and are also sprinkled whole over bread. In the Middle East the seeds are favoured for flavouring bread and desserts and in the making of halva. Dry-roasting the seeds before use enhances their flavour. It is believed that poppyseeds relieve stomach irritations and, when mixed with honey, help cure dysentery. *Available*: widely (grey European poppyseeds are sold in supermarkets; look for the brown or white seeds in Middle Eastern and Indian food stores respectively).

saffron

Each autumn a single purple crocus flower yields three orange–red stigmas, which are picked laboriously by hand and then dried to make saffron. It takes roughly 20 000 stigmas to make up a mere 125 g saffron, hence the luxury price tag. However, saffron is an essential ingredient in any self-respecting spice cupboard. Thankfully, because of its intense qualities, a little goes a long way (for maximum flavour, however, make those pinches generous ones).

Saffron has a sweet, floral aroma and slightly bitter flavour that underlies its distinctive and penetrating spiciness. There is no substitute for it as a spice or colouring agent. Saffron can be used in savoury and sweet preparations and is integral to such dishes as France's bouillabaisse and rouille, Italy's risotto Milanese, Spain's paella and zarzuela (a seafood and saffron casserole), Iran and Iraq's saffron rice, and India's rice pilaf and kulfi, as well as numerous breads, pastries and cakes from the cuisines of the world. It is also an important ingredient in the making of yellow chartreuse (a French liqueur that is light and sweet on the palate) and in perfumes, and is used as a dye for cloth (it is a sacred colour for Buddhist monks). Saffron was valued as a heart tonic in ancient Persia, and its fragrance was thought to induce sleep. It has also been considered an aphrodisiac and a cure for flatulence and poor vision. In India it is used to treat digestive and urinary tract disorders and as a skin remedy.

Thought to have originated during the ancient civilisations of the eastern Mediterranean and Central Asia, saffron is now cultivated widely, in particular in Spain, Turkey, India and Iran and, more recently, Tasmania. It is a commonly held belief that the deeper the colour, the better the quality, and each cook has his or her favourite saffron. I prefer the dark-red, intense variety from Iran or, as a close second, Kashmiri saffron. Spanish saffron is also of extremely good quality – it tends to be slightly paler than its Iranian or Indian counterparts but its flavour is equally intense. I find the Turkish and Tasmanian varieties too pale and insipid in flavour, and too similar to the inadequate safflower, which is often passed off as saffron.

When purchasing saffron, buy stigmas or threads rather than the powder as the latter loses its flavour quickly and can be adulterated with imitations and false colourings. To use saffron threads to the best effect, infuse them in a chosen cooking liquid to ensure even colouring and distribution of flavour. *Available*: widely (gourmet and Middle Eastern food stores, in particular).

salam leaf

From a type of CASSIA originating in and specific to Indonesia and Malaysia, fresh, bright-green salam leaves are as essential in Indonesian cooking as the CURRY LEAF is in Indian cooking. They are used sparingly in curries and soups, as they release an essential oil when simmered with other ingredients, giving an aromatic flavour with slight tobacco overtones. Bay leaves are sometimes suggested as a substitute, but on no account should they be used instead of salam leaves as their flavour is completely different. *Available*: Asian food stores (only dried leaves are currently available).

salt *see* black salt, sea salt

sansho pepper

Sansho pepper is derived from the dried and ground seed pods of a Japanese variety of the prickly ash tree and is that country's equivalent of SICHUAN PEPPER. The seeds themselves are not used as they are too bitter. One of the few spices used in Japanese cooking, sansho pepper gives off a certain amount of heat, has a slight numbing effect on the tongue and is used to counter fattiness in food. The aromatic leaves of the sansho plant, which have minty, basil and liquorice overtones, are used in herbal preparations. *Available*: Japanese or Asian food stores.

sea salt

Sea salt is the universal seasoning used in everyday cooking throughout the world to flavour and preserve food and to heighten the flavour of other ingredients. As opposed to rock salt, which is mined, sea salt is produced by the evaporation of sea water or water from salt marshes, the best varieties coming from England and France, where it is known as gros sel. Excellent sea salt from South Australia has recently appeared on the market, too. More costly to produce than other types of salt, sea salt flakes are odourless but have a strong, salty taste and do not include the iodine and magnesium carbonate found in processed table salt. Kosher salt, available from Jewish food stores, has a very similar texture and taste to sea salt as it contains no additives. *Available*: widely (gourmet food stores, in particular).

sesame seeds

Sesame seeds come from a herbaceous tropical plant native to Assyria and are one of the world's oldest spices, being known since circa 3000 BC. These small, flat seeds have a high oil content and a nutty flavour that becomes pronounced after dry-roasting or frying. The seeds range in colour from pearly white to black. The most commonly used are creamy white – these are referred to as white sesame seeds in the recipes in this book. White sesame seeds are ground to a paste to make tahina in the Middle East and to serve with noodles and rice in China. In the Middle East, sesame seeds are used to make the sweet halva. The flavour of black sesame seeds is stronger and more earthy than the creamy white ones. They are best eaten raw as they become quite bitter when toasted. Black sesame seeds are used in Japanese and Chinese cooking and are compatible with sugar and some fruits in desserts. Sesame seed oil is an important ingredient in many styles of cooking, particularly Chinese, but it must be used with caution as it can taste very bitter if used with a heavy hand. Sesame seeds are considered a laxative and can be used as a hot poultice to relieve aches and pains. *Available*: widely (look for black sesame seeds in Asian food stores).

Sichuan pepper

Sichuan pepper is one of the oldest staple spices used in Chinese cooking. It is technically not a pepper at all but rather the berries from the prickly ash tree native to the Sichuan province of China. The reddish brown berries are dried after picking and are husked to remove small, bitter black seeds before crushing. Sichuan pepper, also known as fagara or Chinese pepper, has a spicy, earthy flavour and produces a slight numbing effect when eaten. It is used in spice preparations – for example, Chinese Five-spice Powder (see page 39) – and is often combined with DRIED ORANGE PEEL and STAR ANISE, and is used to flavour sauces and master stocks for red-braising (see page 339). To maximise flavour, dry-roast Sichuan pepper before grinding. *Available*: Asian food stores.

star anise

A staple in Chinese and Vietnamese cooking, this beautiful spice is the sun-dried fruit of a member of the magnolia family native to those countries. The fruit, an eight-pointed star in which the carpels provide most of the flavour and aroma, imparts a delicate fragrance and a pronounced sweet liquorice flavour. Star anise, unrelated to ANISE, is usually sold whole or sometimes as broken pieces and is an essential ingredient in Chinese Five-spice Powder (see page 39). It is regarded in Asia as promoting good digestion and as a breath freshener. *Available*: widely.

sumac

This reddish ground spice is made from the berries of the sumac bush, which is native to the Middle East and North America and is from the genus that includes poison ivy and oak. An ancient but relatively unknown spice, sumac is used as a souring agent in the same way as lemon juice or TAMARIND (in fact it was used by the Romans before the introduction of lemons). It has a hint of fruitiness, is pleasantly astringent and has almost no aroma. Sumac is used throughout the Middle East in marinades and sprinkled on breads, and is an essential ingredient in the spice mix Za'atar (see page 37). *Available*: Middle Eastern food stores.

tamarind

Literally translating as 'Indian date', tamarind is produced from the pods of the tamarind tree, a native of tropical east Africa that has been cultivated in India since ancient times and that now grows in tropical countries across the globe. The pods contain seeds and a dark-brown, sticky pulp that is dried, with or without the seeds intact, for use as a souring agent in all Asian cooking,

in sauces, curries, soups, with fish and poultry and so on. Tamarind gives food a fruity, sweet–sour flavour. It is considered a mild laxative and digestive aid and is used to treat bronchitis and sore throats.

The most refined way to use tamarind is to make tamarind liquid. Simmer 1 part tamarind pulp to 3 parts water for 30 minutes or so, then pass the pulp and water through a coarse-meshed sieve to remove the fibre and seeds, which can be discarded. Tamarind liquid can be refrigerated for up to a month and used as required. *Available*: Asian food stores.

turmeric

A rhizome related to the GINGER family, turmeric is bright-orange when fresh and becomes a vibrant yellow with drying. Dried and ground turmeric is a common ingredient in Asian cooking, providing a brilliant yellow colour and musky flavour. It is also used fresh as a vegetable in South-East Asia. Essential in the making of curry powder and the North African spice mix Ras el Hanout (see page 37), turmeric has long been respected for its medicinal properties and as a fabric dye. Turmeric, valued for its antiseptic qualities (particularly for burns and minor skin irritations), is made into a tonic for treating liver complaints, is considered a blood purifier, and in India is used as a skin cleanser when mixed with milk. *Available*: widely (look for fresh turmeric in Asian food stores and good greengrocers).

vanilla bean

Vanilla beans or pods grow on a fleshy tropical orchid native to Mexico and Central America. The beans are picked when

immature and yellow and are then sun-dried for up to several months, during which time they ferment and develop their familiar brown, wrinkled appearance and rich, mellow tobacco-like aroma. Each bean produces thousands of tiny, highly fragrant seeds that, along with the pod, add an exotic, intense and characteristic flavour to food, a flavour particularly suited to dessert work, confectionery and chocolate. (It's no coincidence that in the sixteenth century the conquistadores returned to Spain with hauls of cocoa as well as vanilla beans!)

Three types of vanilla bean are available: the Madagascan, a thin but sweet and rich pod; the thick, dark and aromatic Tahitian; and the scarce Mexican, which is smooth and rich. Whichever you choose, select plump vanilla beans that feel slightly moist and sticky. Pure vanilla extract is the only real substitute for a vanilla bean. There are many imitation and poor-quality flavourings on the market that should be avoided at all costs (some are chemically derived from wood by-products!). The pure extract is costly, but a little goes a long way. *Available*: widely (look for the best beans and pure extract in gourmet food stores).

wasabi

Wasabi, which translates as 'mountain hollyhock', is a horseradish that grows wild near spring water in the mountains of northern Japan. It is unrelated to the European white HORSERADISH. The very expensive fresh pale-green root is available only in Japan and is grated before use as a condiment to accompany raw fish and sushi rice. Elsewhere, wasabi is available as a powder or paste, although it is grown in Taiwan and New Zealand on a smaller, less-successful scale. Specific to Japanese cooking, wasabi has a milder aroma and gentler, more aromatic but nonetheless hotter flavour than the sharper white horseradish. It is best to buy powdered wasabi and mix the required quantity with water as the paste can be quite impotent by comparison. *Available*: Asian food stores.

zedoary

Known in India as mango ginger and as white turmeric in other parts of Asia, zedoary is a rhizome from the TURMERIC family. It has the appearance of GINGER and a strong, musky, ginger-like and slightly bitter flavour similar to green mango, and is used in Thai, Indian and Indonesian cooking. Fresh zedoary can be pounded or ground with other aromatics such as ginger, turmeric and garlic to make spice pastes; it is also shredded, chopped or minced and added to Asian salads, and is common in pickles and condiments. Dried zedoary is often sold under its Indonesian name, 'kentjur', and is usually added to broths or sauces for flavouring and then discarded. Zedoary is highly regarded as a blood purifier and a healing agent for the skin. *Available*: Asian food stores (fresh zedoary is rare, and may be sold as 'white turmeric' or sometimes 'mango ginger').

SPICE MIXES

THE BLENDING OF SPICES gives a dish its character, complexity and distinctive flavour. It is a fascinating subject and practice, one that provides constant challenges and helps personalise your cooking through the myriad nuances of taste and texture that can be achieved. Experiment with the intricacies of spice chemistry until the blending becomes instinctive, and know that a properly spiced dish should 'taste awake but not angry', as Bruce Cost writes in his book *Ginger East to West.* Then you will enjoy one of the most pleasant of culinary euphorias: the harmony of flavours. ❋

WELL-KNOWN SPICE BLENDS and mixes hail from many parts of the world, each open to interpretation by the blender. Spice blending is the essence of good cooking, particularly in North Africa and India, where the work of blending spices is regarded as an art, the craft of specialists. ❋

THE USE OF SPICE MIXES in Australia today has revolutionised our food habits and has opened our palates to what Indian author Julie Sahni so aptly describes as a sensual awakening. To indulge is to experience an intoxicating and passionate world, allowing us to enjoy aromatic, fragrant, pungent, mellow, fiery and delicious taste sensations. Spices are the words that come together to make the language of my food.

DRY SPICE MIXES Dry spice mixes do not contain moist or wet ingredients that would otherwise give them a limited shelf-life. Blended dried spices, raw or dry-roasted, can be prepared and stored in small quantities, although they are best made as you need them or as close to that time as possible to guarantee freshness and optimum flavour. ❋ MOST OF THE BLENDS listed in this section can be bought already mixed for convenience, but if you are as driven by the flavour and aroma of freshly ground spices as I am, then these recipes will be invaluable to you as you roast, mix and concoct your own magical spice potions. (I think it's quite possible that I would have been burnt at the stake had I lived in earlier times!)

Paramount's garam masala

This is my favourite garam masala, a rich, aromatic version of the staple Indian spice mix that I have developed over time.

seeds from 16 green cardamom pods
1 teaspoon nigella seeds
1 teaspoon cloves
2 teaspoons black peppercorns
1/4 teaspoon freshly grated nutmeg
1/4 teaspoon ground cassia

Grind whole spices to a fine powder and then stir in remaining spices. Store in a sealed jar. MAKES 2 TABLESPOONS

Bengali garam masala

Many regard the food of the state of Bengal as the best in India – elegant, refined and mild. Spices work their magic with warmth and aromatic appeal without the burning heat of the chilli. Use this garam masala with fish, shellfish, fresh green vegetables or lentils.

1 teaspoon black peppercorns
1 teaspoon white peppercorns
5 cloves
1 stick cinnamon
seeds from 5 green cardamom pods
2 teaspoons cumin seeds
1 1/2 tablespoons coriander seeds

Grind spices to a fine powder. Store in a sealed jar. MAKES 3 TABLESPOONS

Kashmiri garam masala

Garam masala, which simply means 'hot spice', is used throughout India, although particularly in the food of the north, where the winters are very cold. It is not a standardised recipe and is open to interpretation, with the distinct blends of each region giving the masala its own character and taste. The Kashmiri version, which has a pervading sweetness, is used with meat, poultry and root vegetables, and is also good with yoghurt-based sauces.

3 teaspoons nigella seeds
2 teaspoons black peppercorns
1 teaspoon caraway seeds
8 cloves
seeds from 5 black cardamom pods
5 mace blades, ground
1/2 teaspoon freshly grated nutmeg
1/2 teaspoon freshly ground cinnamon

Dry-roast whole spices (except cardamom) separately over gentle heat until slightly coloured and fragrant. Cool. Grind whole spices to a fine powder and then stir in remaining spices. Store in a sealed jar. MAKES 3 TABLESPOONS

Chat masala

'Chat' is an Indian term for appetisers, palate teasers or small morsels eaten as a snack. This spice mix is used to flavour fried pastries, various potato preparations and tomato-based salads. The raw spiciness and tart flavour of the mix best suit fruit or vegetables – I find it works wonders when added to cooked root vegetables, accentuating their rich, earthy flavour.

1 teaspoon black peppercorns
1 teaspoon cumin seeds
1/2 teaspoon ajwain seeds
3 cubeb
1/2 teaspoon dried pomegranate seeds
seeds from 3 green cardamom pods
1 teaspoon ground black salt
1 teaspoon amchoor powder
1 teaspoon ground ginger
1/4 teaspoon asafoetida powder
1 teaspoon chilli powder

Grind whole spices to a fine powder and then stir in remaining spices. Store in a sealed jar. MAKES 2 1/2 TABLESPOONS

Kashmiri korma

A mild blend from northern India, where saffron features prominently in cooking and mustard oil is used for heating the spice mix for deeper complexity. A korma is simply a Murghul term for long, slow braising. The spice mix is usually stirred into a yoghurt, ghee, cream or ground-nut base and is then used to marinate the chosen meat or vegetable.

4 large dried chillies
4 green cardamom pods
1 stick cinnamon
1/2 teaspoon ground turmeric
4 cloves
1/2 teaspoon anise
1/2 teaspoon ground ginger
1/2 teaspoon saffron threads

Dry-roast chillies over gentle heat until fragrant. Cool. Grind to a fine powder. Mix spices and store in a sealed jar. To use, fry spice mix in mustard oil to release flavours and aroma. MAKES 2 TABLESPOONS

Kerala curry powder

This spice mix typifies the flavours abundant in the food of the south-western Indian state of Kerala, where the spices are usually mixed with aromatics and made into a wet paste. This mix can be cooked into minced onion, ginger and garlic and added to coconut milk or stock.

1 teaspoon black peppercorns
seeds from 6 green cardamom pods
5 cloves
1/2 teaspoon ground turmeric
1/2 teaspoon brown mustard seeds

Mix spices and store in a sealed jar. Grind spices to a fine powder as required – this mix relies on freshness for best flavour.
MAKES 1 1/2 TABLESPOONS

Madras curry powder

A moderately hot spice mix from southern India that can be fried in ghee and then made into a sauce with coconut milk, tamarind or a light stock.

1 tablespoon brown mustard seeds
1 tablespoon coriander seeds
1 tablespoon cumin seeds
10 dried bird's-eye chillies
2 teaspoons fenugreek seeds
1 teaspoon black peppercorns
12 fresh curry leaves
1 tablespoon ground turmeric

Dry-roast whole spices over gentle heat until they begin to change colour. Add curry leaves and roast for a minute or two. Cool. Grind to a fine powder, then stir in turmeric. Store in a sealed jar.
MAKES 5 TABLESPOONS

Sri Lankan curry powder

This curry mix comes from the days of the British Empire when the island of Sri Lanka was known as Ceylon. It includes spices used by its neighbour India in Madras Curry Powder (at left), but it has a totally different flavour and aroma as the spices are roasted until dark-brown before being ground. Curries made with this blend tend to be very aromatic, mellow and warming, as opposed to fiery.

2 tablespoons coriander seeds
1 tablespoon cumin seeds
1/2 teaspoon fenugreek seeds
2 teaspoons fennel seeds
1 stick cinnamon
5 cloves
2 black cardamom pods
15 dried bird's-eye chillies
1 teaspoon black peppercorns

Dry-roast spices separately over gentle heat until highly aromatic and very dark but not burnt. Cool. Grind to a fine powder, then store in a sealed jar.
MAKES 5 TABLESPOONS

Malaysian curry blend

The curries of Malaysia, which has a large Indian population, are heavily influenced by the flavours and spice combinations of India and the curry mixes are easily interchangeable. Malay cooks often combine a spice mix such as this with coconut milk or tamarind liquid and then infuse it with a fresh aromatic (for example, lemongrass).

1 teaspoon black peppercorns
1 tablespoon coriander seeds
1 teaspoon fennel seeds
2 teaspoons cumin seeds
6 dried bird's-eye chillies
1/2 teaspoon celery seeds
3 teaspoons ground turmeric
1 teaspoon ground galangal

Dry-roast whole spices over gentle heat until just aromatic. Cool. Grind to a fine powder, then stir in remaining spices. Store in a sealed jar.
MAKES 4 TABLESPOONS

Singapore curry mix

As in Malaysia, there is a strong Indian presence in Singapore, which naturally affects the food culture. This mild blend can be spiced up by adding extra chillies or Chilli Jam (see page 58) and is great to use when making curries using fish heads or oily fish such as mackerel or kingfish.

1 tablespoon cumin seeds
4 tablespoons coriander seeds
1 tablespoon fennel seeds
5 large dried chillies
2 teaspoons black peppercorns
1 stick cinnamon
seeds from 5 green cardamom pods
1 tablespoon ground turmeric

Grind whole spices to a fine powder, then stir in turmeric. Store in a sealed jar.
MAKES 9 TABLESPOONS

West Indian curry blend

This recipe is inspired by one I found in Jill Norman's *The Complete Book of Spices*, where she notes that the practice of blending spices was introduced to the West Indies by Indian Hindu migrants in the nineteenth century. It's an aromatic curry blend with little residual heat and works well with the lighter textures of fish and seafood, especially when baked in banana leaves over charcoal.

2 dried bird's-eye chillies
2 tablespoons coriander seeds
1 teaspoon fennel seeds
1 teaspoon black cumin seeds
1 teaspoon cumin seeds
1 teaspoon black mustard seeds
2 teaspoons fenugreek seeds
1 tablespoon black peppercorns
1 small stick cinnamon
1 tablespoon ground ginger
1 tablespoon ground turmeric

Dry-roast whole spices over gentle heat until lightly coloured and fragrant. Cool. Grind to a fine powder, then stir in remaining spices. Store in a sealed jar.
MAKES 7 TABLESPOONS

Sambar powder

This masala spice mix is specific to the southern Indian food of Tamil Nadu and is used to flavour dal (lentils) and vegetables cooked together to make sambar, an important part of the daily diet. The dal acts as a thickening agent – look for specific dals in Indian food stores. Use sambar powder as a base flavouring for a vegetable soup or curry.

1 teaspoon brown mustard seeds
2 teaspoons cumin seeds
1 teaspoon fenugreek seeds
10 large dried chillies
1 teaspoon coriander seeds
1 teaspoon black peppercorns
1 stick cinnamon
2 pinches asafoetida powder
1 teaspoon ground turmeric
1 tablespoon vegetable oil
1 tablespoon chana dal
1 tablespoon toor dal

Dry-roast whole spices over gentle heat until aromatic. Add asafoetida and turmeric and toss over heat briefly. Cool. Heat oil in pan and fry dals until they change colour. Remove dals with a slotted spoon and cool. Grind roasted spices and dals to a fine powder. Store in a sealed jar. Best used as soon as possible. MAKES 6 TABLESPOONS

Bengali panch phoron (Indian five-spice mix)

Panch phoron is the Indian version of Chinese Five-spice Powder (see page 39). It is highly aromatic and used to flavour the food of Bengal in north-east India, which is noted for its richness and a gentle, warm spiciness attained with very little chilli. The spices are mixed but kept whole until needed, then they are usually fried in hot oil or ground and cooked into aromatics at the start of the cooking process. The spices can also be fried whole in ghee and sprinkled onto cooked food as a garnish. Bengali panch phoron is used to flavour rice, lentils and vegetables.

1 tablespoon brown mustard seeds
1 tablespoon fennel seeds
1 tablespoon cumin seeds
1 tablespoon nigella seeds
2 teaspoons fenugreek seeds

Mix spices and store in a sealed jar. If the recipe requires ground spices, grind only the amount you need.
MAKES 4 TABLESPOONS

Tandoori masala

Many people think Indian food *is* tandoori, especially with the worldwide proliferation of Indian restaurants, which have popularised this particular cooking style, originally the domain of the Punjabi people. The meat, marinated with these spices and yoghurt before being threaded onto skewers, is traditionally baked on the sides of a clay tandoor oven, which gives the food and bread cooked in it a slightly smoky flavour. Tandoori masala is aromatic and gently spicy with a salty, sour flavour. The red colouring so frequently used in the commercial blends has been omitted here.

1 tablespoon coriander seeds
1 tablespoon cumin seeds
1 × 4 cm stick cinnamon
5 large dried chillies
10 cloves
3 mace blades
1 teaspoon ground ginger
2 teaspoons ground turmeric
1 teaspoon sea salt
1 teaspoon ground black salt
$^{1}/_{2}$ teaspoon saffron threads, ground

Dry-roast whole spices over gentle heat until they become fragrant and change colour. Cool. Grind to a fine powder, then mix in remaining spices. Store in a sealed jar. (To make the tandoori marinade, drain yoghurt in a sieve lined with muslin for 24 hours to firm up, then stir in spice mix. Allow 1 tablespoon spice mix to 250 ml yoghurt.) MAKES 5 TABLESPOONS

Ras el hanout

Ras el hanout, a complex and distinctive mix of spices and herbs originating in the Meghribi villages of North Africa, translates literally as 'head of the shop' spice and varies according to who makes it. Most versions list 20 or so spices but specific quantities are a much-guarded secret from one spice shop to the next, where blending is considered a special art. Blends vary with the region and spending power of the buyer. Ras el hanout is used with meat, game, poultry, rice and cous cous.

Ready-made ras el hanout is now available in Australia from selected stores (see page 349). When writing *Paramount Cooking* in 1995, I could only explain where I had found it in Paris! At the time of writing, belladonna berries, ashberries and Spanish fly beetle are unobtainable in Australia (which is why it is easier to buy the blended mix), but they may, too, become available as interest increases. Have a go at making your own blend from the ingredients you can obtain, using this list as a reference point.

cubeb
grains of paradise
black cumin seeds
belladonna berries
allspice
dried rose petals
dried lavender flowers
long pepper
black peppercorns
mace blades
ashberries
nutmeg
seeds from green cardamom pods
cloves
allspice
stick cinnamon
Spanish fly beetle
sea salt
ground turmeric
ground galangal
ground cassia

Grind whole spices to a fine powder, then store in a sealed jar.

African berbere

This complex blend from Ethiopia and the Arabian Gulf States bears a close resemblance to the masala mixes of India and is used in much the same way as a coating for fried meats, in stews, in soups and with baked fish. Bring your next barbecue to life with it!

12 large dried chillies
6 cloves
2 teaspoons coriander seeds
1 teaspoon cumin seeds
1 teaspoon allspice
seeds from 6 green cardamom pods
$^{1}/_{2}$ teaspoon ajwain seeds
2 teaspoons black peppercorns
$^{1}/_{2}$ teaspoon fenugreek seeds
1 teaspoon ground ginger
$^{1}/_{4}$ teaspoon freshly grated nutmeg
1 tablespoon sea salt

Dry-roast whole spices over gentle heat until aromatic and just beginning to colour. Cool. Grind to a fine powder, then mix in remaining spices. Store in a sealed jar. MAKES 5 TABLESPOONS

Za'atar

The North African spice blend za'atar is also used in Jordan, Israel, Greece and Turkey. It is usually sprinkled onto food as a seasoning or garnish, and in Israel it is often served with bread and olive oil for breakfast. Za'atar is sold already blended in Middle Eastern food stores. Traditionally, the herbs hyssop or wild thyme are ground with the spices.

2 tablespoons white sesame seeds
1 tablespoon dried thyme
2 teaspoons dried oregano
1 tablespoon ground sumac

Dry-roast sesame seeds over gentle heat until just coloured. Cool. Grind dried herbs to a fine powder and mix with spices. Store in a sealed jar. MAKES 4$^{1}/_{2}$ TABLESPOONS

Baharat

Almost every spice blend used in the Arab world and Middle Eastern cooking is known as baharat, which literally means 'spices', the equivalent of India's masala. Each blend varies from region to region, family to family, but the overall flavour of baharat is not dissimilar to allspice. The baharat of North Africa is fiery-hot; the version of the Levant can rely more heavily on cinnamon; the Egyptians use more cumin; and the cooks of the Gulf States include more cardamom and nutmeg to make a sweetly aromatic blend, similar to an Indian curry mix. Baharat is generally used as a seasoning for marinades, preserves, meat and vegetables.

2 tablespoons black peppercorns
1 tablespoon coriander seeds
1 stick cinnamon
20 cloves
1 tablespoon cumin seeds
seeds from 4 green cardamom pods
1 teaspoon ground cassia
2 teaspoons freshly grated nutmeg
2 tablespoons ground paprika

Grind whole spices to a fine powder and then mix in remaining spices. Store in a sealed jar. MAKES 8 TABLESPOONS

Tunisian five-spice powder

According to Jill Norman in *The Complete Book of Spices*, this Arabic blend, known as qãlat daqqa, is used to give lamb tagines and vegetable dishes in Tunisian cooking a warm sweetness. It goes particularly well with eggplant.

1 tablespoon black peppercorns
2 teaspoons cloves
1 teaspoon grains of paradise
1 tablespoon freshly grated nutmeg
1 teaspoon freshly ground cinnamon

Grind whole spices to a fine powder and then mix in remaining spices. Store in a sealed jar. MAKES 3 TABLESPOONS

Pickling spice mix

Typical of and particular to English cooking, this pickling spice mix is used to flavour preserved meats, vegetables and fruit. Blends vary greatly according to who makes them, and mixes are readily available on the retail shelf. The spices are cooked into a vinegar solution that is then used as a flavouring or poured over the items to be preserved. The spices are usually left whole to ensure subtlety of flavour.

1 tablespoon coriander seeds
1 tablespoon white peppercorns
2 teaspoons cloves
1 tablespoon yellow mustard seeds
1 tablespoon allspice
10 large dried chillies
2 sticks cinnamon
4 bay leaves

Mix spices and add to vinegar as instructed in your recipe. The spices can be left loose or tied in muslin and discarded later. MAKES 6 TABLESPOONS

Quatre épices

This is the definitive spice mix used in French cooking, particularly with charcuterie (pâtés, rillettes, sausages, and meat and poultry terrines) and meat that requires long, slow cooking. It consists, as its name suggests, of four sweet, aromatic spices.

1 teaspoon cloves
1 tablespoon white peppercorns
2 teaspoons freshly grated nutmeg
1 teaspoon freshly ground cinnamon

Grind cloves and peppercorns to a fine powder, then mix in remaining spices. Store in a sealed jar.
MAKES 2 TABLESPOONS

English pudding spice

An Anglo-Saxon favourite, English pudding spice is used to flavour Christmas fare: sweet fruit puddings, sweet mincemeat that fills festive little pies, and the various cakes that are usually based on dried or candied fruit, nuts and alcohol. Make this mix and then refer to Stephanie Alexander's *The Cook's Companion* for the best Christmas pudding recipe in existence, a family treasure from her grandmother, Emily Bell.

2 teaspoons allspice
12 cloves
2 teaspoons freshly ground cinnamon
2 teaspoons ground ginger
1 teaspoon freshly grated nutmeg
1 teaspoon ground mace

Grind whole spices to a fine powder, then mix in remaining spices. Make as required for maximum flavour.
MAKES 2 TABLESPOONS

Chinese five-spice powder

An essential spice mix used in Chinese cooking. Although it varies from region to region and maker to maker, it is characteristically highly aromatic with a well-balanced aroma and flavour. According to Barbara Tropp in her tome *The Modern Art of Chinese Cooking*, the concoction exemplifies the five flavours essential to the balance of the palate: sweet, salty, sour, bitter and pungent.

Chinese five-spice powder is sprinkled on roasted meats and used in marinades and with red-cooked meats. The ready-made varieties can taste dusty and stale. I don't think I need to harp on any further about the difference between shop-bought ground spices and those you grind yourself: this recipe is living testament to what I am saying.

5 star anise
1 tablespoon fennel seeds
1 tablespoon Sichuan peppercorns
2 teaspoons cloves
1 teaspoon ground cassia
1 teaspoon freshly ground cinnamon

Grind spices to a fine powder, then pass through a fine-meshed sieve and discard husks. Store in a sealed jar.
MAKES 4 TABLESPOONS

Chinese spice salt

A vital accompaniment to Chinese barbecued, roasted and fried meats and poultry. Traditionally served in a small, shallow dish and sprinkled onto food as it is about to be eaten.

2 tablespoons sea salt
1 teaspoon Sichuan peppercorns
2 teaspoons Chinese Five-spice Powder (at left)

Dry-roast sea salt and peppercorns over gentle heat until fragrant and lightly coloured. Cool. Grind to a fine powder, then pass through a fine-meshed sieve and discard husks. Mix with five-spice powder and store in a sealed jar.
MAKES 3 TABLESPOONS

Goma shio (Japanese sesame salt)

Goma shio is one of the few spice flavourings used in the cooking of Japan, which tends to rely on the unadulterated flavour of the protein or vegetable being used. It is a simple seasoning, and the sesame seeds give an added crunch and nutty flavour. Often sold already prepared in Japanese food stores, goma shio is used to flavour vegetables and rice and is taken to the table as a condiment.

2 teaspoons white sesame seeds
1 tablespoon black sesame seeds
3 teaspoons sea salt

Dry-roast white sesame seeds over gentle heat until just coloured. Cool. Grind spices briefly, keeping texture slightly coarse. Store in a sealed jar.
MAKES 2½ TABLESPOONS

Shichimi togarashi (Japanese seven-spice powder)

Shichimi togarashi, used as a condiment or seasoning, is often served with soups, yakitori, kushiyaki, nabemono (one-pot dishes) and udon noodles. It is available ready-mixed, but in Japan it can be made according to personal preference and is available in varieties that range from mild to hot. The formula is flexible, and the traditional Japanese blend includes hemp seeds. I have used black poppyseeds instead in this sanitised Australian version. Use at the table as you would pepper.

1 tablespoon crushed dried mandarin peel
2 teaspoons white sesame seeds
2 teaspoons black sesame seeds
1 sheet nori seaweed, toasted and torn into small pieces
1 teaspoon dried chilli flakes
1 teaspoon black poppyseeds
1 tablespoon ground sansho pepper

Grind dried mandarin peel and sesame seeds in a mortar and pestle. Blend in nori seaweed pieces, chilli flakes and poppyseeds, then mix in sansho pepper. Store in a sealed jar.
MAKES 4 TABLESPOONS

WET SPICE MIXES Wet spice mixes form the basis and provide the soul for much of my cooking. These preparations combine spices and aromatics such as garlic, onion, galangal and lemongrass with oil, ghee, tamarind, coconut milk and the like to make a masala, sambal or rempah, for example, that is cooked into food to give added flavour or is used as a condiment. I think of a spice paste as the catalyst that brings everything together to create what can best be described as an oral orgasm. ❊ THE FOLLOWING PREPARATIONS have been with me throughout my cooking life. They are my starting point and I can't imagine life without them.

Green masala paste

This versatile, pungent and slightly sour paste, which has its origins in southern India, is used in the making of rich sauces and curries.

400 ml malt vinegar
1 tablespoon fenugreek seeds
2 teaspoons cumin seeds
3 cups chopped mint leaves
4 cups chopped coriander leaves
25 cloves garlic, minced
3 tablespoons minced ginger
1 tablespoon minced turmeric
2 tablespoons ground turmeric
1 teaspoon freshly ground cloves
2 teaspoons freshly ground green
    cardamom seeds
300 ml vegetable oil
50 ml sesame oil
50 ml fish sauce

Bring malt vinegar and fenugreek seeds to a boil in a non-reactive saucepan. Remove from heat and set aside for 6 hours or overnight.

Dry-roast cumin seeds over gentle heat until fragrant. Cool, then grind to a fine powder. Blend all ingredients to a smooth, fine paste in an electric blender, in small batches if necessary.

Cook paste in a wide, heavy-based pan over gentle heat for 1 hour, stirring regularly and adding more oil if necessary to prevent sticking. Spoon into a jar, then cover with a film of oil. Cool. Refrigerate for up to a month.
MAKES 600 ML

Chettinad red masala paste

The Chettiars are a group of merchants, bankers and traders from Tamil Nadu in south-eastern India. Their food is particularly hot and spicy, largely due to their long history of trade with South-East Asia, from where they acquired early access to many Chinese spices not commonly found or used in the rest of India. This is my adaptation of the essential flavours of the Chettinad cooking style – I use it as I would any other curry paste.

2 teaspoons white poppyseeds
50 ml water
5 large dried chillies
200 g freshly grated coconut
1 teaspoon fennel seeds
1 stick cinnamon
seeds from 3 green cardamom pods
4 cloves
1 teaspoon ground turmeric
1 teaspoon Paramount's Garam Masala
    (page 34)
125 ml vegetable oil
1 brown onion, minced
2 teaspoons minced ginger
2 teaspoons minced garlic
2 teaspoons Chilli Jam (page 58)
1 star anise

Briefly dry-roast poppyseeds over medium heat, then crush and soak in the water for 30 minutes. Dry-roast chillies over gentle heat until fragrant. Cool, then grind to a fine powder.

Blend poppyseed mixture, coconut, fennel seeds, cinnamon, cardamom seeds, cloves, turmeric and garam masala to a fine paste in an electric blender. Heat oil in a frying pan and sauté onion until just golden. Add ginger and garlic and fry for a couple of minutes, then add remaining ingredients and the prepared spice paste. Add a little water if mixture appears dry. Cook for 5 minutes over moderate heat, stirring regularly to prevent sticking. Spoon into a jar, then cover with a film of oil. Cool. Refrigerate for up to 1 month.
MAKES 400 ML

Goan vindaloo paste

The tiny territory of Goa is situated on the central western coast of India, south of Bombay, and has a history of French and Portuguese colonisation. Vindaloo curries, traditionally made with pork although now made with a wide variety of meat and fish, are considered the hottest in India and have a characteristic sourness provided by vinegar.

10 g dried bird's-eye chillies
3 teaspoons cumin seeds
seeds from 4 green cardamom pods
18 cloves
3 sticks cinnamon
1 tablespoon black peppercorns
1 star anise
3 teaspoons black poppyseeds
$1/2$ teaspoon freshly grated nutmeg
1 teaspoon ground turmeric
1 tablespoon minced ginger
20 cloves garlic, minced
80 ml Tamarind Liquid (page 341)
50 ml cider vinegar

Dry-roast whole spices over gentle heat until aromatic. Cool. Blend all ingredients to a fine paste in an electric blender. Spoon into a jar, then cover with a film of oil. Refrigerate for up to 1 week.
MAKES 200 ML

Madras masala paste

I came across this masala paste, now one of my favourite seasonings, in 1995 when working at the Taj Coromandel Hotel in Madras. Working there was like being in heaven: I soaked up every little bit of information I could about how and why spices are used, which enriched my knowledge and understanding of cooking in general. Use this paste when cooking fish or shellfish.

1 tablespoon coriander seeds
1 teaspoon cumin seeds
seeds from 2 green cardamom pods
$\frac{1}{2}$ teaspoon black peppercorns
1 teaspoon ground turmeric
1 teaspoon chilli powder
$\frac{1}{2}$ teaspoon sea salt
30 ml malt vinegar
50 g ghee
3 cloves garlic, minced
1 teaspoon minced ginger
2 red chillies, minced
3 red shallots, minced
20 ml Tamarind Liquid (page 341)

Dry-roast whole spices over gentle heat until aromatic. Cool, then grind to a fine powder. Combine with dry spices and stir in vinegar to make a paste.

Heat ghee in a frying pan over moderate heat and cook garlic, ginger, chilli and shallot until fragrant. Add spice paste and fry until it begins to colour, then stir in tamarind liquid and let paste absorb it. Spoon into a jar, then cover with a film of oil. Cool. Refrigerate for up to 1 month. MAKES 150 ML

Kerala curry paste

During my time in Madras, I observed the cooking at the Mysore Restaurant, one of the restaurants housed in the hotel. It specialised in the food of the four southern Indian states of Tamil Nadu, Kerala, Karnataka and Andhra Pradesh. Chefs from each state were responsible for their particular dishes, and I found myself eating in the restaurant regularly to taste as much as possible. We often had leftovers for supper, too, after finishing our dinner service.

Kerala runs along the Malabar or south-western coast of India. Spicy black pepper, green cardamom and coconuts are abundant in the area, and these flavour much of the food. This paste is fried in a little coconut oil until aromatic, and then coconut milk is added to make a sauce that forms the base for fish or seafood curries.

seeds from 3 green cardamom pods
2 cloves
$\frac{1}{2}$ teaspoon ground turmeric
1 teaspoon freshly ground black
    peppercorns
2 teaspoons sea salt
100 g freshly grated coconut
8 green bird's-eye chillies, minced
5 cloves garlic, minced
2 teaspoons minced ginger
6 red shallots, minced
10 curry leaves
50 ml vegetable oil

Grind cardamom seeds and cloves to a fine powder, then combine all ingredients. Refrigerate and use within 24 hours. MAKES 200 ML

Paramount curry paste

This paste, another of my interpretations using the principles of curry-making, is a staple at the Restaurant and at home. To make a curry, I cook this paste into coconut milk with a few roasted tomatoes and then sharpen it with some tamarind liquid. For a hotter curry, add 2 tablespoons Chilli Jam (page 58) to the paste before cooking.

1 teaspoon coriander seeds
$\frac{1}{2}$ teaspoon cumin seeds
10 white peppercorns
seeds from 2 green cardamom pods
5 large dried chillies, roughly chopped
5 red shallots, sliced
4 cloves garlic, minced
2 teaspoons minced galangal
1 stalk lemongrass, chopped
2 coriander roots, chopped
10 curry leaves
1 tablespoon Madras Curry Powder
    (page 35)
$\frac{1}{2}$ teaspoon sea salt
50 ml vegetable oil

Dry-roast coriander and cumin seeds over gentle heat until fragrant. Cool, then grind to a fine powder with peppercorns and cardamom seeds. Blend all ingredients to a smooth paste in a food processor. Spoon into a jar, then cover with a film of oil. Refrigerate for up to 1 month. MAKES 150 ML

Nonya spice paste

Nonya or Peranakan food is possibly some of the most fragrant, rich and interesting to be found anywhere in the world, and is part of a long heritage passed down through the maternal side of the family. Originating in Malacca on the south-west coast of the Malay peninsula, Nonya cooking combines Chinese and Malay ingredients and techniques, the result of Chinese migration during the fifteenth century. (An early example of fusion food, perhaps?) Nonya cooking also bears close resemblance to some of the cooking of Thailand and Indonesia, sharing many ingredients and seasonings and some culinary habits. The spice pastes or 'rempah' are fried in oil first and then infused into coconut milk or tamarind to achieve maximum flavour. This paste is fabulous when teamed with wet noodles and a coconut-based sauce.

12 large dried chillies
1 tablespoon belacan (Malaysian shrimp paste)
12 red shallots, sliced
2 stalks lemongrass, chopped
6 fresh kaffir lime leaves, shredded
3 cloves garlic, chopped
75 ml vegetable oil
2 tablespoons salted soy beans, mashed
3 teaspoons fish sauce
25 g palm sugar, shaved

Dry-roast dried chillies and belacan, separately, over gentle heat until fragrant. Blend chillies, belacan, shallots, lemongrass, lime leaves, garlic and half the oil to a paste in a food processor. Heat remaining oil in a frying pan and cook paste over moderate heat for a few minutes until it begins to colour and become fragrant. Add remaining ingredients and fry for another minute or two. Spoon into a jar, then cover with a film of oil. Cool. Refrigerate for up to 1 month. MAKES 175 ML

Satay spice paste

Typical of Nonya and Singaporean cooking, this paste is used as a marinade and flavour booster for meat or poultry, which is then threaded on satay sticks before barbecuing or grilling.

1 teaspoon fennel seeds
1 teaspoon cumin seeds
2 teaspoons coriander seeds
$1/2$ teaspoon black peppercorns
30 g palm sugar, shaved
200 ml coconut milk
2 teaspoons ground turmeric
$1/2$ teaspoon chilli powder
1 teaspoon minced lime zest
2 teaspoons sea salt

Dry-roast whole spices separately over gentle heat until fragrant. Cool, then grind to a fine powder. Stir palm sugar into coconut milk over gentle heat until dissolved, then mix in all spices. Refrigerate for up to 48 hours.
MAKES 300 ML

Paramount laksa paste

Laksa paste, a speciality of Nonya cooking, is great to have on hand and allows you to throw a fabulous soup together at the last minute. The paste needs to be cooked to make it palatable and desirable – the heat brings out the subtle flavours of the spices as they infuse into the added liquid, usually stock and coconut milk or tamarind liquid. We use this laksa paste in the Restaurant and sell it under the Paramount label.

2 teaspoons belacan (Malaysian shrimp paste)
1 teaspoon dried prawns
2 dried bird's-eye chillies
1 teaspoon coriander seeds
2 small red onions, chopped
4 cloves garlic, sliced
1 teaspoon minced lime zest
1 stalk lemongrass, finely sliced
1 teaspoon freshly chopped galangal
1 teaspoon freshly chopped turmeric
4 red bird's-eye chillies
25 g candlenuts
2 coriander roots, chopped
1 teaspoon ground turmeric
1 tablespoon coriander leaves
1 tablespoon laksa (Vietnamese mint) leaves
120 ml vegetable oil

Dry-roast, separately, the belacan, dried prawns, chillies and coriander seeds over gentle heat until fragrant. Cool. Grind roasted prawns and spices to a fine powder. Blend all ingredients to a smooth paste in an electric blender. Spoon into a jar, then cover with a film of oil. Refrigerate for up to 1 month.
MAKES 250 ML

Singapore laksa paste

There are probably as many recipes for laksa pastes as there are cooks – everyone seems to have his or her interpretation. This is my version of a most wonderful laksa I tasted recently in Singapore, cooked at home by one of that city's most ingenious and generous cooks, Melina Yong.

12 large dried chillies
2 teaspoons ground turmeric
2 tablespoons dried prawns
1 tablespoon belacan (Malaysian shrimp paste)
18 red bird's-eye chillies, minced
15 red shallots, finely sliced
8 cloves garlic, minced
12 candlenuts
150 ml vegetable oil

Dry-roast dried chillies and belacan, separately, over gentle heat until fragrant. Cool, then grind chillies to a fine powder. Soak dried prawns in warm water for 10 minutes, then drain. Blend all ingredients to a fine paste in a food processor, adding a little water if necessary. Heat a wok and gently fry paste over moderate heat, stirring frequently, for 10–15 minutes until oil is red and paste is fragrant and thick. Refrigerate in a sealed container for up to 1 month. MAKES 100 ML

Lemongrass stir-fry paste

This most fragrant paste is another staple in my repertoire and one of the products we sell under the Paramount label. It brings a simple stir-fry to life and gives the food a fiery zing. The flavours are released immediately with the application of heat and respond best to a quick, high blast – anything else only results in a stewy mess. Best with fish, poultry and vegetables.

10 stalks lemongrass
12 red bird's-eye chillies
15 cloves garlic
8 coriander roots
6 fresh kaffir lime leaves
200 ml vegetable oil
3 teaspoons freshly ground black pepper
50 ml fish sauce

Finely chop all fresh ingredients, then blend with oil to a fine paste in an electric blender and add pepper and fish sauce. Taste and adjust if necessary. Spoon into a jar, then cover with a film of oil. Refrigerate for up to 1 month.
MAKES 400 ML

Thai red curry paste

The fragrant, rich and spicy curries of Thailand have become so familiar in Australia that they are almost a staple. Avoid the one-dimensional flavours of the tinned and processed spice pastes and make your own. When you are familiar with the real flavours and their depth, you will not be conned by weak imitations.

These curry pastes come from the central plains of Thailand, the richest and largest region. Their colour can be an indication of the flavour of the paste. Yellow curry paste is usually considered the mildest, green the hottest and red the richest. Cooked into coconut cream to produce a thick and moderately hot curry, red curry paste is good with roast duck, red meat or chicken.

6 large dried chillies, chopped
50 ml warm water
2 teaspoons kapi (Thai shrimp paste)
1 teaspoon coriander seeds
1/2 teaspoon white peppercorns, freshly ground
6 red shallots, chopped
6 red bird's-eye chillies, minced
6 cloves garlic, chopped
2 teaspoons minced ginger
1 tablespoon minced galangal
1 stalk lemongrass, chopped
1 teaspoon minced kaffir lime zest
1 tablespoon chopped coriander root
1 tablespoon Chilli Jam (page 58)
30 ml fish sauce

Soak dried chilli in warm water for 15 minutes. Meanwhile, dry-roast kapi and coriander seeds, separately, over gentle heat until fragrant. Cool, then grind coriander seeds to a fine powder. Blend all ingredients to a smooth paste in an electric blender. Spoon into a jar, then cover with a film of oil. Refrigerate for up to 1 month. MAKES 200 ML

Thai green curry paste

The heat of this paste depends on the strength and size of the green chillies used. The paste can be cooked into coconut milk and then stock added later for a lighter, more fragrant result. I use green curry paste with fish, chicken, pork or vegetables.

1 teaspoon kapi (Thai shrimp paste)
1 teaspoon coriander seeds
$1/2$ teaspoon cumin seeds
20 green bird's-eye chillies, minced
5 red shallots, chopped
6 cloves garlic, chopped
2 stalks lemongrass, chopped
1 tablespoon minced galangal
2 tablespoons minced coriander root
3 tablespoons coriander leaves
2 tablespoons Thai *or* holy basil leaves
1 teaspoon minced kaffir lime zest
3 teaspoons fresh green peppercorns
$1/4$ teaspoon freshly grated nutmeg
25 ml fish sauce
50 ml water

Dry-roast kapi, coriander seeds and cumin seeds, separately, over gentle heat until fragrant. Cool, then grind seeds to a fine powder. Blend all ingredients to a fine paste in a food processor. Spoon into a jar, then cover with a film of oil. Cool. Refrigerate for up to 2 weeks.
MAKES 200 ML

Thai yellow curry paste

The mildest Thai curry paste, gaeng kari is directly influenced by the spices and flavours of India. It omits some of the fresh aromatic ingredients found in other Thai pastes such as galangal and kaffir lime and relies on fresh and ground turmeric for its flavour and colour. Shrimp paste is used fresh rather than dry-roasted for added pungency. Yellow curry paste works perfectly with fish, chicken and vegetables and usually relies on a light stock base flavoured with tamarind and lime. Look for small yellow chillies in good greengrocers – both Asian and Mexican varieties are suitable in this preparation.

5 dried bird's-eye chillies
1 teaspoon cumin seeds
2 teaspoons coriander seeds
1 teaspoon white peppercorns
1 tablespoon ground turmeric
1 tablespoon minced turmeric
6 cloves garlic, minced
5 red shallots, minced
2 teaspoons minced coriander root
2 teaspoons minced ginger
2 stalks lemongrass, finely chopped
6 small yellow chillies, minced
1 tablespoon kapi (Thai shrimp paste)
25 ml fish sauce
75 ml vegetable oil
50 ml water

Dry-roast whole spices over gentle heat until fragrant. Cool, then grind to a fine powder. Blend all ingredients to a smooth paste in a food processor. Spoon into a jar, then cover with a film of oil. Cool. Refrigerate for up to 1 month.
MAKES 100 ML

Massaman curry paste

Massaman curry paste, specific to central and southern Thailand, translates as 'Muslim curry' and is named after the Malay traders who influenced the foods of the region over the past century. Curries made with this paste are complex, rich and spicy with a wonderful depth of flavour due to the inclusion of the Indian spices cardamom and cinnamon. The paste is usually cooked into coconut cream with thinner coconut milk added at a later stage, along with roasted peanuts. Use with chicken or beef or other rich, firm meats.

1 tablespoon cumin seeds
2 tablespoons coriander seeds
seeds from 5 green cardamom pods
6 cloves
2 sticks cinnamon
8 dried bird's-eye chillies
2 teaspoons kapi (Thai shrimp paste)
6 fresh red bird's-eye chillies, chopped
20 cloves garlic, chopped
2 small brown onions, chopped
1 tablespoon fresh green peppercorns
5 coriander roots, chopped
50 ml vegetable oil
minced zest of 2 kaffir limes
2 stalks lemongrass, chopped
75 g palm sugar, shaved
75 ml fish sauce
60 ml Tamarind Liquid (page 341)

Dry-roast cumin, coriander and cardamom seeds with the cloves, cinnamon sticks and dried chillies over gentle heat until fragrant. Cool, then grind to a fine powder. Dry-roast kapi over gentle heat until fragrant.

Blend fresh chilli, garlic, onion, peppercorns, coriander root and oil to a fine paste in a food processor. Sauté paste over gentle heat in a frying pan until slightly coloured and softened. Return hot paste to food processor and blend with lime zest, lemongrass and dry-roasted kapi. Mix paste, ground spices and remaining ingredients thoroughly. Spoon into a jar, then cover with a film of oil. Cool. Refrigerate for up to 2 weeks.
MAKES 250 ML

Larp paste

Larp (also spelt larb or laab), popular in the north of Thailand and Laos and traditionally served with sticky or glutinous rice, is a fiery-hot dish that bears a similarity to steak tartare. The spicy, aromatic paste is mixed with raw or lightly cooked meat as it is minced. The most popular Thai versions are made with raw beef or cooked chicken meat, a speciality of Chiang Mai. I also use it with quail: I sear the meat over high heat with a garlic and pepper paste before mixing it with the larp paste and mincing it. I tend to seal beef over hot coals so that the centre remains raw, then I mince the meat with the larp paste and combine it with pickled green mango to make a fabulous summer salad.

5 red shallots
5 cloves garlic
4 large dried chillies
4 cloves
1 teaspoon kapi (Thai shrimp paste)
1 stalk lemongrass, finely sliced
1 tablespoon minced galangal
2 red bird's-eye chillies, minced
3 coriander roots, minced
4 kaffir lime leaves, shredded
$^1/_2$ teaspoon freshly ground white pepper
$^1/_4$ teaspoon freshly grated nutmeg
30 ml fish sauce
30 ml vegetable oil

Dry-roast shallots and garlic over gentle heat for 10 minutes until skins are blackened. Cool, then peel. Dry-roast dried chillies, cloves and kapi, separately, over gentle heat until fragrant. Cool, then crush chillies and grind cloves to a fine powder. Blend all ingredients to a smooth paste in a food processor. Spoon into a jar, then cover with a film of oil. Cool. Refrigerate for up to 2 weeks.
MAKES 125 ML

Chermoula

Chermoula is essential in the cooking of Morocco, where it is used as a fragrant marinade and seasoning for meat, poultry and fish that is to be grilled or baked. The formula is interpreted in many ways, depending on the region in which it is made. This version works particularly well with poultry and meat.

1 teaspoon cumin seeds
2 large dried chillies
$^1/_2$ teaspoon saffron threads
50 ml strained lemon juice
1 red onion, minced
2 teaspoons minced garlic
$^1/_2$ teaspoon ground paprika
$^1/_2$ teaspoon freshly ground black pepper
$^1/_2$ teaspoon freshly ground cinnamon
1 cup coriander leaves, finely chopped
1 cup flat-leaf parsley, finely chopped
125 ml olive oil
1 teaspoon sea salt

Dry-roast cumin seeds and dried chillies, separately, over gentle heat until fragrant. Cool, then grind to a fine powder. Soak saffron threads in lemon juice, then bring slowly to simmering point to bring out colour and flavour. Cool. Mix all ingredients. Refrigerate for up to 48 hours. MAKES 250 ML

Chermoula with preserved lemon

This version of chermoula, with the addition of preserved lemon, is wonderful with fish.

1 teaspoon cumin seeds
10 red shallots, finely sliced
4 large cloves garlic, minced
$^1/_4$ cup flat-leaf parsley, finely chopped
$^1/_2$ cup coriander leaves, finely chopped
$^1/_2$ cup spearmint leaves, finely chopped
2 red bird's-eye chillies, minced
$^1/_2$ teaspoon freshly ground black pepper
1 preserved lemon (rind only), diced
200 ml extra-virgin olive oil

Mix all ingredients thoroughly. Spoon into a jar and cover with a film of oil. Refrigerate for up to 3 days.
MAKES 350 ML

Cajun spice paste

The Cajun people of Louisiana are descendants of the French Acadians who were forced out of Canada by the British in the late eighteenth century. Cajun cooking is a combination of French and Spanish cuisines, a robust style that uses more spices than the Creole cooking of the region, of which gumbo is an example. This spice paste is a staple in the cooking of well-known Cajun stews such as jambalaya. It can also be used as a spice crust for fish and chicken that are to be fried in oil. Oregano and thyme are used in many of the basic seasonings and spice preparations that flavour fish, meat and vegetables in this style of cooking.

1 teaspoon black peppercorns
1 teaspoon cumin seeds
5 cloves
1 teaspoon yellow mustard seeds
10 dried bird's-eye chillies
1 brown onion, minced
5 cloves garlic, minced
1 tablespoon oregano, finely chopped
1 tablespoon thyme, finely chopped
1 teaspoon sea salt
1 teaspoon Tabasco
50 ml strained lime juice

Dry-roast peppercorns, cumin seeds, cloves, mustard seeds and chillies together over gentle heat until fragrant. Cool, then grind to a fine powder. Blend all ingredients to a smooth paste in a food processor. Spoon into a jar, then cover with a film of oil. Refrigerate for up to 48 hours. MAKES 175 ML

Mexican salt-and-pepper recado

This recipe is an adaptation of a spice paste given by Patricia Quintana in her book *The Taste of Mexico*. From the Yucatán region of the Maya people in southern Mexico, a 'recado' is used to flavour soups, broths, meat, sauces and fish. I use this version as a marinade rub for chicken or quail that is to be roasted. The seasoning has quite a potent kick when eaten raw but mellows in the cooking process. Habanero chillies are the hottest known to exist, so handle them with care!

4 habanero chillies
1 teaspoon black peppercorns
2 teaspoons coriander seeds
3 cloves
6 allspice
100 ml vegetable oil
1 brown onion, minced
10 cloves garlic, roasted in their skins
1 teaspoon freshly ground cinnamon
1 tablespoon oregano
1 tablespoon flat-leaf parsley
1 tablespoon sea salt

Preheat oven to 200°C. Roast habanero chillies, turning regularly, until blistered all over – this will only take a short time as the chillies have very thin skin and flesh. Allow to cool a little, then carefully remove skin, stems and seeds.

Dry-roast whole spices over gentle heat until fragrant. Cool, then grind to a fine powder. Heat oil and sauté onion until slightly coloured, then cool. Remove and discard skins from roasted garlic. Blend all ingredients to a paste in a food processor. Spoon into a jar, then cover with a film of oil. Refrigerate for up to 1 week. MAKES 100 ML

SPICE REFERENCE

THE FOLLOWING PREPARATIONS for spiced condiments, oils and sauces are regularly referred to throughout this book, and form an essential reference and repertoire for everyday cooking with spice. The tastes and textures described here are the building blocks for more complex preparations, adding to the vibrant language of spicy food. They are the exclamation marks on the palate! ❋ MANY OF THESE RECIPES can be made in larger quantities than you need at the time and the leftover quantity stored for later use, when time may be of the essence. Doing this will give you greater flexibility and versatility in your taste creations.

CONDIMENTS Pickles, chutneys, relishes, sambals and so on are essential taste sensations to add to the table when serving spicy food. They tickle the palate, enhance the flavours and textures of the dishes, and give an added versatility. Making these condiments is also an insightful lesson into the art of preservation: for those who pursue the ritual of food preparation, preserving is a vital and intrinsic component, but it is sadly overlooked by many today. And every cuisine around the world has its bank of preserves that makes the most of the abundance of the season. ✳ THE PICKLES THAT FOLLOW have a long shelf-life – they are characterised by a pungent heat and rely on spices and vinegar as preservatives. The sambals – chilli preparations with multiple functions – can be cooked or uncooked, which dictates how long they can be stored. The chutneys capture the freshness of their ingredients and are meant to be consumed within a few days or a week of being made. Similarly, the relishes are quick to prepare and rely on fresh, milder flavours that dissipate rapidly. These are best eaten the day they are made.

Eggplant pickle

An absolute essential in my larder. I serve this rich, vibrant and spicy pickle with curries, dosas (rice pancakes) or Parathas (flaky Indian bread – see page 266). I also use it as a base for other preparations, such as the eggplant salad I serve with prawn fritters (see page 88).

6 large dried chillies
hot water
1 tablespoon minced garlic
2 teaspoons minced ginger
1 teaspoon ground turmeric
1 tablespoon brown mustard seeds
500 g small eggplants, washed
200 ml vegetable oil
65 g palm sugar, shaved
2 teaspoons sea salt
100 ml malt vinegar
1 teaspoon Paramount's Garam Masala
  (page 34)

Soak chillies in hot water until soft, about 30 minutes. Drain, but reserve water. Blend chillies, garlic, ginger, turmeric and mustard seeds to a paste with a little chilli water in a food processor.

Slice eggplants into 1 cm thick rounds. Heat oil in a frying pan, then add spice paste and stir for a few minutes to release flavours. Add eggplant and cook until soft, stirring occasionally. Add palm sugar, salt and vinegar and simmer over low heat until thick. Remove from heat, then stir in garam masala. Cool. Spoon into jars, then cover with a film of oil and seal. Keeps for 2 months. MAKES 500 ML

Spiced tomato chilli pickle

I have adapted this recipe from the one for tomato kasaundi in Charmaine Solomon's *The Complete Asian Cookbook* – it is a variation of the traditional tomato pickle served as a condiment with breads and fish dishes in India. This staple pickle has a sweet–sour, spicy flavour characteristic of Indian preserves. I find it most versatile and use it also as a base for sauces.

1 tablespoon brown mustard seeds
125 ml cider vinegar
2 tablespoons cumin seeds
125 ml vegetable oil
pinch of freshly ground cloves
2 teaspoons ground turmeric
2 tablespoons minced ginger
10 cloves garlic
10 red bird's-eye chillies
2 kg ripe tomatoes, peeled and quartered
75 g palm sugar, shaved
60 ml fish sauce

Cook mustard seeds in vinegar over moderate heat for 10 minutes, then set aside for 2 hours.

Dry-roast cumin seeds over gentle heat until fragrant. Cool, then grind to a fine powder. Heat oil in a heavy-based pan, then fry ground cumin and cloves and turmeric gently until fragrant. Remove from heat. Blend mustard-seed mixture, ginger, garlic and chillies until smooth in an electric blender, then add with tomato to oil and spices. Cook for 1 hour over low heat, stirring frequently. Add palm sugar and fish sauce and cook for a further 30 minutes. Taste and adjust if necessary. Spoon into jars, then cover with a film of oil. Keeps for months. MAKES 500 ML

Date and lime pickle

A wonderful condiment to serve with sour curries, roasted meats or fried pastries. It has a strong and powerful flavour, so use it in moderation.

1 kg dates, pitted and diced
500 g Lime Pickle (page 53)
75 g palm sugar, shaved
1.25 litres water
2 teaspoons sea salt
125 ml strained lime juice
75 ml cider vinegar

Bring all ingredients to a simmer over low heat in a wide-based pot. Cook gently for 10 minutes, then remove from heat. Spoon into jars and seal. Store for 2 weeks before using. Keeps indefinitely. MAKES 1 LITRE

Pickled ginger

Essential on any Japanese table, gari or pickled ginger is served with sashimi and grilled meats. It tastes delicate yet pungent. I use it often in salad preparations as it cuts through and lightens any fattiness. 'Green' ginger simply means young, tender ginger.

300 g green ginger, peeled
350 ml rice vinegar
25 ml fish sauce
50 ml strained lime juice
25 ml Sugar Syrup (page 343)

Trim knobs of ginger to uniform size for ease of slicing. Slice ginger extremely finely, using either a sharp, fine-bladed knife or cleaver or a mandolin. The slices should resemble tissue paper. Pack ginger into jars, then combine remaining ingredients and pour over ginger to cover. Mix well, then seal. Refrigerate for up to 3 months. MAKES 600 ML

Pickled chilli cabbage and mustard greens

A staple of the Korean diet, the fiery-hot and wonderfully acidic kimchi is served with everything from rice to roasted meats. It can be bought from most Asian food stores, as it is considered a convenience food and is used in the same way as chilli sambals are in other Asian cuisines. But try making it at home for the best results.

1 Chinese cabbage
1 bunch large mustard greens
1 tablespoon sea salt
1 tablespoon castor sugar

Marinade
5 red shallots, minced
1 tablespoon minced garlic
1 tablespoon minced ginger
6 red bird's-eye chillies, minced
1 teaspoon chilli powder
75 ml fish sauce
25 ml soy sauce
30 g castor sugar
150 ml rice vinegar
50 ml strained lime juice

Remove core from cabbage and discard, then separate leaves. Wash cabbage and mustard greens well and arrange in layers in a deep-sided, non-reactive dish, sprinkling sea salt and castor sugar between each layer. Cover with another dish and put a weight on top, then set aside for 24 hours.

Drain cabbage and greens, then wash and pat dry. Combine marinade ingredients in a large, non-reactive bowl and add cabbage and greens. Cover and refrigerate for 3 days before using. Keeps refrigerated for 2 months, and less time if held at room temperature. To use, shred leaves coarsely and serve with pickling solution. MAKES 600 ML

Lemon or lime pickle

This pickle can be made with lemons or limes – go with whatever is the most abundant at the time and whichever flavour you prefer. It is a wonderful accompaniment to curries and rice dishes, but use it sparingly as the flavour is very intense.

12 lemons *or* limes
1 teaspoon fenugreek seeds
250 ml vegetable oil
50 g large red chillies, halved lengthwise
salt
2 teaspoons brown mustard seeds
1 teaspoon ground turmeric
1/4 teaspoon asafoetida powder

Cut lemons or limes into eighths lengthwise. Dry-roast fenugreek seeds over gentle heat until fragrant, then remove from heat. Heat half the oil and fry chillies for 5 minutes over moderate heat until softened, then remove with a slotted spoon. Reserve oil from pan. Pound chillies, fenugreek seeds and a little salt in a mortar and pestle. Heat remaining oil and fry mustard seeds, turmeric and asafoetida over moderate heat until fragrant. Reduce heat and add lemon or lime wedges, then cover and cook for 15 minutes until softened. Cool. Stir pounded chilli mixture through fruit with the reserved chilli oil, then spoon into jars and seal. Store for 1 month before using. Keeps for 1 year. MAKES 2 LITRES

Hot-and-sour pickled zedoary

When zedoary is in season, make this pickle and add it to salads or noodle dishes or use it to accompany rich curries. Remember that zedoary is usually referred to as white turmeric in Australia and occasionally as mango ginger, which is its name in India.

100 g zedoary, cut into julienne
3 teaspoons minced ginger
6 cloves garlic, minced
2 green bird's-eye chillies, minced
100 ml strained lime juice
30 ml fish sauce

Combine all ingredients and mix thoroughly. Refrigerate in a sealed jar for up to 2 weeks. MAKES 175 ML

Green mango pickle

This zippy, fresh-tasting pickle is wonderful added to spicy salads or as a condiment with curries. You can also make it with green papaya.

2 large green mangoes, washed
2 red bird's-eye chillies, minced
2 cloves garlic, minced
100 ml strained lime juice
60 g palm sugar, shaved
80 ml fish sauce
20 ml coconut vinegar

Slice mangoes, skin on, very finely with a mandolin or similar, then cut into thin julienne strips with a sharp knife. Combine remaining ingredients in a bowl, stirring until sugar has dissolved, then add mango. Refrigerate in sealed jars for up to 2 weeks. MAKES 600 ML

Spiced onion pickle

The addictive flavour of this pickle is great with preserved meats, sausages, fried pastries or grilled fish.

1 tablespoon sea salt
1 kg white pickling onions, quartered
200 ml vegetable oil
50 ml mustard seed oil
1 tablespoon brown mustard seeds
1 teaspoon chilli flakes
1 teaspoon ground turmeric
1 tablespoon amchoor powder
100 ml malt vinegar
100 g brown sugar
6 cloves garlic, sliced
4 green bird's-eye chillies, finely sliced
2 teaspoons minced ginger

Sprinkle salt over onion in a non-reactive bowl and set aside for 15 minutes. Heat both oils in a frying pan and cook mustard seeds until they pop. Stir in chilli flakes, turmeric, amchoor, vinegar and brown sugar – when mixture starts to bubble, add onion and remaining ingredients. Cook gently for 10 minutes until onion starts to soften, then remove from heat. Cool. Spoon into jars, then cover with a film of oil and seal. Keeps for 3 months. MAKES 1 LITRE

Pickled cumquats

Cumquats make great pickles and preserves because they have sweet, thick skins and little juice. Try them with duck, preserved meats, terrines and spicy sausages.

1 kg cumquats, washed
water
1 kg castor sugar
500 ml red-wine vinegar
500 ml shiraz
2 sticks cinnamon
10 cloves
2 teaspoons allspice
2 teaspoons black peppercorns

Put cumquats into a large saucepan and just cover with water. Bring to a boil, then simmer over low heat until fruit has softened, about 30 minutes. Strain and set aside. Bring remaining ingredients to a gentle boil in a large non-reactive pan, stirring until sugar has dissolved. Add cumquats and simmer for 20 minutes. Cover pan with a lid and stand for 12 hours or overnight.

Bring fruit and liquid back to a boil, uncovered, and simmer for 30 minutes. Ladle cumquats into jars, then reduce pickling liquid over high heat by half. Pour syrup over cumquats and seal. Store in a cool place for at least 3 weeks before using. Keeps for at least a year. Refrigerate once opened. MAKES 1.5 LITRES

Ginger chutney

Ginger chutney is one of my favourites to serve with curries and fried meats or pastries. This is how I remember it being made each day at the Mysore Restaurant in Madras when I was a visiting chef at the Taj Coromandel Hotel. This chutney is best eaten quite soon after it is made as the flavours start to dissipate after a few days.

5 large dried chillies
2 teaspoons cumin seeds
1 teaspoon fenugreek seeds
75 ml vegetable oil
1 cup finely sliced ginger
10 green bird's-eye chillies
125 ml Tamarind Liquid (page 341)
150 g palm sugar, shaved
3 teaspoons sea salt

Dry-roast chillies, cumin seeds and fenugreek seeds, separately, over gentle heat until fragrant. Cool, then grind, separately, to a fine powder. Heat oil in a saucepan and cook ginger and green chillies over low heat until softened. Add tamarind liquid, palm sugar and ground chilli and cook until thickened, 20–30 minutes. Stir in salt and ground cumin and fenugreek. Refrigerate in a sealed jar for up to 1 week. MAKES 250 ML

Hot mango chutney

Another essential condiment to serve with a curry and rice, but use it sparingly because its flavour packs a punch!

1 tablespoon sea salt
1 kg green mangoes, peeled and diced
6 large dried chillies
60 ml Chilli Oil (page 61)
1 teaspoon brown mustard seeds
6 cloves garlic, sliced
50 g ginger, finely sliced
1 teaspoon fenugreek seeds
2 teaspoons ground turmeric
200 ml malt vinegar
200 g brown sugar

Sprinkle salt over mango and set aside for 30 minutes. Dry-roast chillies over gentle heat until fragrant. Cool, then grind to a fine powder. Heat chilli oil in a frying pan and cook mustard seeds until they pop, then add garlic, ginger and spices and fry until fragrant. Add vinegar and sugar and bring to a boil, then reduce heat and simmer for 10 minutes. Stir in mango, then cook over low heat until softened, about 20 minutes. Spoon into a jar and seal when cool. Store for 2 weeks before using and keep refrigerated once opened. Keeps for 1 month.
MAKES 500 ML

Coconut mint chutney

Wonderful with rendang and other dry curries, coconut mint chutney gives a fresh and zesty flavour to slow-cooked meats. Look for the different types of dal in Indian food stores. This chutney is best used soon after it has been made.

$1/4$ cup chana dal
250 g freshly grated coconut
3 green bird's-eye chillies, minced
2 tablespoons chopped mint
5 cloves garlic, minced
1 teaspoon minced ginger
$1/2$ teaspoon sea salt
2 teaspoons vegetable oil
$1/4$ teaspoon brown mustard seeds
$1/2$ teaspoon urad dal
2 large dried chillies
10 curry leaves
pinch of asafoetida powder

Dry-roast chana dal for 10 minutes over moderate heat. Cool. Coarsely blend coconut, green chillies, mint, garlic, ginger, salt and chana dal in a food processor. Heat oil in a frying pan and cook mustard seeds, urad dal, dried chillies and curry leaves until seeds start to pop. Stir into coconut mixture, then add asafoetida. Refrigerate in a sealed jar for up to 2 days only. MAKES 350 ML

Mint chutney

Use this fresh and fragrant mint chutney soon after you have made it for the most benefit.

1 cup firmly packed spearmint leaves
6 green onions, sliced
3 green bird's-eye chillies, sliced
1 teaspoon minced ginger
4 cloves garlic, minced
1 teaspoon fish sauce
2 teaspoons castor sugar
1 teaspoon Bengali Garam Masala
  (page 34)
60 ml strained lime juice
50 ml vegetable oil

Blend all ingredients to a smooth paste in a food processor, adding oil slowly. Spoon into a jar, then cover with a film of oil and seal. Refrigerate for up to 3 days.
MAKES 200 ML

Fig and cardamom chutney

A wonderful condiment to serve with game birds, cold or preserved meats, terrines and pâtés.

750 g ripe black figs
50 g brown sugar
100 ml red-wine vinegar
25 ml cider vinegar
seeds from 12 green cardamom pods,
  ground

Peel figs and quarter lengthwise. Cook all ingredients in a non-reactive saucepan over moderate heat for 20 minutes or until thick and all liquid has been absorbed. Refrigerate in a sealed jar for up to 1 week. MAKES 300 ML

Tomato ginger chutney

This chutney gives fried pastries and meats a real flavour boost. I love it with lamb's brain fritters.

10 roma tomatoes, peeled and seeded
50 g small capers, rinsed
1 tablespoon minced ginger
4 cloves garlic, crushed
75 ml extra-virgin olive oil
30 ml red-wine vinegar
1 teaspoon sea salt
1/2 teaspoon freshly ground black pepper

Dice tomatoes, then stir over medium heat in a non-reactive saucepan to evaporate all juice. Stir in capers, ginger and garlic and cook for 2 minutes, then tip into a bowl and stand over ice to stop cooking. Stir until cool. Mix in remaining ingredients, then taste and adjust if necessary. Refrigerate in a sealed jar for up to 1 week. MAKES 300 ML

Tamarind chutney

This powerful chutney is a necessity for me when eating slightly sweet and spicy food, such as samosas, lentil dishes and hot curries.

1/2 teaspoon cumin seeds
175 g coconut sugar, shaved
75 g tamarind pulp
100 ml water
6 fresh dates, pitted and diced
1/2 teaspoon chilli powder
1/2 teaspoon black salt powder

Dry-roast cumin seeds over gentle heat until fragrant. Cool, then grind to a fine powder. Stir coconut sugar and tamarind pulp into water over low heat until sugar has dissolved, then stir in remaining ingredients. Simmer gently for 10 minutes until mixture thickens. Cool. Spoon into jars and seal. Keeps for 2 months. MAKES 300 ML

Sweet-and-sour green tomato chutney

This is a terrific fruity and spicy accompaniment to a sharp cheddar or roasted, grilled or cold meats and shows off the versatility of the tomato.

2 kg green tomatoes, chopped
3 Granny Smith apples, peeled and chopped
500 g white pickling onions, diced
3 cloves garlic, minced
1 tablespoon sea salt
4 tablespoons Pickling Spice Mix (page 38)
600 ml cider vinegar
500 g brown sugar

Put tomato, apple, onion, garlic and salt into a large non-reactive pot and add pickling spices in a muslin bag. Pour in 400 ml of the vinegar and bring to a simmer, then cook gently for 45 minutes until thickened, stirring regularly. Dissolve sugar in remaining vinegar and add to pot. Simmer for 1 hour until thick. Remove bag of spices, then ladle chutney into hot jars and seal. Store for a few weeks before using. Keeps for at least a year. MAKES 1.5 LITRES

Green garlic ginger relish

This relish is mandatory with white-cooked chicken (of Hainanese origin) and the boiled meats of Chinese cooking. I serve it with steamed chicken and snowpea leaves (see page 162). It is best eaten as soon as it is made to savour its piquancy and freshness.

3 heads green garlic, peeled and sliced
75 g ginger, chopped
12 green onions, sliced
1/4 cup coriander leaves
50 ml vegetable oil
50 ml light soy sauce

Blend garlic, ginger, green onions and coriander to a rough paste in a food processor. With the motor running, slowly add oil and soy sauce to make a smooth paste – blend until relish just comes together. Refrigerate in a sealed jar for up to 3 days. MAKES 250 ML

Fresh mango relish

A simple-to-make, fresh-tasting relish that is best consumed soon after it is made. It is terrific with grilled seafood, baked fish or spicy sausages.

2 ripe mangoes, diced
4 red bird's-eye chillies, finely sliced
1 tablespoon chopped coriander leaves
30 ml strained lime juice
30 ml fish sauce

Combine all ingredients, then taste and adjust fish sauce or lime juice, if necessary. Use immediately.
MAKES 200 ML

Mustard horseradish relish

A mainstay that first appeared in *Paramount Cooking*, this versatile relish can be served as a condiment, used to spike a sauce or added to a meat stuffing.

1 tablespoon freshly grated horseradish
2 tablespoons seeded Dijon mustard
1 tablespoon hot English mustard
2 teaspoons castor sugar
1/2 teaspoon salt
1 teaspoon freshly ground white pepper
2 tablespoons small capers, rinsed
3 teaspoons chopped tarragon leaves
5 tablespoons Roasted Garlic Aïoli
  (page 343)

Mix horseradish, mustards, sugar, salt, pepper, capers and tarragon, then whisk in aïoli. Refrigerate in a sealed jar for up to 1 week. MAKES 250 ML

Sambal belacan

Belacan (Malaysian shrimp paste) gives this sambal a distinctive character. I make a version of a gado gado salad where I toss Peanut Lime Sauce (see page 67) through stir-fried vegetables and bean sprouts and then serve this sambal as an accompaniment for those who want an extra chilli fix. A quick-and-easy meal to throw together in minutes if you have the sauce and sambal already made.

50 g belacan (Malaysian shrimp paste)
100 g red bird's-eye chillies, chopped
6 red shallots, sliced
6 cloves garlic, chopped
2 teaspoons minced ginger
50 ml fish sauce
50 g palm sugar, shaved
50 ml strained lime juice

Dry-roast belacan over gentle heat until fragrant. Blend all ingredients to a smooth paste in a food processor. Refrigerate in a sealed jar for up to 2 months. MAKES 200 ML

Sambal oelek

Fiery-hot sambals feature prominently in the food of Malaysia, Indonesia and Singapore as multipurpose condiments or accompaniments. Some are cooked and others are prepared in their raw, fresh state. All sambal preparations leave in the chilli seeds traditionally, as these provide the characteristic heat and flavour. Sambal oelek, the most basic of all sambals, is very easy and quick to make and can be used as a condiment or in place of freshly chopped chilli.

100 g red bird's-eye chillies
200 g large red chillies
30 ml peanut *or* vegetable oil
50 g palm sugar, shaved
40 ml strained lemon juice
50 ml fish sauce

Dry-roast chillies over gentle heat until softened and beginning to colour – do not let them blacken or the sambal will taste bitter. Cool. Roughly chop chillies, discarding stems. Blend all ingredients to a smooth paste in a food processor. Refrigerate in sealed jars for up to 2 months. MAKES 350 ML

Sambal bajak

Being cooked, this sambal is more gentle on the palate, relatively speaking, than the raw varieties. It includes onions for sweetness and belacan and tamarind for sourness. Used mainly in Indonesian cooking and popular with rice dishes such as nasi goreng, it is made with the milder, large Lombok chillies.

30 g belacan (Malaysian shrimp paste)
20 large red chillies, chopped
6 candlenuts
1 tablespoon minced ginger
1 tablespoon minced garlic
10 red shallots, sliced
6 kaffir lime leaves, shredded
50 ml vegetable oil
30 ml Tamarind Liquid (page 341)
250 ml coconut milk
30 g palm sugar
40 ml fish sauce

Dry-roast belacan over gentle heat until fragrant. Blend belacan, chillies, candlenuts, ginger, garlic, shallots, lime leaves and oil to a smooth paste in a food processor. Cook paste over gentle heat until softened, 10–15 minutes. Add remaining ingredients and bring to a boil. Simmer for 30 minutes until a thick paste has formed and a layer of oil is still evident. Stir oil into sambal and remove from heat. Cool. Refrigerate in a sealed jar for up to 2 months. MAKES 300 ML

Chilli jam

We sell chilli jam under the Paramount label and love it for its strong, addictive personality. I always have it at home, too, as well as at the Restaurant, as it is one of the most versatile concoctions imaginable. As mentioned in *Paramount Cooking*, I've been known to spread it on toast! More usually, however, I'll add it to coconut-cream based sauces for poultry or fish, use it as a straight condiment with grilled meat, or stir it into a marinade or warm salad dressing. It's also great added to a stir-fry, as it gives a more mellow, intense heat than fresh chilli, and it complements any meat red-braised in Chinese Master Stock (see page 339) perfectly. Although you can substitute ready-bought sambals, there is no comparison – this chilli jam has a great length of palate and complex flavours you just won't find in commercial preparations. The long, slow cooking intensifies the natural sugars present in the ingredients and much of the intense heat that you find in the raw or fresh pastes is not evident.

1.5 kg large red chillies, chopped
300 g red bird's-eye chillies, chopped
8 large brown onions, chopped
15 large cloves garlic, chopped
1 litre vegetable oil
300 ml Tamarind Liquid (page 341)
125 g palm sugar, shaved

Blend chillies, onion, garlic and oil to a smooth paste in a food processor. Cook paste in a wide, heavy-based pan over low heat until dark red – this will take up to 12 hours of continuous slow cooking and occasional stirring. Stir in tamarind liquid and palm sugar and cook very slowly for 2 hours. Spoon into jars, then cover with a film of oil and seal. Refrigerate for up to 3 months.
MAKES 2 LITRES

Harissa

Harissa is the North African counterpart to an Asian sambal, although is very much hotter as it has not been mellowed by cooking or the addition of sugar. It is served to enhance salads and cooked fish and meats, and is an automatic addition to cous cous. Test the water, so to speak, and then use it accordingly.

75 g large dried chillies, chopped
water
2 teaspoons cumin seeds
$1/4$ teaspoon caraway seeds
2 large cloves garlic, minced
1 teaspoon sea salt
50 ml tomato purée
60 ml olive oil

Soak chillies in a little water for 2 hours, then drain. Dry-roast cumin seeds over gentle heat until fragrant. Cool, then grind to a fine powder with caraway seeds. Purée chillies, garlic and 100 ml water in a food processor, then blend in spices, salt and tomato purée. With the motor running, slowly pour in oil. Spoon into a jar, then cover with a film of oil and seal. Refrigerate for up to 1 month.
MAKES 250 ML

Zhoug

This chilli paste comes from the Yemenite cuisine of the Middle East that crosses ethnic boundaries and the borders of surrounding countries. Usually made with green chillies, and sometimes with red chillies but without the herbs, zhoug is prepared by hand traditionally and is served with a mezze plate as an explosive condiment. A highly coveted essential of the Middle Eastern region.

1 teaspoon cumin seeds
150 g large green chillies, chopped
1 tablespoon minced garlic
$1/2$ cup chopped flat-leaf parsley
$1/2$ cup chopped coriander leaves
50 ml water
pinch of ground cardamom
1 teaspoon sea salt
1 teaspoon freshly ground black pepper

Dry-roast cumin seeds over gentle heat until fragrant. Cool, then grind to a fine powder. Pound chillies and garlic to a rough paste in a mortar and pestle, then work in fresh herbs and water. Pound remaining ingredients into paste. Refrigerate in a sealed jar and use within 48 hours. MAKES 300 ML

Coriander zhoug

I have adapted the more traditional recipe for zhoug (see page 58) to include coriander. We use it often at Paramount in various preparations, such as with steamed or roasted chicken or lamb's brain-and-spinach dumplings (see page 183).

1 teaspoon fennel seeds
2 teaspoons white peppercorns
1 tablespoon minced coriander root
1 tablespoon minced garlic
2 green bird's-eye chillies, minced
1 tablespoon coriander leaves, chopped
1 tablespoon basil leaves, chopped
1 tablespoon laksa (Vietnamese mint)
  leaves, chopped
30 ml vegetable oil
75 ml water

Dry-roast fennel seeds over gentle heat until fragrant. Cool, then grind to a fine powder. Grind and sieve peppercorns, discarding husks. Blend all ingredients to a smooth paste in a food processor. Spoon into a jar, then cover with a film of oil and seal. Refrigerate for up to 2 weeks.
MAKES 225 ML

Hilbeh

Used extensively in the cuisine of Yemen in the southern Arabian Gulf and also in the food of Libya and Egypt, this fenugreek paste is served as a dip with flatbread in the same way hoummus, baba ghannouj and other dips of the Middle East are. Hilbeh can also be cooked into a stock with grains, vegetables, lentils or meat. The fenugreek seeds are soaked first to reduce their bitterness, so don't contemplate skipping this step.

2 tablespoons fenugreek seeds
water
1 tablespoon minced garlic
1 cup coriander leaves
1 teaspoon minced red bird's-eye chilli
$1/2$ teaspoon freshly ground black pepper
$1/2$ teaspoon caraway seeds
1 teaspoon ground turmeric
sea salt
30 ml strained lemon juice
4 roma tomatoes, peeled and seeded

Cover fenugreek seeds with water and soak overnight or for 12 hours to allow the seeds to develop a jelly-like coating. Strain, then purée seeds in an electric blender with garlic, coriander and chilli. Grind pepper and caraway seeds to a fine powder and mix with turmeric. Add spices and remaining ingredients to fenugreek purée and process to a fine paste. Spoon into a jar, then cover with a film of oil. Refrigerate for up to 1 week. Serve at room temperature.
MAKES 200 ML

SPICED OILS Oils flavoured with spices give a boost to any foods with which they are cooked, providing complexity and an added dimension. ❋ WHILE THERE ARE MANY different flavoured oils on the market these days, it is a satisfying exercise to make them yourself. Cooking oils have an amazing ability to absorb and take on flavours – but rather than simply bottling spices in oil, I slowly infuse the spices in the oil over low heat, which draws out and highlights the flavours. ❋ THE FOLLOWING SPICED OILS form an important part of my cooking media, especially when stir-frying, barbecuing or grilling.

Chilli oil

Use this when stir-frying or to brush over food cooked on the barbecue.

1 litre peanut oil
25 g large dried chillies, roughly chopped
50 g dried bird's-eye chillies, roughly chopped
12 fresh red bird's-eye chillies, sliced

Bring all ingredients to a simmer in a saucepan over low heat – do not boil. Cook gently for 30 minutes, then remove from heat. Set aside for 24 hours to infuse. Bring oil to simmering point slowly, then remove from heat. Cool completely. Strain through a fine-meshed sieve, discarding solids. Store in sterilised bottles and seal with a cork. Keeps indefinitely. MAKES 1 LITRE

Sichuan pepper oil

Use in conjunction with Lemongrass Stir-fry Paste (see page 44), or when cooking poultry, especially duck.

10 large dried chillies
$^{1}/_{4}$ cup Sichuan peppercorns
1 litre peanut oil
3 fresh red bird's-eye chillies, finely sliced
2 tablespoons minced ginger
10 green onions, thinly sliced

Dry-roast dried chillies and peppercorns, separately, over gentle heat until fragrant. Bring all ingredients to a simmer in a saucepan over low heat – do not boil. Cook gently for 15 minutes, then remove from heat. Cool completely. Strain through a fine-meshed sieve, discarding solids. Store in sterilised bottles and seal with a cork. Keeps indefinitely. MAKES 1 LITRE

Chilli orange oil

Toss this oil through noodles for added flavour, or add it to stir-fries. It's also great when grilling fish.

zest of 3 oranges
4 pieces dried orange *or* mandarin peel, broken into small pieces
12 large dried chillies, broken into pieces
4 red bird's-eye chillies, finely sliced
4 cloves garlic, sliced
1 stalk lemongrass, finely sliced
1 litre vegetable oil
150 ml sesame oil

Bring all ingredients to a simmer in a large saucepan over low heat – do not boil. Cook gently for 15 minutes, then remove from heat. Cool completely. Strain through a fine-meshed sieve, discarding solids. Store in sterilised bottles and seal with a cork. Keeps indefinitely. MAKES 1 LITRE

Annatto pepper oil

This pepper oil is used when making a yellow curry or when grilling or braising fish.

1 litre olive oil
2 tablespoons annatto seeds
1 tablespoon black peppercorns, coarsely ground

Bring all ingredients to a simmer in a large saucepan over low heat – do not boil. Cook gently for 1 hour until deeply coloured, then remove from heat. Cool completely. Strain through a fine-meshed sieve, discarding solids. Store in sterilised bottles and seal with a cork. Keeps indefinitely. MAKES 1 LITRE

Spiced tomato marron oil

Look for the Mexican ancho chilli in Spanish and gourmet food stores and specialist spice suppliers.

12 tomatoes, halved and seeded
shells and heads from 5 freshwater marrons
1 tablespoon white peppercorns, freshly cracked
6 dried ancho chillies
2 litres olive oil

Preheat oven to 175°C. Roast tomato halves until coloured and syrupy, about 20 minutes. Be careful not to burn them. Roast marron shells and heads separately for 15 minutes. Cook all ingredients in a wide-based saucepan over very low heat for 2 hours. Remove from heat, then allow to cool for 30 minutes. Strain through a fine-meshed sieve, discarding solids. Store in sterilised bottles and seal with a cork. Keeps indefinitely. MAKES 2 LITRES

SAUCES Every sauce I make has a spice component. Assertive and complex yet refined flavours can shine in a sauce, giving balance to a dish, making it complete. The art of sauce-making requires a finely tuned palate that can pick up nuances, the subtlety of the ingredients, and pull them together to create a whole. Sauces give length of palate to the food they accompany, so they should be complementary by their very nature. The spices and aromatics used should build on the flavours used in the rest of the dish; they should certainly not override them. ❋ SPICES WERE USED extensively in sauce-making from Roman times through to the eighteenth and nineteenth centuries, when this practice went into decline. Today the fundamentals of cooking and sauce-making have become part of a global language, and we now have the flexibility to adopt and adapt the rules, to create a new palette of flavours. ❋ A GOOD SAUCE takes time to make: it needs resting, settling and skimming to rid it of any impurities. But the most important part of preparing a good sauce is having an excellent base stock that provides unequalled flavour, something that cannot be found in a packet or tin. Stocks and sauces can be prepared ahead of time and stored in the refrigerator or freezer, making the final cooking, assembly and serving much easier. The sauces in this chapter accompany specific recipes, so read carefully and be patient!

Spicy masala sauce

This sauce has a rich, enduring, mellow spiciness – it's one of my favourites and a staple on our menu. It is best served with any red meat and is fabulous with smoked eggplant, Garam Masala Potato (see page 203), and the sweetness of pumpkin roasted with spices.

2 teaspoons belacan (Malaysian shrimp paste)
2 teaspoons dried prawns
1 teaspoon Sichuan peppercorns
1 teaspoon cumin seeds
2 teaspoons coriander seeds
75 ml vegetable oil
25 ml sesame oil
1 brown onion, diced
4 large cloves garlic, minced
1 tablespoon minced ginger
2 slices galangal, diced
5 red bird's-eye chillies, diced
2 slices turmeric, diced
4 coriander roots, chopped
1 teaspoon ground turmeric
pinch of freshly grated nutmeg
8 curry leaves
1 stick cinnamon
100 ml tomato purée
150 ml coconut milk
50 g palm sugar, shaved
1.5 litres reduced Beef *or* Veal stock (page 339)
25 ml fish sauce

Dry-roast belacan, dried prawns, Sichuan peppercorns, cumin and coriander seeds, separately, over gentle heat until fragrant. Cool, then grind spices and dried prawns, separately, to a fine powder. Heat a wide-based saucepan, then add oils and fry belacan, ground prawns, diced vegetables and aromatics until just beginning to colour. Stir in ground spices, curry leaves and cinnamon stick until fragrant. Stir in tomato purée, coconut milk and palm sugar and cook over gentle heat for a few minutes until mixture starts to bubble.

Add stock, then bring to a boil and reduce heat. Simmer for 1 hour to reduce slightly, skimming when necessary to remove scum and excess oil. When the sauce is ready it will coat the back of a spoon. Strain through a fine-meshed sieve, pressing firmly to extract all juices. Discard solids. Stir in fish sauce, then taste and adjust seasoning. Cool, skimming surface when necessary. Reheat gently as required.
MAKES 1.75 LITRES

Hot-and-sour coconut sauce

This rich, spicy sauce is the perfect accompaniment to red meat – it softens and subdues meat fibres – and root vegetables.

2 teaspoons coriander seeds
$1/2$ teaspoon cumin seeds
$1/2$ teaspoon fenugreek seeds
$1/2$ teaspoon Sichuan peppercorns
$1/2$ teaspoon white peppercorns
2 dried bird's-eye chillies
2 teaspoons dried prawns
50 ml vegetable oil
1 brown onion, minced
5 cloves garlic, minced
1 tablespoon minced ginger
1 teaspoon minced galangal
4 fresh red bird's-eye chillies, minced
4 kaffir lime leaves, shredded
1 stalk lemongrass, finely sliced
1 stick cinnamon, broken into pieces
2 teaspoons ground turmeric
seeds from 4 green cardamom pods, ground
1 teaspoon nigella seeds
150 ml tomato purée
500 ml coconut milk
350 ml Tamarind Liquid (page 341)
1200 ml jellied Beef *or* Veal stock (page 339)

Dry-roast coriander, cumin and fenugreek seeds with Sichuan and white peppercorns, dried chillies and dried prawns over gentle heat until just coloured and fragrant. Cool, then grind to a fine powder.

Heat oil in a deep, wide-based saucepan over moderate heat and sauté onion, garlic, ginger, galangal, minced chilli, lime leaves, lemongrass and cinnamon until fragrant. Stir in roasted spices and cook for a few minutes, then add ground turmeric and cardamom and nigella seeds and cook for another couple of minutes. Stir in tomato purée and coconut milk, then bring slowly to a boil, uncovered. Cook for 5 minutes, then add tamarind liquid and stock and return to a boil. Reduce heat and cook at a moderate simmer for 1 hour or until slightly reduced. Strain through a fine-meshed sieve and discard solids. Cool, skimming surface when necessary. Reheat gently as required. MAKES 2 LITRES

Turmeric tamarind sauce

The flavour of warm spices and the slight tartness of tamarind dominate this sauce, which is served with fried chicken or seared tuna, the natural richness and textures of which allow the sauce to reach its full potential.

25 g belacan (Malaysian shrimp paste)
1 tablespoon minced galangal
1 tablespoon minced turmeric
2 teaspoons coarsely ground dried bird's-eye chillies
5 candlenuts
10 red shallots, chopped
3 kaffir lime leaves
3 stalks lemongrass, finely sliced
3 coriander roots, minced
75 ml vegetable oil
500 ml Tamarind Liquid (page 341)
50 ml fish sauce
60 ml Sugar Syrup (page 343)
1.5 litres Brown Chicken Stock (page 338)

Dry-roast belacan over gentle heat until fragrant. Blend belacan, galangal, turmeric, chilli, candlenuts, shallots, lime leaves, lemongrass, coriander roots and oil to a smooth paste in a food processor. Cook paste in a heavy-based pan over moderate heat until fragrant and slightly coloured. Add remaining ingredients and bring to a boil, then reduce heat and simmer for 45 minutes. Strain through a fine-meshed sieve and discard solids. Taste and adjust seasoning. Cool, skimming surface when necessary. Reheat gently as required.
MAKES 2 LITRES

Chilli prawn sauce

Flavour-packed and pungent to boot with a good mellow chilli heat that rounds out the palate, this sauce is great with white reef fish, shellfish and dumplings.

1 teaspoon belacan (Malaysian shrimp paste)
2 stalks lemongrass, finely sliced
1 large green chilli, diced
3 red bird's-eye chillies, diced
1 teaspoon minced galangal
1 teaspoon minced ginger
4 red shallots, diced
minced zest of 1 kaffir lime
4 kaffir lime leaves, shredded
5 cloves garlic, minced
1 teaspoon Chilli Jam (page 58)
50 ml soy sauce
100 ml Sichuan Pepper Oil (page 61)
150 ml tomato purée
175 ml coconut milk
500 ml Prawn Stock (page 337)
1500 ml Fish Stock (page 337)
25 g palm sugar, shaved
30 ml fish sauce

Blend aromatics to a smooth paste in a food processor with chilli jam and soy sauce. Heat pepper oil in a heavy-based saucepan and fry paste over moderate heat until fragrant, stirring to prevent burning. Stir in tomato purée and coconut milk and cook for 5 minutes. Add stocks and bring to a boil, then stir in palm sugar and fish sauce and reduce heat to a simmer. Cook for 45 minutes. Strain through a fine-meshed sieve and discard solids, then taste and adjust seasoning. Cool, then skim surface of any residual oil. Reheat gently as required.
MAKES 2.2 LITRES

Star anise broth

A light but intensely flavoured broth that is fabulous with tea-smoked fish, oily fish such as salmon, tuna and mackerel, or steamed pork. It has a lingering palate that many have described as the most ethereal taste sensation. Test that theory for yourself.

1 litre White Chicken Stock (page 337)
1 star anise
1 teaspoon dried bonito flakes
3 green onions, sliced
5 slices ginger
3 dried black Chinese mushrooms
1 piece cassia bark
1 teaspoon finely grated tangerine or orange zest
70 ml light soy sauce
50 ml ponzu sauce
50 ml Chinese Shaoxing rice wine
80 ml mirin
250 ml Sweet-and-sour Dressing (page 128)
40 ml Sugar Syrup (page 343)
few drops of sesame oil

Make stock as instructed, reserving 1 tablespoon chicken fat when skimming cooled stock. Crack star anise in a mortar and pestle. Put all ingredients except chicken fat into a large saucepan and bring to a simmer over low-to-moderate heat. Cook gently for 1 hour – do not boil. Strain through a fine-meshed sieve and discard solids. Stir in reserved chicken fat to give added gloss and flavour. MAKES 1.5 LITRES

Pepper glaze

This sauce should be used sparingly as its flavour is intense and its character slightly viscous. It can be flavoured with mustard, porcini, foie gras, beetroot or brandy and cream if you plan to serve it with a classic pepper steak.

vegetable oil
1 brown onion, chopped
3 large cloves garlic, sliced
3 sprigs thyme
1 tablespoon black peppercorns
2 teaspoons Sichuan peppercorns
100 ml brandy
200 ml shiraz
2 litres jellied Veal *or* Beef stock
    (page 339)
freshly ground black pepper (optional)

Stand a stockpot over moderate heat, then brush with a film of oil and fry onion, garlic, thyme and peppercorns until onion has softened and mixture is fragrant. Add brandy and, when hot, carefully touch surface with a lit match to flame it, then add wine. Cook gently until reduced by a third, then add stock and bring to a boil. Reduce to a simmer and cook for 1 hour, or until reduced by a third again, skimming occasionally. Strain through a conical and then a fine-meshed sieve to remove all sediment, then skim again. Taste and add black pepper if necessary. Cool. Reheat gently as required.
MAKES 1.5 LITRES

Chilli tamarind sauce

The heat from the chilli, the sourness from the tamarind and the rich sweetness of the coconut milk create a perfect harmony in this sauce, which best complements baked fish, crispy chicken or slow-braised pork.

25 g belacan (Malaysian shrimp paste)
2 brown onions, chopped
5 cloves garlic, minced
6 red bird's-eye chillies, chopped
2 stalks lemongrass, finely sliced
4 coriander roots, chopped
1 tablespoon minced ginger
75 ml vegetable oil
20 ml sesame oil
750 ml Tamarind Liquid (page 341)
800 ml coconut milk
2 litres Fish Stock (page 337)
50 g palm sugar, shaved
40 ml fish sauce

Dry-roast belacan over gentle heat until fragrant. Blend belacan and aromatics to a smooth paste in a food processor with half of each oil. Stand a saucepan over moderate heat, then add remaining oil and fry paste until fragrant and softened, stirring regularly to prevent sticking. Add tamarind liquid, coconut milk and stock and bring to a boil, uncovered. Boil over moderate heat for 1 hour or until reduced by half. Add palm sugar and fish sauce and simmer for 10 minutes. Taste and adjust seasoning. Strain through a fine-meshed sieve and discard solids. Cool. Remove any residual oil. Reheat gently as required. MAKES 1.75 LITRES

Ginger glaze

This sauce was designed to accompany the now-famous Five-spice Duck and Shiitake Mushroom Pies (see page 260), a constant on the Paramount menu. It builds on the essential flavours used in the pie, giving the dish an added dimension in flavour and texture. The sauce can also be used with other poultry or meat when the pervasive flavour of ginger is desired.

60 ml vegetable oil
20 ml sesame oil
1 brown onion, chopped
2 green onions, chopped
1 tablespoon shredded ginger
3 cloves garlic, chopped
1 red bird's-eye chilli, split
1 star anise
1 teaspoon Sichuan peppercorns
1 teaspoon fennel seeds
1 piece cassia bark
100 ml Stone's Green Ginger Wine
30 ml Chinese Shaoxing rice wine
20 ml Ginger Juice (page 342)
2 litres jellied Duck Stock (page 338)
1 tablespoon shredded drained Pickled
    Ginger (page 52)

Stand a stockpot over moderate heat, then add oils and fry aromatics until softened. Add whole spices and cook until fragrant. Deglaze pot with wines and cook until reduced slightly, about 10 minutes. Add ginger juice and stock and bring to a boil. Cook at a gentle boil until reduced by half and shiny and sticky, skimming occasionally. Strain through a conical and then a fine-meshed sieve to remove any sediment. Discard solids. Cool completely, then remove any residual fat. Reheat to boiling point when required and add pickled ginger at the last minute.
MAKES 1 LITRE

Coriander yoghurt sauce

This sauce is one of my favourites, as you will see by the number of times I use it to accompany various dishes in this book. It has its origins in India and is known there as podina, of which there are many varieties and interpretations. It goes particularly well with fried food, spiced meats and pastries.

1/3 cup coriander leaves
2 tablespoons spearmint leaves
2 green bird's-eye chillies
2 teaspoons diced red onion
1 teaspoon minced ginger
2 teaspoons fish sauce
1 teaspoon strained lime juice
250 ml plain thick yoghurt

Chop herbs and chillies. Blend all ingredients except yoghurt to a paste in a food processor. Add yoghurt and pulse only until mixture comes together. Do not overwork or yoghurt will split and make the sauce too thin. Refrigerate for up to 2 days. MAKES 250 ML

Sweet chilli sauce

This is my version of the popular Thai condiment: a terrific, easy-to-prepare dipping sauce and accompaniment that tastes a million times better than the bottled variety.

200 ml Sugar Syrup (page 343)
150 ml strained lime juice
75 ml fish sauce
2 teaspoons minced red bird's-eye chilli
2 teaspoons minced garlic

Combine ingredients and refrigerate until ready to use. Refrigerate for up to 1 week. MAKES 400 ML

Peanut lime sauce

This is my version of the well-known Indonesian satay sauce – I like to dress a gado gado salad with it and use it with satays or barbecued meats. Be sure to heat the sauce when serving to get the full benefit of the flavours.

4 brown onions, minced
6 large cloves garlic, minced
1/4 cup minced ginger
8 red bird's-eye chillies, minced
30 ml vegetable oil
500 g crunchy peanut butter
800 ml coconut milk
250 ml light soy sauce
300 g brown sugar
200 ml strained lime juice
200 ml rice vinegar
100 ml fish sauce

Sweat aromatics in oil over moderate heat until softened. Add peanut butter and coconut milk and bring to a boil, uncovered, over gentle heat, stirring frequently to prevent sticking. Cook for 15 minutes until thickened. Add remaining ingredients, then bring back to a boil and cook for 5 minutes. Taste and adjust seasoning. Refrigerate in sealed bottles for up to 1 month. MAKES 2 LITRES

Mandarin sauce

An exotic citrus-flavoured sauce that is wonderful with pork or duck, as the citrus counteracts the fat inherent in both meats. The sauce can also be made with the juice of Seville oranges when they are in season.

1 tablespoon vegetable oil
1 teaspoon sesame oil
2 teaspoons minced mandarin zest
8 cloves garlic, sliced
1 small brown onion, finely chopped
3 red bird's-eye chillies, minced
2 teaspoons minced ginger
225 ml Tamarind Liquid (page 341)
200 ml mandarin juice
100 ml soy sauce
50 ml mirin
100 ml fish sauce
100 ml Chinese Shaoxing rice wine
200 ml tawny port
600 ml Brown Chicken Stock (page 338)
200 g palm sugar, shaved

Heat oils in a large saucepan over moderate heat and fry mandarin zest, garlic, onion, chilli and ginger until softened and fragrant. Add remaining ingredients and bring to a boil. Reduce heat and simmer gently for 1 hour. Pass through a fine-meshed sieve and discard solids. Cool, preferably refrigerated overnight, skimming off any residual oil. Reheat gently as required.
MAKES 1.2 LITRES

Spiced green masala sauce

A rich and complex aromatic sauce that draws its inspiration from the flavours and textures of southern India. It is best served with baked or fried white fish and shellfish. Spiced green masala sauce uses two wet pastes as its base, so you need to plan well ahead before starting to make it. The sauce can be made ahead, up until the palm sugar and fish sauce are added, with one simple step left to complete the cooking.

30 g ghee
1 brown onion, minced
3 cloves garlic, minced
2 teaspoons minced ginger
2 red bird's-eye chillies, minced
2 teaspoons Paramount's Garam Masala
   (page 34)
1 teaspoon ground turmeric
1/4 cup Green Masala Paste (page 41)
2 tablespoons Spiced Tomato Chilli
   Pickle (page 52)
150 ml tomato purée
600 ml Fish Stock (page 337)
1/2 teaspoon saffron threads
25 g palm sugar, shaved
30 ml fish sauce
2 tablespoons Saffron Butter (page 342)
2 tablespoons spearmint leaves, shredded
2 tablespoons diced tomato

Melt ghee in a wide, heavy-based saucepan over moderate heat and fry aromatics until softened. Add ground spices and fry until fragrant, then stir in masala paste and tomato pickle. Cook for a few minutes until mixture starts to bubble, then add tomato purée and bring to a simmer. Add stock and saffron threads and cook gently for 45 minutes until slightly thickened. Stir in palm sugar and fish sauce and cook for 10 minutes, stirring until sugar has dissolved. To serve, bring to a boil and add saffron butter, mint and diced tomato and stir over high heat to work in butter. As soon as butter has been incorporated, remove pan from heat – the sauce will split if overcooked. Serve immediately.
MAKES 1 LITRE

Tomato cardamom sauce

A gentle, fragrant sauce that is well suited to chicken and fish. I use it with roasted chicken and saffron rice pilaf (see page 164), and it would also be good with Spiced Chicken Sausages (see page 158).

12 tomatoes
50 g ghee
2 brown onions, minced
6 cloves garlic, minced
2 teaspoons minced ginger
4 red bird's-eye chillies, minced
seeds from 8 green cardamom pods
1 teaspoon Paramount's Garam Masala
   (page 34)
2 tablespoons Spiced Tomato Chilli
   Pickle (page 52)
500 ml Brown Chicken Stock (page 338)
1 teaspoon sea salt
1 teaspoon freshly ground black pepper

Preheat oven to 200°C and roast tomatoes in a baking tray for 20 minutes. Cool. Pass roasted tomatoes through a conical sieve, pressing to extract as much juice and pulp as possible. Discard seeds and skin. Set aside. Melt ghee in a wide, heavy-based saucepan and fry aromatics until fragrant and softened. Add spices and fry for a few minutes, stirring, until fragrant. Add reserved tomato pulp and pickle and cook over high heat until bubbling, then cook for 10 minutes to reduce slightly. Add stock and simmer for 30 minutes. Season with salt and pepper. Cool, skimming surface when necessary. Reheat gently as required. MAKES 600 ML

Nam prik

Nam prik literally translates as 'chilli water' and is an essential dipping sauce for Thai food – fiery-hot with chilli, sour with lime. A nam prik can be cooked or uncooked, and both versions should be treated with respect. The sauce is usually served with raw vegetables (especially cucumber), crispy fish and sweet pork and is intended to arouse the palate and excite the appetite.

2 teaspoons kapi (Thai shrimp paste)
1 tablespoon minced garlic
8 red shallots, finely sliced
1/2 stalk lemongrass, finely sliced
1 tablespoon dried prawns
1 tablespoon water
5 red bird's-eye *or* scud chillies,
   finely sliced
25 g palm sugar, shaved
60 ml fish sauce
50 ml strained lime juice
25 ml Ginger Juice (page 342)
1/2 teaspoon minced kaffir lime zest

Dry-roast kapi over gentle heat until fragrant. Blend kapi, garlic, shallots, lemongrass, dried prawns and water in a food processor. Alternatively, pound ingredients in a mortar and pestle. Transfer mixture to a bowl and stir in remaining ingredients. Taste and adjust seasoning. Refrigerate in a sealed jar for up to 2 weeks. MAKES 200 ML

Spiced lemon sauce

This tangy, rich sauce can be served with livers, a variety of poultry dishes, Spiced Chicken Sausages (see page 158) or with a strongly flavoured fish that has been baked with Chermoula (see page 46). I use it in a chicken hotpot, too (see page 159).

6 tomatoes
1 teaspoon cumin seeds
50 ml vegetable oil
1 brown onion, minced
6 cloves garlic, minced
2 teaspoons minced ginger
zest of 1 lemon
4 red bird's-eye chillies, sliced
1 tablespoon Ras el Hanout (page 37)
1 teaspoon paprika
1 teaspoon ground turmeric
$\frac{1}{2}$ teaspoon freshly ground black pepper
100 g chicken livers, trimmed
1.5 litres Brown Chicken Stock
   (page 338)
1 preserved lemon, diced
30 ml strained lemon juice
$\frac{1}{2}$ teaspoon sea salt

Preheat oven to 200°C and roast tomatoes in a baking tray for 20 minutes. Dry-roast cumin seeds over gentle heat until fragrant. Cool, then grind to a fine powder. Heat oil in a deep, heavy-based saucepan and fry aromatics until softened and fragrant. Add spices and fry for a minute, then add livers and cook over moderate heat, stirring to coat with spices. Add roasted tomatoes and stock to pan and bring to a boil. Reduce heat to a simmer and cook for 1 hour until reduced and slightly thickened. Pass through a fine-meshed sieve, pressing to extract as much liquid as possible. Discard solids. Cool, skimming off any residual fat. To serve, stir in preserved lemon and lemon juice and bring to a simmer. Add salt, then taste and adjust seasoning. Allow sauce to sit for 1 hour or so before serving to allow lemon flavour to infuse fully. MAKES 1.3 LITRES

COOKING WITH SPICE

SALADS Salads feature strongly in the eating habits of modern Australia and have been popularised by many of the world's food cultures, offering contrasting textures, flavours and temperatures within the one dish. We have established a repertoire of exciting, spicy and tantalising salads in this country that has helped define our culinary status and inventiveness. With considered composition, a salad can be a spectacular, alluring and satisfying starting point for or feature of a meal. Much of the preparation can be done beforehand and it often takes only moments to complete the final cooking or assembly of a salad – a great bonus when cooking for friends or guests.

1 Preheat oven to 200°C and roast capsicums, turning regularly, until skin blisters, then peel. Finely dice capsicums and mix with capers, olives, parsley and red onion. Stir in half the olive oil and season with salt and pepper.

2 Dry-roast fennel seeds over gentle heat until fragrant. Cool, then grind to a fine powder. Mix ground fennel, cracked black pepper and crushed chilli flakes, then sprinkle over tuna to coat it lightly.

3 Wash spinach and blanch over moderate heat with just the water clinging to the leaves. Plunge spinach into iced water to stop the cooking process, then squeeze out excess water.

4 Heat a frying pan, then add remaining oil and sear tuna briefly over high heat on both sides. The cooking should be fast: the fish should remain raw or glassy in the centre. Remove tuna from pan and rest briefly. Toss cooked spinach in same pan until warmed through, then add lemon juice and season with a little salt and pepper.

5 Put warmed spinach onto centre of each plate. Finely slice tuna and pile it on top, then spoon roasted capsicum salad around fish and serve immediately.

1 red capsicum	1 tablespoon minced red onion	1 tablespoon freshly cracked black pepper
1 yellow capsicum	150 ml peppery extra-virgin olive oil	1 teaspoon crushed chilli flakes
1 tablespoon rinsed small capers	sea salt	500 g best-quality tuna, cut into 6 slices
12 kalamata olives, diced	freshly ground black pepper	300 g spinach, stems removed
1 tablespoon shredded flat-leaf parsley	$^1/_2$ teaspoon fennel seeds	25 ml strained lemon juice

Seared tuna with spinach and roasted capsicum caper salad

This salad is light and refreshing with clean, well-balanced flavours. Choose the best-quality

sashimi tuna available – yellowfin, bluefin, big eye or albacore.

1 Dry-roast Sichuan peppercorns over gentle heat until fragrant. Cool, then grind to a fine powder.

2 Remove wings, neck and tail end from duck. Wipe duck dry outside and inside with paper towel. Mix Sichuan pepper, Chinese five-spice powder and 1 teaspoon sea salt and rub into skin and cavity of duck. Put duck on a tray lined with a dry tea towel, then cover with another tea towel and refrigerate for 12 hours to cure.

3 Put duck, breast-side down, into a large bowl and add ginger and 2 of the green onions, chopped. Cover duck with baking paper, then seal bowl with foil. Steam in a large Chinese steamer for 1 hour 30 minutes, turning duck every 30 minutes to ensure even cooking. Insert a skewer into the thigh – if juices run pale pink, the duck is ready.

4 Remove duck from bowl and discard green onions and ginger. Strain accumulated cooking juices through a fine-meshed sieve into a jug and refrigerate until set to a jelly. Remove fat from jelly and set aside for another use. Melt jelly over gentle heat, then whisk in vinegar and olive oil until amalgamated and add salt and pepper to taste. Set aside.

5 Slice asparagus diagonally and blanch in boiling water until crisp-tender, then plunge into iced water to stop cooking. Drain on paper towel.

6 Chargrill or barbecue eggplants until blackened and blistered on all sides, then peel and cut into long strips. Set aside.

7 Heat vegetable oil in a deep-fryer to 180°C and fry duck for 5 minutes until crisp, keeping it submerged with tongs. Drain duck on paper towel. Remove breast and leg meat and slice. Discard carcass.

8 Heat a heavy-based frying pan until very hot. Smear scallops with a little olive oil and sear them on both sides until coloured, about 2 minutes all up. The flesh should be quite translucent inside.

9 Using your hands, gently mix warm duck and scallops, duck sherry dressing, smoked eggplant, asparagus, sliced remaining green onions, red onion, parsley and rocket leaves and pile onto serving plates. Serve immediately.

½ teaspoon Sichuan peppercorns	5 green onions	vegetable oil for deep-frying
1 × 1.7 kg Peking duck	40 ml sherry vinegar	18 large scallops
1 teaspoon Chinese Five-spice Powder (page 39)	120 ml extra-virgin olive oil	1 small red onion, diced
sea salt	freshly ground black pepper	1 tablespoon flat-leaf parsley
4 slices ginger	12 asparagus spears	2 handfuls small rocket leaves, washed
	6 Japanese eggplants	

Sichuan-spiced duck and seared scallops with smoked eggplant, asparagus and rocket salad

An all-time classic salad at Paramount that combines a true symphony of flavours. It borrows the Chinese idea of mixing poultry and shellfish and combining hot and cold ingredients. The preparation is quite involved but if spread over a couple of days the final cooking and assembly are reasonably straightforward. (See photograph opposite.)

1 Dry-roast cumin seeds over gentle heat until fragrant. Cool, then grind to a fine powder.

2 Char eggplants over direct flame using tongs until blackened and blistered on all sides. Peel, then squeeze out bitter juices from flesh and chop finely.

3 Heat a frying pan, then add oil and sauté onion and garlic until pale golden.

4 Mix onion and garlic with eggplant and remaining ingredients. Taste and adjust seasoning if necessary.

5 Serve immediately or at room temperature.

$^1/_2$ teaspoon cumin seeds
2 eggplants
60 ml olive oil
2 tablespoons diced brown onion

5 cloves garlic, minced
2 tablespoons coriander leaves, chopped
1 teaspoon minced ginger
1 teaspoon sea salt

$^1/_2$ teaspoon freshly ground black pepper
25 ml strained lemon juice

Smoked eggplant and coriander salad

One of my favourite eggplant preparations, this salad can be served alone or as an accompaniment to grilled or barbecued fish or chicken or spiced lamb and venison. I often also use it to stuff a boned leg of lamb or a venison loin.

1 Shallow-fry garlic cloves in oil over moderate heat until softened and golden, turning to ensure even cooking. Remove with a mesh spoon, then drain and set aside.

2 Bring coconut milk, palm sugar and fish sauce to a boil in a saucepan. Reduce to a simmer, then add chicken and poach over very gentle heat (below a simmer) for 8 minutes, keeping chicken immersed. Remove pan from heat immediately and allow to cool for 15 minutes.

3 Cut chicken into long strips and set aside.

4 Bring coconut milk back to a boil and stir in chilli jam and lime juice. Taste and adjust seasoning if necessary. Remove from heat and cool for 10 minutes, then pour coconut sauce over chicken.

5 Blanch snake beans in boiling water, then drain. Cut cucumber into fine julienne. Mix with remaining ingredients, except chicken and peanuts.

6 Divide salad between serving plates, then top with chicken and ladle over some sauce. Sprinkle with crushed peanuts and serve immediately.

12 cloves garlic
vegetable oil
500 ml coconut milk
60 g palm sugar, shaved
50 ml fish sauce
6 free-range, corn-fed chicken breasts
1 tablespoon Chilli Jam (page 58)

30 ml strained lime juice
6 snake beans, cut into 5 cm lengths
1 cucumber, seeded
3 large red chillies, finely sliced
$1/4$ cup freshly shaved coconut
3 green onions, finely sliced
3 red shallots, finely sliced lengthwise

6 kaffir lime leaves, shredded
minced zest of 1 kaffir lime
$1/4$ cup coriander leaves
2 tablespoons shredded laksa
   (Vietnamese mint) leaves
100 g baby spinach leaves
6 teaspoons crushed roasted peanuts

Coconut chicken with chilli and spinach salad

A rich and creamy, restorative warm salad that's easy to prepare and a winner every time –

the chilli jam gives the tastebuds a kick-start!

1 Dry-roast rice over gentle heat until slightly coloured. Cool, then grind to a fine powder.

2 Mix vegetable oil, lemongrass, lime leaves, garlic and crushed chilli and marinate beef, refrigerated, for 12 hours.

3 Combine dressing ingredients and set aside.

4 Sear beef with its marinade in a frying pan over high heat for 1 minute a side only – the centre should be quite raw. Cut beef into small pieces and put it into a food processor with the larp paste, mint, basil, 6 teaspoons of the roasted ground rice and 50 ml of the dressing. Pulse until mixture comes together and beef is coarsely minced.

5 To make the salad, peel pomelo, then remove all membrane. Chop flesh into small segments. Remove seeds and membrane from large chillies, then slice finely. Put salad ingredients into a bowl, then add minced beef mixture and enough lime dressing to moisten. Mix thoroughly.

6 Pile salad onto serving plates and top with a little extra pickled green mango, then sprinkle with remaining roasted ground rice. Serve immediately.

2 tablespoons jasmine rice
60 ml vegetable oil
1 stalk lemongrass, minced
2 kaffir lime leaves, shredded
2 cloves garlic, crushed
2 dried bird's-eye chillies, crushed
1 × 500 g fillet of beef, cut into 6 slices
6 teaspoons Larp Paste (page 46)
24 spearmint leaves, chopped
24 Thai *or* holy basil leaves, chopped
2 tablespoons Green Mango Pickle
  (page 53)

Lime dressing
150 ml strained lime juice
50 ml fish sauce
25 ml Sugar Syrup (page 343)
1 red bird's-eye chilli, minced

Pomelo salad
1 pomelo
3 large red chillies
3 red shallots, finely sliced
24 spearmint leaves
24 Thai *or* holy basil leaves
24 baby spinach leaves, washed
2 tablespoons Green Mango Pickle
  (page 53)

Fragrant beef tartare with pomelo, chilli, lemongrass, roasted rice and pickled green mango

Here I take the idea and flavours of Thai larp, an exotic steak tartare, and interpret it to suit my palate

and preferred cooking style. Chicken can be substituted for the beef, if you like, but cook it a little longer

(until just cooked through) before mincing it with the spice paste. (See photograph opposite –

the seasoned beef is pictured here with the components that make up the salad.)

1 Dry-roast cumin seeds over gentle heat until fragrant.

2 Cool, then grind to a fine powder.

3 Mix all ingredients in a bowl, then taste and adjust seasoning if necessary.

4 Sprinkle a few extra nigella seeds on top to serve, if desired.

$^1/_2$ teaspoon cumin seeds

500 ml thick plain yoghurt

2 small cucumbers, seeded and diced

1 small red onion, diced

$^1/_4$ cup chopped coriander leaves

1 teaspoon fish sauce

2 teaspoons nigella seeds

Cucumber yoghurt salad with nigella

This is my version of the well-known Indian salad raita. Serve it with hot curries, fried pastries,

tandoori-cooked meats or spiced fish – the yoghurt and spices are beautifully cooling on the palate.

1 Combine ingredients for pickled green papaya in a non-reactive bowl, then cover and refrigerate for a couple of days before using.

2 Shortly before serving, mix dressing ingredients and taste. The sweet, salty and sour flavours should be in harmony – adjust if necessary.

3 To make the salad, shred radish and seed cucumber before slicing it finely lengthwise. Mix salad ingredients in a bowl and set aside.

4 Heat a chargrill pan over high heat. Brush beef with oil and seal very quickly on all sides, ensuring meat remains very rare in centre. Remove from pan and rest in a warm place for 10 minutes.

5 Meanwhile, dry-roast dried prawns and jasmine rice, separately, until fragrant and rice has coloured. Cool, then grind separately to a fine powder. Mix ground prawns and rice with remaining aromatics and spices, then add beef and rest for 5 minutes, turning once.

6 Cut beef into 1 cm thick slices and toss with salad. Add enough dressing to moisten salad and pile onto serving plates. Top with pickled green papaya and drizzle with a little extra dressing if necessary. Serve immediately.

1 × 500 g fillet of beef, trimmed
30 ml vegetable oil
1 teaspoon dried prawns
1 teaspoon jasmine rice
1 stalk lemongrass, minced
1 red bird's-eye chilli, minced
2 coriander roots, minced
2 kaffir lime leaves, shredded
zest of 1 kaffir lime
2 teaspoons minced galangal
1 teaspoon minced ginger
1 teaspoon white sesame seeds

Pickled green papaya
$1/2$ cup shredded green papaya
50 ml strained lime juice
40 ml fish sauce
30 g palm sugar, shaved
1 red bird's-eye chilli, minced

Tamarind dressing
100 ml Tamarind Liquid (page 341)
20 g palm sugar, shaved
75 ml strained lime juice
1 teaspoon Ginger Juice (page 342)

25 ml fish sauce
1 teaspoon sesame oil

Pickled ginger salad
1 × 6 cm piece daikon radish, peeled
$1/2$ cucumber, peeled
6 teaspoons drained Pickled Ginger
  (page 52)
12 red shallots, finely sliced
1 tablespoon shredded laksa
  (Vietnamese mint) leaves
2 cups watercress leaves

Seared beef fillet with lemongrass, ginger and pickled green papaya salad

This hot-and-sour salad first appeared in *Paramount Cooking* but deserves inclusion in this chapter for its fragrant spicing and pungent flavours. You can also substitute other red meats such as kangaroo, venison or lamb for the beef.

1 Remove skin from fish and clean thoroughly, scraping all flesh and scales away with a knife. Mix salt, pepper and chilli powder, then sprinkle some over fish skin. Stretch skin out on a wire rack to dry – this will take up to 24 hours. Cut dried fish skin into pieces about 5 cm square. Set aside.

2 To make the salad, preheat oven to 180°C. Split chillies in half lengthwise, brush with a little oil and roast for 10–15 minutes until softened. Allow to cool a little, then peel and slice finely, discarding seeds and membrane. Shallow-fry garlic cloves in oil until softened and golden, turning to ensure even cooking. Remove with a mesh spoon and drain. Mix all salad ingredients in a bowl and set aside.

3 Mix dressing ingredients and set aside.

4 Cut fish into 6 pieces. Brush with olive oil and sprinkle with the remaining salt, pepper and chilli powder. Cook under a hot griller for 3–4 minutes (do not turn it) – the fish should be quite rare and juicy. Cut each piece of fish into 3 chunks. Toss fish and dressing through salad.

5 Just before serving, heat oil in a deep-fryer to 180°C and fry dried fish skin until doubled in size and like crackling. Drain on paper towel. Sprinkle with a little extra salt and pepper.

6 Pile salad onto plates, then sit a piece of fish crackling on top of each and spoon on ocean trout roe. Serve immediately.

1 × 500 g fillet of Tasmanian ocean trout, skin on
1 teaspoon sea salt
$^{1}/_{2}$ teaspoon freshly ground black pepper
$^{1}/_{2}$ teaspoon chilli powder
$^{1}/_{4}$ cup olive oil
vegetable oil for deep-frying
100 g ocean trout roe

Chilli, shallot and mint salad
6 large red chillies
olive oil
12 cloves garlic
6 red shallots, finely sliced
1 small cucumber, seeded and cut into julienne
1 handful mâche (lamb's lettuce) leaves
$^{1}/_{4}$ cup shredded spearmint leaves
2 tablespoons shredded laksa (Vietnamese mint) leaves

Lime chilli dressing
$^{1}/_{2}$ teaspoon chilli flakes
2 pinches freshly ground black pepper
100 ml strained lime juice
100 ml coconut vinegar
25 ml fish sauce
25 ml Sugar Syrup (page 343)
3 drops sesame oil
25 ml olive oil

Grilled Tasmanian ocean trout with roasted chilli, shallot and mint salad, ocean trout roe and fish crackling

The spices and the richness of the trout flesh bring the elements of this salad together perfectly, with the roe offering the palate refreshing bursts of sea salt. The fish crackling gives an added texture and flavour to the composition.

(See photograph opposite.)

1 Preheat oven to 180°C.

2 Roast onion and garlic cloves in an oiled baking tray until soft and coloured, about 30 minutes.

3 Heat a chargrill or barbecue. Toss octopus with 75 ml of the olive oil in a bowl to coat, then cook briefly over high heat until pink and tender, 5–6 minutes. Set aside.

4 Toss onion and garlic with remaining olive oil, pimiento, vinegar, salt and pepper, then add octopus and rocket. Arrange salad on serving plates and drizzle with rouille. Serve immediately.

3 small red onions, cut into eighths	200 g roasted pimiento strips	100 g small rocket leaves
12 cloves garlic	50 ml aged balsamic vinegar	1 quantity Saffron Rouille (page 344)
500 g baby octopus, cleaned	$^1/_2$ teaspoon sea salt	
225 ml fruity extra-virgin olive oil	$^1/_2$ teaspoon freshly ground black pepper	

Chargrilled octopus with saffron rouille and roasted onion and pimiento salad

Hanging around the fabulous La Boquería market (Mercat de Sant Josep) off the Ramblas in Barcelona inspired the

flavours, textures and colour of this salad. Look for jars of roasted pimiento strips (also called piquillo peppers)

in Spanish or gourmet food stores – they are a necessity if the success of this salad is to be ensured.

1 Mix crabmeat and lime dressing in a non-reactive bowl.

2 Marinate for 10 minutes.

3 Add remaining ingredients to bowl, tossing thoroughly to combine.

4 Serve immediately.

500 g freshly cooked blue-swimmer
  crabmeat
180 ml Lime Dressing (page 79)
1 small cucumber, finely sliced
2 green onions, finely sliced

2 tablespoons freshly shaved coconut
2 tablespoons chopped mint leaves
2 tablespoons coriander leaves
1 tablespoon Thai *or* holy basil leaves
4 kaffir lime leaves, shredded

2 teaspoons drained Pickled Ginger
  (page 52), shredded
$1/4$ cup Green Mango Pickle (page 53)
2 red bird's-eye chillies, minced

Crab and coconut salad with chilli and pickled green mango

Sweet, rich coconut flesh and just-cooked blue-swimmer crabmeat have a natural affinity, and in this salad chilli and sour green mango add a subtle complexity and fullness of palate to the combination. The salad relies on perfect produce, but any fresh crab can be used successfully. I presented this dish as part of a Paramount menu at the Park Hyatt in Tokyo in June 1997 and made it with a local favourite, zuwaigan or Pacific snow crab, which had the most luscious flavour and texture.

To achieve the amount of crabmeat needed here, you'll need about six blue-swimmers. Otherwise, look for vacuum-packed crabmeat from top-class fishmongers.

1 To make the coconut dressing, bring coconut cream, lemongrass, palm sugar and fish sauce to a boil in a saucepan, uncovered, then reduce to a simmer and stir in sambal and lime juice. Taste and adjust seasoning.

2 Reduce heat to very low and poach scallops in dressing for 3 minutes. Remove from heat. Do not leave scallops in dressing for more than 2 minutes or they will overcook.

3 Mix remaining ingredients except fried shallots and garlic in a bowl. Add scallops and coconut dressing and toss.

4 Pile salad onto serving plates (or divide between scrubbed scallop shells), positioning scallops on top. Sprinkle with the fried shallots and garlic and serve immediately.

30 scallops
2 large red chillies, finely sliced
1/4 cup freshly shaved coconut
3 red shallots, finely sliced lengthwise
6 kaffir lime leaves, shredded
minced zest of 1 kaffir lime
1 small cucumber, seeded and cut into
 julienne

1 teaspoon drained Pickled Ginger
 (page 52), minced
2 tablespoons coriander leaves
2 tablespoons shredded Thai *or*
 holy basil leaves
1/4 cup small mizuna leaves
2 tablespoons Fried Shallots (page 342)
2 tablespoons Fried Garlic (page 342)

Coconut dressing
150 ml coconut cream
1 stalk lemongrass, minced
30 g palm sugar, shaved
30 ml fish sauce
2 teaspoons Sambal Bajak (page 57)
30 ml strained lime juice

Spiced scallops with shaved coconut, basil and shallots

The quality of the scallops is of vital importance if this dish is to succeed as it should. I like to use either the creamy scallops from Victoria's Port Phillip Bay or the iodine-flavoured Coffin Bay scallops from South Australia, both of which can be used with their roe intact, or the big white scallops from Queensland's Hervey Bay or those from Tasmania's north coast. Choose fleshy, fresh scallops that have not been soaked in water after they have been removed from their shells.

If desired, you can serve this salad on betel or shiso leaves, which are edible and then become part of the salad.

Alternatively, you can serve smaller portions as an appetiser on scallop shells. (See photograph opposite.)

1 Make batter as instructed and set it aside for the designated time.

2 To make the salad, heat oil in a deep-fryer to 180°C.

3 Fry eggplant until golden, then drain on paper towel. Mix eggplant with remaining salad ingredients in a bowl, then cover and refrigerate until ready to use.

4 Peel prawns, leaving their tails intact but removing their intestinal tracts, then butterfly them open.

5 Heat oil in a deep-fryer to 180°C.

6 Dip prawns in batter to coat, holding onto the tail, and deep-fry, a few at a time, for 2 minutes or until batter has set. Drain on paper towel until all prawns are cooked.

7 Serve immediately with pickled eggplant salad garnished with coriander.

1 quantity Chickpea Batter (page 344)
24 green king prawns
vegetable oil for deep-frying
2 tablespoons coriander leaves

Pickled eggplant yoghurt salad
vegetable oil for deep-frying
2 eggplants, cut into 1 cm dice
2 tablespoons Eggplant Pickle (page 52)

500 ml thick plain yoghurt
2 teaspoons fish sauce
$^1/_4$ cup coriander leaves

Prawn fritters with pickled eggplant yoghurt salad

Use extra-large or jumbo prawns for these fritters, as their size stands up to the cooking

better than smaller kinds, resulting in better flavour and texture.

1 Dry-roast dried chillies, fennel seeds and Sichuan peppercorns, separately, over gentle heat until fragrant. Cool, then grind separately to a fine powder.

2 Quarter eggplants lengthwise, then cut each quarter across into 2 cm thick slices. Sprinkle eggplant with salt and drain on paper towel in a single layer for 30 minutes.

3 Heat oil in a deep-fryer to 180°C. Blot salt and moisture from eggplant with paper towel, then deep-fry in small batches until golden. Drain on paper towel.

4 Heat a large wok and add 30 ml vegetable oil, then toss in garlic, ginger and fresh chilli and swirl around quickly. Add ground spices, shredded fungus and fried eggplant and toss. Immediately add rice wine, vinegar, soy sauce, stock and castor sugar and bring to a boil over high heat. This will take a minute or two at most.

5 Reduce heat to a simmer and cook for 3 minutes to allow eggplant to absorb some of the liquid.

6 Remove pan from heat and stir in remaining ingredients. Serve immediately.

6 dried bird's-eye chillies
$^{1}/_{2}$ teaspoon fennel seeds
$^{1}/_{2}$ teaspoon Sichuan peppercorns
3 large eggplants
sea salt
vegetable oil for deep-frying
1 tablespoon minced garlic
2 teaspoons minced ginger

3 fresh red bird's-eye chillies, minced
5 fresh black wood fungus, shredded
30 ml Chinese Shaoxing rice wine
30 ml rice vinegar
40 ml light soy sauce
30 ml White Chicken Stock (page 337)
   or water
25 g castor sugar

2 teaspoons sesame oil
2 teaspoons fish sauce
6 green onions, finely sliced
$^{1}/_{2}$ cup coriander leaves

Chilli and garlic eggplant salad

Eggplant features so regularly in my cooking not just because it is my favourite vegetable but because it is so versatile and it is amenable to being paired with spicy and aromatic flavours. This hot salad can stand alone or be served with other salads with barbecued meats and fish. It also makes a wonderful vegetable accompaniment for soy-braised or white-cooked chicken, baked or grilled fish, seared tuna or crispy, fried quail.

1 To make the dressing, stir palm sugar into tamarind liquid over gentle heat until dissolved. Remove from heat and stir in remaining ingredients.

2 Remove bug tails from shells and lift out intestinal tracts. Arrange bug tails on a baking tray, then brush with chilli oil and sprinkle with black pepper. Cook under a hot griller for 3 minutes until flesh turns white, then turn over and grill other side for 1 minute. Remove from heat.

3 Mix remaining ingredients except trout roe and dressing in a bowl.

4 Cut each bug tail into 2–3 pieces and toss with enough dressing to flavour. Add to salad and mix well to combine. Arrange salad on plates, then spoon over trout roe and serve immediately.

18 large green Moreton Bay bug tails
Chilli Oil (page 61)
freshly ground black pepper
1 cucumber, finely sliced
2 red shallots, finely sliced
2 green onions, finely sliced
2 tablespoons chopped spearmint leaves
2 tablespoons coriander leaves
1 tablespoon Thai *or* holy basil leaves

6 kaffir lime leaves, shredded
12 cape gooseberries, halved
2 teaspoons drained Pickled Ginger
  (page 52), shredded
1/4 cup Green Mango Pickle (page 53)
60 g bean sprouts
3 red bird's-eye chillies, finely sliced
3 handfuls mitzuba *or* mizuna leaves
1/2 cup trout roe

Sweet tamarind dressing
30 g palm sugar, shaved
200 ml Tamarind Liquid (page 341)
25 ml Sugar Syrup (page 343)
150 ml strained lime juice
25 ml Ginger Juice (page 342)
50 ml fish sauce
25 ml sesame oil

Grilled Moreton Bay bug tails with tamarind, chilli, cape gooseberries and trout roe

Make this fabulous salad in early spring when the cape gooseberries and trout roe are in season. You can sometimes get roe from freshwater brook trout, the ultimate, but it is not always readily available – in this case, use ocean trout roe or freshwater salmon roe. The sweetness of the fruit and the fresh crunch of the roe enhance the tamarind and lift the salad, and your tastebuds, into another realm! (See photograph opposite.)

1 Mix curing ingredients, then rub liberally into fish. Put fish onto a tray, then cover and refrigerate for 2 hours. Drain off any accumulated liquid.

2 Heat some olive oil in a frying pan and seal fish for 1 minute a side only. Set aside.

3 To make the pickling mix, dry-roast dried prawns, rice and sesame seeds, separately, over gentle heat until fragrant and rice and seeds have coloured. Cool, then grind separately to a fine powder. Combine all pickling mix ingredients, then taste and adjust seasoning or sharpness if necessary.

4 Arrange fish in a non-reactive dish, then ladle over 200 ml pickling mix and leave for at least 2 hours. The fish can be left overnight or for up to 24 hours, but ensure that it is given enough time to come back to room temperature before serving.

5 To serve, toss remaining ingredients except salmon roe with 75 ml pickling mix, just enough to moisten. Cut fish into bite-sized chunks and toss through salad.

6 Pile salad onto plates, then spoon over salmon roe and serve immediately.

6 × 100 g fillets Tasmanian salmon
olive oil
1 red onion, diced
3 cloves garlic, finely sliced
2 large red chillies, finely sliced
6 red radishes, cut into julienne
1 cucumber, seeded and cut into julienne
12 sorrel leaves, shredded
1 small fennel bulb, finely shaved into
  rounds
2 tablespoons coriander leaves
100 g mizuna *or* rocket leaves
6 teaspoons salmon roe

Curing mix
2 teaspoons sea salt
$^1/_2$ teaspoon cumin seeds, coarsely crushed
2 kaffir lime leaves, minced
$^1/_4$ teaspoon crushed fennel seeds
$^1/_4$ teaspoon freshly cracked black pepper
seeds from 1 green cardamom pod,
  ground

Pickling mix
$^1/_2$ teaspoon dried prawns
$^1/_2$ teaspoon jasmine rice
$^1/_2$ teaspoon white sesame seeds
50 ml strained lime juice
1 teaspoon minced lemongrass
4 coriander roots, minced
10 g castor sugar
30 ml fish sauce
$^1/_2$ teaspoon soy sauce
3 teaspoons Ginger Juice (page 342)
3 teaspoons Chinese Shaoxing rice wine
200 ml fruity extra-virgin olive oil

Tasmanian salmon escabèche with radish, basil and cucumber salad and salmon roe

The method I use to prepare the fish for this salad is of Persian and Spanish origins – the fish

(preferably freshwater salmon or trout) is spiced, fried and then pickled before serving.

The salad ingredients provide textural contrast to the fish, making this a favourite summer dish.

1 Cut all vegetables into julienne and mix in a bowl.

2 Add green onion, chilli, bean sprouts and herbs and toss to combine.

3 Just before serving, add dressing and toss to coat salad.

1 cucumber
1 daikon radish
2 carrots
1 green zucchini
1 yellow zucchini
1 red capsicum

1 yellow capsicum
$1/2$ Chinese cabbage
12 snowpeas
12 green beans
4 green onions, finely sliced
  on the diagonal

4 large red chillies, finely sliced
200 g bean sprouts
50 g garlic chives, cut into 2 cm lengths
$1/2$ cup coriander leaves
$1/2$ cup laksa (Vietnamese) mint leaves
1 quantity Lime Chilli Dressing (page 82)

Vegetable salad with lime chilli dressing

An easy-to-prepare salad based on the idea of a coleslaw but including Asian flavours and ingredients to make it more interesting and refreshing. Find the crunchiest and freshest vegetables and use a sharp knife with a deft hand, or get yourself a Japanese slicer – the best results lie in the finesse of the slicing. The salad can be served as a light accompaniment to grilled or barbecued meats and fish, fried chicken or roast duck.

SOUPS

S O U P S   Soups are staples in every cuisine of the world and each includes a spice element in its make-up: this is what gives a soup its mysterious, elusive character. Rich and hearty or light and elegant, soups are comforting and endearing by their very nature. As a food source, they provide sustenance for the body *and* soul.   T H E   S O U P S   W I T H   the most fiery bite are those served in the tropical regions of the world – hot food causes the body to perspire, thus cooling it down. So don't shy away from a laksa in the middle of an Australian summer – it is one of the best things you can eat (and it's a great cure for a hangover!). With basic stock and spices to hand, soups are also among the easiest things to prepare quickly. Here I share with you the soups I use the most, at home and work, all with varying degrees of spiciness.

1 Preheat oven to 200°C and roast tomatoes for 20 minutes.

2 Put crabs into freezer for 15 minutes to stun them. Bring a large stockpot of water to a rolling boil, then drop crabs into boiling water for a minute or two to kill them. Refresh crabs in iced water to stop the cooking process. Crack shells and claws with a meat mallet or hammer.

3 Bring stock, tomatoes, crabs, aromatics and spices to a boil in a stockpot over moderate heat. Reduce to a simmer and cook gently for 45 minutes.

4 Add lime juice and fish sauce and simmer for 10 minutes. Taste and adjust if necessary. Strain through a fine-meshed sieve, pressing firmly to extract all liquid. Discard solids.

5 Just before serving, reheat soup. Roll crab cake mixture into 18 small balls with lightly floured hands. Heat oil in a deep-fryer to 180°C and fry cakes for 3–4 minutes until golden and puffy. Drain on paper towel.

6 Ladle hot soup into bowls, then add crab cakes and basil leaves and serve immediately.

8 tomatoes
3 live blue-swimmer crabs
2 litres Fish Stock (page 337)
2 stalks lemongrass, minced
6 kaffir lime leaves, shredded
1 teaspoon minced lime zest

6 coriander roots, minced
4 green onions, finely chopped
2 teaspoons minced ginger
12 black peppercorns,
  freshly cracked
40 ml strained lime juice

30 ml fish sauce
300 g Crab Cake Mixture (page 125)
vegetable oil for deep-frying
2 tablespoons lemon basil leaves

Crab and lemongrass broth with crab cakes

A light, refreshing soup that draws on the tropical, clean flavours of Asia, making it perfect for the warmer months

of the year. This recipe includes the crab cakes featured on page 125 – remember to use

the freshest crabmeat for the best effect.

1 To make the spice paste, blend ingredients to a smooth paste in a food processor. Heat a little oil in a stockpot and fry spice paste over moderate heat, stirring, until aromatic and slightly coloured.

2 Add all broth ingredients except pepper and bring to a boil, then reduce heat and simmer for 10 minutes. Strain through a fine-meshed sieve and discard solids. Reheat broth in rinsed-out pot and stir in pepper.

3 To serve, cook noodles in boiling water, then strain and divide between bowls.

4 Combine chilli and vegetables and add to noodles.

5 Ladle hot broth into bowls to cover noodles and vegetables and stir with a chopstick to combine. Serve immediately.

vegetable oil
200 g Egg Noodles (page 340) *or* bought
  egg noodles (Hokkien, ramen,
  fettuccine)
2 large red chillies, finely sliced
1 green zucchini, cut into julienne
12 snowpeas, finely sliced
6 green onions, sliced
100 g bean sprouts
1 carrot, peeled and cut into julienne
3 shiitake mushrooms, finely sliced

Spice paste
1 tablespoon minced galangal
1 tablespoon minced turmeric
2 red bird's-eye chillies, chopped
6 candlenuts
3 stalks lemongrass, minced
10 red shallots, sliced
5 kaffir lime leaves, shredded
4 cloves garlic, sliced
50 ml vegetable oil
1 teaspoon sesame oil

Turmeric lemongrass broth
1.5 litres Spiced Vegetable Stock
  (page 340)
300 ml Tamarind Liquid (page 341)
100 ml light soy sauce
30 ml strained lemon juice
75 ml Sugar Syrup (page 343)
1 teaspoon freshly ground white pepper

Turmeric lemongrass broth with noodles and vegetables

A fabulous spicy vegetable-based soup that will delight vegetarians and meat-eaters alike.

1 To make the soup, shell prawns (reserving shells and heads), then remove intestinal tracts. Butterfly prawns open and set aside.

2 Heat oil in a wide, heavy-based saucepan and fry prawn heads and shells over moderately high heat until a pinkish red. Tip shells and heads onto a plate.

3 In the same pan, fry aromatics and herbs until fragrant and slightly coloured. Return prawn heads and shells to pan and stir to incorporate. Add stock and bring to a simmer over gentle heat, then cook for 45 minutes.

4 Strain through a fine-meshed sieve, discarding solids.

5 Return soup to rinsed-out pan. Stir in fish sauce and lime juice while soup is still very hot. Taste and adjust seasoning if necessary.

6 To serve, reheat soup over gentle heat and simmer prawns for 2 minutes only, just until opaque. Finely slice tomato lengthwise. Ladle soup and prawns into bowls and add tomato, laksa and lime leaves and chilli, then swirl with a chopstick to combine. Serve immediately.

2 tomatoes, peeled and seeded
3 teaspoons laksa (Vietnamese mint)
  leaves
3 kaffir lime leaves, shredded
1 large red chilli, finely sliced

Soup
1 kg green king prawns
30 ml vegetable oil
1 stalk lemongrass, sliced
4 red bird's-eye chillies
3 kaffir lime leaves, shredded
minced zest of 1 kaffir lime
2 teaspoons minced galangal

2 teaspoons minced ginger
5 cloves garlic, minced
3 red shallots, sliced
2 coriander roots, chopped
1 tablespoon chopped spearmint leaves
2 litres Fish Stock (page 337)
75 ml fish sauce
85 ml strained lime juice

Hot-and-sour prawn soup

A rich, clear broth with refreshing aromatic flavours I have interpreted from the Thai classic tom yam gung.

(See photograph opposite.)

1 Make dashi stock as instructed and keep warm.

2 Soften miso pastes in 150 ml hot dashi stock and whisk until blended.

3 Bring 1 litre dashi stock and ponzu sauce to a simmer in a saucepan and carefully stir in softened miso until dissolved. Do not boil – remove pan from heat as soon as it comes to a mere simmer.

4 Divide tofu, seaweed and sliced mushrooms between bowls, then sprinkle with a little sansho pepper and ladle in hot miso broth. Add green onion and pickled ginger and serve immediately.

1 quantity Dashi Stock (page 337)
75 g shiromiso (white) paste
40 g akamiso (red) paste
60 ml ponzu sauce
6 fresh tofu squares

30 g fresh wakame seaweed, washed and shredded
12 shimeji *or* 6 shiitake mushrooms, sliced
sansho pepper

3 green onions, finely sliced
1 teaspoon drained Pickled Ginger (page 52), shredded

Tofu in miso broth with green onions, mushrooms and ginger

Japan must surely lead the way when it comes to purity of flavour. After the complexity of flavours and multi-dimensional nature of so much of the food available in Australia, it is with occasional relief that we turn to the clean flavours and the aesthetics of Japanese-inspired dishes. As I learned when working in Tokyo recently, the varieties of miso and tofu available are fantastic, each offering a different flavour and result and each used for a different purpose. Shiromiso or white miso, in fact a pale-yellow colour, has a sweet, delicate flavour; the most commonly used and darker akamiso has a more earthy, salty character. Use the fresh, silken Japanese tofu when making this soup as it provides the best texture.

1 Wash chicken thoroughly to remove any blood. Put chicken into a stockpot and cover with water (you may need to add a little more). Add green onions, ginger and peppercorns and bring to a boil.

2 Reduce heat to a simmer and cook for 1 hour or until chicken is cooked. Do not boil as meat will toughen. Test thigh with a skewer – if juices run pale pink, chicken is cooked. Remove chicken from pot with a strainer or slotted spoon and set aside to cool for 10 minutes.

3 Strain cooking liquid through a fine-meshed sieve, discarding solids, then return to rinsed-out pot and add fish sauce. Taste and adjust seasoning if necessary.

4 Pull chicken apart while still warm, discarding skin and bones. Shred meat with your fingers and sprinkle with Chinese spice salt.

5 To serve, bring broth to a gentle boil. Meanwhile, bring a saucepan of water to a boil and blanch noodles for a few minutes until softened, then drain. Blanch cabbage leaves for 30 seconds, then drain. Add corn kernels to broth and cook for 2 minutes.

6 Crack a raw egg into each bowl, then pour in boiling broth and stir with a chopstick until egg forms threads.

7 Divide chicken and remaining ingredients between bowls. Serve immediately.

1 × 1.8 kg free-range, corn-fed chicken
3 litres water
6 green onions, chopped
6 slices ginger
1 teaspoon white peppercorns, cracked

120 ml fish sauce
1 teaspoon Chinese Spice Salt (page 39)
500 g fresh Chinese egg noodles
12 Chinese cabbage leaves
kernels from 2 corn cobs

6 eggs
$\frac{1}{4}$ cup chopped garlic chives
2 teaspoons drained Pickled Ginger
   (page 52), shredded
3 large green chillies, finely sliced

Chicken, sweetcorn and noodle soup

A delicious soup that can easily be considered a meal in a bowl. The base can be made ahead of time,

making the last-minute cooking and assembly very simple. Using the best-quality chicken you can

will make all the difference to the flavour and outcome of this dish.

1 Dry-roast dried prawns over gentle heat until fragrant. Cool, then grind to a fine powder.

2 Heat oil in a large saucepan, then sauté mustard seeds and curry leaves briefly over moderate heat until seeds start to pop. Stir in onion, garlic, ginger, chilli and minced turmeric, then cook for 1–2 minutes to soften. Add coconut cream and fenugreek seeds and cook, uncovered, for 5 minutes.

3 Stir in remaining ingredients except fish sauce and coriander and bring to a boil. Reduce heat and simmer gently until pumpkin has cooked, about 15 minutes. Stir in fish sauce, then taste and adjust if necessary.

4 To serve, stir in coriander leaves and ladle soup into deep bowls.

1 teaspoon dried prawns
25 ml vegetable oil
1 teaspoon brown mustard seeds
12 curry leaves
1 large brown onion, minced
6 cloves garlic, minced

1 tablespoon minced ginger
2 green chillies, minced
1 teaspoon minced turmeric
250 ml coconut cream
1 teaspoon fenugreek seeds
600 g butternut pumpkin, peeled and cut into 1 cm cubes

1 teaspoon ground turmeric
600 ml coconut milk
1 litre Spiced Vegetable Stock (page 340)
150 ml fish sauce
¼ cup coriander leaves

Pumpkin, fenugreek and coconut soup

A spicy, rich vegetable soup with familiar curry flavours. Try it with Curry Crackers (see page 270),

Parathas (pages 266 and 267) or Onion Nigella Bread (page 269).

1 Wash chicken to remove all blood. Bring a stockpot of water to a boil, then immerse chicken and blanch for 5 minutes. Remove and drain, then cut into quarters.

2 Finely chop 6 slices of the galangal, ginger, coriander roots, shallots, 3 of the chillies, 6 of the lime leaves and 2 stalks of the lemongrass.

3 Bring coconut cream to a boil in a large saucepan and boil, uncovered, for a few minutes. Stir in chopped aromatics, lime zest and chilli jam, then return to a boil. Add stock and fish sauce and return to a boil once more. Add chicken pieces, then reduce heat and simmer gently for about 20 minutes until chicken is cooked. Remove chicken carefully with a strainer or slotted spoon and set aside until cool enough to handle.

4 Strain soup through a fine-meshed sieve, discarding solids, then return to rinsed-out pan and add lime juice. Taste and adjust if necessary.

5 Slice remaining chillies and finely shred remaining lemongrass and kaffir lime leaves.

6 To serve, shred chicken while warm, discarding bones and skin, then pile meat into each bowl. Ladle soup over chicken and garnish with sliced chilli, shredded lemongrass and kaffir lime leaves, basil and coriander leaves. Mince remaining galangal and add to bowls, then stir and serve immediately.

1 × 1.8 kg free-range, corn-fed chicken	6 red bird's-eye chillies	2 litres White Chicken Stock (page 337)
water	12 kaffir lime leaves	100 ml fish sauce
8 slices galangal	3 stalks lemongrass	75 ml strained lime juice
3 slices ginger	1 litre coconut cream	2 tablespoons Thai *or* holy basil leaves
6 coriander roots	zest of 1 kaffir lime, minced	2 tablespoons coriander leaves
6 red shallots	2 teaspoons Chilli Jam (page 58)	

Spiced chicken, lemongrass and coconut soup with chilli jam

I fell in love with the flavours and textures of tom kha gai years ago on my first visit to Thailand. I have since

adapted the fragrance and balance of flavours of this classic to suit my own style of cooking.

1 Steam or poach chicken breast in stock gently for 15 minutes until just cooked through. Cool, then shred.

2 Bring coconut milk, laksa paste and chilli jam slowly to a boil in a saucepan, uncovered, then reduce heat and simmer for 10 minutes until oil rises to surface.

3 Add stock, then return to a boil, uncovered. Reduce heat and simmer gently for 15 minutes. Season with lime juice and fish sauce, then taste and adjust if necessary.

4 Put noodles and chicken into separate noodle baskets or conical sieves and lower into soup to warm through.

5 Divide noodles and chicken between bowls, then shred lime leaves very finely and add with bean sprouts. Ladle soup into each bowl to cover noodles and stir with a chopstick to combine.

6 Sprinkle remaining ingredients over top and serve immediately. Offer extra chilli in a separate bowl for the addicts!

1 × 250 g free-range corn-fed chicken
  breast, skin removed
500 ml White Chicken Stock (page 337)
450 ml coconut milk
¼ cup Paramount *or* Singapore laksa
  paste (page 43 or 44)

1 teaspoon Chilli Jam (page 58)
20 ml strained lime juice
30 ml fish sauce
500 g fresh rice noodles
3 kaffir lime leaves
125 g bean sprouts

3 teaspoons Fried Shallots (page 342)
3 teaspoons coriander leaves
3 red bird's-eye chillies, finely sliced
24 laksa (Vietnamese mint) leaves

Chicken laksa

This soup is of Nonya origin and has become a familiar part of the Australian urban diet. We seek out the best laksa places everywhere as if we're hunting for gold, demonstrating our appetite and love for spicy, rich food. Make the paste and stock ahead of time and you can whip up a delicious meal in minutes. Laksa translates easily into large numbers: you can increase the quantities according to how many you are feeding without fear of losing out on quality or flavour.

(See photograph opposite.)

1 To make the soup, preheat oven to 200°C and roast tomatoes for 20 minutes. Set aside. Dry-roast fennel seeds over gentle heat until fragrant. Cool, then grind to a fine powder. Melt butter in a stockpot and sauté onion, garlic and sliced fennel for 5 minutes until softened. Stir in ground fennel, paprika, potato and tomatoes. Pour in stock and parsley, then bring slowly to a boil. Simmer for 45 minutes.

2 Pass soup through a conical sieve, pressing to extract as much liquid and potato as possible (the potato is needed to thicken the soup).

3 To make the custards, preheat oven (*not* fan-forced) to 125°C. Whisk eggs with mirin, fish sauce and pepper. Bring stock to a simmer in a saucepan, then add saffron and infuse off the heat for 5 minutes. Stir hot stock into eggs, then skim off any bubbles. Pour custard into 6 × 125 ml oiled dariole moulds, then stand these in a baking tray of hot water. Cover tray with foil and bake custards for 30 minutes until just set. Remove custards from water bath and cool for 15 minutes.

4 While the custards are cooling, bring soup to a simmer in a clean saucepan, then stir in saffron and infuse for 5 minutes. Stir in seasonings and cream and simmer for 10 minutes. Taste and adjust if necessary.

5 To serve, reheat noodles in boiling water for 30 seconds, then divide between bowls. Sit rock lobster meat on top of noodles and ladle in soup. To turn out each custard, run a small, sharp knife around the rim to loosen, then give mould a firm tap on its base and slide custard out onto a wide spatula. Carefully position custard on top of lobster, then add saffron rouille and sprinkle with parsley. Serve immediately.

300 g Egg Noodles (page 340), cooked
300 g cooked southern rock lobster
   tail meat, finely sliced
6 teaspoons Saffron Rouille (page 344)
1 tablespoon shredded flat-leaf parsley

Rock lobster saffron soup
6 tomatoes
$^1/_2$ teaspoon fennel seeds
75 g unsalted butter
1 brown onion, minced

4 cloves garlic, sliced
$^1/_2$ fennel bulb, sliced
2 teaspoons Spanish paprika
250 g waxy potatoes, peeled and cut into
   2 cm cubes
2 litres Crayfish Stock (page 337)
1 tablespoon chopped flat-leaf parsley
1 teaspoon saffron threads
2 teaspoons sea salt
1 teaspoon freshly ground black pepper
100 ml thick (45%) cream

Lobster savoury custards
4 large eggs
20 ml mirin
20 ml fish sauce
pinch of freshly ground white pepper
400 ml Rock Lobster Stock (page 337)
pinch of saffron threads

Spiced rock lobster and saffron soup with egg noodles, lobster savoury custard and saffron rouille

A rich, satisfying soup that can be a meal in itself when served with loads of crusty bread. Shellfish and saffron seem perfect partners in the food world of relationships, the richness and strong flavour of each working well together – just think of the great French bouillabaisse. The little savoury custards take their cue from the delicate and lightly textured Japanese chawan mushi custard. I choose southern rock lobsters here, but any of the other varieties available – eastern, tropical or western – can be substituted.

1 To make the consommé, put all ingredients into a stockpot and bring very slowly to a simmer. Do not boil or consommé will become cloudy. Cook gently for 1 hour, then remove chicken with a slotted spoon. With such gentle cooking, the meat should be very relaxed and tender, but not falling off the bone. Allow to cool enough to handle, then shred meat while still warm. Discard skin and bones. Set meat aside.

2 Strain consommé through a muslin-lined sieve or a jelly bag to eliminate all sediment. Discard solids. Taste and adjust seasoning, then skim surface if necessary.

3 To make the won tons, mix oyster sauce, soy sauce and Chinese spice salt, then brush over scallops. Put a few shreds of wood fungus in the centre of 12 won ton wrappers. Sit scallops on top and brush edges of wrapper with egg white. Cover with remaining wrappers and press edges to seal, ensuring there are no air pockets.

4 To serve, reheat consommé in a clean saucepan. Divide chicken and shredded wood fungus between bowls. Bring a saucepan of water to a boil, then cook won tons, 6 at a time, for 2 minutes. Place 2 won tons in each bowl, then carefully ladle in hot consommé. Sprinkle with garlic chives and serve immediately.

3 fresh black wood fungus, shredded
$^1/_4$ cup finely chopped garlic chives

Chicken and scallop consommé
2 litres White Chicken Stock (page 337)
2 free-range, corn-fed chicken legs and thighs (on the bone)
2 dried scallops, shredded
2 teaspoons dried Chinese anchovies

2 cloves garlic, sliced
1 teaspoon minced ginger
$^1/_2$ teaspoon freshly cracked white peppercorns
4 green onions, cut into 1 cm lengths
2 dried Chinese black mushrooms
65 ml Chinese Shaoxing rice wine
50 ml fish sauce
2 coriander roots, minced

Scallop won tons
1 teaspoon oyster sauce
$^1/_2$ teaspoon soy sauce
2 pinches Chinese Spice Salt (page 39)
12 scallops
50 g fresh black wood fungus, shredded
24 won ton wrappers
1 egg white

Chicken and scallop consommé with scallop won tons and garlic chives

This clear but intense soup is one of our favourites at Paramount. It employs the best Chinese cooking techniques and

flavours, with our own twist, of course. A perfect combination of flavour and textural elements.

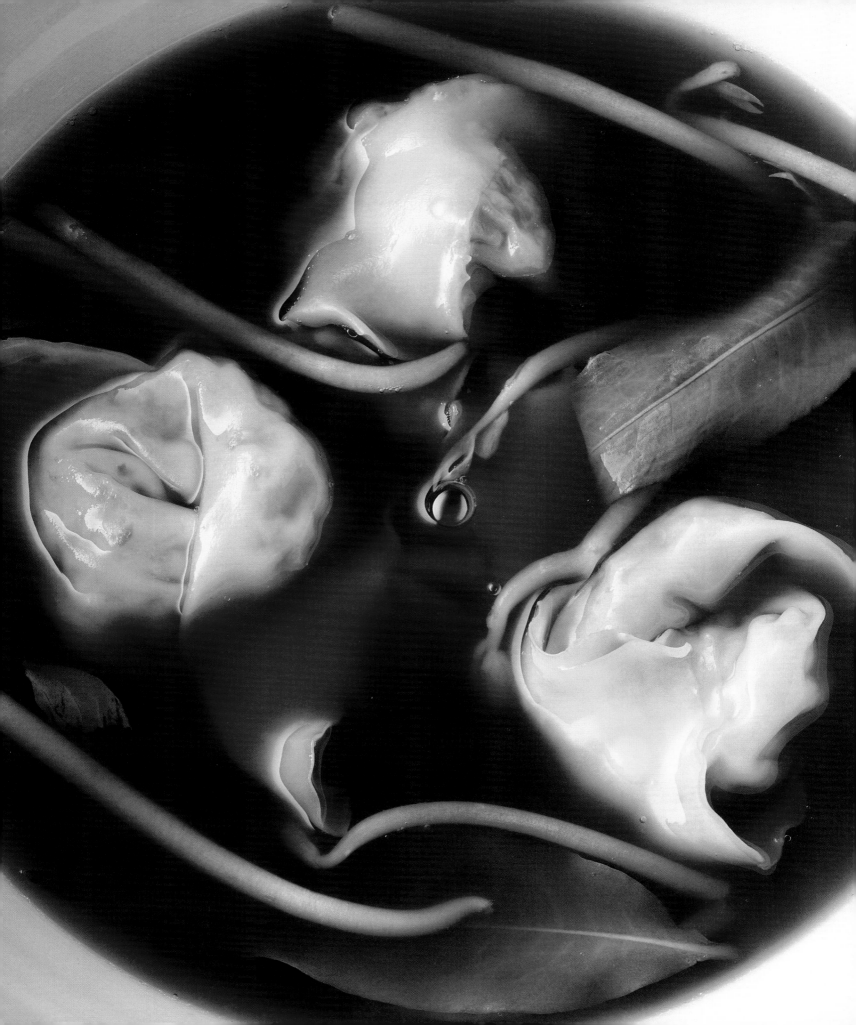

1 To make the consommé, dry-roast the Sichuan peppercorns over gentle heat until fragrant, then crack. Put remaining consommé ingredients into a stockpot and bring to a simmer over very gentle heat – do not boil or consommé will become cloudy. Simmer for 1 hour, then carefully strain through a muslin-lined sieve or a jelly bag to ensure consommé is clear and free of sediment.

2 To make the dough, mix wheat starch and cornflour in a bowl, then stir in boiling water with a chopstick until combined. Rest dough, covered with a cloth, for 5 minutes. Knead in lard, then rest again for 30 minutes.

3 Meanwhile, make the stuffing. Heat oil in a frying pan and sauté shallots, garlic and coriander root until fragrant. Remove from heat and stir in shredded meat, mint and seasonings. Allow to cool.

4 To make the dumplings, roll dough into a long sausage shape and cut into 24 pieces. Rub your bench and rolling pin with a little extra lard to keep dough moist. Roll each piece of dough into a thin, flat round and cut with a 5 cm round pastry cutter. Spoon 1 teaspoon filling into the centre of each round and fold in half, pressing edges to seal. Sit each dumpling on a small piece of baking paper, then steam in a large Chinese steamer, with plenty of room between them, for 15 minutes until pastry is translucent.

5 Put 3 freshly steamed dumplings into each bowl. Add bean sprouts, mint and laksa leaves and sliced chilli, then ladle in hot consommé. Serve immediately.

100 g bean sprouts
6 large spearmint leaves, shredded
1 tablespoon laksa (Vietnamese mint) leaves
1 large red chilli, cut into very fine julienne

Oxtail consommé
1 teaspoon Sichuan peppercorns
2 litres settled, clear Oxtail Stock (page 339)
3 green onions, sliced
4 slices ginger

1 stalk lemongrass, sliced
1 large red chilli, split lengthwise
5 kaffir lime leaves, shredded
1 star anise, cracked
2 pieces cassia bark
40 ml fish sauce

Dumpling dough
125 g wheat starch
10 g cornflour
150 ml boiling water
5 g lard

Dumpling stuffing
20 ml vegetable oil
2 red shallots, minced
2 cloves garlic, minced
1 coriander root, minced
120 g shredded oxtail meat reserved from stock
2 teaspoons shredded mint leaves
$\frac{1}{2}$ teaspoon freshly ground black pepper
$\frac{1}{4}$ teaspoon Chinese Spice Salt (page 39)

Oxtail consommé with dumplings, bean sprouts, mint and chilli

Oxtail consommé is one of my favourite winter classics: in the morning the kitchen is filled with the perfume of the stock, which has been gently simmering away all night. When making the stock, remember to put aside some of the oxtail meat to make the dumplings for this soup. The dumplings take their inspiration from the Chinese gow gee of yum cha tradition that have a gorgeous, silky, almost translucent pastry. (See photograph opposite.)

1 To make the consommé, preheat oven to 180°C and roast garlic wrapped in foil for 30 minutes or until soft. Cool, then slice thickly.

2 Rub cracked peppers liberally into skin and flesh of the 8 duck pieces. Heat oil in a heavy-based frying pan and seal duck quickly over high heat. Set aside. In the same pan, fry onion, chilli and ginger until softened and beginning to colour. Deglaze pan with rice wine – remove pan from heat when wine comes to a boil.

3 Put duck, onion mixture, roasted garlic, lime leaves, green onion tops, stock and soy sauce into a stockpot and bring to a boil over gentle heat. Reduce heat and simmer for 1½ hours, skimming surface occasionally. Do not boil or consommé will become cloudy.

4 Strain consommé through a muslin-lined sieve or a jelly bag to ensure stock is clear and free of sediment, pressing firmly to extract as much liquid as possible. Discard solids (the meat can be removed from the bones and reserved for another use, if desired). Allow to cool, then refrigerate. Remove fat from cooled consommé.

5 Strain cooled consommé into a clean saucepan, avoiding any sediment. Bring to a simmer, then add 2 teaspoons Chinese spice salt and fish sauce and cook for 3 minutes. Taste and adjust seasoning if necessary.

6 To serve, remove meat from roast duck, then cut into strips and sprinkle with 1 teaspoon Chinese spice salt. Divide meat and remaining ingredients between bowls, then ladle in hot consommé and swirl with a chopstick to combine. Serve immediately.

1 Chinese roast duck, quartered
1 teaspoon Chinese Spice Salt (page 39)
6 Chinese cabbage leaves, finely sliced
1 cup watercress leaves
2 slices ginger, cut into julienne
3 green onions, finely sliced
12 fine slices bamboo shoot
3 teaspoons finely chopped garlic chives
3 teaspoons chopped coriander leaves

Duck consommé
2 heads garlic
1 teaspoon black peppercorns, freshly cracked
2 teaspoons Sichuan peppercorns, freshly cracked
1 × 2 kg duck, cleaned and cut into 8 pieces
50 ml vegetable oil
2 brown onions, chopped

2 large red chillies, sliced
2 teaspoons chopped ginger
100 ml Chinese Shaoxing rice wine
6 kaffir lime leaves, shredded
6 green onions (green part only), chopped
4 litres White Chicken Stock (page 337)
100 ml light Chinese soy sauce
2 teaspoons Chinese Spice Salt (page 39)
60 ml fish sauce

Peppered duck consommé with roast duck and watercress

This is a delightful duck preparation, although a little time-consuming, as is the way with all good duck-cooking.

If you want to make this a meal in a bowl, add some cooked Pepper Noodles (see page 341) to the soup.

1 Sprinkle spice salt over snapper and grill for 5 minutes, turning halfway through cooking, or until fish is crisp on the outside but still soft and translucent inside.

2 Break fish into chunks.

3 Bring stock to a boil, then add lime juice and fish sauce. Taste and adjust if necessary.

4 Add noodles and heat through.

5 Heat oil in a frying pan and cook garlic and ginger over moderate heat until they begin to colour.

6 Add crabmeat and black pepper and toss over high heat to coat crab with aromatics.

7 Add fish and remove pan from heat.

8 Ladle stock and noodles into deep bowls and carefully stir in fish and crab with a chopstick without breaking the fish.

9 Add pickled ginger and green onion and serve immediately.

2 teaspoons Chinese Spice Salt (page 39)
1 × 500 g snapper fillet *or* other fleshy
    white fish
600 ml Crab Stock (page 337)
30 ml strained lime juice

30 ml fish sauce
500 g fresh udon noodles, blanched
30 ml vegetable oil
3 cloves garlic, minced
1 tablespoon minced ginger

500 g freshly picked blue-swimmer *or*
    mud crabmeat
$1/2$ teaspoon freshly ground black pepper
1 tablespoon Pickled Ginger (page 52)
6 green onions, finely sliced

Snapper and crab with udon noodles and ginger

Udon noodles, generally served in a broth or soup, are a lunchtime ritual in Japan, especially in winter when the hearty

servings and warming flavours give sustenance. Fresh udon noodles are available from Japanese food stores.

Alternatively, you can use thick rice noodles, fresh ramen noodles or fettuccine.

FISH AND SHELLFISH

FISH AND SHELLFISH Australia's waters – our oceans, reefs, bays, rivers, streams, lakes and dams – provide a variety and abundance of fish and shellfish envied around the world. Yet many of us are not confident about cooking fish, or about combining it with exotic flavours. ❋ SPICES AND AROMATICS can work their magic to enhance the flavour and texture of fish and seafood just as they do any other ingredient. Spicing is as much about subtlety of hand as it is about complexity and strength of flavour. The spices should not take over but instead should play a supporting role – an overpowering blend won't work with a delicately flavoured fish but the right spice can take it to another realm. The flavours and textures of fish and shellfish vary dramatically, so it is of vital importance that the right spices are used with the right species. It is your responsibility as the cook to work with empathy, knowledge and care when marrying flavours and textures for the best results. Learn about the varieties and differences of the seafood world just as you have learnt about the various spice elements and how they best respond to cooking, then bring them together with understanding. You've learnt how to take the best care of spices, now do the same with fish and shellfish.

1 Make and cook noodles as instructed, then refresh under cold running water to stop cooking. Drain, then toss with a little oil and set aside.

2 Clean each squid by removing tentacles and discarding internal sac. Set tentacles aside for garnish. Discard transparent pen from body. Cut wings away from body and reserve for stuffing. Wash bodies and tentacles thoroughly under cold running water and dry with paper towel.

3 To make the stuffing, chill bowl of a food processor, then blend prawn meat and egg whites to a paste and season with fish sauce, lime juice and pepper. Finely dice water chestnuts and reserved squid wings, then stir thoroughly into prawn paste with lime leaves, green onion and pickled ginger.

4 Spoon stuffing into a piping bag and three-quarters fill each squid tube – leave room for stuffing to expand during cooking or tubes will split. Sew each tube shut with a needle and thread. Refrigerate until ready to cook.

5 To make the dressing, blend all ingredients except the oils in a food processor. With the motor running, slowly pour in the combined oils. Taste and adjust seasoning if necessary.

6 Cut cucumber, radish and pickled ginger into fine julienne, then toss with noodles and add enough dressing to moisten.

7 Bring stock to a boil in a stockpot, then reduce to a gentle simmer and poach squid in a single layer for 10 minutes. Turn squid over with a mesh spoon and poach for another 10 minutes. Remove from heat, then allow to sit for a few minutes. Cut into 5 mm thick slices.

8 While squid is poaching, heat vegetable oil in a deep-fryer to 180°C. Fry reserved tentacles for 30 seconds until crisp and tender. Drain on paper towel.

9 Arrange noodles on each plate, then top with slices of warm, stuffed squid and finish with fried tentacles.

1 quantity Black Ink Noodles (page 341)
vegetable oil
6 squid (each body 10 cm long)
1 cucumber
1/4 daikon radish
3 teaspoons drained Pickled Ginger
   (page 52)
2 litres Fish Stock (page 337)

Squid stuffing
350 g green prawn meat, deveined
50 g *or* 2 egg whites

25 ml fish sauce
20 ml strained lime juice
1 teaspoon freshly ground white pepper
75 g fresh water chestnuts, blanched
4 kaffir lime leaves, shredded
2 green onions, finely sliced
1 teaspoon minced Pickled Ginger
   (page 52)

Ponzu dressing
1 egg yolk
25 ml strained lime juice

25 ml Cucumber Juice (page 343)
35 ml ponzu sauce
1 teaspoon rice vinegar
1 teaspoon wasabi paste
zest of 1 kaffir lime, minced
1 teaspoon minced Pickled Ginger
   (page 52)
2 teaspoons fish sauce
1 teaspoon sesame oil
100 ml olive oil
75 ml vegetable oil

Stuffed squid with black ink noodles and ponzu dressing

Stuffing squid is a time-consuming task, not the sort of thing you want to do at the last minute. However, the results are well worth the effort: the squid's body acts as a 'sausage' casing for the prawn stuffing and the very gentle poaching leaves the squid beautifully tender and flavoursome.

1 To make the salsa verde, soak breadcrumbs and lemon zest in half the olive oil for 10 minutes. Blend breadcrumb mixture and remaining ingredients to a paste in a food processor, dripping in the remaining oil as you go.

2 To make the stuffing, soak burghul in lemon juice with garlic for 15 minutes. Heat olive oil in a frying pan and fry pancetta and chilli until crisp. Combine all stuffing ingredients, then add 2 tablespoons salsa verde and mix thoroughly.

3 Put sardine fillets on a board skin-side down, then put a teaspoon of stuffing in centre of each. Roll up fillets and wrap 2 slices pancetta around each to secure. Refrigerate for 1 hour before cooking.

4 Heat some olive oil until smoking in a saucepan, then quickly deep-fry parsley until crisp. Remove with a slotted spoon and drain on paper towel.

5 Preheat oven to 180°C. Heat 20 ml olive oil in a heavy-based baking tray or skillet and bake sardine rolls, lying on one side, for 3 minutes, then turn over and bake for another 3 minutes.

6 To serve, spread salsa verde on centre of each plate, then arrange 3 sardine rolls on this and add a dollop of aïoli. Sprinkle with fried parsley and serve immediately.

18 sardine fillets
36 slices pancetta
olive oil
2 tablespoons flat-leaf parsley
6 teaspoons Roasted Garlic Aïoli
   (page 343)

Burghul stuffing
50 g burghul
25 ml strained lemon juice
3 cloves garlic, minced
2 teaspoons extra-virgin olive oil
3 slices pancetta, finely chopped
1 red bird's-eye chilli, minced
$1/2$ teaspoon freshly ground black pepper
$1/2$ teaspoon sea salt
50 g fresh sourdough breadcrumbs
50 g Parmigiano-Reggiano, grated
25 g small capers, rinsed

Salsa verde
25 g stale bread, crumbed
zest of $1/2$ lemon, minced
100 ml extra-virgin olive oil
1 firmly packed cup flat-leaf parsley,
1 tablespoon rinsed small capers
1 teaspoon minced garlic
2 anchovy fillets, chopped
30 ml strained lemon juice
$1/4$ teaspoon chilli powder
$1/2$ teaspoon freshly ground black pepper

Fremantle sardine fillets stuffed with pancetta, capers and burghul with salsa verde

These gorgeous parcels of rich flavours are reminiscent of the Mediterranean. The fresh sardines and anchovies being fished and processed in Western Australia are plentiful and readily available all year round. You could just as easily use pilchards or herrings in place of the sardine fillets.

1 Preheat oven to 200°C and roast tomatoes for 20 minutes.

2 Put crabs into freezer for 15 minutes before cooking to stun them. Bring a large stockpot of water to a rolling boil, then cook crabs for 4 minutes. Refresh crabs in iced water to stop the cooking process. Remove outer shell, then cut off and crack claws. Cut bodies into quarters using a cleaver or poultry shears.

3 Heat a large wok, then add oil and stir-fry ginger, garlic, shallots, chilli and crab pieces until shells turn red. Add roasted tomatoes, soy sauce, lime juice, chilli paste, palm sugar, fish sauce and stock and bring to a boil over high heat, tossing continuously. This will take about 3 minutes, by which time the crab will be cooked and coated with sauce. Add basil, then taste and adjust seasoning if necessary.

4 Serve in large bowls with lots of boiled rice or crusty bread. And don't forget cloth napkins, generous fingerbowls and bowls for the shells, either.

6 tomatoes
2 × 1 kg live mudcrabs, washed
100 ml vegetable oil
1 tablespoon minced ginger
1 tablespoon minced garlic
8 red shallots, finely sliced

3 red bird's-eye chillies, finely sliced
1 tablespoon light soy sauce
25 ml strained lime juice
1 tablespoon Sambal Bajak (page 57)
    or Chilli Jam (page 58)
40 g palm sugar, shaved

25 ml fish sauce
100 ml Fish Stock (page 337)
1/2 cup Thai or holy basil leaves,
    shredded

Chilli mudcrab

This dish cannot be served or eaten elegantly, making it well suited to eating at home where it doesn't matter how messy you get! You have to be prepared to release some of those primal urges to achieve full enjoyment and satisfaction. If you cannot get hold of mudcrabs, others (blue-swimmer, spanner, sand or the huge King Island crabs) can easily be substituted, but you'll need to alter the cooking time depending on their weight and size, so ask your fishmonger. You could also use flower crabs (in Singapore), Pacific snow crabs (Japan and the north-west coast of the USA), Dungeness (UK and Europe) or stone crabs (Florida, USA). The most important ingredient here is freshness. (See photograph opposite.)

1 Stun lobsters in freezer for 30 minutes, then plunge briefly into a stockpot of rapidly boiling water (this is to kill rather than cook them).

2 Remove tail meat and discard heads, shells and claws (make stock for another use). Cut each tail in half lengthwise.

3 Preheat oven to 200°C.

4 Bring masala paste, chilli jam, coconut milk, tomato purée and fish sauce to a simmer in a saucepan, stirring to combine.

5 Coat lobster liberally with masala sauce and wrap 2 pieces tail meat in a banana leaf, folding over to secure. Bake parcels seam-side down for 8–10 minutes or until meat is just cooked. Unwrap to serve. Spoon a little sauce over unwrapped lobster to moisten it.

6 Spread fresh banana leaves on plates, then spoon on masala lobster and garnish with fried shallots. Serve immediately.

3 × 1 kg live rock lobsters
2 tablespoons Madras Masala Paste
  (page 42)

1 teaspoon Chilli Jam (page 58)
200 ml coconut milk
50 ml tomato purée

25 ml fish sauce
12 fresh banana leaves
1/4 cup Fried Shallots (page 342)

Masala lobster

I use southern rock lobsters from New South Wales for this dish during the summer months but you can successfully substitute freshwater marrons (from Margaret River, Western Australia, or Kangaroo Island, South Australia), king prawns, scampi or Moreton Bay bug tails. Cooking times will vary according to the size of the shellfish you are using, so ask your fishmonger.

1 Mince prawn meat and snapper fillet or pulse to a coarse paste in a food processor, then mix thoroughly with remaining ingredients except sugarcane.

2 Trim sugarcane and cut each length into thin sticks.

3 Mould prawn paste around top half of each stick.

4 Grill over a hot barbecue or chargrill for 4–5 minutes until golden, turning regularly.

5 Pile onto a plate lined with a banana leaf and serve immediately.

350 g green prawn meat
1 × 250 g snapper fillet
2 tablespoons Satay Spice Paste (page 43)

2 teaspoons Sambal Belacan (page 57)
6 kaffir lime leaves, shredded
1/2 teaspoon freshly ground black pepper

2 teaspoons fish sauce
3 × 12 cm lengths fresh sugarcane

Satay prawn sugarcane sticks

A fabulous barbecued snack, appetiser or entrée that is simple to prepare and cook. Make loads because they seem to disappear in an instant! The prawn paste, flavoured by the juices of the sugarcane during cooking, has enough flavour and spice in its own right, so I tend to serve the sticks unadorned. They are also fantastic with scampi, shrimps or yabbies (freshwater crayfish). You could offer a bowl of Sweet Chilli Sauce (see page 67) or Cucumber Yoghurt Salad with Nigella (see page 80), however, if you want to. Look for fresh sugarcane in Asian food stores.

1 Heat oil in a saucepan and fry shallots for 10 minutes until golden, then drain on paper towel. Cut asparagus into 3 cm lengths and blanch briefly in boiling water, then drain. Cut snake beans into 2 cm lengths. Finely slice chilli into rounds, then cut snowpeas into julienne. Wash and drain snowpea leaves. Cut each beancurd square into quarters. Divide vegetables and beancurd into 6 portions and set aside.

2 To make the curry sauce, heat coconut cream in a saucepan over moderate heat, uncovered, until it separates, about 10 minutes. Add curry paste and chilli jam and cook until fragrant, stirring regularly. Stir in palm sugar and fish sauce and cook for 2 minutes. Add coconut milk and stock and bring to a boil, then reduce heat and simmer gently, uncovered, for 10 minutes. Remove from heat, then taste and adjust seasoning if necessary. Heat through before starting to cook tuna.

3 Cut tuna into 3 cm cubes, then divide into 6 portions. Stand a wok over high heat and add 25 ml chilli oil. Sear 1 portion tuna quickly on all sides. This should take 1 minute. Add 100 ml curry sauce and bring to a boil. Add 1 portion prepared vegetables and beancurd and stir carefully to combine. Cook for 30 seconds, just enough to heat through, then spoon into a warm bowl. Set aside while cooking remaining portions. Sprinkle with fried shallots and serve immediately.

vegetable oil
24 golden shallots
18 spears thin asparagus
3 snake beans
1 large red chilli
6 snowpeas
100 g snowpea leaves
6 squares fresh beancurd *or* tofu
1 × 500 g piece yellowfin tuna

150 ml Chilli Oil (page 61)
2 tablespoons Fried Shallots (page 342)

Fragrant curry sauce
125 ml coconut cream
4 tablespoons Paramount Curry Paste
  (page 42)
2 teaspoons Chilli Jam (page 58)
25 g palm sugar, shaved

50 ml fish sauce
150 ml coconut milk
200 ml White Chicken Stock (page 337)

Wok-seared tuna with beancurd, asparagus and fragrant curry sauce

The success of this dish lies in the cooking. All the ingredients should be prepared ahead and then divided into six portions (or however many serves you are making), before being cooked separately. If you attempt to cook everything in a large wok, you will end up with an unsatisfying stew. The cooking is so quick that the cooked portions can easily rest for a couple of minutes while the remaining serves are dealt with. You can speed up the process by buying several small, inexpensive non-stick woks from an Asian food store and cooking more than one portion at a time. Substitute any other oily fish, such as bonito, tunny fish or mahi mahi (dolphin fish), for the tuna.

1 Cut six 20 cm × 20 cm squares each of baking paper and foil. Arrange foil squares on a flat surface, then top with squares of baking paper.

2 Remove any bones from fish with fish tweezers, then remove and discard skin.

3 Put 1 tablespoon chermoula onto each baking paper square, then put fish on top and spread with 1 tablespoon chermoula. Fold paper over fish to make a secure parcel, then wrap in foil. Marinate parcels, refrigerated, for 3–5 hours.

4 Wash spinach thoroughly, then blanch in boiling water for 30 seconds and refresh immediately in iced water. When cold, squeeze out water and set aside.

5 Preheat oven to 200°C. Bake fish parcels on an oven tray for 6–8 minutes, depending on thickness. The fish should retain its moisture and be just cooked.

6 Meanwhile, cook spinach gently in a saucepan with butter, salt, pepper and nutmeg, stirring regularly. Do not let it dry out.

7 Stir preserved lemon into extra-virgin olive oil.

8 Remove fish from oven and unwrap. Divide spinach between plates and slide fish on top, then pour over any remaining juices from the parcels. Spoon lemon oil over fish and serve immediately.

6 × 150 g pieces blue eye
1 cup Chermoula with Preserved Lemon
  (page 46)
3 bunches spinach, stems removed

75 g unsalted butter
$\frac{1}{2}$ teaspoon sea salt
$\frac{1}{2}$ teaspoon freshly ground black pepper
pinch of freshly grated nutmeg

$\frac{1}{2}$ preserved lemon, finely chopped
60 ml extra-virgin olive oil

Blue eye with chermoula, preserved lemon and spinach

This recipe lends itself to a wide variety of fish, so the choice is really up to you – just make sure you ask for slices from a thick fillet. When it is in perfect condition, I often use salmon, ocean trout or snapper in place of blue eye (trevalla). In other parts of the world, fish like sea bass or groper would be perfect. The marinade and cooking process keeps the flesh moist, sealing in the juices and imparting a gentle, zesty flavour.

1 Stun lobster in freezer for 30 minutes, then plunge briefly into a stockpot of rapidly boiling water (this is to kill rather than cook it). Remove tail meat and discard head and shell (make stock for another use). Cut tail meat into 50 g medallions.

2 Meanwhile, make rice pilaf as instructed and keep warm.

3 Dry-roast dried prawns and rice, separately, over gentle heat until fragrant and rice is slightly coloured. Cool, then grind separately to a fine powder and combine. Cut fish into 50 g chunks, then coat with ground dried prawns and rice.

4 Toss scrubbed mussels into a wide, heavy-based saucepan over high heat, then cover and steam until shells open. This will only take about 1 minute. Remove open mussels (discard any that haven't opened) and plunge into iced water to stop the cooking process. When cool, remove mussels from shells, then debeard them and set aside. Discard shells. Repeat process with clams. They may take a minute or so longer to open as they have tougher shells.

5 Shape crab cake mixture into 6 patties about 4 cm round and 2 cm thick. Dust with rice flour.

6 Heat oil in a deep-fryer to 180°C. Deep-fry fish and crab cakes separately for 3 minutes or until golden, then remove and drain on paper towel.

7 Bring chilli prawn sauce to a gentle simmer in a clay pot or saucepan. Gently cook lobster medallions in sauce for 2 minutes, then add mussels and clams and heat through for 30 seconds. Toss in tatsoi leaves and allow to wilt. Remove pot from heat, then add fish, crab cakes, coriander and chilli and serve immediately, with the cardamom rice pilaf alongside in another pot. Serve chilli jam in a small side dish and add with discretion.

1 × 1 kg live rock lobster
1 quantity Cardamom Rice Pilaf
  (page 211)
1 tablespoon dried prawns
1 tablespoon jasmine rice
1 × 300 g red emperor fillet *or*
  other reef fish

1 kg black mussels, scrubbed
1 kg surf clams, scrubbed
120 g Crab Cake Mixture (page 125)
1 tablespoon rice flour
vegetable oil for deep-frying
500 ml Chilli Prawn Sauce (page 65)
30 tatsoi leaves

$^{1}/_{4}$ cup coriander leaves
3 red bird's-eye chillies, finely sliced
3 teaspoons Chilli Jam (page 58)

Hot-and-sour seafood hotpot with rice pilaf and chilli jam

This dish can be served in individual Chinese clay pots or from a large pot in the centre of the table that people share as part of a communal offering, in the typical Asian tradition. If you are serving from the clay pot at the table, be sure to sit it on a mat that will withstand the heat. Clay pots are inexpensive, come in a variety of sizes and are readily available from Asian food stores. The combination of fish and shellfish you use will be determined by the varieties available in your locality. Try snapper, wrasse, red sea bream, rouget or pompano in place of the red emperor.

1 Dry-roast dried chillies and coriander seeds, separately, over gentle heat until fragrant. Cool, then grind separately to a fine powder.

2 Mix ground chilli, turmeric and black pepper with salt and rub into fish.

3 Heat oil in a deep frying pan and fry fish quickly on both sides until coloured and spices become fragrant. Remove fish and set aside.

4 Add ginger, garlic, onion, green chilli, ground cardamom and ground coriander and sauté briefly.

5 Stir in stock and half the coconut milk, then bring to a boil, uncovered. Reduce sauce to a simmer, then add curry leaves and fish.

6 Simmer, uncovered, over low heat until fish is cooked, about 6 minutes. Add remaining coconut milk and reheat, but do not boil.

7 Fry mustard seeds in a little oil until they start to pop, then add to fish with lime juice and coriander leaves.

8 Divide fish and sauce between plates and serve immediately.

2 large dried chillies
1 teaspoon coriander seeds
1 teaspoon ground turmeric
1/4 teaspoon freshly ground black pepper
1 teaspoon sea salt
1 × 1 kg snapper fillet, cut into 6 pieces
70 ml vegetable oil

2 teaspoons minced ginger
8 cloves garlic, minced
2 brown onions, finely sliced
6 green bird's-eye chillies, finely sliced
seeds from 5 green cardamom pods, ground
150 ml Fish Stock (page 337)

300 ml coconut milk
18 curry leaves
1 teaspoon brown mustard seeds
20 ml strained lime juice
handful of coriander leaves

Snapper baked with green chilli and coconut

This is my version of a Kerala fish 'molee', the term given to a fish stew or curry common on the west coast of India in which fish is spiced and braised in coconut milk. Many types of fish are suitable for this dish – any of the snapper varieties or blue eye (trevalla), morwong, hapuku, jewfish, rock cod (also known as bar cod), wrasse, pompano or mahi mahi (dolphin fish). Choose a firm-fleshed fillet from a large fish for the best results.

1 To make the crab cakes, blend all ingredients except crabmeat with 1 tablespoon rice flour to a paste in a food processor, then transfer to a bowl and stir in crabmeat.

2 Roll mixture into small balls, flatten slightly and coat with extra rice flour. Refrigerate on a tray in a single layer until ready to cook.

3 Heat oil in a deep-fryer to 180°C.

4 Cook crab cakes in small batches – this maintains the temperature of the oil and prevents the cakes becoming soggy – until golden and puffed, about 3–4 minutes. Drain on paper towel while cooking remaining mixture.

5 Stir cucumber into chilli sauce and serve in a bowl for dipping.

6 Pile crab cakes onto a large plate and serve immediately.

vegetable oil for deep-frying
2 tablespoons diced cucumber
200 ml Sweet Chilli Sauce (page 67)

Crab cake mixture
1 × 300 g snapper fillet, finely chopped
50 ml coconut milk
6 green onions, finely sliced
2 teaspoons soy sauce
1 teaspoon minced ginger
2 teaspoons Chilli Jam (page 58)

1 tablespoon chopped coriander leaves
1 egg
25 ml fish sauce
1 teaspoon freshly ground white pepper
rice flour
400 g freshly picked spanner crabmeat

Deep-fried spanner crab cakes with sweet chilli and cucumber

These crab cakes are a variation on the ubiquitous Thai fish cake. You can easily substitute prawn meat for the crab if you wish – the method remains the same. The mixture can be made ahead of time but be sure that you cook the cakes as you need them as they fall flat and do not respond at all well to reheating. Other alternatives for spanner crab are blue-swimmer, mud, Dungeness and spider crab. (See photograph opposite.)

1 To make the dressing, whisk all ingredients together.

2 Shell prawns, leaving tails intact but discarding heads. Discard intestinal tracts and butterfly prawns open.

3 Cut pork into small, thin slices.

4 Heat oils in a wok and fry shallots for 2 minutes until coloured, then add spice paste and stir over high heat until bubbling. Toss prawns, pork, capsicum, snowpeas and bok choy with paste.

5 Add dressing and continue to toss over high heat to cook ingredients quickly – all up, cooking should only take a few minutes.

6 Stir in basil, then pile onto plates and serve immediately.

30 green king prawns
300 g Chinese sweet pork
60 ml vegetable oil
1 teaspoon sesame oil
6 red shallots, finely sliced
¼ cup Nonya Spice Paste (page 43)

1 red capsicum, finely sliced
12 snowpeas, cut in half lengthwise
12 baby bok choy, blanched
1 cup lemon *or* Thai basil leaves

Sweet tamarind dressing
100 ml Tamarind Liquid (page 341)
20 ml Sugar Syrup (page 343)
20 g palm sugar, shaved
75 ml strained lime juice
25 ml fish sauce
2 teaspoons Ginger Juice (page 342)

Stir-fried prawns and bok choy with sweet pork, basil and shallots

A straightforward dish that uses the quick-and-easy method of stir-frying. Sweet pork (red roast pork or cha siu) is available from Chinese roast-meat shops, where ducks, chickens and various meats hang in the window. The meat is glazed with maltose and soy before being roasted, giving the surface a caramelised, reddish appearance. Buy the meat in one piece and slice it as you are about to cook it. If you have several small, non-stick woks, available from Asian food stores, you can cook a few serves at a time, ensuring the stir-fry doesn't stew. In this case, divide the prepared ingredients into six portions before starting to cook. Scampi can be substituted for the prawns.

1 Preheat oven to 200°C and roast shallots in a little oil for 15–20 minutes until golden and softened. Bring turmeric tamarind sauce to a simmer in a saucepan and add shallots.

2 Cut tuna into 6 thick slices. Sprinkle cracked pepper over tuna. Heat a little oil in a frying pan and quickly seal tuna over high heat for 2 minutes, then flip fish over and cook other side for 1–2 minutes, depending on thickness of fish. The tuna should be rare or glassy in the middle. Remove from heat immediately.

3 Meanwhile, cut zucchini and leek into julienne and plunge into boiling water with noodles for 1 minute. Add tatsoi leaves to noodles, then drain immediately.

4 Divide noodles and vegetables between plates, then ladle sauce and shallots around. Cut each piece of tuna into 4–5 slices and arrange carefully on top of the noodles. Serve immediately.

18 golden shallots, peeled
vegetable oil
400 ml Turmeric Tamarind Sauce
  (page 65)
750 g sashimi-quality yellowfin tuna

2 teaspoons freshly cracked
  black pepper
1 yellow zucchini
1 leek, cut into 5 cm lengths

300 g Saffron Noodles (page 341),
  cooked
½ cup tatsoi leaves

Rare-roasted tuna with saffron noodles, roasted shallots and turmeric tamarind sauce

Although I recommend yellowfin tuna here, any of the tuna species can be used, as can other oily fish such as mackerel, swordfish or bonito. The texture and flavour of the fish combines perfectly with the sweetness of the noodles and the earthiness and gentle spiciness of the sauce. Once the basic preparation is done, this dish is very quick to cook and assemble, relying on everything being ready at the same time.

1 To make the dressing, gently simmer all ingredients in a saucepan for 15 minutes. Strain, then discard solids and cool.

2 Preheat oven to 200°C and roast shallots for 15–20 minutes in a little oil until softened and coloured. Meanwhile, blanch bok choy in boiling water until just tender, then drain. Shave cucumbers down their length with a vegetable peeler, discarding seed core.

3 Cook noodles in rapidly boiling water for 3 minutes or until just cooked through. Strain and immediately refresh under cold running water to stop cooking. Toss to remove as much water as possible, then add a little olive oil to prevent sticking.

4 Butterfly each fish fillet open, then roll up each fillet down its length and wrap with 3 slices pancetta to secure. Tie with kitchen twine. Line a steamer tray that will fit inside a wok with baking paper (don't cover tray completely – some steam holes need to be left open), then arrange fish rolls on this.

5 Combine ingredients for smoking mixture. Line a wok with foil and stand over a high flame until hot. Add $^{1}/_{4}$ cup smoking mixture – when it starts to smoke, stand steamer tray of fish in wok and cover with a tight-fitting lid. Smoke for 3 minutes, then flip rolls over and smoke for 2–3 minutes depending on thickness of fillets. The fish must stay rare in the middle. Transfer fish to a plate until ready to serve. Let smoking mixture cool completely outside before discarding.

6 To assemble, bring star anise broth to a simmer, then add noodles and blanched bok choy to heat through.

7 Bring some dressing to a simmer in a frying pan, add fish and cook for 3–4 minutes until glazed on both sides, then add roasted shallots, cucumber and fennel and heat through.

8 Arrange noodles and bok choy on each plate, then ladle about 75 ml star anise broth over each portion of noodles and add cucumber and fennel. Sit fish roll on vegetables, then scatter shallots around and spoon salmon roe on top. Serve immediately.

18 red shallots, peeled
olive oil
12 baby bok choy, washed
2 continental cucumbers, peeled
250 g soba noodles
6 × 150 g pieces Tasmanian salmon
18 slices pancetta
450 ml Star Anise Broth (page 65)
1 fennel bulb, finely sliced into rounds
6 tablespoons salmon roe

Sweet-and-sour dressing
4 red bird's-eye chillies, chopped
4 small cloves garlic, chopped
200 ml vegetable oil
120 ml light soy sauce
200 ml cider vinegar
300 ml Sugar Syrup (page 343)

Tea smoking mixture
1 tablespoon oolong tea leaves
1 tablespoon jasmine tea leaves
zest of 1 orange
2 pieces dried tangerine peel
2 tablespoons jasmine rice
2 tablespoons brown sugar
3 star anise
2 teaspoons Sichuan peppercorns
3 pieces cassia bark

Tea-smoked Tasmanian salmon with pancetta, soba noodles, pickled cucumber and star anise broth

This is one of the most popular fish items on the Restaurant menu, and it combines flavours and textures sublimely. Although there are a few steps to carry out beforehand, the final execution is relatively simple. Don't forget to keep the kitchen well ventilated and the fan on while smoking the fish! The smoking mixture given here is sufficient for two 'smokes' and it seems to keep forever. Salmon or trout from anywhere in the world can be used for this dish – such as wild salmon from Scotland and the wonderful red sockeye salmon from Canada. Ask the fishmonger to cut the salmon from the middle or thickest part of the fillet. (See photograph opposite.)

1 Make sticky black rice as instructed and keep warm.

2 Dry-roast dried prawns and rice together over gentle heat until fragrant and rice has coloured. Cool, then grind to a coarse powder.

3 Thoroughly coat fish with prawn and rice crust.

4 Preheat oven to 200°C.

5 Heat oil in an ovenproof frying pan and fry fish over moderately high heat until sealed, about 4 minutes, then flip carefully.

6 Bake fish in oven for 5 minutes, depending on thickness. The fish should yield to the touch when just cooked – don't let it become firm and tough.

7 Meanwhile, reheat sticky black rice in a steamer – steam it in oiled moulds, if you like, for a more definite form. Divide rice between plates.

8 Reheat chilli tamarind sauce. Wilt tatsoi leaves in boiling water for a few seconds, then add to rice. Sit fish on top and spoon some hot chilli tamarind sauce around.

9 Sprinkle with sliced chilli and serve immediately.

1 cup Aromatic Sticky Black Rice
 (page 212)
1 tablespoon dried prawns

1 tablespoon jasmine rice
6 × 150 g pieces blue eye
120 ml vegetable oil

300 ml Chilli Tamarind Sauce (page 66)
6 handfuls tatsoi leaves
2 large red chillies, finely sliced

Baked blue eye with a prawn crust, sticky black rice and chilli tamarind sauce

Here, a crust of dry-roasted dried prawns and jasmine rice gives a pungent flavour and crunchy texture to the delicate white flesh of the blue eye, a sensational combination. Try it also with sea bass, sea bream, dorade or any fish from the snapper family. Ask the fishmonger for slices cut from the middle or thickest part of the fillet.

1 To make the spiced coconut milk, bring coconut milk to a boil, uncovered, in a wide, heavy-based saucepan for a few minutes. Add aromatics and simmer for a few minutes, then stir in stock and fish sauce and cook gently for 15 minutes. Strain through a fine-meshed sieve and add lime juice. Taste and adjust if necessary.

2 Bring spiced coconut milk to a boil in rinsed-out pan, then add fish fillets and bug tails.

3 Reduce heat and simmer very gently, uncovered, for 5 minutes until fish and bugs are just cooked through. Remove to a warm plate with a slotted spoon.

4 Add blanched bok choy to coconut milk and reheat for 1 minute.

5 Spoon 2 bok choy into each bowl, then arrange fish and bug tails on top and ladle coconut sauce around. Sprinkle sauce with coriander, chilli and shredded lime leaf.

6 Spoon a little coriander pesto on top of fish and bug tails, then add fried shallots and serve immediately.

600 g red emperor *or* coral trout fillets
300 g green Moreton Bay bug tails
12 baby bok choy, blanched
¼ cup coriander leaves
3 large red chillies, finely sliced
3 kaffir lime leaves, shredded
6 teaspoons Coriander Peanut Pesto
  (page 343)
3 teaspoons Fried Shallots (page 342)

Spiced coconut milk
1 litre coconut milk
1 tablespoon minced galangal
2 teaspoons minced ginger
3 red bird's-eye chillies, minced
3 coriander roots, minced
6 red shallots, sliced lengthwise
6 kaffir lime leaves, shredded
2 stalks lemongrass, minced

zest of 1 kaffir lime, minced
500 ml Prawn Stock (page 337)
100 ml fish sauce
75 ml strained lime juice

Reef fish and bug tails in spiced coconut milk with fried shallots and coriander pesto

A tropical fish stew full of fragrant flavours and beautifully soft textures. Choose the best variety available – rouget, wrasse, hake, sea bass or halibut can be used in place of the red emperor or coral trout.

1 Wash spinach thoroughly, then blanch in boiling water for 30 seconds and refresh immediately in iced water. When cold, squeeze out water and refrigerate.

2 To make the anchovy butter, blend all ingredients in a food processor until smooth. Roll up tightly in foil to make a sausage, then refrigerate until firm.

3 To make the anchovy sauce, preheat oven to 180°C and roast garlic cloves wrapped in foil for 30 minutes until soft. Boil eggs for 2 minutes only. Squeeze garlic from skins into bowl of a food processor and blend with hot eggs and anchovy fillets. Add sherry vinegar and lemon juice, then slowly drizzle in oil with the motor still running until sauce emulsifies. Season, then taste and adjust if necessary. Refrigerate, sealed, until ready to use.

4 Coat surfaces of tuna with pepper. Stand a heavy-based frying pan over a high heat and quickly sear peppered tuna on both sides, leaving it rare in the middle. This will take only a few minutes at most – overcooking will render tuna white, dry and flaky.

5 Meanwhile, cook spinach gently in a saucepan with butter, salt, pepper and nutmeg, stirring regularly. Do not let it dry out.

6 To serve, spoon anchovy sauce onto each plate, then add hot spinach. Slice each tuna steak into 5 crosswise, then arrange on spinach. Top with a slice or two of anchovy butter – the heat of the tuna will melt the butter. Serve immediately.

3 bunches spinach, stems removed
6 × 150 g tuna steaks (2 cm thick),
   cleaned
coarsely ground black pepper
olive oil
50 g unsalted butter
½ teaspoon sea salt
½ teaspoon freshly ground black pepper
¼ teaspoon freshly grated nutmeg

Anchovy butter
250 g unsalted butter, softened
10 anchovy fillets
30 ml strained lemon juice
½ teaspoon freshly ground black pepper
1 tablespoon chopped flat-leaf parsley

Anchovy sauce
8 cloves garlic
2 large (61 g) eggs
6 anchovy fillets, chopped
25 ml sherry vinegar
1 teaspoon strained lemon juice
300 ml extra-virgin olive oil
½ teaspoon sea salt
½ teaspoon freshly ground white pepper

Tuna pepper steak with spinach and anchovy sauce

Something quite delightful happens on the palate when fresh tuna and anchovies are combined, so if you haven't tasted this particular pairing before, give it a go and see if you agree. Swordfish and anchovies are also a great pairing. Apart from the fact that you will experience a particularly sexy partnership, I recommend trying this recipe just because it's so straightforward. (See photograph opposite.)

1 Wash spinach thoroughly, then blanch in boiling water for 30 seconds and refresh immediately in iced water. When cold, squeeze out water.

2 Heat half the saffron butter in a frying pan and sear scallops for 1½ minutes a side until just cooked. Do not overcook or the scallops will shrink and toughen.

3 Season scallops lightly with salt and pepper and remove to a warm plate.

4 Bring pickle to a simmer in a saucepan over moderate heat. Stir in remaining saffron butter with coriander, mint and tomato.

5 Melt butter in a saucepan, then add spinach and reheat gently, stirring. Add salt and pepper to taste. Divide spinach between plates, then spoon over spiced tomato chilli pickle and top with scallops. Serve immediately.

2 bunches spinach, stems removed
125 g Saffron Butter (page 342)
24 scallops
sea salt

freshly ground black pepper
½ cup Spiced Tomato Chilli Pickle
  (page 52)
¼ cup coriander leaves

2 tablespoons shredded mint
3 tomatoes, peeled, seeded and diced
30 g unsalted butter

Saffron-braised scallops with spiced tomato chilli pickle

Look for plump scallops from Queensland or Victoria or beautiful Coffin Bay scallops from South Australia when they are in season when making this recipe. Avoid scallops that have been washed or soaked in water when removed from their shells – this bloats the meat, causing it to shrink when heat is applied. If you buy scallops in their shells, carefully remove the meat with a small knife by cutting the attached muscle, then wipe it clean with paper towel.

1 To prepare the dressing, blend sun-dried capsicum to a paste in a food processor. Whisk paste into vinegar with salt and pepper, then whisk in olive oil until emulsified.

2 Make and cook noodles as instructed, then toss with a little oil to prevent sticking.

3 To prepare chilli salt, dry-roast chillies, salt and peppercorns together over gentle heat until fragrant and slightly coloured. Cool, then grind to a fine powder. Mix ground spices with rice flour.

4 Cut poblano chillies in half lengthwise, then brush with oil and grill until skin blisters. Rub off skin, then remove seeds and cut into fine strips. Toss noodles, poblano chillies, pimiento, onion and basil with dressing in a saucepan and warm slightly to allow flavours to infuse.

5 Brush eel with sweet soy sauce and cook under a hot griller for 2 minutes until caramelised, then remove from heat.

6 Heat oil in a deep-fryer to 180°C. Cut squid tubes into strips, coat with chilli salt and deep-fry in small batches for 30 seconds until squid curls and crisps. Remove with a mesh spoon and drain briefly on paper towel.

7 Divide noodles between plates, then add a piece of grilled eel and carefully arrange crispy squid strips on top. Drizzle over extra dressing if needed and serve immediately.

1 quantity Black Ink Noodles (page 341)
extra-virgin olive oil
6 roasted poblano chillies
2 tablespoons roasted pimiento strips,
    finely sliced
1 small red onion, diced
1/4 cup basil leaves, shredded
2 Japanese grilled double eel fillets,
    cut into 6 pieces
2 teaspoons sweet soy sauce
vegetable oil
300 g squid tubes, cleaned

Sun-dried capsicum dressing
1 tablespoon sun-dried red capsicum
50 ml aged balsamic vinegar
1/2 teaspoon sea salt
1/2 teaspoon freshly ground black pepper
150 ml extra-virgin olive oil

Chilli salt
3 large dried chillies
3 teaspoons sea salt
1 teaspoon black peppercorns
50 g rice flour

Chilli salt squid with sweet grilled eel, black ink noodles and pimiento

This composition is a union of savoury, luscious flavours and textures redolent of the Mediterranean: the sweetness of the roasted pimiento highlights the natural sweetness of the squid and the chilli salt crust provides a spicy edge. Look for roasted pimiento and poblano chillies in Spanish or gourmet food stores. Grilled eel fillets imported from Japan are available from some Asian food stores. If you find it difficult locating them, use local hot-smoked eel, fresh mackerel or sardine fillets.

1 Peel potatoes and slice into paper-thin rounds. Infuse saffron in a saucepan of boiling water, then blanch potato rounds briefly. Remove potato with a slotted spoon and cool on a tray.

2 To make the saffron cream, bring cream and saffron to a simmer and cook gently for 5 minutes until cream is infused with colour and flavour of saffron. Allow cream to cool, then whisk it into egg yolk with salt and pepper.

3 Paint skin of fish with saffron cream, then arrange overlapping rows of potato over skin, painting with saffron cream as you go, to give appearance of fish scales. Refrigerate fish for 1 hour.

4 Toss scrubbed mussels into a wide, heavy-based saucepan over high heat, then cover and steam until shells open. This will only take about 1 minute. Remove open mussels (discard any that haven't opened) and plunge into iced water to stop the cooking process. When cool, remove mussels from shells and set aside. Discard shells.

5 Wash spinach thoroughly, then blanch in boiling water for 30 seconds and refresh immediately in iced water. When cold, squeeze out water and set aside.

6 Preheat oven to 180°C with a heavy-based baking tray in it. Heat oil in a frying pan and fry fish potato-side down in batches over high heat for 2 minutes. Transfer fish to hot baking tray, potato-side down, and bake for 10–12 minutes, depending on thickness of fish, or until opaque. Remove from oven and turn fish over with a spatula – rest for a minute or two while assembling dish.

7 Reheat spinach with 50 g ghee in a saucepan, then season with salt and pepper. Bring green masala sauce to a simmer in a saucepan, then add saffron butter, mussels, tomato and mint, stirring until butter has been incorporated. Spoon spinach onto plates, then ladle around sauce, portioning mussels equally. Sit fish, potato-side up, on top of spinach. Brush potato 'scales' with a little extra melted ghee and serve immediately.

6 kipfler *or* pink fir apple potatoes
small pinch of saffron threads
6 × 150 g pieces wild barramundi
  (skin on)
1 kg black mussels, scrubbed
2 bunches spinach, stems removed
50 ml vegetable oil
ghee

salt
freshly ground black pepper
300 ml Spiced Green Masala Sauce
  (page 68)
150 g Saffron Butter (page 342)
2 tablespoons diced tomato
1 tablespoon shredded mint

Saffron cream
50 ml thick (45%) cream
generous pinch of saffron threads
1 egg yolk
2 pinches sea salt
2 pinches freshly ground black pepper

Wild barramundi with saffron potato crust, black mussels and green masala sauce

The season for wild barramundi in North Queensland and the Northern Territory starts in early February and lasts through to winter. It is a delightful fish, being quite large and having moist, tight flesh. Barramundi of a similarly large size are also being farmed in Queensland – these are saltwater-purged before killing. Remember, however, that the farmed species never have quite the same flavour as those caught in the wild. (I never use the smaller, plate-sized farmed barramundi as I find they have little character or flavour.) Other fish that can be prepared in this manner include nile perch, sea perch, halibut and sea bream. Ask the fishmonger for slices taken from the middle or thickest part of the fillet. (See photograph opposite.)

1 Make the rice pilaf as instructed and keep warm.

2 To make the red chilli paste, combine all ingredients thoroughly, then cook over gentle heat, uncovered, for 10 minutes. Remove from heat and allow to cool. Taste and adjust seasoning if necessary.

3 Spread red chilli paste in centre of 6 square banana leaves. Put fish on top, then pour on more paste, about a tablespoon per serve. Wrap fish securely in banana leaf and secure with a skewer or tie with string.

4 Put fish parcels onto a plate that will fit inside a Chinese steamer and pour over any remaining paste.

5 Bring a large saucepan of water to a rolling boil, then steam fish, covered, for 20 minutes or until cooked through. Check after 15 minutes by pressing on flesh – it should have a little spring and not be tight. Fish should be translucent and white, not opaque, when ready.

6 Meanwhile, reheat the rice pilaf in a steamer if it has been prepared beforehand.

7 To serve, put a banana leaf rectangle on each plate, then carefully transfer barramundi from its parcel to a plate with a spatula and pour over chilli paste. Spoon rice pilaf alongside, then sprinkle coriander leaves over fish and fried garlic over rice. Serve immediately.

1 quantity Cardamom Rice Pilaf
  (page 211)
6 × 20 cm squares banana leaf, washed
6 × 150 g pieces wild barramundi
6 × 18 cm × 10 cm rectangles
  banana leaf, washed
2 tablespoons coriander leaves
2 tablespoons Fried Garlic (page 342)

Red chilli paste
5 tablespoons Massaman Curry Paste
  (page 45)
500 ml coconut milk

2 tablespoons Chilli Jam (page 58)
40 ml fish sauce

Wild barramundi baked in banana leaf with red chilli paste, fried garlic and rice pilaf

This recipe is designed for thick fish fillets that do not have an abundance of natural oil – the gentle method of baking the fish in the banana leaf helps retain the natural juices, which keep the fish moist and soft. I like to use wild barramundi in this dish as it holds up well to the heady flavours of the chilli paste, but Murray cod, snapper, rock cod (also known as bar cod), dhufish, sea perch, groper or sea bass can also be used. Ask the fishmonger to cut slices from the middle or thickest part of the fillet.

1 Dry-roast cumin seeds over gentle heat until fragrant. Cool, then grind to a fine powder.

2 Cook onion, ginger, garlic, green chilli and curry leaves in coconut oil until softened and fragrant.

3 Cut cheeks away from mangoes, then cut into 2 cm dice, skin on, and discard seeds. Add mango and coconut milk to aromatic base and bring to a boil, uncovered. Stir in ground spices and simmer gently until sauce takes on sourness of green mango.

4 Add fish and fish sauce and cook until fish just loses its transparency, 6–7 minutes. Carefully remove fish from sauce with a mesh spoon and set aside.

5 Add coconut cream and return to a boil, uncovered. Taste and adjust seasoning if necessary.

6 Remove pan from heat, then stir fish back into sauce with coriander and serve immediately with steamed rice or Coconut Rice (page 215).

2 teaspoons cumin seeds
1 brown onion, finely sliced
30 g minced ginger
4 cloves garlic, minced
6 large green chillies, halved lengthwise
1 tablespoon curry leaves

30 ml coconut oil
2 small green mangoes
250 ml coconut milk
1 teaspoon ground chilli
1 teaspoon ground turmeric

1.5 kg coral trout fillets, cut into
  3 cm cubes
30 ml fish sauce
200 ml coconut cream
1/4 cup coriander leaves

Coral trout and green mango curry

The richness of the coconut cream used in this curry is offset by the sourness of the green mangoes. Any white-fleshed

reef fish is suitable if you cannot get fresh coral trout: try sea bream, sea bass, groper, black bream, ocean perch or any fish

from the snapper family. Like any fish recipe, always choose the freshest fish available, not necessarily the one prescribed

in the recipe, to give yourself as much flexibility as possible. You can substitute a lighter oil for the initial cooking, too,

if you don't want to use the heavier coconut oil.

1 Heat oil in a deep-fryer to 180°C and fry leek until crisp and golden, about 1 minute. Drain on paper towel. Toast both halves of nori sheet over direct flame for a few seconds, then shred very finely. Set aside.

2 To make the dressing, whisk all ingredients together.

3 Shave fennel into fine rounds, then shave cucumber into long strips, discarding seed core. Shred pickled ginger, then mix with fennel, cucumber and red onion. Blanch bok choy in boiling water until just tender, then drain and add to vegetables.

4 Toss dressing through salad and mix well, then divide salad between plates.

5 Season flour with salt and pepper and coat oysters.

6 Heat oil in a deep-fryer to 180°C, then fry 5 oysters at a time for 20 seconds, just enough to heat through. Remove with a mesh spoon, then drain on paper towel while cooking remaining oysters.

7 Divide oysters between plates and top with shredded leek and nori. Serve immediately.

vegetable oil for deep-frying
$1/2$ leek, very finely shredded
1 nori seaweed sheet, cut in half
2 small fennel bulbs
1 large cucumber, peeled
2 teaspoons Pickled Ginger (page 52), shredded

1 tablespoon diced red onion
6 baby bok choy
2 tablespoons coarse rice flour
1 teaspoon sea salt
1 teaspoon freshly ground black pepper
30 Pacific oysters, freshly opened

Blackbean dressing
15 g black beans, soaked and rinsed
9 red shallots, finely sliced
2 teaspoons minced ginger
$1/4$ teaspoon freshly ground black pepper
$1/4$ teaspoon sesame oil
50 ml soy sauce
30 ml mirin
30 ml strained lime juice
120 ml extra-virgin olive oil

Salt-and-pepper oyster fritters with shaved fennel and blackbean dressing

Not often is it desirable or necessary to cook oysters, but the ocean-dwelling Pacific variety from Tasmania or South Australia can withstand a flash of heat without detriment to its flavour or texture. These fritters taste like a mouthful of surf and have a great texture, both of which are complemented by the saltiness of the blackbeans in the dressing. Do not use creamy rock oysters or flat belon (angasi) oysters for this dish, as their texture and taste will be lost in the translation.

(See photograph opposite.)

1 To make the spice crust, dry-roast chilli and whole spices except mustard and nigella seeds over gentle heat until fragrant and slightly coloured. Cool, then grind to a fine powder. Stir in mustard and nigella seeds, ground cassia and ginger, salt and chickpea flour.

2 Coat fish thoroughly with spice crust.

3 Heat oil in a frying pan and cook fish for 3 minutes until fish is a paler pink at the base. Turn fish over and cook for another 2 minutes. The fish should be rosy-rare in the middle.

4 Serve with mint chutney and cucumber salad.

6 × 100 g pieces Tasmanian salmon
150 ml vegetable oil
$^{1}/_{2}$ cup Mint Chutney (page 55)
$^{1}/_{2}$ cup Cucumber Yoghurt Salad with
 Nigella (page 80)

Spice crust
1 large dried chilli
2 teaspoons cumin seeds
1 teaspoon coriander seeds
$^{1}/_{2}$ teaspoon black peppercorns
seeds from 2 green cardamom pods

1 teaspoon brown mustard seeds
2 teaspoons nigella seeds
$^{1}/_{4}$ teaspoon ground cassia
$^{1}/_{4}$ teaspoon ground ginger
2 teaspoons sea salt
20 g chickpea flour

Spice-crusted salmon with mint chutney

This spice crust gives the fish a wonderfully fragrant piquancy. To allow the spices to speak for themselves,

I serve this dish without a sauce, just adding a couple of condiments instead. Salmon or trout from

anywhere in the world may be used.

1 Cook noodles in boiling water for 2 minutes, then strain and set aside.

2 Steam mussels and clams open, separately, in a wide, heavy-based pan over high heat.

3 Plunge mussels and clams into iced water to cool, then remove meat from shells. Discard any unopened shells. Strain and reserve any cooking liquid in pan.

4 Heat oil in a wok and fry garlic, chilli and green onion briefly until softened.

5 Deglaze wok with rice wine, then add reserved cooking liquid, stock, vinegar, mirin and fish sauce and bring to a boil. Taste and adjust seasoning if necessary.

6 Add clams, mussels, noodles and shredded cabbage to wok and stir over high heat until warmed through, about 1 minute. Stir in basil and ladle into deep bowls to serve.

400 g dried somen noodles
1 kg black mussels
1 kg wild surf clams
60 ml vegetable oil
12 cloves garlic, minced

4 large dried chillies, crushed
6 green onions, cut into 1cm lengths
50 ml Chinese Shaoxing rice wine
200 ml Fish Stock (page 337)
25 ml Chinese Chinkiang black vinegar

50 ml mirin
30 ml fish sauce
6 Chinese cabbage leaves, finely
  shredded
$^{1}/_{2}$ cup Thai *or* holy basil leaves

Garlic clams and mussels with somen noodles

A simple preparation full of soft, silky textures and fresh sea flavours. You can also use pippies, scallops or other molluscs,

if you like. If you can get fresh green-lip abalone, steam it until softened, then slice it very finely and

toss it through the noodles for a fabulous textural and flavour combination.

POULTRY

POULTRY Spices and poultry are natural partners: spices render fat, enhance the texture of the meat, and help preserve, all the while creating new taste sensations and giving a complexity of flavour not possible otherwise. Just about every poultry preparation in existence has some spice element to it. Those that don't aren't worth consideration in my mind. ❋ CHICKENS, DUCK, PIGEONS, squab, quail, pheasants, turkeys and geese are some of the birds that make up the diverse poultry family. Of these, chicken is the most consumed poultry item in Australia today, with duck as second runner. Thankfully, breeders with integrity have restored the glamour appeal of real chicken – free-range, corn-fed birds are now challenging the ill effects wrought on the industry by the battery-farm chook. ❋ AS CONSUMERS, we must opt for the best quality, and cook with respect, care and a sense of adventure, using spices and flavourings to further enhance the flavour and texture of our poultry. Asian cuisines have been doing this forever. Chicken and duck hold an elevated position on the Asian table, particularly in Chinese cooking, where countless celebratory recipes, using a range of techniques from red-braising to steaming and deep-frying, give these birds the prestige they deserve.

1 To prepare the pickled lamb's tongues, soak tongues for 24 hours in cold water with a pinch of salt, changing the water every 4 hours or so. Drain.

2 Heat oil in a large, heavy-based pan and fry fennel, onion, garlic and ginger over moderate heat until softened and fragrant. Stir in speck and mustard seeds and cook for a few minutes, then add tongues and toss to coat with aromatics. Add remaining ingredients and bring to a boil over gentle heat. Simmer for 2 hours or until tongues are soft. Remove pan from heat and allow tongues to cool completely in their pickling stock. Remove cooled tongues and dislodge any spices attached to the meat. Slice finely just before serving.

3 While tongues are cooking, make and cook spaghetti as instructed. Drain, then dress with a little oil to prevent sticking.

4 To make the garlic sauce, preheat oven to 180°C and roast garlic wrapped in foil for 30 minutes until soft. Squeeze roasted garlic from cloves into a mortar and pestle or food processor and pound or blend with salt and pepper. Heat stock and reduce by a third until slightly thickened. Whisk garlic paste, pomegranate molasses and lemon juice into sauce as you are about to serve it. Taste and adjust seasoning if necessary.

5 Reheat spaghetti by immersing it in boiling water for 10 seconds, then drain. Quickly wilt tatsoi leaves in boiling water, then drain.

6 Heat a heavy-based frying pan, then add 50 ml olive oil and fry livers quickly over high heat, just long enough to sear both sides, leaving centres pink and soft. Remove livers from pan immediately and sprinkle with pepper.

7 Arrange a nest of mustard spaghetti on each plate, then add wilted tatsoi leaves and sit 3 livers on top. Add slices of pickled tongue and spoon over garlic sauce. Snip mustard cress with scissors, then sprinkle over dish and serve immediately.

1 quantity Mustard Spaghetti (page 341)
olive oil
2 cups small tatsoi leaves
18 corn-fed chicken livers, trimmed
1 teaspoon freshly ground black pepper
1 punnet mustard cress

Pickled lamb's tongues
3 lamb's tongues
cold water
sea salt
50 ml olive oil

1 tablespoon diced fennel
1 tablespoon diced onion
1 teaspoon minced garlic
1 teaspoon minced ginger
30 g diced speck *or* bacon
1 teaspoon brown mustard seeds
1 stick cinnamon
2 mace blades
5 allspice
1 clove
1 teaspoon black peppercorns
50 g palm sugar, shaved

200 ml rice vinegar
400 ml White Chicken Stock (page 337)
25 ml fish sauce

Garlic sauce
24 cloves garlic
$\frac{1}{2}$ teaspoon sea salt
$\frac{1}{2}$ teaspoon freshly ground black pepper
400 ml Brown Chicken Stock (page 338)
30 ml pomegranate molasses
25 ml strained lemon juice

Chicken livers with pickled lamb's tongue, mustard spaghetti and garlic sauce

This is a magical balance of flavours and textures and a wonderful way to present and eat offal, or 'fancy meats' as they are now sometimes labelled for marketing purposes. There are a few steps involved, but much of the work for each component can be prepared ahead of time, leaving the final cooking to the last minute.

1 Dry-roast dried chillies over gentle heat until fragrant. Cool, then grind to a fine powder.

2 Preheat oven to 180°C.

3 Heat half the olive oil in a frying pan and sauté onion and garlic over moderate heat until just softened.

4 Thickly slice Jerusalem artichokes and arrange in a single layer in a buttered ovenproof dish, then add onion and garlic and stir to combine.

5 Bake for 15 minutes until artichokes are cooked and golden. Deglaze dish with pomegranate molasses, then remove from heat and stir in parsley.

6 Reheat pepper glaze gently.

7 Dust livers with ground chilli. Heat remaining oil in a heavy-based frying pan and sear livers quickly on both sides over high heat, leaving centres pink and juicy. Remove from heat.

8 Arrange roasted artichokes on plates, then sit livers on top, spoon a little hot pepper glaze around and add a dollop of harissa. Serve immediately.

6 large dried chillies
100 ml olive oil
2 small red onions, finely sliced
6 cloves garlic, sliced

500 g Jerusalem artichokes, scrubbed
butter
40 ml pomegranate molasses
2 tablespoons flat-leaf parsley

200 ml Pepper Glaze (page 66)
18 corn-fed duck livers, trimmed
6 teaspoons Harissa (page 58)

Duck livers with roasted Jerusalem artichokes and harissa

The fiery chilli paste harissa works its magic with the rich livers in this dish, and the sharpness of the pomegranate molasses and the creaminess of the tubers combine in an ancient cooking equation that continues to make perfect chemistry.

1 Dry-roast cumin seeds over gentle heat until fragrant. Cool, then grind to a fine powder.

2 Spatchcock quail by cutting away their backbones and flattening them out, then trim wing tips back to first joint. Mix oil, lemon juice, pepper and ground cumin and pour over birds.

3 Heat a chargrill or barbecue, then cook quail skin-side to the grill for about 4 minutes, basting with the oil mix as they cook. Turn and cook 2–3 minutes on the other side – the flesh should still look pink. Arrange quail on a flat plate or tray and spoon over the chermoula.

4 Toss tomato, onion and mint together and arrange on a serving platter. Sit the chermoula quail on top, then sprinkle with salt and serve immediately.

1 teaspoon cumin seeds
6 large quail
175 ml olive oil
25 ml strained lemon juice

$1/2$ teaspoon freshly ground black pepper
$1/4$ cup Chermoula (page 46)
6 vine-ripened tomatoes, sliced
1 red onion, diced

1 cup spearmint leaves, shredded
1 teaspoon sea salt

Grilled quail with chermoula and tomato mint salad

The flavours of Morocco were the inspiration for this warm, spiced quail and salad combination. Be sure to use large, plump quails and vine-ripened tomatoes for the best results. Other poultry such as chicken, guinea fowl or pheasant can also be used – make sure you alter the cooking times accordingly.

1 Bring stock, soy sauce, star anise, peppercorns, cassia, ginger and green onions to a boil in a stockpot, then reduce heat to a mere simmer. Cook for 10 minutes, then immediately strain through a fine-meshed sieve.

2 Return stock to rinsed-out pot, then immerse birds and allow them to 'swim' in stock for 8 minutes off the heat. Remove squab from pot and drain on paper towel. Allow birds to dry in a warm, draughty area (this will take about 2 hours) – hang on metal hooks, if you have any, or by their necks with string.

3 Dissolve maltose in rice vinegar and rice wine in a saucepan over moderate heat, stirring until liquid and boiling. Remove from heat. Dip each squab into maltose mixture to coat, using a pastry brush to ensure birds are completely covered. Hang squab to dry as beforehand for 1 hour, making sure birds are not touching. Repeat lacquering process, then hang birds to dry for 2 hours or overnight.

4 Heat oil in a deep-fryer to 180°C and cook squab, 2–3 at a time depending on size of pot, for 4 minutes. Remove from oil with a mesh spoon to avoid puncturing the crisp skin and drain on paper towel.

5 Cut each squab into quarters and sprinkle liberally with spice salt. Serve immediately with wedges of lemon alongside.

2 litres White Chicken Stock (page 337)
100 ml soy sauce
3 star anise
1 teaspoon freshly cracked Sichuan
   peppercorns

2 pieces cassia bark
5 slices ginger
4 green onions, chopped
6 × 600 g squab
250 g maltose

300 ml Chinese rice vinegar
100 ml Chinese Shaoxing rice wine
vegetable oil for deep-frying
Chinese Spice Salt (page 39)
1 lemon, cut into wedges

Crispy-skinned squab with Chinese spice salt

This dish always reminds me of the first time I visited Hong Kong many years ago and was taken for lunch by a local resident to Lamma, a small island a short ferry ride from Hong Kong Island. We trekked up a grassy path to a hillside house and sat in the courtyard where a hundred or so pigeons were hanging on the clothesline, waiting to be cooked to order. Service ended when the pigeons were all eaten – it was all that was served, the house speciality! I use hand-raised, corn-fed squab in place of everyday pigeon to guarantee juiciness and perfect texture. It's a good idea to provide a bowl for bones and refuse and a large fingerbowl of water, as well as cloth napkins. This is a very tactile dining experience.

1 Cut chicken into 12 pieces on the bone.

2 To make the marinade, bring all ingredients to a boil in a stockpot. Simmer for 10 minutes, then add chicken pieces and simmer gently for 6 minutes.

3 Remove from heat and allow chicken to cool in marinade for 5 hours.

4 Remove chicken from marinade using a slotted spoon and dry with paper towel. (Reserve marinade for later use – just bring it back to a boil before cooling and refrigerating it. It can be kept indefinitely if boiled each week, as for the Chinese Master Stock on page 339.)

5 When ready to cook, make turmeric rice as instructed and keep warm.

6 Heat oil in a deep-fryer to 180°C and fry chicken pieces for 5 minutes until crisp and golden, then drain on paper towel.

7 Serve with rice and sambal alongside.

1 × 1.8 kg free-range, corn-fed chicken	*Tamarind marinade*	2 teaspoons freshly cracked black pepper
1 quantity Turmeric Rice (page 213)	500 ml Tamarind Liquid (page 341)	40 ml soy sauce
3 tablespoons Sambal Bajak (page 57)	30 ml fish sauce	1.5 litres White Chicken Stock (page 337)
	80 g coconut sugar, shaved	

Fried tamarind chicken with sambal and turmeric rice

This is a popular Nonya way of preparing chicken for eating as a snack or as part of a meal. You will never

want to eat fast-food fried chicken again after tasting this delicious version!

1 Melt ghee in a wide, heavy-based pan and fry onion, garlic and ginger over moderate heat until fragrant.

2 Stir in curry paste, chilli jam and curry leaves and fry for a minute for flavours to amalgamate. Add tomato, tamarind liquid and coconut milk and bring to a boil. Simmer for 5 minutes.

3 Chop potatoes and add to pan with chicken legs, then simmer gently until both are cooked, about 40 minutes.

4 Stir in fish sauce and lemon juice, then taste and adjust if necessary.

5 Stir through coriander leaves and serve immediately with steamed rice.

2 tablespoons ghee
1 brown onion, diced
3 large cloves garlic, minced
1 teaspoon minced ginger
5 tablespoons Paramount Curry Paste
  (page 42)
3 teaspoons Chilli Jam (page 58)

18 curry leaves
6 tomatoes, peeled, seeded and chopped
150 ml Tamarind Liquid (page 341)
400 ml coconut milk
300 g kipfler *or* other waxy potatoes,
  washed

12 free-range, corn-fed chicken
  drumsticks
50 ml fish sauce
30 ml strained lemon juice
$1/4$ cup coriander leaves

Chicken, tamarind and coconut curry

A rich, hot-and-sour curry that is best made the day before it is needed, so that the flavours develop fully, and then reheated gently when you are ready to eat. Use chicken meat that is still on the bone as opposed to breast meat, which tends to dry out too quickly.

1 Dry-roast cumin seeds over gentle heat until fragrant. Cool, then grind to a fine powder. Combine ground spices and sprinkle evenly over livers to coat lightly. Set aside.

2 Make the garam masala potato as instructed and keep warm.

3 Blanch peas for 2 minutes in boiling water, then mix into potato with curry leaves and a pinch of the garam masala. Toss over moderate heat for a minute, then add spinach and allow to wilt but not cook. Remove from heat.

4 Melt ghee in a cast-iron frying pan, then cook seasoned livers over high heat for 2 minutes only – the livers should remain quite pink and tender.

5 Spoon potato onto warm plates and top with livers.

6 Sprinkle over a little extra garam masala and serve immediately.

1 teaspoon cumin seeds
seeds from 1 green cardamom pod,
   ground
1/4 teaspoon freshly ground black pepper
24 large corn-fed duck livers, trimmed

1 quantity Garam Masala Potato
   (page 203)
100 g shelled peas
12 curry leaves

1 teaspoon Paramount's Garam Masala
   (page 34)
100 g baby spinach leaves, stems removed
50 g ghee

Duck livers with garam masala potato, peas and spinach

The rich flavour and texture of duck livers are the perfect partners for spicy potato, making this dish a great way

to start a meal. You can use other red meat in place of the livers, if you wish. I have used beef, venison and kangaroo,

searing the meat quickly in a hot pan so it remains quite rare and juicy, then slicing it to arrange on the potato.

(See photograph opposite.)

1 Bring stock to a simmer in a stockpot and add chicken. Cover pot with a lid and remove from heat. Allow chicken to sit in the hot stock for 25 minutes, stirring occasionally to ensure pieces remain submerged and are evenly coated.

2 At the end of this time, test meat with a small, sharp knife at the thickest part – it should be quite pink and relaxed, but not at all bloody. (If it appears underdone, leave in stock for another 5 minutes or so.) Remove meat from stock, then drain on paper towel and allow to cool for 2 hours. Reserve master stock for later use.

3 Meanwhile, make the eggplant salad as instructed.

4 Heat oil in a deep-fryer to 180°C, then fry chicken legs in batches for 5 minutes until crisp. Drain on paper towel.

5 Divide eggplant salad between plates, then sit the crisp chicken legs on top and sprinkle with spice salt and fried garlic. Add a dollop of chilli jam to each plate and serve immediately.

2 litres Chinese Master Stock (page 339)
12 free-range, corn-fed chicken
   drumsticks

1 quantity Chilli and Garlic Eggplant
   Salad (page 89)
vegetable oil for deep-frying

2 teaspoons Chinese Spice Salt (page 39)
1 tablespoon Fried Garlic (page 342)
6 teaspoons Chilli Jam (page 58)

Twice-cooked chicken with chilli and garlic eggplant salad and chilli jam

This is the most divine way to eat chicken as far as I am concerned. The first step can be carried out

the day beforehand, making the final cooking easier and quicker.

1 Dry-roast pine nuts over gentle heat until golden, tossing to avoid burning.

2 Cut each chicken breast into quarters lengthwise.

3 Mix oil, onion, garlic, cardamom, cloves, sumac, salt and pepper in a bowl and add chicken. Marinate for 1 hour.

4 To make the garlic tahini dressing, preheat oven to 180°C. Roast garlic cloves, wrapped together in foil, for 30 minutes until softened. Allow to cool, then squeeze garlic from skins. Mix garlic, lemon juice and tahini in a bowl, then whisk oil in slowly until emulsified. Add salt and pepper to taste.

5 Heat a chargrill plate and add chicken and its marinade. Cook for 8–10 minutes, turning halfway through cooking, until chicken is tender and onions have coloured.

6 Arrange spinach on a platter, then add tomato and sprinkle with pine nuts. Spoon dressing over salad, then pile on chicken and serve immediately.

60 g pine nuts
600 g free-range, corn-fed chicken breasts
75 ml olive oil
1 brown onion, finely sliced
4 cloves garlic, sliced
seeds from 3 green cardamom pods,
    ground

2 cloves, ground
1 tablespoon ground sumac
1 teaspoon sea salt
$^1/_2$ teaspoon freshly ground black pepper
100 g baby spinach leaves, washed
4 tomatoes, finely sliced

Garlic tahini dressing
16 large garlic cloves
75 ml strained lemon juice
75 g tahini
150 ml extra-virgin olive oil
sea salt
freshly ground black pepper

Barbecued chicken with sumac, spinach, tomatoes and pine nuts

The rich and heady spice combinations of the Middle East give a new, alluring dimension to familiar ingredients.

Here the spice sumac gives barbecued chicken an interesting, sour note.

1 To make the duck-neck sausages, cook duck as instructed, discarding bones and skin to achieve 500 g meat. Chop meat into medium–fine dice. Dry-roast peppercorns and fennel and cumin seeds, separately, over gentle heat until fragrant. Cool, then grind separately to a fine powder. Heat oils in a wide, heavy-based pan and fry onion, garlic, ginger and chilli until softened and slightly coloured. Stir in ground spices until fragrant, about 1 minute. Add diced fennel, fungus, thyme and water chestnuts and stir to combine. Tip mixture into a large bowl and allow to cool.

2 Add duck meat and pork fat to cooled spice mixture and combine thoroughly. Season with salt and pepper. Secure each duck neck at one end with kitchen twine. Spoon duck mixture into a piping bag fitted with a wide nozzle and pipe into duck necks until three-quarters full, taking care to apply even, steady pressure. Leave a little space for the mixture to expand during cooking, then tie open ends with twine.

3 Bring stock to a simmer in a wide, heavy-based pan and add sausages. Reduce heat and simmer sausages gently for 15 minutes, then turn them over with a slotted spoon and cook for another 15 minutes. Do not let stock boil during cooking or the sausages may split. Remove sausages from stock with a slotted spoon and drain on paper towel for 30 minutes before proceeding. The sausages can be refrigerated overnight in an airtight container, if desired.

4 Peel celeriac with a knife and grate into acidulated water. Blanch grated celeriac for 30 seconds in a large saucepan of boiling water to soften. Remove from heat immediately, then strain. Run cold water over celeriac to stop the cooking process, then drain thoroughly. Mix grated celeriac and apple into mustard horseradish relish.

5 Whisk sherry vinegar, salt, pepper and oil until combined. Set aside.

6 To cook the sausages, preheat oven to 200°C. Seal sausages in a lightly oiled, cast-iron or heavy-based frying pan over high heat for 2 minutes, then turn over. Transfer pan to oven for 5 minutes, then turn sausages and cook for another 4 minutes until crisp and golden. Drain sausages on paper towel.

7 Spoon some celeriac relish onto each plate. Cut each sausage into 3–4 pieces and arrange on top of celeriac. Drizzle with sherry vinaigrette and serve immediately.

2 litres White Chicken Stock (page 337)
2 heads celeriac
1 Granny Smith apple, grated
3 tablespoons Mustard Horseradish
  Relish (page 57)
30 ml sherry vinegar
$^{1}/_{2}$ teaspoon sea salt
$^{1}/_{2}$ teaspoon freshly ground black pepper
90 ml extra-virgin olive oil

Duck-neck sausages
500 g cooked duck meat (page 260)
1 teaspoon Sichuan peppercorns
2 teaspoons fennel seeds
2 teaspoons cumin seeds
60 ml vegetable oil
20 ml sesame oil
1 brown onion, minced
10 cloves garlic, minced
2 teaspoons minced ginger
3 red bird's-eye chillies, minced

$^{1}/_{2}$ cup diced fennel
50 g fresh black wood fungus,
  shredded
2 teaspoons thyme leaves
75 g fresh water chestnuts, blanched
  and chopped
150 g pork fat, coarsely minced
2 teaspoons sea salt
1 teaspoon freshly ground black pepper
12 duck-neck skins, cleaned

Spiced duck-neck sausages with celeriac, mustard and horseradish

These sausages are time-consuming to make, I must admit, but their flavour is unparalleled and the final result is worth every bit of effort you put in. You need to start two days before you want to serve the sausages. I have referred here to the recipe for Five-spice Duck and Shiitake Mushroom Pies for the duck meat needed for the stuffing. Seek out a speciality poultry supplier for the duck-neck skins used as the sausage casing. (See photograph opposite.)

1 Dry-roast fennel seeds over gentle heat until fragrant. Cool, then grind to a fine powder.

2 Finely mince chicken meat and combine with pork fat in a large bowl. Set aside.

3 Heat oil in a wide, heavy-based pan and sauté minced onion, garlic, coriander root and chilli over moderate heat until softened, about 2 minutes.

4 Stir in ras el hanout, paprika and ground fennel and cook for a few minutes until fragrant and beginning to colour. Remove from heat and season with fish sauce and pepper. Allow to cool completely.

5 Stir cooled spice mixture and parsley thoroughly into minced chicken.

6 To make the sausages, tie a knot in one end of sausage casing. Spoon chicken mixture into a piping bag fitted with a wide nozzle and pipe into casing, taking care to apply even, steady pressure and to leave a little space for mixture to expand during cooking. Twist filled casing every 12 cm to give sausages their shape. Secure filled and twisted casing with a knot.

7 To cook the sausages, bring stock to a gentle simmer in a stockpot. Poach sausages in a single layer for 15 minutes. Remove from stock and hang sausages on a hook over a tray and allow to cool completely. Refrigerate sausages on tray, covered, until ready to use.

1 teaspoon fennel seeds
1 kg free-range, corn-fed chicken leg
  meat (off the bone)
200 g pork fat, coarsely minced
50 ml vegetable oil
1 brown onion, minced

10 cloves garlic, minced
8 coriander roots, minced
4 red bird's-eye chillies, minced
1 tablespoon Ras el Hanout (page 37)
1 tablespoon sweet paprika
30 ml fish sauce

1 teaspoon freshly ground black pepper
$1/4$ cup shredded flat-leaf parsley
300 g sausage casings
3 litres White Chicken Stock (page 337)

Spiced chicken sausages

Part of our weekly ritual at the Restaurant involves making sausages, an important part of any good cook's repertoire.

Although it is easy to buy 'gourmet' sausages, there is a great feeling of satisfaction and accomplishment when you

make your own. Of course, it requires the luxury of time, an ingredient not always available to a cook in a hurry.

But for those of you who can proceed at a leisurely pace, try making these sausages to have on hand to throw on

the barbecue, use in a particular recipe (such as the chicken hotpot on page 159) or feature in a simple dinner.

Once made, the sausages keep for 2 weeks in the refrigerator.

1 Make the sauce as instructed and keep warm.

2 Preheat oven to 180°C. Cut 6 parsnips into thick batons about 5 cm in length and set aside. Cut remaining parsnips into rounds and place in a well-buttered ovenproof dish and top with a few knobs of butter. Season with salt and pepper and spoon cream loosely through parsnip. Cover with foil and bake for 30 minutes or until softened. Pass baked parsnip through a food mill or fine sieve to make a smooth purée. Set aside.

3 Bring stock to a boil in a stockpot, then add lemon zest and reduce heat to a mere simmer, so the surface is not bubbling. Cut chicken into 12 pieces on the bone. Rub ras el hanout over chicken pieces and add to pot with parsnip batons, then poach gently for 10 minutes. Remove pot from heat but leave chicken in stock for 1 hour to cook through. Remove chicken and parsnips carefully with a mesh spoon and set aside until cool enough to handle. Reserve stock for another use.

4 Preheat oven to 200°C. Stand a heavy-based frying pan over moderately high heat, then add sausages and transfer pan to oven for 5 minutes. Turn sausages and cook for another 5 minutes. Remove sausages and drain on paper towel. Reduce oven temperature to 180°C.

5 Put chicken pieces into a large ovenproof pot. Slice each sausage in two and add to pot with parsnip batons. Bring spiced lemon sauce to a simmer and gently pour over chicken. Cover and bake for 10 minutes to allow meat to absorb flavours in sauce. Meanwhile, gently reheat creamed parsnip in a steamer or in a covered dish in the oven.

6 Remove pot from oven, then add parsley. Serve from the pot at the table with creamed parsnip alongside.

1 quantity Spiced Lemon Sauce (page 69)	$^{1}/_{2}$ teaspoon freshly ground white pepper	1 × 2 kg free-range, corn-fed chicken
18 parsnips, peeled	50 ml thick (45%) cream	2 teaspoons Ras el Hanout (page 37)
50 g unsalted butter	2 litres Brown Chicken Stock (page 338)	6 Spiced Chicken Sausages (page 158)
1 teaspoon sea salt	zest of 1 lemon	$^{1}/_{4}$ cup flat-leaf parsley

Chicken hotpot with spiced chicken sausage, preserved lemon and creamed parsnip

Perfect in winter, this is a dish to warm your soul as well as your tastebuds. It can be prepared in one large pot
and served from the centre of the table, in the best tradition of home-cooking.

1 To make the marinade, dry-roast chillies over gentle heat until fragrant. Cool, then grind to a fine powder and combine with remaining marinade ingredients.

2 'Spatchcock' chicken by cutting away backbone and then flattening out bird. Coat chicken liberally with marinade, then cover and leave for 2 hours.

3 Preheat oven to 200°C.

4 Melt ghee in a baking tray, then add onion and ginger and fry for 1 minute to soften.

5 Add chicken with its marinade and bake, skin-side up, for 30–35 minutes until chicken and onion have coloured and meat is cooked, turning chicken and stirring onion every 10 minutes to prevent burning. Cover tray with foil towards end of cooking if chicken is browning too quickly. Test thigh or leg of chicken with a skewer – if juices are pale pink, the chicken is cooked.

6 To serve, chop chicken into pieces with a cleaver. Fry onions further over high heat for a few minutes until darker in appearance and sweeter in flavour. Arrange fried onion and ginger on a platter, then put chicken pieces on top. Sprinkle with a little garam masala and serve immediately with steamed rice.

1 × 2 kg free-range, corn-fed chicken
75 g ghee
3 brown onions, finely sliced
1 tablespoon finely sliced ginger
Bengali Garam Masala (page 34)

Marinade
3 large dried chillies
1 tablespoon ground turmeric
1 teaspoon ground ginger

1 teaspoon Bengali Garam Masala
  (page 34)
1 teaspoon sea salt
2 teaspoons minced garlic
75 ml thick plain yoghurt

Spicy roast chicken with fried onion

An alternative to the traditional roast chicken, this version is still cooked in the manner that we all grew up with

but the spicy marinade gives it a serious facelift. Try it out for your next Sunday roast!

1 Dry duck thoroughly inside and out with a clean cloth. Press firmly on breastbone to break bones – this helps render fat during cooking. Rub 1 tablespoon Chinese spice salt into skin and cavity. Sit duck on a tray, then cover and refrigerate for a few hours.

2 To smoke the duck, cut legs from frame and sit legs and frame on a Chinese steamer tray lined with baking paper. Pierce a few holes in the paper to allow smoke to get through. Line a large wok with foil and stand over a high heat. Add smoking mixture – when it starts to smoke, stand steamer tray in wok and cover with a tight-fitting lid. Smoke duck for 6 minutes, then remove lid and quickly turn pieces over. Replace lid and smoke a further 5 minutes. Remove duck from wok. Allow smoking mixture to cool completely outside before discarding.

3 Put smoked duck into a large bowl and pour in stock, mirin and rice wine. Cover bowl with baking paper and seal with foil. Sit bowl over a large saucepan of gently boiling water and steam duck for 15 minutes. Carefully lift off foil and paper and turn duck over in cooking liquid, then replace paper and foil and steam duck for a further 10 minutes. Remove bowl from pan, then take out duck pieces and allow to cool. Strain cooking juices through a fine-meshed or muslin-lined sieve and refrigerate until set. Remove fat from juices (reserve fat for later use) and reserve duck juices for the dressing.

4 Remove breast meat from cooled carcass and trim off any excess fat. Remove leg meat from bones and trim.

5 To assemble, heat vegetable oil in a deep-fryer to 180°C. Fry eggplant rounds until golden on both sides, about 5 minutes, then drain on paper towel. Deep-fry pieces of duck meat for 4 minutes until crisp, then remove with a mesh spoon and drain on paper towel. Slice duck meat finely. Warm reserved duck juices gently, then combine with sherry vinegar and extra-virgin olive oil and season with salt and pepper. Taste and adjust if necessary.

6 Heat olive oil in a cast-iron or heavy-based frying pan and quickly sear livers on both sides over high heat for about 1 minute, so they remain pink and tender inside.

7 Sit an eggplant round on each plate and spoon on some smoked eggplant purée. Arrange 2 duck livers on the purée, then lie the sliced duck meat over livers and sprinkle with a little Chinese spice salt. Spoon warm dressing over duck, then sprinkle with green onion and shredded parsley and serve immediately.

1 × 2 kg corn-fed duck	vegetable oil for deep-frying	25 ml olive oil
Chinese Spice Salt (page 39)	6 × 1.5 cm thick, round slices eggplant	12 large corn-fed duck livers
$1/4$ cup Tea Smoking Mixture (page 128)	25 ml sherry vinegar	6 tablespoons Smoked Eggplant Purée
100 ml White Chicken Stock (page 337)	75 ml fruity extra-virgin olive oil	(page 198)
20 ml mirin	$1/2$ teaspoon sea salt	3 green onions, sliced on the diagonal
20 ml Chinese Shaoxing rice wine	$1/2$ teaspoon freshly ground black pepper	1 tablespoon shredded flat-leaf parsley

Sichuan-smoked duck with duck livers and smoked eggplant

The Chinese are the masters of duck-cooking, I believe. This is another favourite duck preparation that draws its flavours and inspiration from their cooking techniques. The textures and flavours of this dish combine in a symphony for the palate.

1 Chop 2 of the green onions and put into cavity of chicken with ginger, then truss legs. Rub sea salt and white pepper into skin of chicken.

2 Put chicken into a large bowl, breast-side up, then pour in stock, rice wine and mirin. Cover chicken with baking paper, then seal bowl with foil.

3 Stand bowl over a large saucepan of gently boiling water and steam chicken for 50 minutes. Check thigh joint with a skewer – if juices run pale pink, the chicken is ready. (If not quite ready, steam a little longer.) Remove chicken from bowl and set aside.

4 Strain cooking juices, then skim off fatty layer and discard. Stir soy sauce into juices and keep warm until ready to serve.

5 Joint chicken, then cut meat from bone into thick slices and keep warm.

6 Bring a small saucepan of water to a boil and steam snowpea leaves until wilted, 30 seconds only, then divide between plates. Sit a few slices of chicken on snowpea leaves, then moisten with reserved juices and add a dollop of green garlic relish. Finely shred tops of remaining green onions and sprinkle over finished dish. Serve immediately.

5 green onions
1 × 2 kg free-range, corn-fed chicken
3 slices ginger
1 teaspoon sea salt

1 teaspoon freshly ground white pepper
125 ml White Chicken Stock (page 337)
25 ml Chinese Shaoxing rice wine
25 ml mirin

25 ml soy sauce
100 g snowpea leaves
6 teaspoons Green Garlic Ginger Relish
  (page 56)

Steamed chicken with snowpea leaves and green garlic ginger relish

This dish is so simple and clean-tasting: it relies on the pure flavour of good-quality chicken highlighted by

the zesty freshness of the green garlic relish. (See photograph opposite.)

1 Make the rice pilaf as instructed, then allow to cool.

2 Make the sauce as instructed and set aside.

3 Preheat oven to 200°C.

4 Tunnel-bone chickens using a small, sharp knife, removing all bones except last leg joint and wing bones. Stuff cavity of each bird with cooled pilaf to return bird to its original shape and size. Run a skewer through each chicken to secure legs and close off neck opening, so rice is enclosed. Rub birds with annatto pepper oil and sprinkle with salt and pepper.

5 Roast chickens for 25 minutes until golden, basting occasionally with oil and juices from pan. Test leg meat with a skewer – if juices run pale pink, the chickens are cooked.

6 Remove chickens from oven and sit on a wire rack to drain, then remove skewers.

7 Reheat tomato cardamom sauce gently. Sit a roasted chicken on each plate, then spoon sauce around and serve immediately.

1 quantity Saffron and Cashew Rice Pilaf
  (page 210)
300 ml Tomato Cardamom Sauce
  (page 68)

6 × 500 g free-range, corn-fed small
  chickens
50 ml Annatto Pepper Oil (page 61)
2 teaspoons sea salt

2 teaspoons freshly cracked black pepper

Roasted corn-fed chicken with saffron and cashew rice pilaf and tomato cardamom sauce

For this heady, warming winter dish, I bone out the birds first and then stuff them with the pilaf and proceed with the roasting. If you don't feel like tunnel-boning the chickens yourself, or cannot find a butcher or supplier who will do it for you, don't worry. You can still stuff the birds with their bones intact and then roast them – just add extra cooking time and carve the meat away from the bone to serve. Alternatively, you can roast the chickens in the usual fashion, cook the rice pilaf during this time and serve both separately at the table: the flavours will be the same.

Spiced Onion Pickle (see page 54) is a great accompaniment.

1 Dry-roast chillies, coriander and cumin seeds and peppercorns over gentle heat until fragrant and lightly coloured, then tip onto a plate.

2 Dry-roast coconut and turmeric over gentle heat, tossing frequently to prevent browning, and add to roasted spices.

3 Fry shallots in a little coconut oil in the same pan, then add to plate too.

4 Blend all these ingredients to a smooth paste with garlic in a food processor.

5 Heat remaining coconut oil in pan, then add fenugreek seeds and brown over moderate heat. Add onion and cook until coloured, about 5 minutes. Add curry leaves and chicken and cook for a few minutes, stirring to coat chicken with aromatics.

6 Stir spice paste into chicken and add stock, then cover and cook over gentle heat for about 25 minutes until chicken is tender. Stir in coriander and add salt to taste, then serve immediately.

12 dried bird's-eye chillies
1 tablespoon coriander seeds
2 teaspoons cumin seeds
1 teaspoon black peppercorns
500 g freshly grated coconut
1 teaspoon ground turmeric

6 red shallots, peeled
100 ml coconut oil
10 cloves garlic, chopped
1 teaspoon fenugreek seeds
2 small brown onions, diced
1 tablespoon curry leaves

750 g free-range, corn-fed chicken
  breasts, cut into chunks
250 ml White Chicken Stock (page 337)
¼ cup coriander leaves
sea salt

Spiced coconut chicken curry

This hot-and-sour curry is deliciously rich and quick and simple to make – it can also be made ahead of time and reheated gently. Serve it with steamed rice and pappadams or Parathas (see pages 266 and 267).

1 Remove legs from each quail and set aside, then trim wing tips back to first joint. Leave breasts attached to carcasses.

2 Bring master stock to a boil in a wide, heavy-based pan, then remove from heat and add quail breasts. Position a smaller lid in pan to act as a weight and keep birds submerged, then set aside for 10 minutes.

3 Remove quail from stock with a mesh spoon, then drain thoroughly and cool completely.

4 Prepare chilli garlic eggplant salad as instructed, then keep warm until ready to serve.

5 Remove leg meat from bones (discard bones).

6 Combine 30 ml vegetable oil, larp paste and basil, then add leg meat and mix thoroughly to coat meat with spice paste. Heat a heavy-based frying pan and sear leg meat over high heat for about 2 minutes, just enough to seal. Mince leg meat and flavourings in a food processor.

7 Heat vegetable oil in a deep-fryer to 180°C. Fry quail breasts for 3 minutes until crisp, then remove from oil carefully with a slotted spoon and drain on paper towel. Slice quail breasts from carcasses, discarding bones, then cut each breast in half.

8 To assemble, spoon warm eggplant salad onto plates and top with warm minced quail larp. Arrange 4 pieces of quail breast on larp, then sprinkle with spiced salt and top with fried garlic.

6 large quail	vegetable oil	½ teaspoon Chinese Spice Salt (page 39)
2 litres Chinese Master Stock (page 339)	6 teaspoons Larp Paste (page 46)	2 tablespoons Fried Garlic (page 342)
1 quantity Chilli and Garlic Eggplant Salad (page 89)	2 teaspoons shredded Thai *or* holy basil leaves	

Red-cooked quail breasts with quail larp, chilli and eggplant salad and fried garlic

Finger-licking good, these quail breasts boast great flavours that are a real palate teaser. The hard work is done

in the kitchen beforehand for the ultimate pleasure of those for whom you are cooking.

(See photograph opposite.)

1 Dry-roast cumin seeds over gentle heat until fragrant. Cool, then grind to a fine powder.

2 Heat half the oil in a wide, heavy-based pan and brown duck legs on both sides, about 8 minutes. Remove legs, then tip oil and fat from pan.

3 Heat remaining oil in pan and sauté onion, garlic and ginger until softened. Add ground cumin, cinnamon stick, ras el hanout and pepper and fry until fragrant, stirring constantly.

4 Pour in stock and bring to a boil, then add duck legs, lemon juice, saffron and harissa and stir. Reduce heat to a mere simmer, then cover pan and braise slowly for 30 minutes.

5 Turn duck legs in cooking juices, then add preserved lemon and cook for a further 25 minutes until duck is cooked and tender to the touch. Discard cinnamon stick. Taste and adjust seasoning if necessary.

6 Remove duck legs from pan, then arrange on a platter and keep warm.

7 Bring cooking juices to a rapid boil, then add olives and cook for 5 minutes to thicken sauce slightly. Pour sauce over duck legs, then sprinkle with coriander and serve immediately.

2 teaspoons cumin seeds	1 stick cinnamon	2 teaspoons Harissa (page 58)
50 ml olive oil	1 tablespoon Ras el Hanout (page 37)	1 preserved lemon, finely sliced
12 duck legs	1 teaspoon freshly ground black pepper	12 green kalamata olives, pitted and
2 brown onions, minced	2 litres Duck Stock (page 338)	halved
8 cloves garlic, minced	50 ml strained lemon juice	$^1/_4$ cup coriander leaves
1 tablespoon minced ginger	1 teaspoon saffron threads	

Braised duck with saffron, preserved lemon and harissa

This dish blends African and Mediterranean flavours with natural ease and makes you dream of the kasbah! It is an adaptation of an earlier favourite using the same flavours with squab, as appeared in *Paramount Cooking*.

1 Heat ghee in a heavy-based saucepan and fry masala paste gently for 2 minutes until slightly aromatic. Add chicken and stir well to coat with paste.

2 Sauté gently for 5 minutes to seal.

3 Stir in tomato, salt and stock, then cook over moderately low heat for 15 minutes until chicken is tender. Add lime juice, curry leaves and coriander. Taste and adjust if necessary.

4 Serve immediately with steamed rice or a pilaf.

30 g ghee
3 tablespoons Chettinad Red Masala
   Paste (page 41)

1 kg free-range, corn-fed chicken breasts,
   cut into chunks
4 tomatoes, peeled, seeded and chopped
2 teaspoons sea salt

500 ml White Chicken Stock (page 337)
25 ml strained lime juice
10 curry leaves
handful of coriander leaves

Red masala chicken

A rich, hot, red curry made in the best Indian tradition. If you have made the masala paste in advance, the rest of the cooking is straightforward and quick. Serve this curry with cooling Cucumber Yoghurt Salad with Nigella (see page 80) and some spicy pickles or as part of a larger feast featuring several other compatible dishes.

MEAT

MEAT   The firm, fibrous texture and the rich flavour of red meat provide a great backdrop for complex spicing and allow the cook a freer, more liberal hand than do more subtle, softer sources of protein. Beef is perfectly partnered with pepper, ginger, garlic, cardamom and paprika, among other spices and aromatics; lamb responds well to the spectrum of warm spices; and venison and kangaroo are magical with horseradish, mustard, chilli, juniper berries and pepper. Keep in mind that while meat responds best to big, bold flavours, care and restraint in the selection and combination of spices still give the best results.   JUST AS YOU should seek out those who supply the freshest spices, next time you buy meat, visit your local butcher rather than relying on the plastic-wrapped packets of indeterminate contents available from a floridly lit supermarket express lane where there is no psychological link between the source and the product. In our haste for shopping convenience, we have allowed the skills and practices of generations to slip away. Be selective when buying red meat – ask your butcher for advice about cuts, and think about the endless flavour partnerships you can create to give your cooking an added dimension.

1 Make the pilaf and the sauce as instructed and keep warm.

2 Preheat oven to 200°C.

3 Dry-roast cumin seeds over gentle heat until fragrant. Cool, then grind to a fine powder. Combine ground cumin and cardamom and ½ teaspoon freshly ground black pepper and coat lamb.

4 Heat oil in a heavy-based frying pan and seal meat over moderately high heat on both sides. Transfer pan to oven for 2 minutes, then rest meat on a plate in a warm place for 6 minutes.

5 Meanwhile, steam rice for 10 minutes in moulds if desired. Reheat spinach in a saucepan with a little butter, salt and pepper. Return lamb to oven for 1 minute, then remove from pan and cut into 4–5 slices.

6 Turn out rice or spoon pilaf onto plates, then sit some spinach alongside and arrange lamb beside or on top. Sprinkle fried shallots over rice and serve immediately.

1 quantity Cardamom Rice Pilaf
  (page 211)
500 ml Hot-and-sour Coconut Sauce
  (page 64)
1 teaspoon cumin seeds

seeds from 3 green cardamom pods,
  ground
freshly ground black pepper
6 × 150 g lamb loin fillets, trimmed
50 ml vegetable oil

150 g spinach leaves, stems removed
  and blanched
butter
sea salt
2 tablespoons Fried Shallots (page 342)

Spiced lamb with cardamom rice pilaf and hot-and-sour coconut sauce

This dish can be as formal or informal as you like. For a structured presentation, I pack the cooked pilaf into small dariole moulds, then steam them for 6 minutes (longer if they have been refrigerated) just before serving, so that the preparation can be done ahead of time. Otherwise you can go for a more casual approach by simply spooning the hot pilaf onto plates and arranging the sliced lamb on top. The final presentation is purely a matter of style and preference – what is important is that you concentrate on getting the wonderful flavours right.

1 Dry-roast coriander and cumin seeds over gentle heat until fragrant. Cool, then grind to a fine powder. Blend garlic, ginger, onion, chilli jam, spices, tomato paste and 100 ml of the oil to a smooth paste in a food processor. Marinate lamb fillets in paste for 2 hours.

2 Preheat oven to 180°C.

3 Heat remaining oil in a large frying pan and cook lamb over moderate heat for 3 minutes, then turn and cook another 2 minutes. Transfer lamb to oven for 3 minutes, then rest meat on a plate for 5 minutes in a warm place.

4 Cut baguette into 1 cm thick rounds, then spread with a little cucumber yoghurt. Slice lamb and arrange on bread, then add a little extra yoghurt.

5 Garnish with coriander and sprinkle with a few nigella seeds.

1 teaspoon coriander seeds
$^{1}/_{2}$ teaspoon cumin seeds
2 teaspoons minced garlic
2 teaspoons minced ginger
1 brown onion, minced
2 teaspoons Chilli Jam (page 58)

1 teaspoon ground turmeric
$^{1}/_{2}$ teaspoon freshly ground black pepper
3 tablespoons tomato paste
150 ml vegetable oil
300 g lamb loin *or* backstrap fillets,
    trimmed

1 baguette
1 quantity Cucumber Yoghurt Salad
    with Nigella (page 80)
2 teaspoons coriander leaves
nigella seeds

Lamb masala

I prepare this spicy lamb to serve on slices of freshly baked Onion Nigella Bread (see page 269) as a tasty appetiser or canapé. Top it with a dollop of Cucumber Yoghurt Salad with Nigella (see page 80) to complete the composition.

1 Dry-roast sesame seeds over gentle heat until just coloured. Toast nori sheet over direct flame for a few seconds, then chop finely. Combine sesame seeds, toasted nori, oils, mirin, pepper and bonito, then add meat and refrigerate for at least 5 hours, ensuring meat is covered.

2 To make the pikelet mixture, cut potatoes into 2 cm cubes. Blend all ingredients except cream briefly in a food processor. Add cream and pulse until just incorporated. Pour mixture into a plastic jug, then cover and refrigerate until ready to use.

3 To make the nori omelettes, toast nori sheets over direct flame, then cut into strips. Lightly whisk eggs (don't aerate them), then season with salt, pepper, sesame oil and fish sauce and stir in nori strips. Heat a 20 cm non-stick frying pan and brush it lightly with oil. Ladle in just enough egg mixture to cover base of pan, spreading it thinly. Cook until just set over moderate heat, then turn out onto a clean tea towel. Continue process with remaining mixture, stacking omelettes on top of each other as you go. Roll omelette stack into a roulade, then wrap firmly in plastic film and secure ends. Allow to cool at room temperature for 30 minutes.

4 To cook the kangaroo, heat a heavy-based chargrill pan until extremely hot, then remove fillet from marinade and sear quickly on all sides to just seal – this should take 2 minutes all up. Transfer meat to a plate to rest for a few minutes before slicing.

5 To cook the pikelets, heat a non-stick frying pan and oil lightly, then pour pikelet mixture into 6 oiled egg rings. Cook over moderate heat until bubbles start to appear in batter, then flip pikelets over and cook other side, removing egg rings as you do so.

6 Cut omelette roll into 1.5 cm thick slices. Place a hot pikelet in centre of each plate and top with an omelette round. Finely slice kangaroo and carefully arrange 4–5 slices on top of omelette, then season with a little sansho pepper, add a dollop of horseradish cream and sprinkle with chopped chives. Serve immediately.

$^1/_2$ teaspoon white sesame seeds
1 nori seaweed sheet
100 ml olive oil
20 ml sesame oil
1 teaspoon mirin
$^1/_4$ teaspoon freshly ground white
   peppercorns
$^1/_2$ teaspoon dried bonito flakes
1 × 250 g striploin fillet of kangaroo,
   trimmed
$^1/_4$ teaspoon sansho pepper
6 teaspoons Horseradish Cream (page 343)
3 teaspoons finely chopped chives

Pikelet mixture
350 g desiree potatoes, peeled
1 large (61 g) egg
1 tablespoon plain flour
2 teaspoons chopped chives
1 teaspoon freshly grated horseradish
1 teaspoon wasabi powder
1 teaspoon sea salt
$^1/_2$ teaspoon freshly ground black pepper
50 ml thick (45%) cream

Nori omelettes
2 nori seaweed sheets
10 large (61 g) eggs
pinch of sea salt
$^1/_2$ teaspoon freshly ground black pepper
1 teaspoon sesame oil
1 teaspoon fish sauce
vegetable oil

Peppered kangaroo fillet with nori omelette, wasabi potato pikelet and horseradish cream

This dish is a wonderful way to introduce the fantastic texture and flavour of kangaroo – lean, cholesterol-free meat that demands simple, quick cooking in order to maintain juiciness. Kangaroo meat is now available in the United Kingdom at stores such as Harvey Nichols and Harrods. (See photograph opposite.)

1 Preheat oven to 180°C. Dry-roast cumin and coriander seeds and dried chillies, separately, over gentle heat until fragrant. Cool, then grind to a fine powder.

2 Brush brisket with some of the oil, then sprinkle with pepper and brown in a large, heavy-based cast-iron casserole in oven, about 10 minutes each side. Remove meat and reduce oven temperature to 150°C.

3 Add remaining oil to pot and sauté onion, garlic, ginger and minced chilli until fragrant. Stir in ground spices and 2 teaspoons freshly ground black pepper and cook for a few minutes. Pour in stock and bring to a boil. Reduce to a simmer, then return beef to pot and cover with foil. Cook slowly in oven for 1 hour, turning meat in stock during cooking, then add potato and cook for 1 hour more.

4 Stir in chopped rind of half the preserved lemon, then cook for another hour (3 hours all up) until meat is very tender. Remove meat from stock and rest on a plate until cool enough to handle.

5 Strain stock through a fine-meshed sieve, discarding solids. Bring strained stock to a boil in a saucepan and reduce by half or until thickened and unctuous but not sticky. Mince remaining preserved lemon and add to sauce. Taste for seasoning and adjust with salt and pepper if necessary. The lemon usually provides enough salt but a little extra pepper may be required.

6 Carefully remove any fat, tendons and muscle tissue from brisket and cut meat into even chunks.

7 To prepare the cous cous, bring stock to a boil in a saucepan. Remove from heat, then add saffron and infuse for 5 minutes. Pour cous cous into a bowl and stir in stock and butter until all liquid has been absorbed. Set bowl over a steamer, then cover with a lid and steam cous cous for 7–8 minutes, stirring occasionally to fluff up grains. Remove from heat and season lightly with salt and pepper.

8 To make the gremolata, chop parsley, then mince with onion, garlic and preserved lemon.

9 Reheat finished sauce by bringing it to a boil in rinsed-out casserole, then reduce heat and add meat and simmer very gently for 10 minutes. Spoon meat and sauce over cous cous, then sprinkle with gremolata and serve immediately.

1 teaspoon cumin seeds	2 teaspoons Ras el Hanout (page 37)	500 g cous cous
2 teaspoons coriander seeds	1 teaspoon hot paprika	50 g unsalted butter
2 large dried chillies	3 litres Beef Stock (page 339)	salt
1 × 2 kg piece beef brisket	12 kipfler *or* other waxy potatoes,	freshly ground black pepper
200 ml olive oil	thickly sliced	
freshly ground black pepper	1 preserved lemon	*Preserved lemon gremolata*
2 brown onions, minced		$^1/_2$ cup flat-leaf parsley
6 cloves garlic, minced	*Saffron cous cous*	1 tablespoon minced red onion
1 tablespoon minced ginger	750 ml White Chicken Stock (page 337)	2 cloves garlic, minced
1 red bird's-eye chilli, minced	$^1/_2$ teaspoon saffron threads	2 teaspoons minced preserved lemon

Slow-braised beef brisket with spiced potato, preserved lemon and saffron cous cous

A perfect dish for cold winters that is full of heady spicing and big flavours and uses an under-valued cut of meat.

Start the preparation, then leave the pot ticking over for ages – it just gets better and better. In the Restaurant, I cook an 8 kg brisket from a big animal overnight in a very low oven – all the work is done while I sleep!

1 Rub ground chilli and pepper into beef.

2 Heat oil in a heavy-based frying pan and seal beef for 3 minutes over moderately high heat, then turn over and cook for another 2 minutes. Remove pan from heat and allow meat to rest for 10 minutes.

3 While meat is resting, preheat oven to 200°C and bring prepared dal to a simmer in a saucepan.

4 Reheat pepper glaze gently.

5 When ready to serve, transfer beef to oven for 3 minutes, then cut each piece in two. Spoon some dal onto each plate, then sit beef on top, add some chilli jam and ladle the pepper glaze around. Serve immediately.

2 teaspoons ground roasted chilli
2 teaspoons freshly cracked black pepper
6 × 200 g ribs of beef *or* pieces Scotch
    fillet, trimmed

60 ml vegetable oil
1 quantity Chilli Cumin Dal (page 192)

300 ml Pepper Glaze (page 66)
3 teaspoons Chilli Jam (page 58)

Roasted rib of beef with chilli cumin dal

Here rich, succulent meat combines with the full-bodied yet mellow spiciness of lentils,

creating a wonderful and complex partnership.

1 Dry-roast dried chillies, cumin seeds and coriander seeds, separately, over gentle heat until fragrant. Cool, then grind separately to a fine powder.

2 Bring coconut milk to a simmer in a wide, heavy-based pan, then add aromatics and spices and simmer gently, uncovered, for 5 minutes.

3 Add stock and bring to a boil, then reduce heat and stir in beef and simmer gently for 45 minutes.

4 Quarter potatoes, then add to beef and simmer for 45 minutes until soft. If liquid disappears during cooking, add a little water to keep meat and potato moist. By the end of cooking, all liquid should have been absorbed. Season with fish sauce, adding a little more if necessary.

5 Stir coriander through curry when you are ready to serve. Offer jasmine rice separately.

6 large dried chillies
2 teaspoons cumin seeds
1 tablespoon coriander seeds
1 litre coconut milk
2 brown onions, minced
1 tablespoon minced ginger
8 cloves garlic, minced

3 coriander roots, minced
1 stalk lemongrass, minced
4 kaffir lime leaves, shredded
2 teaspoons minced turmeric
2 teaspoons minced galangal
8 red bird's-eye chillies, finely sliced
12 curry leaves

1 tablespoon ground turmeric
1 litre Beef Stock (page 339)
1 kg rump steak, cubed
6 large desiree or pink-eye potatoes, peeled
50 ml fish sauce
1 cup coriander leaves

Beef and potato rendang

This dry curry is of Malay origin – the meat and potatoes are cooked slowly in an aromatic sauce until all the liquid has been absorbed. It is even better made a day or two in advance and then gently reheated, as it becomes more flavoursome again. The curry base is rich with a deep complexity, perfect for red meats that require long, slow cooking to render them tender and velvety in texture. Traditionally, rendang is made with mutton or goat but I have chosen rump here. It also works with any of the cheaper cuts of beef (blade, round or skirt steak or topside), the slow cooking softening the connective tissues. (See at top of photograph opposite.)

1 Soak sweetbreads overnight in lightly salted water, refrigerated, to remove excess blood.

2 To make the gratin, preheat oven to 190°C and generously butter a 24 cm square gratin dish. Whisk egg yolks, then stir in cream, salt and pepper. Arrange overlapping slices of potato over base of dish, then brush with egg mixture. Repeat this process until gratin is about 4 cm thick, then brush top with melted butter. Press a sheet of baking paper over gratin, then seal dish with foil. Bake for 45 minutes or until cooked and soft – test with a skewer. Remove from oven, then allow to cool a little and turn out onto a board. Trim edges. Reset oven to 200°C.

3 Bring a large saucepan of water flavoured with a little white wine, peppercorns and bay leaf to a gentle simmer and poach sweetbreads gently for 5 minutes. Remove from heat, then transfer sweetbreads to a bowl of cold water for 5 minutes. Peel sweetbreads of any membrane and connective tissue.

4 Roll each piece of veal into a perfect medallion and wrap each with 4 slices pancetta. Heat half the oil in a frying pan and cook veal for 3 minutes, then turn over and cook for a further 2 minutes. Transfer pan to oven for 3 minutes, then remove and rest in a warm place for 10 minutes. Leave oven on.

5 Heat remaining oil in a clean pan and fry sweetbreads with garlic and cracked pepper until crisp, about 5 minutes, turning over to colour on both sides. Tip sweetbreads onto a plate and keep warm.

6 Melt butter in pan and quickly fry foie gras until lightly coloured on both sides. This will take only a minute or so, as the foie gras is very soft and will start to disintegrate if left on the heat for too long.

7 Bring pepper glaze to a gentle simmer. Return veal to oven for 1–2 minutes to reheat. Meanwhile, cut gratin into 6 squares for serving. Put a square of gratin on each plate, then cut veal in half crosswise and position on top. Sit a slice of foie gras on the veal, then top with a peppered sweetbread. Sprinkle tarragon leaves into pepper glaze and ladle sauce around meat. Serve immediately.

6 veal sweetbreads	80 ml olive oil	*Potato gratin*
sea salt	3 cloves garlic, minced	butter
water	1 teaspoon freshly cracked black pepper	2 egg yolks
white wine	50 g unsalted butter	100 ml thick (45%) cream
4 black peppercorns	200 g Strasbourg foie gras, cut into	1 teaspoon sea salt
1 bay leaf	6 slices	1 teaspoon freshly ground black pepper
6 × 150 g milk-fed veal tenderloins	400 ml Pepper Glaze (page 66)	6 large potatoes, peeled and finely sliced
24 slices pancetta	1 tablespoon French tarragon	

Milk-fed veal with pancetta, sweetbreads, foie gras and pepper glaze

Refined and full flavours come together here to create an exquisite whole while still allowing each ingredient to shine.

A perfect and elegant dish to serve to those who appreciate their meat.

1 Soak brains overnight in lightly salted water, refrigerated. Peel away all membrane and remove any blood, separating the lobes in the process to give you 12 pieces. Soak again for 1 hour in fresh water, then drain.

2 Poach soaked brains very gently in clean water (with a pinch of salt) or stock for 5–10 minutes until just firm, then remove with a slotted spoon to drain on paper towel. Cut each lobe in half lengthwise to give 24 slices.

3 Dry-roast dried prawns and chillies separately, over gentle heat until fragrant. Cool, then grind to a fine powder.

4 Mix ground dried prawns and ground chilli with $^1/_2$ teaspoon salt, $^1/_2$ teaspoon freshly ground black pepper, breadcrumbs and ginger. Mix eggs and milk in another bowl until combined. Dip brains into egg mixture, then coat with spiced breadcrumbs. Refrigerate crumbed brains on a tray for 1 hour until coating is firm.

5 Heat oil in a deep-fryer to 180°C. Deep-fry crumbed brains, a few at a time, for 3 minutes until crisp. Remove with a slotted spoon and drain on paper towel.

6 Heat a saucepan and melt butter. Reheat spinach over gentle heat, then season with a little salt and pepper. Spread 1 tablespoon chutney in centre of each plate, then add spinach and arrange brain fritters on top. Serve immediately.

6 sets veal brains
sea salt
water *or* White Chicken Stock (page 337)
1 teaspoon dried prawns
2 dried bird's-eye chillies

freshly ground black pepper
1 cup fine breadcrumbs
pinch of ground ginger
2 eggs
30 ml milk

vegetable oil for deep-frying
20 g unsalted butter
2 bunches spinach, stems removed and
    blanched
$^1/_2$ cup Tomato Ginger Chutney (page 56)

Veal brain fritters with tomato ginger chutney

Veal brains have larger lobes than the more commonly available lamb's brains, which can just as easily be used

for this recipe. The crunchy exterior of these fritters, lifted by a gentle spiciness, offsets the creaminess of the brains

perfectly – both combining beautifully with the freshness of the chutney. A dish for those who appreciate textures.

1 Soak brains overnight in lightly salted water, refrigerated. Peel away all membrane and remove any blood, separating the lobes in the process to give you 12 pieces. Soak again for 1 hour in fresh water, then drain. Poach soaked brains very gently in clean water with a pinch of salt for 5 minutes until just firm, then remove with a slotted spoon to drain on paper towel.

2 To make the pepper broth, bring all ingredients slowly to a simmer in a large stockpot. Cook over gentle heat for 1 hour. Strain stock through a fine-meshed sieve, discarding solids. Taste and adjust seasoning if necessary.

3 Spread brains with zhoug, then wrap each brain in 2 spinach leaves. Spread 12 gow gee wrappers out on bench, then put wrapped brains in centre of each wrapper. Brush edges of pastry with egg white. Position remaining gow gee wrappers over brains and press edges together to seal. Bring a large saucepan of salted water to a boil, then cook dumplings for 3 minutes until they float to the surface. Remove with a mesh spoon and drain on paper towel.

4 Meanwhile, reheat pepper broth. Slice sausages into thin, diagonal slices (allow about 4–5 slices per serve) and cook under a hot griller until crisp.

5 Spoon 2 dumplings into each bowl and ladle in some broth. Float sliced sausage in broth, dollop some relish on dumplings and top with green onion. Serve immediately.

6 sets lamb's brains
sea salt
water
6 teaspoons Coriander Zhoug (page 59)
24 large spinach leaves, blanched
24 gow gee wrappers
1 egg white
2 Thai pork sausages
6 teaspoons Green Garlic Ginger Relish
  (page 56)
3 green onions, finely sliced diagonally

White pepper broth
1 teaspoon coriander seeds
1 litre White Chicken Stock (page 337)
$1/2$ teaspoon minced coriander root
2 teaspoons freshly cracked white
  peppercorns
1 dried scallop, shredded
3 slices ginger

1 tablespoon chopped green onion tops
1 star anise, cracked
3 dried Chinese black mushrooms
3 teaspoons soy sauce
25 ml Chinese Shaoxing rice wine
25 ml fish sauce
25 ml mirin

Lamb's brains-and-spinach dumplings with crispy pork sausage, green onions and green garlic ginger relish

Lamb's brains have a gorgeous, creamy texture and subtle flavour that beg to sit with some lively company. This dish is our most popular offal item at the Restaurant – its depth of flavours and textures make it a meat-lover's delight.

Look for gow gee wrappers and Thai pork sausages in Asian food stores. (See photograph opposite.)

1 Preheat oven to 180°C. To make the sweet potato purée, butter a gratin dish, then add sweet potato and season with salt and pepper. Cover dish with foil and bake for 30–40 minutes until soft. Pass sweet potato through a food mill or blend in a food processor until smooth. Taste and adjust seasoning if necessary. Set aside.

2 Bring a stockpot of water to a boil and blanch pork necks for 2 minutes. Remove meat from pot and refresh immediately under cold running water. Repeat this process.

3 Bring master stock to a simmer in rinsed-out pot and add pork necks. Remove pot from heat immediately, then place a weight over meat to keep it submerged, cover with a lid and let meat sit in the hot stock for 1 hour in a warm place. Remove meat and drain, reserving the precious stock for another use. Allow meat to cool totally. This part can be done a day ahead and the meat refrigerated overnight.

4 Make the sweet potato pastries as instructed, then deep-fry in hot oil as instructed for 6 minutes when you are about to serve the pork, so every component is ready at the same time.

5 Meanwhile, reheat sweet potato purée gently in a bowl over a steamer. Reheat mandarin sauce gently in a saucepan.

6 Bring sweet-and-sour dressing to a rapid boil in a frying pan. Slice each pork neck into 3 thick medallions and add to pan with mandarin zest. Reduce heat to moderate, then cook meat and zest for 5 minutes to warm through and caramelise, turning meat to coat all sides.

7 Spoon sweet potato purée onto each plate. Cut each pork medallion in two and arrange on purée, then sit 2 sweet potato pastries alongside. Ladle mandarin sauce around and top with chilli. Serve immediately.

water
2 × 600 g pork necks (from suckling
  pigs)
2 litres Chinese Master Stock (page 339)
12 Deep-fried Sweet Potato Pastries
  (page 250)

1 quantity Mandarin Sauce (page 67)
300 ml Sweet-and-sour Dressing
  (page 128)
3 teaspoons mandarin zest, blanched
2 large red chillies, cut into julienne

Sweet potato purée
50 g unsalted butter
600 g sweet potato, peeled and sliced
$1/2$ teaspoon sea salt
$1/2$ teaspoon freshly ground black pepper

Glazed pork neck with sweet potato pastries and mandarin sauce

This sublime pork preparation has become a constant on our Paramount menu because of its explosive flavours and refined elegance. Sweet-and-sour pork never tasted this good! I refer you to the recipe for Deep-fried Sweet Potato Pastries Stuffed with Prawn, Crab and Water Chestnuts with Sweet Chilli Sauce on page 250 for the delicious pastries that accompany the pork in this dish.

1 To prepare the pork belly, rub salt into pork and refrigerate on a tray, covered, for 3 hours. Bring a stockpot of water to a boil and blanch pork belly for 2 minutes. Remove meat from pot and refresh immediately under cold running water. Repeat this process twice, blanching pork 3 times altogether. Put pork, skin-side up, into a large bowl. Mix remaining ingredients, then pour over pork. Cover with baking paper and then seal bowl with a large sheet of foil. Place bowl over a large saucepan or steamer of gently simmering water. Steam pork for 10 hours or overnight, topping up water in steamer as necessary.

2 Remove pork carefully from bowl and discard any pieces of ginger or onion stuck to the meat. While meat is hot, remove any bones, then put pork on a tray to cool. Strain cooking liquid through a fine-meshed sieve, then refrigerate until set. Remove and discard fatty layer and reserve pork jelly for the consommé.

3 To prepare the consommé, put all ingredients, except tamarind dressing, into a stockpot with 250 ml reserved pork jelly and bring slowly to a simmer. Cook gently for 1 hour, then add tamarind dressing. Remove from heat and strain through a fine-meshed or muslin-lined sieve. Taste and adjust seasoning if necessary. Allow consommé to settle and become quite cold, then remove any sediment or fat.

4 To serve, boil cubed potato until soft, then drain. Bring consommé to a simmer. Bring a saucepan of water to a boil and stand a steamer over it. Cut steamed pork into 3 cm cubes and steam for 2–3 minutes until warmed through.

5 Divide bok choy between large bowls, then add potato, pork, pickled ginger and sliced green onion. Ladle in consommé and serve immediately.

3 waxy potatoes, peeled and cut into
  cubes
12 bok choy, blanched
2 teaspoons shredded Pickled Ginger
  (page 52)
3 green onions, finely sliced

Steamed pork belly
sea salt
1 × 2 kg piece pork belly
water
3 green onions, chopped
6 slices ginger
50 ml soy sauce
60 ml mirin
60 ml Chinese Shaoxing rice wine
40 ml fish sauce

Star anise consommé
2 litres White Pork Stock (page 340)
2 star anise, cracked
1 teaspoon white peppercorns,
  freshly cracked
$1/2$ teaspoon fennel seeds, cracked
1 teaspoon Sichuan peppercorns,
  freshly cracked
2 teaspoons minced ginger
2 bird's-eye chillies, sliced
75 ml Tamarind Dressing (page 81)

Steamed pork belly with star anise consommé

The Chinese are the masters of pork-cooking, understanding its texture and versatility better than anyone. This method of preparation is an adaptation of a northern Chinese speciality known as Dongpo or Tungpo pork. In an essay from *Chinese Gastronomy* on the fragrance of pork, Hsiang Ju Lin and Tsuifeng Lin write that 'the square of fat is regarded with much passion, tenderness and expectation . . . the delicacy of the pork fat which, if prepared accordingly, tastes fresh and clean like fresh sweet butter'. They are right. Pork prepared this way is one of the most divine things I know – it's about trapping the clarity of flavour.

1 Make the eggplant purée and masala sauce as instructed.

2 Dry-roast cumin seeds over gentle heat until fragrant. Cool, then grind to a powder.

3 Heat oil in a deep-fryer to 180°C and fry eggplant slices until golden on both sides, about 5 minutes. Drain on paper towel.

4 Coat lamb with ground cumin and sauté in a lightly oiled frying pan over moderately high heat for 2 minutes on each side, then rest in a warm place for up to 10 minutes. Return lamb to oven for 3 minutes, then remove from heat and cut each fillet into 4 diagonal slices.

5 Meanwhile, reheat eggplant purée in a bowl in a steamer until just warm. Remove from heat immediately. Bring masala sauce to a boil in a saucepan.

6 Spoon eggplant purée onto each plate and sit a fried eggplant round on top. Arrange lamb on eggplant, then ladle sauce around meat. Serve chilli jam in a side dish.

1 cup Smoked Eggplant Purée (page 198)	vegetable oil	3 teaspoons Chilli Jam (page 58)
400 ml Spicy Masala Sauce (page 64)	6 thick, even slices eggplant	
1 tablespoon cumin seeds	6 × 150 g lamb loin fillets, trimmed	

Lamb with roasted cumin crust, smoked eggplant purée and spicy masala sauce

A Paramount classic, this dish features a combination of flavours and textures that is often repeated and requested. You can use any red meat – beef, venison or kangaroo – with the same accompaniments with equal success. Whichever you use, choose good-quality meat packed with flavour and some visible fat for tenderness. Eggplant and spices seem inseparable in my repertoire and are in constant use in my daily cooking. (See photograph opposite.)

1 Preheat oven to 200°C.

2 Rub kangaroo with cracked pepper.

3 Cut beetroots into 1 cm cubes.

4 Heat butter and 50 ml olive oil in a frying pan until foaming, then add beetroot and toss to coat. Cook over low heat until beetroot has softened and become glazed, stirring regularly. Season with salt and pepper and set aside.

5 Heat a heavy-based frying pan until very hot, then add a splash of olive oil and immediately toss in peppered kangaroo fillets and cook for 2 minutes each side to seal. Remove meat from pan and rest in a warm place for 8 minutes.

6 While meat is resting, gently reheat pickled spiced beetroot in a steamer and bring pepper glaze to a boil in a saucepan. Add beetroot cubes to pepper glaze and simmer for 5 minutes, then stir in grated horseradish just before serving.

7 To serve, flash meat in oven for 1 minute to reheat.

8 Divide pickled spiced beetroot between plates, then cut each piece of kangaroo into 4 thick slices and arrange on top. Spoon pepper glaze and beetroot cubes around meat, then add a dollop of horseradish cream and serve immediately.

6 × 150 g striploin fillets of kangaroo,
  trimmed
3 teaspoons freshly cracked black pepper
18 small beetroots, peeled
50 g unsalted butter

olive oil
pinch of sea salt
pinch of freshly ground black pepper
¾ cup Pickled Spiced Beetroot
  (page 207)

400 ml Pepper Glaze (page 66)
2 teaspoons freshly grated horseradish
6 teaspoons Horseradish Cream
  (page 343)

Kangaroo fillet with pepper crust, pickled beetroot and horseradish

A perfect partnership between three bold flavours. Instead of cooking the fillets in larger pieces as suggested,

you can also slice the meat thinly, coat it with the pepper and cook it in the same way you would a schnitzel

or minute steak – very quickly over high heat. This method may also give those who squirm at

rare, relaxed meat some psychological advantage.

1 To make the celeriac gratin, preheat oven to 190°C and generously butter a 24 cm square gratin dish. Whisk egg yolks, then stir in cream, salt and pepper. Arrange overlapping slices of celeriac over base of dish, then brush with egg mixture. Add a layer of potato and brush with egg mixture. Repeat this process until gratin is about 4 cm thick, then brush top with melted butter. Press a sheet of baking paper over gratin, then seal dish with foil. Bake for 45 minutes or until cooked and soft – test with a skewer. Remove from oven and allow to cool a little, then turn out onto a board. Trim edges.

2 To make the sauce, slice mushrooms finely and reheat pepper glaze. Heat a saucepan, then add butter and cook garlic for a minute. Add mushrooms and fry over moderate heat, stirring, until softened. Stir tarragon into mushrooms with the simmering pepper glaze. Bring to a boil, then stir mustard into cream and mix this into sauce. Remove from heat immediately – do not let sauce reboil or it may split. (If making sauce ahead of time, reheat gently to simmering point when ready to serve.)

3 Preheat oven to 200°C. Roll venison in cracked pepper to coat lightly. Heat a heavy-based frying pan, then add oil and sear meat over high heat for 3 minutes. Turn over and cook for a further 3 minutes. Remove pan from heat and rest meat for 8–10 minutes. When ready to serve, transfer pan and meat to oven for 2 minutes, then remove meat from pan.

4 To assemble, cut gratin into 6 squares and sit one on each plate. Thinly slice venison across fillet and arrange meat over gratin, then spoon sauce around. Serve immediately.

1 × 1 kg venison striploin fillet, trimmed
2 teaspoons freshly cracked black pepper
50 ml olive oil

Celeriac gratin
unsalted butter
2 egg yolks
100 ml thick (45%) cream
1 teaspoon sea salt
1 teaspoon freshly ground white pepper
2 heads celeriac, peeled and diced
4 waxy potatoes, peeled and diced

Mushroom mustard sauce
200 g boletus mushrooms
300 ml Pepper Glaze (page 66)
50 g unsalted butter
1 tablespoon minced garlic
3 teaspoons chopped French tarragon
1 tablespoon smooth Dijon mustard
75 ml thick (45%) cream

Seared venison with celeriac gratin and mushroom mustard sauce

Gentle spicing and rich, full flavours come together in this celebration of the best of autumn and winter,

flavours that lend themselves to full-bodied cabernets and nights by the fire. Look for boletus mushrooms

in better greengrocers and the markets in autumn. Alternatively, use dried ones (available from

gourmet food stores) – reconstitute in warm water.

VEGETABLES

VEGETABLES Vegetables have a natural affinity with spices and are great textural carriers for wonderful flavours. The close relationship between vegetables and the spice world is well documented and practised in Asian and Mediterranean diets, something we are now becoming more and more familiar with in Australia, and we are incorporating those principles into our daily eating routines. No more are we restricted to the meat-and-three-veg syndrome: vegetables have grown up and can sit proudly at centre stage or can act as versatile and enticing partners to fish, poultry or red meat. ❋ WE ARE MOST FORTUNATE – in fact, spoilt – that the various climates across this huge country give us such a wide variety of premium-quality vegetables throughout the year. Vegetables are one of the most important food sources we have at our disposal and are central to any healthy, well-balanced diet – especially when they have been spiced up.

1 Lightly dry-roast nigella seeds over gentle heat, then set aside. Dry-roast cumin seeds over gentle heat until fragrant. Cool, then grind to a fine powder.

2 Heat ghee in a frying pan and cook onion, ginger, garlic and chilli over moderate heat until they are softened and aromatic, about 5 minutes.

3 Stir in ground cumin, nigella seeds, korma, ground cardamom and salt and cook for a few minutes until fragrant.

4 Stir dal into spices, then add water and cook over moderate heat until lentils have softened, about 30 minutes. Add more water if lentils become dry and have not cooked enough.

5 Season with lime juice, fish sauce and pepper. Taste and adjust if necessary.

6 Stir in coriander and diced tomato and serve.

2 teaspoons nigella seeds
2 teaspoons cumin seeds
60 g ghee
1 small brown onion, minced
1 tablespoon minced ginger
6 cloves garlic, minced
6 red bird's-eye chillies, minced

2 teaspoons Kashmiri Korma (page 34)
seeds from 2 green cardamom pods,
　ground
1 teaspoon sea salt
400 g masoor dal, washed
600 ml water
50 ml strained lime juice

50 ml fish sauce
1 teaspoon freshly ground black pepper
coriander leaves
3 tomatoes, peeled, seeded and finely
　sliced

Chilli cumin dal

A fragrant and tasty lentil dish that can be eaten on its own or served with roasted meats or grilled fish.

Other lentils can be substituted for the masoor or red gram dal – you will just need to alter the cooking time

according to the size of the lentil used.

1 Put eggs into a saucepan of cold water and bring to a boil, stirring occasionally. Simmer for 5–6 minutes. Remove from heat and plunge into cold water. Peel carefully.

2 Dry-roast belacan over gentle heat until fragrant.

3 Heat oil in a frying pan and sauté shallots and lemongrass until softened.

4 Stir in belacan, spice paste, chilli jam and palm sugar.

5 When paste starts to smell fragrant, stir in coconut milk and bring to a simmer. Add fish sauce and lime juice and simmer for 10 minutes. Add eggs and cook for 10 minutes until sauce thickens.

6 Remove from heat, then taste and adjust seasoning if necessary.

7 Spoon eggs and sauce into a serving bowl and sprinkle with fried shallots.

6 large (61 g) eggs
25 g belacan (Malaysian shrimp paste)
50 ml vegetable oil
4 red shallots, finely sliced
1 tablespoon minced lemongrass

1 tablespoon Nonya Spice Paste
  (page 43)
2 teaspoons Chilli Jam (page 58)
30 g palm sugar, shaved
200 ml coconut milk

25 ml fish sauce
25 ml strained lime juice
$^{1}/_{4}$ cup Fried Shallots (page 342)

Spiced eggs in coconut milk

An interesting way to serve boiled eggs, perhaps as part of a series of dishes that complement each other –

a great way of providing protein content for a vegetable-based diet. You can use duck eggs to make it a richer dish,

or quail eggs as an alternative. Cooking times will vary according to the size of the eggs.

1 Heat oil in a deep-fryer to 180°C and fry eggplant dice until golden. Remove with a slotted spoon and drain on paper towel.

2 Melt ghee in a large saucepan and fry onion for a few minutes, then add garlic, ginger and chilli and fry for a further 5 minutes over moderate heat until beginning to colour.

3 Stir in korma, then add mushrooms and fry for 2 minutes.

4 Add potato and stock and bring to a boil. Reduce heat and simmer for 10 minutes or until potatoes are half-cooked. Add remaining vegetables and cook for a further 10 minutes or until all vegetables are cooked.

5 Stir in yoghurt and heat through – do not let sauce boil as yoghurt will split. Season with salt and pepper, then taste and adjust if necessary.

6 Spoon curry into a bowl, sprinkle with garam masala and coriander and serve with rice and Parathas (pages 266 and 267), or pappadams if you don't have the time or inclination to make the bread.

vegetable oil for deep-frying
1 eggplant, diced
60 g ghee
2 brown onions, minced
6 cloves garlic, crushed
1 tablespoon minced ginger
4 large red chillies, minced

2 tablespoons Kashmiri Korma (page 34)
12 button mushrooms, sliced
3 pink-eye potatoes, peeled and sliced
300 ml Spiced Vegetable Stock
  (page 340)
50 g beans, halved
6 pieces broccoli

2 small green zucchini, sliced
100 ml thick plain yoghurt
2 teaspoons sea salt
1 teaspoon freshly ground black pepper
2 teaspoons Kashmiri Garam Masala
  (page 34)
2 tablespoons coriander leaves

Vegetable korma

A simple, aromatic vegetable curry that is gentle and warming on the palate. Serve the curry as soon as

the vegetables are cooked as reheating it will cause them to discolour.

1 Sprinkle half the curry powder over eggplant and marinate for 30 minutes.

2 Heat chilli oil in a large wok and fry shallots, garlic, ginger and chilli over moderately high heat until softened, about 30 seconds, then add remaining curry powder.

3 Add spiced eggplant and seal.

4 Stir in tamarind liquid, fish sauce and tomato and cook for 10 minutes until eggplant is soft.

5 Stir in yoghurt and coriander and cook until warmed through – do not boil or yoghurt will split.

6 Remove from heat and serve immediately.

2 tablespoons Madras Curry Powder
   (page 35)
12 Japanese eggplants, quartered
   lengthwise
50 ml Chilli Oil (page 61)

12 red shallots, finely sliced
6 cloves garlic, minced
2 teaspoons minced ginger
2 large red chillies, finely sliced
50 ml Tamarind Liquid (page 341)

30 ml fish sauce
4 tomatoes, peeled, seeded and quartered
200 ml thick plain yoghurt
2 tablespoons coriander leaves

Eggplant masala

As you may have guessed by now, I have an obsession with eggplant. This is a great vegetable accompaniment

to a meat, fish or chicken curry. (See at bottom right of photograph on page 179.)

1 Make the peanut lime sauce as instructed and keep warm.

2 Dry-roast peanuts over gentle heat until coloured and fragrant. Cool, then chop roughly and set aside.

3 Peel eggs, then cut in half lengthwise and set aside.

4 Divide each of the aromatics and vegetables into 6 even portions.

5 For each serve, heat a wok, then add 2 teaspoons chilli oil and fry garlic, chilli and ginger for a minute until fragrant. Add capsicum, green onion, carrot, zucchini, snowpeas, snake beans and mushrooms and toss over heat for a minute or two until vegetables start to wilt. Add cabbage and bean sprouts with tamarind dressing and toss to combine. Stir watercress through hot vegetables, then remove wok from heat.

6 Spread hot peanut lime sauce on each plate and pile on stir-fried vegetables, then top with half a boiled egg per serve. Sprinkle with roasted peanuts and serve immediately. Serve extra peanut lime sauce in a separate bowl.

200 ml Peanut Lime Sauce (page 67)
2 tablespoons raw peanuts
3 large (61 g) eggs, hardboiled
3 cloves garlic, sliced
2 teaspoons minced ginger
2 large red chillies, cut into julienne
1 green capsicum, cut into julienne

1 red capsicum, cut into julienne
3 green onions, cut into 2 cm lengths
1 small carrot, cut into julienne
1 green zucchini, cut into julienne
9 snowpeas, cut into julienne
3 snake beans, cut into 4 cm lengths
    and blanched

12 oyster mushrooms, halved
3 Chinese cabbage leaves, coarsely
    shredded
100 g bean sprouts
60 ml Chilli Orange Oil (page 61)
120 ml Tamarind Dressing (page 81)
2 cups watercress sprigs

Stir-fried chilli vegetables with peanut lime sauce

This dish builds on the idea of the well-known Indonesian salad gado gado, in which vegetables are traditionally served raw

with a satay sauce. Here, the vegetables are stir-fried and served with a hot peanut lime sauce. Use the best-quality, freshest

vegetables for the greatest flavour impact. To ensure the vegetables do not stew, I suggest cooking each serve separately.

This is easiest if you have several small, non-stick woks at the ready – these are available from

Asian food stores and are inexpensive. (See photograph opposite.)

1 Dry-roast cumin seeds over gentle heat until fragrant.

2 Cool, then grind to a fine powder.

3 Char eggplants over a direct flame until skin has blackened. Allow to cool enough to handle, then peel carefully. Squeeze flesh to remove any bitter juices.

4 Blend warm eggplant pulp to a smooth paste in a food processor with ground cumin, garlic, salt, tahini and lemon juice. With the motor still running, slowly drizzle in olive oil.

5 Taste and adjust if necessary.

6 Pass purée through a fine-meshed sieve to ensure a velvety-smooth paste.

7 Eat immediately!

½ teaspoon cumin seeds	1 teaspoon sea salt	150 ml extra-virgin olive oil
3 large eggplants	175 ml tahini	
5 cloves garlic, minced	50 ml strained lemon juice	

Smoked eggplant purée

This purée is the commonly known baba ghannouj, that wonderfully versatile Middle Eastern dish made with eggplant, tahini (a sesame paste) and subtle spicing. One spoonful is never enough. Serve as a dip with bread or as an accompaniment to spiced meats.

1 Heat half the vegetable oil in a frying pan and fry sambar powder over a moderate heat until crisp. Add coconut and cook for 1 minute. Blend mixture to a smooth paste in a food processor.

2 Cook dal in boiling water with ground turmeric until softened, about 15 minutes. Remove from heat and strain, reserving 150 ml cooking water.

3 Heat remaining oil in a saucepan and fry curry leaves and shallots for 2 minutes, then add eggplant, beans and zucchini and sauté for 2 minutes until vegetables have started to soften.

4 Add reserved cooking water, tamarind liquid, palm sugar, salt and sambar paste, then bring to a boil. Cook over a low heat for 6 minutes, stirring occasionally.

5 Add cooked dal and simmer for 10 minutes. Taste and adjust seasoning if necessary. Melt ghee and spoon it over sambar – and serve immediately.

50 ml vegetable oil
2 tablespoons Sambar Powder (page 36)
$^{1}/_{3}$ cup freshly grated coconut
2 cups masoor dal
2 teaspoons ground turmeric

8 curry leaves
6 red shallots, finely sliced
1 eggplant, diced
12 small green beans, cut into short
   lengths

6 small green zucchini, diced
300 ml Tamarind Liquid (page 341)
30 g palm sugar, shaved
2 teaspoons sea salt
50 g ghee

Vegetable sambar

Sambar powder is a spice blend used in the cooking of southern India to flavour vegetable and lentil preparations.

Sambar is served as a starting point for a meal – a fiery-hot liquid with mellow spicing that falls

somewhere between a soup and a curry. Serve with plain rice.

1 To make the sauce, soak black beans for 30 minutes, then drain.

2 Heat both oils in a wok and fry garlic, ginger and chilli for a minute over moderately high heat until fragrant. Add black beans, rice wine, ginger juice, sweet soy sauce and water and bring to a boil, then simmer for 3 minutes. Add salt, then taste and adjust if necessary.

3 To make the chilli salt crust, dry-roast dried chillies, peppercorns and sea salt over gentle heat until slightly coloured. Cool, then grind to a fine powder and mix with rice flour.

4 Steam broccoli for 5 minutes until tender. The stems will take longer than the leaves, so remove the leaves as they cook or add halfway through to ensure even cooking.

5 Meanwhile, heat oil in a deep-fryer to 180°C. Coat beancurd squares with chilli salt crust and fry a few at a time for 3 minutes until pale golden and crisp on the surface. They will float to the top when cooked. Remove carefully with a mesh spoon and drain on paper towel.

6 Stir garlic chives into blackbean sauce. Arrange steamed broccoli on each plate and spoon over some sauce, then sit the fried beancurd on top and add chilli jam, chilli julienne and sliced green onion.

1 bunch Chinese broccoli, cut into 10 cm lengths
vegetable oil for deep-frying
6 fresh beancurd *or* tofu squares
3 teaspoons Chilli Jam (page 58)
1 large red chilli, cut into julienne
6 green onions, sliced diagonally

Blackbean sauce
2 teaspoons dried black beans
30 ml vegetable oil
½ teaspoon sesame oil
5 cloves garlic, minced
2 teaspoons minced ginger
4 red bird's-eye chillies, finely sliced
25 ml Chinese Shaoxing rice wine
25 ml Ginger Juice (page 342)
75 ml sweet soy sauce

150 ml water
1 teaspoon sea salt
50 g garlic chives, cut into 1 cm lengths

Chilli salt crust
12 large dried chillies
12 black peppercorns
2 teaspoons sea salt
2 tablespoons coarse rice flour

Chilli salt beancurd with steamed vegetables and blackbean sauce

Fresh beancurd or tofu, a popular feature in the cooking of China, Japan and Korea, is a major source of protein for the vegetarian diet and there are many fantastic ways of preparing it. This is one of my favourite beancurd dishes, the spicy crust contrasting beautifully with the soft, steamed centre. (See photograph opposite.)

1 Make the batter as instructed, then leave it to stand for 2 hours.

2 Cut vegetables into small dice, then combine. Check batter – if it is too thick, add a little water. Add diced vegetables to batter and stir to combine.

3 Heat vegetable oil in a deep-fryer to 180°C.

4 Drop a few small spoonfuls of vegetable batter into the hot oil and fry for 3–4 minutes until golden, turning them over with a slotted or mesh spoon to ensure even cooking.

5 Remove pakoras from oil and drain on paper towel.

6 Sprinkle pakoras with coriander and serve with eggplant pickle.

1 quantity Chickpea Batter (page 344)
75 g broccoli
75 g sweet potato, peeled

75 g potato, peeled
75 g green zucchini
1 green capsicum

vegetable oil for deep-frying
coriander leaves
¼ cup Eggplant Pickle (page 52)

Vegetable pakoras with eggplant pickle

These little fried spicy vegetable balls make an interesting start to a meal or can be served as palate-teasers with drinks. The mixture can be made ahead of time, leaving the cooking to the last minute. Fry the pakoras in small batches in hot oil so that they cook quickly and remain crisp.

1 Dry-roast cumin seeds and coriander seeds, separately, over gentle heat until fragrant. Cool, then grind to a fine powder.

2 Cut potatoes into 1 cm dice. Boil potato in hot, salted water until just soft and still holding its shape. Strain.

3 Meanwhile, melt ghee in a frying pan over moderate heat and fry mustard seeds until they start to pop. Add ginger and chilli and stir quickly until mixture just begins to colour.

4 Add nigella seeds and ground cumin, coriander and turmeric, stirring constantly to prevent spices sticking or burning.

5 Toss potato with spices to coat, then add 2 teaspoons salt and remaining ingredients. Cook for 2 minutes, then remove from heat and serve.

$^{1}/_{4}$ teaspoon cumin seeds
2 teaspoons coriander seeds
1 kg kipfler *or* other waxy potatoes, washed
sea salt
50 ml ghee

1 teaspoon brown mustard seeds
1 tablespoon minced fresh ginger
2 green bird's-eye chillies, minced
$^{1}/_{4}$ teaspoon nigella seeds
1 teaspoon ground turmeric
pinch of asafoetida powder

$^{1}/_{2}$ teaspoon amchoor powder
1 teaspoon Kashmiri Garam Masala (page 34)
2 tablespoons curry leaves

Garam masala potato

This recipe celebrates the heavenly combination of warm spicing and the wonderful texture and flavour of

creamy, waxy potatoes. It can be served as a vegetable dish or as one of a variety of spiced dishes

or it can act as a strong support to red meats such as venison, kangaroo, beef, oxtail or liver.

1 Peel pumpkin, potatoes and turnips and wash, then cut each vegetable into 5 mm thick, large slices. Using a pastry cutter, cut an 8 cm round from each vegetable slice. For each gratin, you need 3 slices of each vegetable per person – that's 9 slices per serve and 54 slices altogether.

2 Mix remaining ingredients to make a paste.

3 Preheat oven to 160°C.

4 Line a baking tray with baking paper. Brush a slice of pumpkin with paste, then sit a slice of potato on top and brush this with paste. Sit a slice of turnip on top, then repeat this process twice to complete each gratin, so you have 9 layers in all. Wrap the outside of each gratin with a strip of baking paper and slide over a stainless steel ring so gratin holds its shape during cooking. Sprinkle extra chat masala on top.

5 Bake for 30 minutes until vegetable layers are soft – test with a skewer. To serve, carefully lift off rings and remove paper wrapping, then use a spatula to lift the gratins onto plates.

1 butternut pumpkin
6 desiree *or* pink-eye potatoes
2 large turnips
50 g ghee, melted

2 teaspoons minced garlic
2 egg yolks
2 teaspoons Chat Masala (page 34)
50 ml thick plain yoghurt

1 teaspoon sea salt
$\frac{1}{2}$ teaspoon freshly ground black pepper

Potato, pumpkin and turnip gratin with chat masala

Chat masala is a perfect spice companion for the earthy flavours of root vegetables. If you don't want to go to the bother of making individual gratins (for which you need stainless steel rings, available from good kitchen suppliers), you can easily make one large one in a baking dish. Just overlap the sliced vegetables, brushing the layers with the spice paste as you go, and adjust the cooking time – a 24 cm square gratin will need about 45 minutes' cooking at 190°C.

(See photograph opposite.)

1 Wash dal, then soak in cold water for 30 minutes. Strain.

2 Dry-roast dried chillies and coriander seeds, separately, over gentle heat until fragrant. Cool, then grind to a powder.

3 Cut pumpkin and sweet potato into 2 cm cubes.

4 Cut cauliflower into small pieces.

5 Heat oil in a wide, heavy-based saucepan and fry fenugreek and mustard seeds, then add onion, garlic, green chilli, ginger, curry leaves and turmeric and fry until onion softens and colours slightly.

6 Add dal, vegetables, coconut milk, roasted spices and fish sauce and bring gently to a boil. Simmer until vegetables are soft but still holding their shape.

7 Add lemon juice and coriander, then taste and adjust seasoning if necessary. Serve immediately.

100 g chana dal	1 teaspoon fenugreek seeds	1 teaspoon ground turmeric
2 large dried chillies	1 teaspoon brown mustard seeds	300 ml coconut milk
1 teaspoon coriander seeds	2 onions, minced	30 ml fish sauce
250 g butternut pumpkin, peeled	4 cloves garlic, minced	25 ml strained lemon juice
150 g sweet potato, peeled	6 large green chillies, minced	¼ cup coriander leaves
100 g cauliflower	2 teaspoons minced ginger	
50 ml vegetable oil	10 curry leaves	

Pumpkin, sweet potato and cauliflower with chana dal, fenugreek and coconut

Rich, coconut-based sauces are commonplace in southern Indian cooking, which also places heavy emphasis on dal and vegetable-cooking in strict Hindu tradition.

1 Dry-roast fennel seeds over gentle heat until fragrant. Cool, then grind to a powder.

2 Cook beetroots whole in a large saucepan of boiling water until soft, then peel. Refresh beetroots in cold water and coarsely grate into a large bowl.

3 Put remaining ingredients, including ground fennel, into a non-reactive saucepan and bring to a boil. Simmer for 45 minutes until liquid has reduced by a third.

4 Pour hot liquid over grated beetroot and allow to cool.

5 Refrigerate in an airtight container for up to 2 weeks.

$^1/_2$ teaspoon fennel seeds
12 large beetroots
700 ml malt vinegar
150 g dark-brown sugar

6 cloves
1 tablespoon minced ginger
6 cloves garlic, minced
3 red bird's-eye chillies, minced

20 black peppercorns,
 freshly cracked
2 teaspoons sea salt

Pickled spiced beetroot

This is a terrific vegetable to serve with roasted or barbecued kangaroo, venison or beef. It can also be served as an

appetiser with fresh goat's cheese or the creamy Persian-style fetta being made in Victoria

at Meredith Dairy and Yarra Valley Dairy.

NOODLES AND RICE

NOODLES AND RICE   Noodles and rice have played an integral part in Asian and Mediterranean diets for centuries and have gained considerable prominence in the everyday eating habits of modern-day Australia. As staple foods, both have become as important as bread, adding necessary starch and fibre to our diet. ❊ RICE AND NOODLES respond beautifully when combined with spices, whether as a textural background for more exotic flavours or as a dominant ingredient in famed dishes such as risotto or laksa. They provide the sustaining dishes we turn to when in need of comfort or step into the shadows to let protein star, all the while providing balance and harmony to a meal. Most importantly, rice and noodles can be prepared with relative ease. ❊ IT IS BELIEVED in Asian cultures that you have not eaten unless you have had rice. It is rice that takes centre stage at the table and other foods are there to accompany it. Noodles are a symbol of longevity and are eaten every day in China and Japan to sustain life. That's reason enough to eat more rice and noodles – and to try out the myriad spice combinations that these versatile starches welcome so readily. ❊ SPECIFIC USES REQUIRE specific varieties of rice and noodles: don't be tempted to make risotto with anything other than arborio rice or to substitute Chinese egg noodles for the Japanese udon. Treat quality ingredients with the respect they deserve and you will be rewarded with culinary success every time.

1 Dry-roast cardamom and cumin seeds, separately, over gentle heat until fragrant. Cool, then grind to a fine powder. Dry-roast cashew nuts until coloured, then cool and chop.

2 Bring stock to a simmer in a saucepan and add saffron, then leave to infuse.

3 Melt ghee in a wide, heavy-based pan and fry onion, garlic, ginger and chilli until softened.

4 Stir in spices, then add rice and stir to coat. Pour in hot stock, then cover with a lid and cook over moderate heat until all liquid has been absorbed, about 15 minutes. Remove pan from heat and remove whole spices.

5 Stir in salt and rosewater, then add cashews, tomato and capsicum dice. Serve immediately.

seeds from 12 green cardamom pods
1 teaspoon cumin seeds
50 g raw cashew nuts
1 litre White Chicken Stock (page 337)
1 teaspoon saffron threads
50 g ghee
1 brown onion, minced

6 cloves garlic, minced
25 g minced ginger
2 green bird's-eye chillies, minced
$^{1}/_{2}$ teaspoon brown mustard seeds
3 cloves
1 stick cinnamon
1 bay leaf

2 cups basmati rice
1 teaspoon sea salt
20 ml rosewater
2 tablespoons finely diced tomato
1 tablespoon finely diced roasted
  red capsicum

Saffron and cashew rice pilaf

A wonderfully rich Indian pilaf I like to serve with gently spiced lamb or chicken or with a robust vegetable curry.

Its vibrant colour and different textures give a festive appearance.

1 Preheat oven to 180°C.

2 Wash rice a few times, then soak it in cold water for 15 minutes and strain.

3 Melt 1 tablespoon ghee in a wide, heavy-based pan, then fry onion and garlic until they start to colour. Stir in spices, then add drained rice, stirring to coat with spices and ghee, and finally water.

4 Cover with a lid and cook for 15–20 minutes in oven until all liquid has been absorbed and rice is cooked. Season to taste with salt and pepper. Remove whole spices.

5 Stir in a little extra ghee to gloss up rice, then add fried shallots and serve immediately.

1 cup basmati rice
ghee
1 brown onion, minced
3 cloves garlic, minced
1 teaspoon nigella seeds

seeds from 3 green cardamom pods,
  ground
1 bay leaf
1 stick cinnamon
4 cloves

500 ml water
1 teaspoon sea salt
$\frac{1}{2}$ teaspoon freshly ground black pepper
2 tablespoons Fried Shallots (page 342)

Cardamom rice pilaf

This pilaf is my staple, the one I turn to when I want to serve a spicy rice.

(See at bottom of photograph on page 214.)

1 Reconstitute dried mandarin peel in a little warm water, then drain and mince. Dry-roast fennel seeds over gentle heat until fragrant. Cool, then grind to a fine powder.

2 Heat oil in a saucepan and fry onion, garlic, ginger and chilli over moderate heat until softened. Add ground fennel, mandarin peel and dates and stir to combine. Stir in rice.

3 Stir in 200 ml stock until absorbed by rice. Add another 200 ml stock and stir until it has been absorbed, then continue this way, as you would when making risotto, until all the liquid has been absorbed and rice is cooked. Season with fish sauce and pepper. Serve immediately.

2 pieces dried mandarin *or* orange peel	2 cloves garlic, minced	250 g sticky black rice, washed
1 teaspoon fennel seeds	1 tablespoon minced ginger	1 litre White Chicken Stock (page 337)
75 ml vegetable oil	1 large red chilli, minced	20 ml fish sauce
1 brown onion, minced	2 Chinese black dates, pitted and minced	$^1/_2$ teaspoon freshly ground black pepper

Aromatic sticky black rice

Black rice takes longer to cook than white rice because it still has its bran layer, giving it a darker appearance and a slightly

nutty flavour. Black rice is traditionally cooked with sugar, and often coconut milk, and is served as a dessert in Malaysia,

Thailand, Singapore and Indonesia. I give this rice a savoury application for a different approach and serve it with chicken

and fish. As the rice cooks, it swells and the grains stick together but remain separate – the fibres should not break down

into a gluggy mass. The spices and smokiness of the black dates and aromatics used in this recipe

enhance the earthy character of the rice. (See at top right of photograph on page 214.)

1 Bring stock to a simmer and infuse with ground turmeric.

2 Mix rice, turmeric and galangal slices, lime leaves, lemongrass and salt in a saucepan. Stir coconut milk and turmeric chicken stock into rice mixture.

3 Cover with a lid and bring to a boil over moderate heat, then reduce heat to low and cook for 15 minutes until rice has absorbed all liquid, stirring occasionally to prevent sticking.

4 Remove whole spices from rice before serving. Taste and adjust seasoning if necessary.

250 ml White Chicken Stock (page 337)
2 tablespoons ground turmeric
2 cups jasmine rice, washed

4 slices turmeric
2 slices galangal
2 kaffir lime leaves

1 stalk lemongrass, cut into 4 diagonally
1 tablespoon sea salt
750 ml coconut milk

Turmeric rice

This Balinese speciality, served at ceremonial and festive dinners, is known as nasi kuning and is usually presented in a large conical form, the tip of which is wrapped in banana leaf or edible silver leaf. Cook it for a special dinner and accompany it with a variety of other spicy dishes that complement each other.

(See at top left of photograph on page 214.)

1 Wash rice thoroughly a few times in cold water.

2 Put all ingredients into a saucepan and stir well.

3 Cover with a lid and bring to a boil over moderate heat.

4 Stir to prevent sticking, then reduce heat and simmer for 15 minutes until liquid has been absorbed by rice and grains are soft but not broken.

400 g jasmine rice 1 teaspoon sea salt	400 ml coconut milk	300 ml water

Coconut rice

Although this rice is not cooked with any spice, it always accompanies spicy food, so I have included it here

for your convenience. It is mostly used with Nonya and Singaporean cooking.

1 Bring water to boil in a saucepan, then add rice and salt and cover. Reduce heat and simmer for 10 minutes or until rice is cooked and has absorbed all liquid.

2 Melt ghee in a frying pan and fry mustard seeds over moderately high heat until they pop. Add asafoetida, chilli and ginger and fry briefly until aromatic.

3 Stir in yoghurt over low heat until warmed (do not boil or yoghurt will split), then remove pan from heat and stir in the cooked rice and coriander.

500 ml water
250 g basmati rice, washed
1 teaspoon sea salt
1 tablespoon ghee

1 teaspoon brown mustard seeds
pinch of asafoetida powder
1 red bird's-eye chilli, minced
1 teaspoon minced ginger

plain thick yoghurt
1 tablespoon chopped coriander leaves

Yoghurt rice

Also known as curd rice, yoghurt rice is a popular accompaniment to the fiery, spicy food of Madras,

as it is considered to be cooling for the body.

1 Cut chicken into 3 cm cubes. To make the yoghurt marinade, dry-roast coriander seeds and cumin seeds, separately, over gentle heat until fragrant. Cool, then grind to a fine powder. Mix all marinade ingredients thoroughly in a large bowl. Add chicken, then cover and marinate, refrigerated, for 5 hours or overnight.

2 Wash rice several times, then drain. Put rice, 2 teaspoons salt, water, cinnamon stick and cloves into a saucepan. Soak for 1 hour.

3 Cook rice over a low heat, covered, until nearly all the water has been absorbed, about 35 minutes. Lift lid and stir a couple of times, then remove from heat and discard whole spices. Leave rice in the covered pan while you proceed with the next step.

4 Heat ghee in a large, heavy-based pan and fry onion, garlic, ginger and chilli for a few minutes until slightly coloured. Stir in chicken and its marinade and cook for a few minutes over moderate heat. Add stock, then cover pan and cook gently for 30 minutes. Remove pan from heat and discard cinnamon stick.

5 Preheat oven to 150°C. Brush another large pan or ovenproof dish with some saffron butter, then spread half the cooked rice over base and pour over half the saffron butter and stir to combine. Spoon cooked chicken over rice, then top with remaining rice and drizzle over rest of saffron butter. Press a sheet of baking paper over surface, then enclose contents of dish with foil and cover with a lid. Bake slowly, with a water bath on the shelf below, for 30 minutes. Remove from oven, then taste and adjust seasoning if necessary.

6 Spoon chicken biryani onto a large platter and garnish with fried onion rings, nuts and sultanas. Serve immediately.

500 g free-range, corn-fed chicken breasts
500 g basmati rice
sea salt
1.5 litres cold water
$^{1}/_{2}$ stick cinnamon
3 cloves
20 g ghee
1 brown onion, finely diced
3 cloves garlic, minced
2 teaspoons minced ginger
6 red bird's-eye chillies, minced
150 ml White Chicken Stock (page 337)
100 g Saffron Butter (page 342)

Yoghurt marinade
1 teaspoon coriander seeds
1 teaspoon cumin seeds
150 ml thick plain yoghurt
50 g ground almonds
seeds from 5 green cardamom pods,
   ground
2 large dried chillies, ground
$^{1}/_{2}$ teaspoon freshly ground black
   peppercorns

3 cloves, ground
1 teaspoon nigella seeds
pinch of freshly grated nutmeg
$^{1}/_{2}$ stick cinnamon
2 teaspoons sea salt

Garnish
$^{1}/_{4}$ cup fried onion rings
50 g almond flakes, fried
2 tablespoons sultanas *or* raisins, fried

Spiced chicken biryani

The most exotic of Indian basmati rice preparations, biryani can have meat, shellfish or vegetables cooked into it, making it a complete meal. It is considered a grand and ceremonial dish and is the Indian equivalent of a risotto or paella.

1 Bring stock to a boil in a saucepan, then reduce heat to maintain a gentle simmer.

2 Heat a wide, heavy-based pan and add oil, then sauté onion, garlic and chilli over moderate heat until soft and golden. Stir in tomato. Add rice and cook for a minute or two, stirring constantly, until rice is coated with oil. Pour in wine, then, when it has been absorbed, stir in saffron.

3 Start to add simmering fish stock, 100 ml at a time, stirring frequently to prevent sticking. Allow rice to absorb stock before adding more. With each addition, the rice will steam and swell to absorb the liquid. As it cooks, the rice should become creamy and the grains remain intact and separate.

4 About 3 minutes from the end of cooking, add prawn meat and basil leaves with the last 100 ml stock, stirring constantly. Cook until prawns are translucent, then stir in the butter and season to taste with salt and pepper. Serve immediately.

900 ml Fish Stock (page 337)
100 ml olive oil
2 tablespoons minced brown onion
2 teaspoons minced garlic
2 red bird's-eye chillies, minced

3 tomatoes, peeled, seeded and diced
350 g superfino arborio rice, rinsed
150 ml semillon *or* other dry white wine
1 teaspoon saffron threads
18 green king prawns, peeled and halved

20 basil leaves, torn
75 g unsalted butter, diced
$1^{1}/_{2}$ teaspoons sea salt
1 teaspoon freshly ground black pepper

Saffron prawn risotto

This is one of my all-time favourite risotto recipes. The grains of rice look like golden jewels on the plate and the flavour is complex and ambrosial. For the best results, use the highest grade superfino arborio rice and the freshest prawns; make a decent fish stock, and cook with the wine you would choose to drink with the dish, not Château Cardboard!

Like any risotto, it must be eaten as soon as it is made – it cannot be cooked ahead of time and reheated with any success. Have everything ready and allow yourself 20 minutes or so to stand and stir the rice as you add the stock. (See photograph opposite.)

1 Poach or steam chicken breasts until tender, then shred.

2 Fry bacon until crisp, then drain on paper towel. Set aside.

3 Rinse rice under running water for a few minutes until water runs clear. Drain.

4 Bring stock to a boil in a large saucepan, then add rice, bacon, cassia bark and celeriac.

5 Reduce heat, then cover and simmer very gently, preferably on a heat mat, for 1.5–2 hours, stirring occasionally to prevent sticking. (Alternatively, cook, covered, in an oven set at 160°C for about the same time.) The congee should be thick but still slightly liquid and the rice grains should be starting to break down. Remove cassia bark.

6 Stir chicken, prawn meat, ginger, cream, diced butter, salt and pepper into rice and simmer for 15 minutes, stirring regularly to prevent sticking. Remove from heat and stir lemon juice, sesame oil and green onion through rice until well incorporated. Taste and adjust seasoning if necessary.

7 Spoon congee into large bowls, then sprinkle with coriander leaves and serve immediately.

500 g free-range, corn-fed chicken breasts	18 green prawn tails, deveined	$^{1}/_{2}$ teaspoon sesame oil
75 g bacon, diced	1 teaspoon minced ginger	4 green onions, finely sliced
250 g short-grain rice	150 ml pouring (35%) cream	2 tablespoons coriander leaves
2.5 litres White Chicken Stock (page 337)	75 g unsalted butter, diced	
2 pieces cassia bark	2 teaspoons sea salt	
2 heads celeriac, peeled and cut into 1 cm cubes	1 teaspoon freshly ground white pepper	
	45 ml strained lemon juice	

Chicken and prawn congee

Congee, a savoury rice porridge also known as rice gruel or soft rice, is traditionally eaten by the Chinese for breakfast.
It is generally not a highly spiced dish, relying more on subtle flavours and smooth textures for its appeal. The basic rice
preparation can be flavoured with any protein – I have made this quite a glamorous and rich version by including chicken
and prawns as well as cream and butter. Serve it as a mainstay for lunch or as an entrée for a more elaborate dinner.

1 Peel prawns and remove shells from scampi tails. Cut scampi tails in half and set aside. Simmer prawn and scampi shells in stock for 20 minutes, then remove from heat and strain. Discard shells.

2 Heat oil in a paella pan or wide, heavy-based frying pan and sauté onion, garlic and chilli flakes until softened. Add tomato, paprika, chilli and half the parsley and cook for 10 minutes until mixture resembles a stew.

3 Cut squid tubes into rings, then stir into aromatic base with rice, scampi meat and prawns. Add hot fish stock and bring to a simmer over high heat.

4 Stir in squid ink, then reduce heat and cook gently for 12 minutes until rice has absorbed all liquid.

5 Season with salt and pepper, then taste and adjust if necessary. Add pimiento and remaining parsley and cook for 3 minutes. Serve immediately.

6 tiger prawns
12 scampi *or* 3 marron tails
2 litres Fish Stock (page 337)
250 ml olive oil
1 red onion, minced
8 cloves garlic, minced
1 teaspoon chilli flakes

4 tomatoes, chopped
$^{1}/_{2}$ teaspoon Spanish paprika
1 sun-dried ñoras chilli *or* 2 dried cascabel chillies, chopped
2 tablespoons shredded flat-leaf parsley
300 g small squid tubes, cleaned

750 g calasparra (Spanish short-grain) rice
3 teaspoons squid ink
sea salt
freshly ground black pepper
2 tablespoons roasted pimiento strips, finely chopped

Squid ink paella with shellfish and pimiento

Paella is the national rice dish of Spain and has many regional variations. It is more common on the southern Mediterranean coast of Spain, especially in the Valencia region. This particular dish is generally referred to as arroz negro. The recipe given here is an adaptation of a family recipe from Eduardo Gonzalez, who originally hails from Salamanca, Alicante, and now lives in Sydney.

1 Cut rice noodle sheets into 1 cm wide strips.

2 Bring a saucepan of water to a boil, then cook yabbies for 2 minutes until shells begin to change colour. Remove yabbies from pan immediately and plunge into iced water to stop the cooking. When cool, remove tail and claw meat from shells. Reserve shells to make stock for another use.

3 Heat marron oil in a wok and fry shallots, garlic and chilli for a minute or so over gentle heat. Add curry paste and fry for 1 minute, then stir in coconut milk, fish sauce and palm sugar.

4 Bring to a boil, then cook for 3 minutes over moderate heat.

5 Stir in noodles, yabby meat, scallops and snake beans and bring to a boil (this should only take about a minute).

6 Remove from heat and stir in lime juice, green onion, laksa leaves and basil and ladle into bowls. Sprinkle with fried shallots and serve immediately.

500 g fresh rice noodle sheets
24 yabbies
60 ml Spiced Tomato Marron Oil
  (page 61)
8 red shallots, finely sliced
3 cloves garlic, minced
4 red bird's-eye chillies, finely sliced

3 tablespoons Paramount Curry Paste
  (page 42)
120 ml coconut milk
40 ml fish sauce
30 g palm sugar, shaved
18 scallops
6 snake beans, cut into 2 cm lengths
  and blanched

25 ml strained lime juice
2 tablespoons finely sliced green onion
  tops
2 tablespoons laksa (Vietnamese mint)
  leaves
2 tablespoons Thai *or* holy basil leaves
1/4 cup Fried Shallots (page 342)

Curried coconut scallops and yabbies with rice noodles

A pungent, intense variation on the laksa theme. You can also make this with prawns, lobster, scampi, bug tails or chicken.

(See photograph opposite.)

1 Soak porcini in water for 15 minutes, then strain through a fine-meshed sieve, reserving soaking liquid. Bring stock to a boil in a saucepan, then reduce heat to maintain a gentle simmer. Add strained porcini soaking water to stock.

2 Heat a wide, heavy-based pan and add olive oil, 50 g of the butter, garlic, minced truffle and pancetta and fry gently for a few minutes until fragrant and soft.

3 Stir in porcini and tarragon and cook for 3 minutes.

4 Add rice and cook for a minute or two, stirring constantly, until rice is coated with oil. Pour in wine, then, when it has been absorbed, start to add the simmering stock, 100 ml at a time, stirring frequently to prevent sticking. Allow rice to absorb stock before adding more. With each addition, the rice will steam and swell to absorb the liquid. As it cooks, the rice should become creamy and the grains remain intact and separate.

5 When rice is cooked, stir in remaining butter with sliced truffle and truffle oil, then season to taste with salt and pepper. Serve immediately.

50 g dried porcini mushrooms
150 ml warm water
800 ml Brown Chicken Stock (page 338)
50 ml olive oil
125 g unsalted butter
2 tablespoons minced garlic

1 teaspoon minced fresh black truffle
50 g pancetta, finely chopped
2 teaspoons chopped French tarragon
350 g superfino arborio rice, rinsed
150 ml red wine (preferably a cabernet
   or cabernet blend)

50 g fresh black truffle, finely sliced
20 ml truffle oil
2 teaspoons sea salt
1 teaspoon freshly ground black pepper

Black truffle and porcini risotto

This rich, earthy risotto can be eaten on its own or served with chicken or veal. To make it a total indulgence,

cook some foie gras or corn-fed duck liver and add it to the risotto at the last minute. Sublime.

1 Prepare the duck meat as instructed, discarding skin and bones and shredding meat.

2 Cut rice noodle sheets into thin strips.

3 Heat oil in a wok and fry onion over gentle heat, then add garlic and ginger and sauté until lightly coloured. Add five-spice powder and mushrooms and fry until mushrooms have softened.

4 Add water chestnuts and stock and bring to a boil. Reduce to a simmer, then add prepared duck meat and rice noodles and cook for 2 minutes until noodles are soft.

5 Stir in fish sauce and pepper, then taste and adjust seasoning if necessary.

6 Add green onion and garlic chives and serve immediately in deep bowls.

1.5 kg cooked duck meat (page 260)
500 g fresh rice noodle sheets
60 ml Sichuan Pepper Oil (page 61)
1 brown onion, finely sliced
4 cloves garlic, minced
1 tablespoon minced ginger

3 teaspoons Chinese Five-spice Powder
  (page 39)
300 g shiitake mushrooms, sliced
12 fresh water chestnuts, blanched and
  sliced
100 ml Duck Stock (page 338)

20 ml fish sauce
$\frac{1}{2}$ teaspoon freshly ground black pepper
3 green onions, finely sliced
50 g garlic chives, cut into 2 cm lengths

Braised five-spice duck with shiitake mushrooms, garlic chives and rice noodles

Lovers of the Paramount Five-spice Duck and Shiitake Mushroom Pies (see page 260) will recognise the flavours here,

this time translated to a quick-and-easy noodle dish with soft and silky textures. I refer you to the pie recipe

for the preparation of the duck meat.

1 Soak dried black mushrooms in hot water until softened, about 15 minutes, then drain, reserving soaking liquid. Strain liquid and reserve 100 ml.

2 Slice black, shiitake and oyster mushrooms and mix.

3 Cut asparagus into pieces diagonally and blanch in boiling water for 1 minute, then refresh in iced water. Cook soba noodles in boiling, salted water until softened, about 4 minutes, then strain and toss with sesame oil.

4 Heat pepper oil in a wok and fry garlic briefly over gentle heat until softened. Add sliced mushrooms and toss over high heat to coat evenly with oil.

5 Add reserved mushroom soaking liquid, rice wine, mirin, tamari and fish sauce and cook until bubbling.

6 Add asparagus, noodles, enoki mushrooms and green onion and cook until warmed through.

7 Sprinkle on sansho pepper to taste, then add coriander and serve immediately.

6 dried Chinese black mushrooms
200 ml hot water
150 g shiitake mushrooms
50 g oyster mushrooms
12 asparagus spears
500 g dried soba noodles

sea salt
2 teaspoons sesame oil
50 ml Sichuan Pepper Oil (page 61)
12 cloves garlic, minced
50 ml Chinese Shaoxing rice wine
100 ml mirin

50 ml tamari soy sauce
50 ml fish sauce
50 g enoki mushrooms
4 green onions, finely sliced
$\frac{1}{2}$ teaspoon sansho pepper
$\frac{1}{4}$ cup coriander leaves

Soba noodles with mushrooms and asparagus

The rich, earthy flavours of mushrooms and soba noodles combine beautifully with light spicing in this dish. Other mushrooms can be used, especially wild, forest mushrooms when they are in season. Dried porcini or boletus mushrooms can be substituted for the Chinese black mushrooms for a different flavour. (See photograph opposite.)

1 Heat oil in a wok and fry a few slices of beancurd at a time over high heat, turning carefully with a mesh spoon, until golden and puffed.

2 Remove carefully and drain on paper towel. Discard oil.

3 Heat pepper oil in wok and fry spice paste and candlenuts over gentle heat until fragrant. Add stock, coconut milk and sweet potato and bring to a boil. The purée will thicken the sauce as it cooks.

4 Reduce heat, stir in chicken and cook for 2 minutes. Add noodles, bean sprouts, green onion, cucumber, chilli and celery leaves and cook for 2 minutes until warmed through. Add fish sauce, then taste and adjust if necessary.

5 Ladle into deep bowls and top with the fried beancurd, coriander, fried shallots and lime wedges.

vegetable oil for deep-frying
6 fresh beancurd *or* tofu squares, sliced
60 ml Sichuan Pepper Oil (page 61)
3 tablespoons Nonya Spice Paste
  (page 43)
6 candlenuts, ground
300 ml White Chicken Stock (page 337)

100 ml coconut milk
100 g sweet potato, cooked and puréed
600 g free-range, corn-fed chicken
  breasts, finely sliced
500 g fresh hokkien noodles, blanched
200 g bean sprouts
6 green onions, finely sliced

1 small cucumber, chopped
2 large green chillies, finely sliced
1/2 cup Chinese celery leaves
40 ml fish sauce
1/4 cup coriander leaves
2 tablespoons Fried Shallots (page 342)
1 lime, cut into 6 wedges

Spicy chicken noodles with beancurd

This is a soupy noodle dish, requiring a spoon and chopsticks for eating. It is my version of mee rebus, a well-known Malay noodle dish thickened with sweet potato, which has a similar richness to laksa lemak.

1 Dry-roast fennel seeds over gentle heat until fragrant. Cool, then grind to a fine powder.

2 Combine rice wine, fish sauce and oyster sauce.

3 Cut rice noodle sheets into 1 cm wide strips and divide into 6 portions. Divide aromatics, spices, vegetables, basil and chicken into 6 portions.

4 For each portion, heat a wok, then add some pepper oil and fry shallots, garlic, chilli and ground fennel until fragrant and softened. Add a little chilli jam and a portion of chicken and toss over high heat to coat meat.

5 Add capsicum and snowpeas and toss to combine, then add a little of the mixed sauces.

6 When the sauce starts to bubble, add a serve of rice noodles, snowpea leaves and basil and toss over heat until noodles soften, about 1 minute.

7 Pile onto a plate and serve immediately.

$^1/_2$ teaspoon fennel seeds
50 ml Chinese Shaoxing rice wine
50 ml fish sauce
50 ml oyster sauce
500 g fresh rice noodle sheets
5 red shallots, finely sliced

12 cloves garlic, minced
6 red bird's-eye chillies, finely sliced
1 red capsicum, finely sliced
6 snowpeas, shredded
50 g snowpea leaves
1 cup Thai *or* holy basil leaves

500 g free-range, corn-fed chicken
  breasts, thinly sliced
60 ml Sichuan Pepper Oil (page 61)
2 teaspoons Chilli Jam (page 58)

Chilli and basil chicken with rice noodles

A fresh and zesty noodle dish that is ideal for a quick meal as it is satisfying and complete. It's the sort of thing we often

make for our staff lunch. I like to make a portion at a time to ensure the stir-fry doesn't stew – having a couple of

inexpensive, small, non-stick woks, available from Asian food stores, to hand is a good idea.

If you don't, it doesn't matter: the dish takes so little cooking there's barely time for the waiting serves to get cold.

1 Shallow-fry 24 of the garlic cloves in oil over moderate heat until softened and golden, turning to ensure even cooking. Remove with a mesh spoon, then drain on paper towel and set aside.

2 Season beef with ground cassia and pepper.

3 Slice remaining garlic. Heat 50 ml oil in a deep, heavy-based pan and fry sliced garlic, shallots and ginger over gentle heat until softened. Stir in ground fennel, chilli jam, cassia bark and cinnamon stick, then add meat and toss over high heat for 5 minutes to coat with spices.

4 Pour in stock and sweet soy and simmer gently for 1 hour until meat is tender. Remove meat from pan and allow to rest for 30 minutes or until cool. Cut meat into 4 cm long strips.

5 Strain stock through a fine-meshed sieve and discard solids. Season with fish sauce, then taste and adjust if necessary. If possible, refrigerate stock overnight, then remove fat from surface.

6 To serve, bring stock to a boil, then add meat, roasted garlic cloves, noodles and spinach.

7 Pour into deep bowls, dividing contents evenly, and sprinkle with garlic chives. Serve immediately.

30 cloves garlic
vegetable oil
1 × 500 g piece rump steak
1/4 teaspoon ground cassia
1 teaspoon freshly ground black pepper
5 red shallots, sliced

5 slices ginger
1 teaspoon fennel seeds, ground
2 teaspoons Chilli Jam (page 58)
2 pieces cassia bark
1 stick cinnamon
1.5 litres Beef Stock (page 339)

150 ml sweet soy sauce
100 ml fish sauce
500 g fresh hokkien noodles, blanched
50 g baby spinach leaves
50 g garlic chives, chopped into 2 cm
  lengths

Cassia beef noodles with spinach and garlic chives

A bowlful of hearty and warming flavours that meld beautifully. Although it's not essential to do so, preparing the meat

a day in advance will result in a clearer stock and cleaner flavour. If you have any stock left over,

keep it for future use – it's too precious to throw away! (See photograph opposite.)

1 Steam clams open in a wide, heavy-based pan over high heat. Plunge clams into iced water to cool. Discard any unopened shells, then remove clam meat from shells.

2 Blanch sausages in boiling water for 3 minutes, then remove and slice finely.

3 Cut rice noodle sheets into 1 cm wide strips and blanch in boiling water for 1 minute to soften. Drain.

4 Combine ginger, garlic, sesame oil, soy sauces, rice wine, fish sauce, palm sugar and white pepper in a bowl, then add prawn meat and sausage and marinate for 10 minutes.

5 Heat a wok, then add vegetable oil and fry curry powder for a second. Immediately stir in prawn meat, sausages and their marinade and toss over high heat for 2 minutes.

6 Add noodles, green onion, chilli, pork and clams and toss over high heat to combine. Mix in bean sprouts and coriander and serve immediately.

750 g wild surf clams
2 Chinese pork sausages
500 g fresh rice noodle sheets
1 tablespoon minced ginger
3 cloves garlic, minced
25 ml sesame oil
50 ml light soy sauce
50 ml sweet soy sauce

30 ml Chinese Shaoxing rice wine
25 ml fish sauce
30 g palm sugar, shaved
$1/2$ teaspoon freshly ground white pepper
300 g green prawn meat, roughly
   chopped
60 ml vegetable oil

1 tablespoon Madras Curry Powder
   (page 35)
6 green onions, cut into 1 cm lengths
3 large red chillies, finely sliced
250 g Chinese red-cooked pork, sliced
200 g bean sprouts
$1/2$ cup coriander leaves

Fried rice noodles with pork, prawns and clams

This is a take on the Chinese/Malaysian classic char kueh teow, sold at the wonderful hawker street stalls in Singapore.
The ideal way to cook these noodles is by the portion in a large, industrial-sized wok over high heat so that you get a smoky
flavour through the food. Buy red-cooked pork from a Chinese barbecue shop – look for the braised ducks and
other delicacies hanging in the window.

1 Heat oil in a wok and fry spice paste over moderate heat until fragrant, about 2 minutes. Add sauce and bring to a boil, then add prawns and cook for 2 minutes, tossing wok constantly, until prawns begin to change colour.

2 Add noodles, snowpea sprouts, bean sprouts and choy sum leaves and allow leaves to wilt in sauce. Taste and adjust seasoning if necessary.

3 Ladle into deep bowls, then sprinkle with fried shallots and serve immediately.

60 ml Sichuan Pepper Oil (page 61)
3 tablespoons Nonya Spice Paste
  (page 43)
300 ml Hot-and-sour Coconut Sauce
  (page 64)

30 large green prawns, shelled and
  deveined
500 g flat egg noodles, blanched
100 g snowpea sprouts, trimmed
200 g bean sprouts

18 choy sum leaves, washed
$\frac{1}{4}$ cup Fried Shallots (page 342)

Hot-and-sour prawns with flat egg noodles

A versatile noodle dish that borrows from the Chinese lo mein principle where the meat, fish or vegetables are simply

tossed in a velvety sauce to coat rather than drown the noodles. This way, the flavours are kept fresh and vibrant.

1 Cook noodles for 2 minutes, then strain and set aside.

2 Dry-roast peppercorns over gentle heat until fragrant. Cool, then grind to a fine powder.

3 Shell prawns, leaving tails intact, then remove intestinal tracts.

4 Cut cucumbers in half lengthwise, then remove seeds and finely slice across.

5 Lightly dust prawns with ground Sichuan pepper.

6 Heat chilli orange oil in a wok and fry shallots, then add stir-fry paste, sambal belacan and prawns and toss over high heat to coat prawns thoroughly.

7 After 1 minute or so, as prawns begin to change colour, add tamarind dressing and bring to a boil.

8 Toss in cucumber, green onion, chilli, bean sprouts and noodles, then remove immediately from heat and stir in laksa leaves. Pile onto plates and serve.

400 g dried somen noodles
1 teaspoon Sichuan peppercorns
24 green king prawns
3 small cucumbers
60 ml Chilli Orange Oil (page 61)
4 red shallots, finely sliced

3 tablespoons Lemongrass Stir-fry Paste (page 44)
1 tablespoon Sambal Belacan (page 57)
180 ml Sweet Tamarind Dressing (page 126)
6 green onions, finely sliced

2 large red chillies, cut into julienne
200 g bean sprouts
$^1/_2$ cup laksa (Vietnamese mint) leaves

Chilli prawns with somen noodles and bean sprouts

This is what I turn to when I crave a good chilli fix – the aromatic flavourings used here are extremely addictive.

(See photograph opposite.)

1 Make and cook the noodles as instructed, then strain and dress with a little olive oil to prevent sticking.

2 Shuck oysters and reserve all strained juices for dressing (you need 100 ml). Discard shells.

3 To make the oyster dressing, mix all ingredients in a bowl, including oyster juices, and taste for balance between acid and salt. Adjust if necessary. Keep refrigerated until ready to use.

4 Divide ingredients into 6 portions, then, for each serve, put a portion of noodles, bok choy and dressing into a bowl and balance of ingredients into another bowl. You should have 12 bowls altogether, 2 bowls per serve.

5 Stand woks over high heat, then tip in first portion of noodles, dressing and bok choy and toss until warmed, being careful that noodles don't stick. Add second bowl of ingredients, stirring with tongs to combine quickly, and toss over heat until warmed through, about 1 minute. Pile onto plates and serve immediately.

1 quantity Seaweed Noodles (page 341)
olive oil
36 large Pacific oysters, unshucked
12 baby bok choy, blanched
3 teaspoons finely sliced Pickled Ginger
  (page 52)
1/4 cup coriander leaves

6 green onions, cut into 1 cm lengths
2 large green chillies, finely sliced
100 g snowpea sprouts
6 teaspoons Coriander Peanut Pesto
  (page 343)

Oyster dressing
250 ml Fish Stock (page 337)
60 ml Tamarind Liquid (page 341)
20 ml fish sauce
10 ml light soy sauce
20 ml mirin
30 ml strained lime juice

Seaweed noodles with Pacific oysters and coriander pesto

A favourite of mine, this stir-fry first appeared in *Paramount Cooking* but is worthy of inclusion here because of its combination of flavours and textures. Choose the best and largest Pacific oysters available (leave the creamy rock oyster for eating direct from the shell) and open them as you are about to cook, so that you can capture their juices to flavour the dressing.

As already mentioned, I recommend acquiring two or three small, non-stick woks, which can be on the go at one time.

I also recommend you use 12 bowls to sort the ingredients. If you've prepared everything in advance, the final cooking and assembly takes just a few minutes and makes you look like an absolute whizz.

1 Remove breast and leg meat from duck, keeping skin intact but discarding bones. Cut meat into thick chunks.

2 Heat pepper oil in a wok and fry shallots and ginger over gentle heat for a minute until softened. Add star anise broth and bring to a boil.

3 Stir in bok choy and noodles, then cook for a few minutes until warmed through.

4 Add duck meat.

5 Ladle into deep bowls, then sprinkle with green onion and add a dollop of relish. Serve immediately.

1 Chinese roast duck
25 ml Sichuan Pepper Oil (page 61)
6 red shallots, finely sliced
3 teaspoons minced ginger

400 ml Star Anise Broth (page 65)
12 baby bok choy, blanched and halved
500 g fresh rice noodles
4 green onions, finely sliced

6 teaspoons Green Garlic Ginger Relish
   (page 56)

Roast duck with star anise noodles and green garlic ginger relish

Another soupy noodle dish that takes only minutes to prepare – if you have the broth and a fresh roast duck on hand!

These refreshing yet intoxicating flavours will have you coming back for more.

1 Shallow-fry garlic cloves in oil until golden and softened, then drain on paper towel. Dry-roast sesame seeds over gentle heat until just coloured, then cool. Set aside.

2 To make the dressing, combine all ingredients and set aside.

3 Bring master stock to a boil in a stockpot. Cut chicken into 8 pieces (2 drumsticks, 2 thigh joints and the breast frame cut into quarters), keeping meat on bone. Put chicken into stock, then reduce heat and simmer very gently for 5 minutes. Remove pot from heat, then cover and let chicken sit in stock for 30 minutes. Check that meat is cooked, testing each piece with a skewer – if juices run pale pink, the chicken is ready. Leave a little longer if meat is too pink. Remove cooked chicken from stock and cut meat into strips, discarding bones. Sprinkle meat with spice salt.

4 Quarter eggplants lengthwise, then score flesh and brush with oil. Grill until softened and golden.

5 Cook noodles in boiling water for 2 minutes until soft, then strain and refresh under cold running water. Put noodles into a bowl with half the dressing.

6 In another bowl, mix garlic cloves with herbs, green onion and watercress, then add chicken and spoon in enough dressing to coat leaves and meat lightly.

7 Pile noodles onto plates, then sit 2 grilled eggplant halves on each pile. Arrange chicken and salad on top of eggplant, then drizzle with a little extra dressing and sprinkle with sesame seeds. Serve immediately.

12 cloves garlic
vegetable oil
2 teaspoons white sesame seeds
3 litres Chinese Master Stock (page 339)
1 × 1.5 kg free-range, corn-fed chicken
1 teaspoon Chinese Spice Salt (page 39)
6 Japanese eggplants
500 g dried somen noodles

¼ cup spearmint leaves, shredded
2 tablespoons torn basil leaves
3 green onions, finely sliced
2 cups watercress sprigs

Soy dressing
40 ml soy sauce
2 teaspoons sesame oil
40 ml strained lemon juice
50 ml Chinese rice vinegar
65 ml mirin
60 ml Sugar Syrup (page 343)
4 cloves garlic, minced

Soy-braised chicken with sesame noodles, eggplant, mint and watercress

A warm noodle salad that balances restrained flavours and textures, leaving the palate feeling clean and light.

(See photograph opposite.)

1 Make and cook the pepper noodles as instructed, then strain and toss with a little oil to prevent sticking.

2 Blanch asparagus in boiling water for 1 minute, then refresh in iced water. Cut cuttlefish tubes lengthwise into 2 cm wide strips and score flesh diagonally with a sharp knife.

3 Heat pepper oil in a wok and fry garlic, coriander root and black pepper over moderate heat for a few seconds until fragrant. Add green peppercorns and cuttlefish and toss over high heat briefly, then add green onion, tamarind dressing and asparagus.

4 Toss in noodles, tatsoi leaves, snowpea sprouts and laksa leaves and combine quickly with tongs. Pile noodles onto plates, then sprinkle with fried garlic and serve immediately.

1 quantity Pepper Noodles (page 341)
vegetable oil
12 asparagus spears, chopped
600 g cleaned cuttlefish tubes
90 ml Sichuan Pepper Oil (page 61)
1 tablespoon minced garlic

2 teaspoons minced coriander root
1 teaspoon freshly ground black pepper
$1/4$ cup fresh green peppercorns
9 green onions, cut into 2 cm lengths
200 ml Sweet Tamarind Dressing
    (page 91)

1 cup small tatsoi leaves
$1/4$ cup snowpea sprouts, trimmed
$1/4$ cup laksa (Vietnamese mint) leaves
2 tablespoons Fried Garlic (page 342)

Cuttlefish, green peppercorns and asparagus with pepper noodles

This noodle dish is full of fresh, lively flavours that explode in the mouth. The secret is to use fresh green peppercorns

that are grown in North Queensland. They make erratic appearances on the market – so when you see them

at Asian food stores or vegetable suppliers, grab some and try this out.

1 Dry-roast sesame seeds over gentle heat until just coloured. Cool.

2 Cook noodles in boiling water until soft, about 4 minutes, then drain and toss with a little oil to prevent sticking.

3 Shallow-fry garlic in oil until golden and softened, then drain on paper towel. Set aside.

4 To make the dressing, mix all ingredients and set aside.

5 To make the stir-fry paste, blend all ingredients to a smooth paste in a food processor.

6 Remove tentacles from octopus and cut in half or into quarters, depending on their size. Marinate octopus in stir-fry paste for 10 minutes.

7 Heat a wok and fry octopus and its marinade over high heat until octopus starts to change colour, about 2 minutes. Add noodles, garlic, peppercorns and just enough sesame soy dressing to moisten. Cook for another minute, then remove wok from heat.

8 Mix watercress, cucumber, capsicum, chilli, coriander and green onion in a bowl and add balance of dressing. Add cooked octopus and noodles and toss to combine.

9 Pile onto serving plates and sprinkle with sesame seeds.

3 teaspoons white sesame seeds
300 g fine egg noodles
vegetable oil
18 cloves garlic
600 g baby octopus, cleaned
6 teaspoons fresh green peppercorns
  (on stems)
$^1/_2$ cup watercress sprigs
1 small cucumber, very finely sliced
$^1/_2$ green capsicum, cut into julienne
1 teaspoon finely sliced green chilli

$^1/_2$ cup coriander leaves
3 green onions, sliced diagonally

Sesame soy dressing
25 ml sesame oil
75 ml tamari soy sauce
100 ml Chinese rice vinegar
125 ml mirin
125 ml Sugar Syrup (page 343)
3 teaspoons fish sauce

Stir-fry paste
1 tablespoon minced garlic
2 teaspoons minced coriander root
1 teaspoon freshly ground black pepper
2 teaspoons crushed fresh green
  peppercorns
5 green bird's-eye chillies, finely sliced
1 teaspoon sesame oil
25 ml soy sauce

Stir-fried octopus, sesame noodles and green chilli with coriander, cucumber and watercress salad

Well-balanced flavours and textures create perfect harmony in this dish. Look for baby octopus that have not seen the inside of a cement mixer (a common implement for tenderising!) – the difference in texture is unbelievable. You can use large octopus just as successfully, but you need to cook it whole beforehand and then slice it before proceeding.

PASTRIES

PASTRIES   Pastries with rich and spicy secret fillings are an all-time favourite of mine. And as spicy pastries feature in many different cuisines, I am obviously not alone in my desires and needs. ❖ PASTRY USUALLY RELIES on some type of fat to keep it moist and succulent – butter, ghee, oil, yoghurt, lard or egg – although there are exceptions to the rule, such as Vietnamese rice-paper wrappers and Chinese and Japanese beancurd skins. Spices are the perfect foil to rich pastry as they cut through fat, and the more delicate wrappings unite and show off subtle flavour combinations while also adding textural interest. ❖ WHATEVER THE ORIGIN, pastry work is an art form. The ritual of making small and delicate parcels takes skills not required in other forms of preparation. Hone those skills and be rewarded by the responses received when the perfectly formed morsels are consumed.

1 To make the pigeon filling, dry-roast cumin and coriander seeds, separately, over gentle heat until fragrant. Cool, then grind to a fine powder.

2 'Spatchcock' pigeons by cutting away their backbones and then flattening out birds. Rub pepper into skin. Heat oil in a wide, heavy-based, deep pan and sear pigeons skin-side down until they begin to brown. Remove from pan and set aside. Sauté onion, garlic, ginger and chermoula in pan until fragrant, then stir in ground spices and cinnamon stick.

3 Return pigeons to pan and coat with spices and aromatics, then cook over moderate heat for a few minutes. Add stock and bring gently to a simmer. Reduce heat, then add saffron and simmer for 45 minutes over a low heat until pigeons are cooked and flesh is tender. Remove birds from pan and set aside to cool. Cook stock over high heat until reduced by half.

4 When birds are cool enough to handle, remove meat, discarding skin and bones. Finely dice meat.

5 Bring 100 ml reduced stock to a boil in a saucepan, then whisk in eggs and salt and cook over moderate heat until eggs begin to set and appear creamy. Remove from heat and stir in herbs. Allow to cool completely, then mix in diced meat.

6 To assemble pastries, fold each filo sheet in half to make a long rectangle, then brush with melted butter. Combine ground almonds, icing sugar and orange-flower water and sprinkle a little down length of each pastry strip. Spread pigeon stuffing over nut paste. With the pastry strip longest side to you, take the top left-hand corner and fold it down over the filling. Fold the triangle you have just made back on itself, then continue folding to make a complete triangular pastry. Brush with melted butter.

7 Preheat oven to 180°C, then bake pastries for 20–25 minutes until golden. Remove from oven and allow to sit for 5 minutes. Dust with extra icing sugar and cinnamon and serve immediately.

6 sheets filo pastry
butter, melted
90 g toasted flaked almonds, ground
2 tablespoons sieved icing sugar
25 ml orange-flower water
freshly ground cinnamon

Pigeon filling
1 teaspoon cumin seeds
1 teaspoon coriander seeds
3 × 400 g pigeons
$^{1}/_{2}$ teaspoon freshly ground black pepper
75 ml olive oil
1 brown onion, finely chopped
1 tablespoon minced garlic
1 teaspoon minced ginger

1 tablespoon Chermoula (page 46)
1 stick cinnamon
1 litre White Chicken Stock (page 337)
$^{1}/_{2}$ teaspoon saffron threads
3 large (61 g) eggs
1 teaspoon sea salt
1 tablespoon chopped flat-leaf parsley
1 tablespoon chopped coriander

B'stilla – spiced pigeon pastries

A highlight of Moroccan festive dinners and banquets, these heavenly, sweet, spicy pastries are served as a first course and are traditionally made with fine sheets of warkha pastry. Claudia Roden writes in her *New Book of Middle Eastern Food* that making this pastry 'requires much skill and an almost inherited experience'.

Good-quality filo pastry can be substituted easily.

1 To make the pastry, blend butter, flour and salt in a food processor until mixture resembles breadcrumbs. Add water and blend to a dough. Knead pastry into a ball by hand, then pat into a round and refrigerate for 1 hour.

2 Cut potatoes into small dice, then boil until tender and drain.

3 Poach or steam chicken until tender, then cool and dice finely.

4 Heat 1 tablespoon vegetable oil in a frying pan and fry onion and garlic over gentle heat until lightly coloured. Add curry powder and fry for a couple of minutes, then stir in sambal. Remove pan from heat and allow to cool.

5 Mix chicken, potato, coriander, salt and pepper into cooled curry base.

6 Roll pastry out thinly and cut into 6 cm rounds.

7 Put 2 teaspoons filling into centre of each round, then fold over pastry to make a semi-circle and crimp or pleat edges to seal.

8 Heat oil in a deep-fryer to 180°C and fry pastries, a few at a time, for 4 minutes until golden – keep pastries submerged in hot oil with a slotted spoon to ensure even cooking. Remove from oil with a slotted spoon and drain on paper towel.

9 Serve hot curry puffs with a relish or chutney of your choice.

150 g waxy potatoes, peeled
1 × 250 g free-range, corn-fed chicken
  breast
vegetable oil
1 brown onion, minced
3 cloves garlic, minced

1 tablespoon Malaysian Curry Blend
  (page 35)
2 teaspoons Sambal Belacan (page 57)
2 tablespoons coriander leaves
½ teaspoon sea salt
½ teaspoon freshly ground black pepper

Pastry
175 g cold unsalted butter, diced
500 g plain flour
½ teaspoon sea salt
200 ml water

Chicken and potato curry puffs

Another versatile Indian fried pastry where the quality of the pastry is as important as its filling. These pastries can be made ahead of time, then refrigerated and cooked at the last minute.

1 Make and rest the samosa pastry as instructed.

2 To make the filling, peel pumpkin and potatoes and cut into 5 mm dice. Melt ghee and sauté pumpkin, potato, garlic, ginger and chilli until softened and fragrant. Remove from heat, then stir in chat masala, chopped coriander and salt. Allow to cool completely.

3 Roll pastry into a long sausage. Cut pastry into 18 pieces, then roll pastry out thinly into rounds.

4 Spoon some filling into centre of each round, then fold in half and then in half again to make a triangle, pressing edges together firmly with fingertips to seal.

5 Heat oil in a deep-fryer to 180°C and fry a few samosas at a time for 5 minutes until golden and crisp – keep samosas submerged in hot oil with a slotted spoon to ensure even cooking.

6 Drain on paper towel and serve hot with a dollop of coriander yoghurt sauce.

1 quantity Samosa Pastry (page 345)
vegetable oil for deep-frying
6 tablespoons Coriander Yoghurt Sauce
   (page 67)

Pumpkin and potato filling
175 g butternut pumpkin
175 g waxy potatoes
30 g ghee
1 teaspoon minced garlic

1 teaspoon minced ginger
2 red bird's-eye chillies, minced
2 teaspoons Chat Masala (page 34)
2 tablespoons chopped coriander leaves
1/2 teaspoon sea salt

Spiced potato and pumpkin samosas with coriander yoghurt sauce

These samosas are made the same way as those on page 248 but include the warm flavours of pumpkin and chat masala.

The coriander sauce served alongside provides a clean lift to these deliciously moreish pastries.

1 To make the wrappers, combine flours and salt in a bowl. Beat eggs in another bowl and add oil and water. Blend dry and wet ingredients in a food processor to form a batter, then refrigerate for 1 hour.

2 To cook the wrappers, heat a non-stick frying pan and brush with the minimum amount of oil possible, then pour in a little batter and swirl to coat base. The procedure is the same as when making crêpes – it is important to keep the batter as fine and even as possible. Do not flip wrapper; instead, turn out onto a plate when set.

3 Stack popiah on top of each other, covering them with a cloth until you have finished cooking. You should have 20 wrappers in all.

4 Mix all other ingredients together, except lettuce, and heat gently in a saucepan until warmed through.

5 Arrange popiah wrappers on a bench, then sit a piece of lettuce on each and spoon some filling into each leaf. Wrap up each popiah as you would a spring roll, folding in the edges as you go. Serve immediately.

vegetable oil
150 g cooked crabmeat
3 tablespoons Fried Shallots (page 342)
2 teaspoons Sambal Bajak (page 57)
2 teaspoons salted soy beans, mashed
10 snowpeas, finely sliced
1 small cucumber, cut into julienne

50 g bean sprouts
4 Chinese cabbage leaves, shredded
12 basil leaves, shredded
$\frac{1}{2}$ teaspoon sea salt
10 butter lettuce leaves, halved
   lengthwise

Popiah wrappers
180 g fine rice flour
25 g superfine *or* cake flour
$\frac{1}{2}$ teaspoon sea salt
4 large (61 g) hen's eggs *or* 3 duck eggs
1 teaspoon vegetable oil
500 ml warm water

Popiah

A popular snack in Singapore and Malaysia, with their origins in Nonya cooking, popiah (called bao bing in China) are made with tissue-thin wrappers and filled with vegetables or fish and seasoned with chilli. They are like a fresh, uncooked spring roll. I first became addicted to these tasty morsels when I lived in Adelaide, where the hawker-style food stalls at the Central Market make them to order. Popiah are best when made fresh and eaten at room temperature; something seems to be lost when they are refrigerated. The wrappers are very easy to make, but you can substitute Vietnamese rice-paper wrappers instead if you don't have time (you need to dunk these in warm water to make them pliable before filling them).

1 Make and rest the pastry as instructed.

2 To make the filling, bring a saucepan of water to a boil and cook peas and potato, separately, until tender, then drain and set aside. Melt ghee in a frying pan and sauté onion, garlic, ginger and chilli until softened and beginning to colour. Stir in turmeric and garam masala, then remove from heat and cool. Mix all filling ingredients in a bowl, then taste for seasoning and adjust if necessary.

3 Roll pastry into a long sausage. Cut pastry into 18 pieces, then roll pastry out thinly into rounds.

4 Spoon some filling into centre of each round, then fold in half and then in half again to make a triangle, pressing edges together firmly with fingertips to seal.

5 Heat oil in a deep-fryer to 180°C and fry a few samosas at a time for 5 minutes until golden and crisp – keep samosas submerged in hot oil with a slotted spoon to ensure even cooking.

6 Drain on paper towel and serve hot with a dollop of cucumber yoghurt salad.

1 quantity Samosa Pastry (page 345)
vegetable oil for deep-frying
6 tablespoons Cucumber Yoghurt Salad
   with Nigella (page 80)

Chickpea and potato filling
2 tablespoons fresh green peas
125 g waxy potatoes, diced
1 tablespoon ghee
1 small brown onion, diced
3 cloves garlic, minced
1 teaspoon minced ginger
1 green bird's-eye chilli, minced

1 teaspoon turmeric powder
1 teaspoon Paramount's Garam Masala
   (page 34)
150 g cooked chickpeas, roughly chopped
1 tablespoon diced tomato
1 teaspoon sea salt
1 tablespoon coriander leaves

Chickpea and potato samosas with cucumber yoghurt salad

Samosas, those well-known fried pastries, are sold as street snacks in India for immediate gratification. The fillings can be made with vegetables or meat – I have given two vegetable versions here, the ones I prefer and use the most.

(See photograph opposite.)

1 To make the pastry, preheat oven to 100°C. Steam sweet potato on a tray in a Chinese steamer, covered, for 15 minutes or until soft. Transfer tray to oven for 5 minutes to remove any excess moisture. Blend sweet potato to a smooth paste in a food processor with remaining ingredients just until dough comes together. Remove dough and knead for a few minutes. Shape pastry into 18 balls the size of a golf ball.

2 To make the stuffing, dice water chestnuts and shiitake mushrooms finely. Mix all ingredients thoroughly.

3 To assemble, dust hands and bench with rice flour and flatten each ball into a round 5 mm thick and 6–7 cm in diameter. Spoon 1 teaspoon filling into centre of each round, then fold pastry over to make a crescent shape and press edges together to seal.

4 Heat vegetable oil in a deep-fryer to 180°C and fry pastries, a few at a time, for 6 minutes. Swirl a slotted spoon through hot oil to prevent pastries sticking together during cooking.

5 Drain on paper towel and serve with sweet chilli sauce alongside.

rice flour
vegetable oil for deep-frying
200 ml Sweet Chilli Sauce (page 67)

Sweet potato pastry
500 g sweet potatoes, peeled and sliced
1 tablespoon castor sugar
1½ tablespoons tapioca flour
3 teaspoons sweet potato flour, sieved

pinch of Chinese Five-spice Powder
   (page 39)
25 ml vegetable oil

Prawn and crab stuffing
10 fresh water chestnuts, blanched
6 shiitake mushrooms
100 g minced green prawn meat
100 g cooked blue-swimmer crabmeat

2 cloves garlic, minced
1 teaspoon minced ginger
3 green onions, finely sliced
2 red bird's-eye chillies, minced
2 teaspoons finely chopped coriander
   leaves
½ teaspoon sea salt
½ teaspoon ground Sichuan pepper

Deep-fried sweet potato pastries stuffed with prawn, crab and water chestnuts with sweet chilli sauce

I love the myriad pastries that are showcased on the trolleys of the Chinese yum cha. The skill involved in making these delectable but time-consuming morsels, which we consume so rapidly for such little cost, leaves me in awe, as does the variety. I constantly strive to emulate the array of flavours and textures achieved by these chefs. The following offering, a favourite at Paramount for some time now, is my own version of a yum cha pastry.

1 Drain ricotta overnight in a muslin-lined sieve over a bowl.

2 To make the pastry, dry-roast cumin seeds over gentle heat until fragrant. Cool, then grind to a fine powder. Blend ground cumin, flour and salt in a food processor. Add butter and blend until mixture resembles breadcrumbs. Add yoghurt and blend until dough forms a ball. Wrap pastry in plastic film and refrigerate for 1 hour.

3 Cut pastry into quarters and roll each piece on a floured surface until 5 mm thick. Using an 8 cm pastry cutter, cut rounds from pastry. Refrigerate pastry rounds until ready to assemble.

4 To complete the filling, dry-roast cumin seeds over gentle heat until fragrant. Cool, then grind to a fine powder. Sauté onion and garlic in butter in a frying pan over moderate heat until softened, then stir in ground cumin. Remove pan from heat and allow to cool. Stir remaining ingredients, except egg wash, into cooled mixture until combined.

5 Preheat oven to 200°C.

6 Put a small spoonful of mixture onto each pastry round. Brush edges of pastry with egg wash, then fold each pastry round in half and press edges together to seal. Brush tops of pastries with egg wash and arrange on a buttered baking tray.

7 Bake for 10 minutes until pastries are golden, then serve immediately.

250 g fresh ricotta
1 teaspoon cumin seeds
1 tablespoon minced red onion
3 cloves garlic, minced
20 g unsalted butter
$^{1}/_{2}$ cup blanched, chopped spinach
2 eggs, lightly beaten

$^{1}/_{2}$ teaspoon sea salt
$^{1}/_{2}$ teaspoon freshly ground black pepper
$^{1}/_{4}$ teaspoon freshly grated nutmeg
1 tablespoon shredded flat-leaf parsley
2 teaspoons chopped oregano
egg wash

Yoghurt pastry
$^{1}/_{4}$ teaspoon cumin seeds
200 g plain flour
$^{1}/_{2}$ teaspoon sea salt
120 g unsalted butter, chopped
100 ml thick plain yoghurt

Spiced ricotta and spinach pastries

The most superior ricotta cheese available on the Australian market, in my mind, is the goat's milk ricotta produced in Western Australia under Gabrielle Kervella's Fromage Fermier label. Its creaminess, firmness and flavour are perfect – especially for these delicious pastries. However, many other brands are readily available – just be sure to select a cheese that is firm, not wet or sloppy in appearance, as the water content will play havoc with the pastry.

1 Remove breasts from quail (to give you 12 pieces meat), then discard skin and butterfly meat open. Set aside. Remove meat from legs and mince, discarding skin. Heat sesame oil in a frying pan and sear quail mince briefly over moderately high heat, about 1 minute. Deglaze pan with rice wine, then remove meat from pan.

2 Heat 2 teaspoons vegetable oil in pan and cook mushroom, ginger, garlic and coriander root over moderate heat until softened. Remove from heat and stir into quail mince. Add green onion, water chestnuts and coriander leaves and mix thoroughly. Season with salt and pepper and allow mixture to cool completely.

3 Spoon cooled mixture onto each butterflied quail breast and fold meat back into its original shape to enclose stuffing.

4 Immerse beancurd skins in cold water until pliable, about 20 seconds, then squeeze out excess water. Using 2 skins per parcel, and with the narrow end facing you, put one stuffed quail breast on the end closest to you, then roll up in the same way as you would a spring roll, making sure edges are firmly tucked in as you go. Brush edges with egg wash to seal. Refrigerate for 1 hour before cooking.

5 Heat vegetable oil in a deep-fryer to 180°C and cook 6 pastries for 6 minutes until crisp. (Don't cook any more pastries than this or the temperature of the oil will drop and the pastry will become soggy.) Remove pastries from hot oil with a mesh spoon, then drain on paper towel. Cut pastries in half diagonally.

6 Spoon coriander yoghurt sauce onto plates, then sit 2 pastries (4 halves) on top and sprinkle with extra coriander leaves. Serve immediately.

6 large quail
1 teaspoon sesame oil
25 ml Chinese Shaoxing rice wine
vegetable oil
100 g shiitake mushrooms, finely
   chopped
2 teaspoons minced ginger

3 cloves garlic, minced
2 coriander roots, minced
6 green onions, finely sliced
18 fresh water chestnuts, blanched and
   minced
2 tablespoons chopped coriander leaves
$^1/_2$ teaspoon sea salt

$^1/_2$ teaspoon freshly ground black pepper
12 × 10 cm square beancurd skins,
   cut in half
egg wash
6 tablespoons Coriander Yoghurt Sauce
   (page 67)

Quail breasts stuffed with shiitake mushrooms and water chestnuts deep-fried in beancurd skins with coriander yoghurt sauce

This is a spectacular and elegant way to present these small birds, and a dish we often feature on the Restaurant menu.

Apart from the gorgeous flavour and texture of these pastries, people love them because they do not have

any small bones that involve tedious fiddling. (See photograph opposite.)

1 Cut eggplants into 1 cm dice.

2 Heat oil in a deep-fryer to 180°C and fry eggplant until golden. Drain on paper towel.

3 Heat 1 tablespoon vegetable oil in a frying pan and fry garlic, onion and chilli over moderate heat for a few minutes until fragrant. Combine onion mixture, eggplant, pickled ginger, coriander leaves, eggplant pickle and fish sauce in a bowl. Dice water chestnuts finely and mix in thoroughly.

4 Spread 2 spinach leaves on a bench so that they overlap. Form 1 tablespoon eggplant mixture into a log, then put in middle of leaves. Roll up so filling is encased by spinach. Repeat this process until you have made 12 parcels.

5 Open out beancurd skins to double thickness and cut into 15 cm squares.

6 Soak each beancurd skin in warm water for 20 seconds to soften, then sit a spinach parcel at one end. Roll over twice, then fold in sides and brush edges with egg wash and roll up to secure. The pastries should resemble spring rolls.

7 Heat oil in a deep-fryer to 180°C and fry pastries, a few at a time, for 5 minutes. Drain on paper towel and serve with a dollop of coriander yoghurt sauce.

2 eggplants
vegetable oil for deep-frying
5 cloves garlic, minced
1 red onion, minced
3 red bird's-eye chillies, minced

2 teaspoons Pickled Ginger (page 52),
  shredded
$^1/_4$ cup coriander leaves, chopped
3 tablespoons Eggplant Pickle (page 52)
1 teaspoon fish sauce
50 g fresh water chestnuts, blanched

24 large spinach leaves, blanched
12 × 10 cm square beancurd skins,
  cut in half
egg wash
6 tablespoons Coriander Yoghurt Sauce
  (page 67)

Spiced eggplant and spinach beancurd-skin pastries with coriander yoghurt sauce

This is one of my favourite vegetable pastries. The filling can just as easily be used with spring roll, filo or shortcrust pastry: the decision is yours. If you use filo or shortcrust, then bake the pastries in the oven as opposed to frying them in oil.

1 Heat 1 tablespoon vegetable oil and the chilli oil in a wok and quickly fry coriander root, pepper, garlic and capsicum until just softened and aromatic. Remove wok from heat and allow mixture to cool.

2 Stir in diced scallops, fish sauce and coriander leaves.

3 Put 1 teaspoon mixture in centre of each won ton wrapper. Brush edges with egg white, then fold wrapper over filling and press edges together. Bring ends together and press to seal.

4 Heat vegetable oil in a deep-fryer to 180°C and fry won tons, a few at a time, for 2 minutes until crisp and golden.

5 Drain on paper towel and serve hot with sweet chilli sauce alongside for dipping.

vegetable oil
few drops of Chilli Oil (page 61)
2 teaspoons minced coriander root
1 teaspoon freshly ground black pepper

2 cloves garlic, minced
1 tablespoon minced green capsicum
250 g scallops, diced
30 ml fish sauce

2 tablespoons chopped coriander leaves
30 won ton wrappers
egg white
150 ml Sweet Chilli Sauce (page 67)

Scallop and coriander won tons with sweet chilli sauce

These gorgeous little flavour-packed mouthfuls are easy to make and cook. Serve the won tons as suggested with the chilli

sauce as an appetiser, or add them, fried or steamed, to a fish-based soup. Alternatively, boil the won tons and serve them

with a hot and spicy chilli sauce and garlic chives as an entrée. Consistent, good-quality won ton wrappers

are made daily at Asian and Chinese food stores.

1 Blanch vermicelli in boiling water until softened, then drain and toss with a little oil to prevent sticking.

2 Cut vegetables and pickled ginger into fine shreds, then mix with vermicelli, bean sprouts, green onion and laksa leaves. In another bowl, mix crabmeat, fish sauce and lime juice.

3 Soak rice-paper wrappers, one at a time, in warm water until softened.

4 Spread wrappers on a clean tea towel and smear a little chilli jam on centre of each. Put some vegetable mixture down the centre, then add sliced pork and top with crabmeat.

5 Roll wrapper over filling, keeping it firm and tucking in the sides as you go. Before completely rolled, sit a couple of garlic chives along the fold to extend beyond the wrapper, then roll wrapper over to secure. Continue this process with remaining filling and wrappers.

6 Serve at room temperature.

100 g rice vermicelli
vegetable oil
1 small carrot
1 large red chilli
1 cucumber, peeled
1/2 daikon radish
3 teaspoons Pickled Ginger (page 52)

50 g bean sprouts
12 green onions, sliced diagonally
1 tablespoon shredded laksa
   (Vietnamese mint) leaves
300 g cooked blue-swimmer crabmeat
1 teaspoon fish sauce
1 teaspoon strained lime juice

18 rice-paper wrappers
2 teaspoons Chilli Jam (page 58)
120 g Chinese red-cooked pork,
   finely sliced
36 garlic chives

Crab and pork rice-paper rolls with chilli

Delicate Vietnamese fresh rice-paper or goi cuon rolls rely on absolute freshness and quality ingredients for their success.

The flavours are clean and cooling, and chilli is added for a zesty spiciness – great food for summer when you desire

something light, fresh and tasty. Do not refrigerate the rolls once they have been made as they will dry out.

They can stand for an hour at room temperature before serving.

1 Peel prawns, leaving their tails intact, then butterfly them open.

2 Mix garlic, coriander root, chilli, pepper, fish sauce and peanut oil in a small bowl until well blended. Brush butterflied prawns liberally with this marinade.

3 Position a prawn on each wrapper, with the tail sticking out one end, and roll up securely, tucking edges in as you go.

4 Heat vegetable oil in a deep-fryer to 180°C.

5 Fry rolls, a few at a time, for 3 minutes until golden – the prawns should just be cooked.

6 Remove with a slotted spoon and drain on paper towel briefly before serving.

18 large tiger prawns
2 teaspoons minced garlic
1 teaspoon minced coriander root

1 teaspoon minced large green chilli
$^{1}/_{2}$ teaspoon freshly ground black pepper
20 ml fish sauce

25 ml peanut oil
18 × 11 cm square spring roll wrappers
vegetable oil for deep-frying

Garlic and pepper tiger prawn spring rolls

Use the best-quality, firm-fleshed tiger prawns you can find when making these simple yet pungent pastries.

1 Dry-roast pine nuts over gentle heat until just coloured, then cool.

2 Heat oil in a frying pan and fry onion and garlic over gentle heat until lightly coloured.

3 Add lamb and spices and cook over moderately high heat until meat changes colour.

4 Remove pan from heat and stir in pine nuts, egg, parsley, mint, salt and pepper until thoroughly combined. Allow mixture to cool completely.

5 Preheat oven to 180°C.

6 Cut pastry sheets into thirds to form rectangles 30 cm long by about 8 cm wide. Brush filo with melted butter, then, with the narrow end towards you, spoon some filling across one end, roll over a few times and then fold sides in. Continue to roll tightly until pastry takes on the shape of a cigarette. Put rolled pastries onto a buttered baking tray and proceed until all 30 pastries have been assembled.

7 Brush tops of pastries with melted butter and bake for 20 minutes until golden. Serve immediately.

30 g pine nuts
30 ml olive oil
2 brown onions, minced
6 cloves garlic, minced
250 g lamb (shoulder or leg),
   coarsely minced

$^1/_2$ teaspoon freshly ground allspice
$^1/_2$ teaspoon cumin seeds, ground
$^1/_4$ teaspoon cayenne pepper
1 egg, beaten
1 tablespoon shredded flat-leaf parsley
1 tablespoon finely shredded mint leaves

1 teaspoon sea salt
$^1/_2$ teaspoon freshly ground black pepper
10 sheets filo pastry
125 g unsalted butter, melted

Lamb böreks

A popular Turkish savoury pie, but also found in other parts of the Middle East, böreks are made with layers of buttered filo pastry that enclose a filling of spiced meat or cheese. Buy a good-quality (preferably locally made) filo and keep it covered with a damp tea towel while rolling the pastries, as it dries out very quickly.

1 To make the pancakes, put flour into a bowl, then whisk in remaining ingredients with a chopstick until incorporated.

2 Continue to stir for a few minutes until dough becomes soft and pliable. Roll dough into a long sausage, then cut into 12 pieces. Roll out each piece of pastry thinly on a lightly floured bench.

3 Cook one pancake at a time in a lightly oiled frying pan over low heat until it bubbles, then flip over and cook other side briefly. Remove from heat and cover with a tea towel while making remaining pancakes.

4 Remove duck meat from carcass, discarding bones, and sprinkle with spice salt.

5 Put some duck meat, sliced cucumber, green onion and 1 teaspoon hoi sin sauce onto each pancake and roll up. Serve immediately.

vegetable oil
1 Chinese roasted duck
Chinese Spice Salt (page 39)

1 continental cucumber, cut into julienne
12 thin green onions (green part only)
12 teaspoons hoi sin sauce

Pancake pastry
150 g sifted plain flour
175 ml boiling water
2 teaspoons vegetable oil
few drops of fish sauce

Barbecued duck and cucumber pancakes

A quick-and-easy snack to make at home, a very humble version of the classic Chinese Peking duck. All it takes is a visit to your local Chinese barbecue shop – look for the roasted duck, braised chicken and red-cooked pork hanging in the window.

1 Prick duck all over with a skewer to release fat and fry in vegetable oil on both sides until skin is golden – use a deep, heavy-based pan just big enough to hold the duck and stock later on. Discard oil.

2 Cook onion, garlic, ginger, chilli and green onion in a little fresh oil over gentle heat until fragrant. Stir in star anise, peppercorns and fennel until fragrant.

3 Add stock and bring to a boil. Reduce heat to low, then add duck and simmer until meat is tender and almost falling off the bone, about 1½ hours – turn duck a couple of times during this time to ensure even cooking. Remove duck from stock and allow to cool enough to handle. While duck is still warm, remove meat from bones, discarding fat, skin and bones. Shred meat by hand into uniformly small pieces.

4 Strain stock through a fine-meshed sieve. Cool, then skim off any fat and reserve for ginger glaze, if preparing it ahead, or save for another use.

5 To make the shiitake mushroom mixture, soak dried black mushrooms in hot water until softened, about 15 minutes, then drain and slice finely. Heat oil in a frying pan and cook onion, garlic and ginger until fragrant. Stir in shiitake and black mushrooms and cook for 15 minutes until softened and any liquid has evaporated. Stir in green onion and cook until just softened, then add five-spice powder, parsley, salt and pepper. Allow to cool thoroughly.

6 To make the pies, mix duck meat with an equal amount of mushroom mixture until well incorporated. Form mixture into balls slightly larger than a tennis ball.

7 Make one pie at a time to keep pastry as cool as possible. Roll out pastry to 5 mm thick. Cut a base 14 cm in diameter and a lid 16 cm in diameter. Brush base with egg wash, then sit a ball of filling on top and cover with lid. Press edges together with your fingers to give a domed effect, then smooth edges with a paring knife. Brush lid with egg wash and score 6–7 arcs around dome working from top centre down. Repeat this procedure with remaining pastry and filling until you have 6 pies. Refrigerate pies until firm before baking, at least 1 hour.

8 Preheat oven to 220°C. Bake pies for 16 minutes until golden. Meanwhile, gently reheat ginger glaze. Slide pies onto plates with a spatula and serve immediately with ginger glaze.

1 × 1.7 kg corn-fed duck	2 litres Duck Stock (page 338)	1 brown onion, minced
vegetable oil	1 quantity Crème Fraîche Pastry	2 cloves garlic, minced
1 large brown onion, diced	(page 344)	2 teaspoons minced ginger
3 cloves garlic, chopped	egg wash	200 g shiitake mushrooms, finely sliced
1 teaspoon chopped ginger	300 ml Ginger Glaze (page 66)	3 green onions, finely sliced
1 large red chilli, split lengthwise		2 teaspoons Chinese Five-spice Powder
2 green onions, chopped	*Shiitake mushroom mixture*	(page 39)
1 star anise	50 g dried Chinese black mushrooms	2 teaspoons shredded flat-leaf parsley
1 teaspoon Sichuan peppercorns	hot water	1 teaspoon sea salt
1 teaspoon fennel seeds	50 ml vegetable oil	1 teaspoon freshly ground black pepper

Five-spice duck and shiitake mushroom pies

The five-spice duck pie is a constant on the Restaurant menu and made its debut in *Paramount Cooking*.

Its outward appearance pays homage to the French pithivier, a hand-moulded dome, while its filling looks towards China for its inspiration. The humble meat pie has special significance to Australians, but this version offers proof that it can employ refined technique and achieve elegant status. You can prepare the duck a day in advance, reserving the cooking liquid to make the Ginger Glaze, if you like. Otherwise, freeze the leftover stock for the next time you make these delicious pies!

(See photograph opposite.)

1 Remove tenderloin fillet from underside of each chicken breast. Roughly chop tenderloins and set breasts aside.

2 Sauté chopped chicken in 2 teaspoons vegetable oil and the sesame oil over moderate heat with mushroom, ginger, coriander root and garlic until chicken is just cooked and mushroom and aromatics are softened. Deglaze pan with rice wine and remove from heat.

3 Stir in green onion, water chestnuts and coriander leaves, then season with salt and pepper. Transfer to a food processor and pulse briefly to mince. Allow mixture to cool thoroughly.

4 Butterfly chicken breasts open, then cover each one with spinach leaves. Spoon some stuffing onto centre of each chicken breast, then roll up to enclose stuffing.

5 Immerse beancurd skins in cold water until pliable, about 20 seconds, then squeeze out excess water. Spread beancurd skins out on a bench and put one stuffed chicken breast onto each sheet, then roll up in the same way as you would a spring roll, making sure edges are firmly tucked in as you go. Brush edges with egg wash to seal. Refrigerate for 1 hour before cooking.

6 Heat vegetable oil in deep-fryer to 180°C and fry 3 pastries at a time for 12 minutes until pastry is crisp (meat should be just cooked and tender). Don't cook any more pastries at a time than this or the temperature of the oil will drop and the pastry will become soggy.

7 Remove from hot oil with a mesh spoon, then drain on paper towel and cut in half to serve.

6 free-range, corn-fed chicken breasts
vegetable oil
1 teaspoon sesame oil
100 g shiitake mushrooms, diced
2 teaspoons minced ginger
2 coriander roots, minced

2 cloves garlic, minced
25 ml Chinese Shaoxing rice wine
6 green onions, finely sliced
18 fresh water chestnuts, blanched and
  minced
1 tablespoon chopped coriander leaves

$^1/_2$ teaspoon sea salt
$^1/_2$ teaspoon freshly ground black pepper
100 g spinach leaves, blanched
12 beancurd skins
egg wash

Chicken breasts stuffed with spinach, water chestnuts and ginger deep-fried in beancurd skins

Using a similar approach as the quail pastries in this chapter (see page 252), these juicy parcels make a wonderful main

course because of their larger size. Try them with a chutney or with Turmeric Tamarind Sauce (see page 65)

for a more formal presentation.

1 To make the rosewater syrup, bring all ingredients except rosewater to a boil in a saucepan, then simmer for 10 minutes until sugar has dissolved and syrup is thick. Strain syrup through a fine-meshed sieve, discarding solids. Stir rosewater into syrup and refrigerate until cold.

2 To make the pistachio spice mixture, finely chop almonds and pistachios or pulse in a food processor until finely crushed. Combine nuts, brown sugar, ground cardamom and cinnamon.

3 Open out filo sheets, then cut 12 × 6 cm rounds from each sheet. Keep filo rounds not in use covered by a damp tea towel to prevent them drying out. Put 2 filo rounds, one on top of the other, on a baking tray lined with baking paper. Brush top with melted butter and sprinkle over some spiced nut mixture. Repeat this process 5 times, finishing with a filo layer, so that pastry has used 12 filo rounds. Brush top with butter. Continue making pastries with remaining filo, butter and spiced nut mixture.

4 Preheat oven to 180°C and bake pastries for 12 minutes or until golden.

5 Remove pastries from oven and immediately brush generously with cold rosewater syrup. As syrup is absorbed by pastries, brush again. Sprinkle finely ground pistachios over surfaces of pastries so nuts stick to syrup. Allow pastries to cool before eating.

12 sheets filo pastry
200 g butter, melted
extra 2 tablespoons finely ground
   pistachio nuts

Pistachio spice mixture
50 g blanched almonds
125 g pistachio nuts
125 g brown sugar
seeds from 2 green cardamom pods,
   ground
1 teaspoon freshly ground cinnamon

Rosewater syrup
200 g castor sugar
100 ml water
25 ml strained lemon juice
zest of 1 lemon
1 stick cinnamon
2 green cardamom pods, cracked
25 ml rosewater

Spiced nut pastries

The astonishing array of syrupy, sweet pastries you see in Middle Eastern and Greek shops are made luscious with butter and fragrant with spices and rose- or blossom water. For this recipe, I have taken the flavours and textures of the well-known baklava but have given it a different form. The rosewater syrup must be chilled when brushed over the pastries – if it is not, the pastries will become soggy. Although the pastries keep for a few days, be sure to eat them as soon as possible to make the most of their sticky irresistibility.

BREADS

BREADS   Just as spices have been central to everyday cooking through the ages, bread in its many forms has long been a staple across the globe. Together they form a long-celebrated partnership. ❋ THE SIMPLEST BREADS, whether leavened or not, are the flatbreads that feature in daily diets from India, Central Asia, Europe, Africa, the Mediterranean and the Middle East to Mexico and South America. These breads cook quickly, thus requiring less fuel, making them economic in all aspects of their production. ❋ AT THE OTHER END of the spectrum is the wild child of the bread world – the ancient pain de campagne, levain or sourdough. It uses no added yeast; instead, the 'starter' collects natural yeasts from the air. Needing commitment, loving and nurturing for assured success, these are the breads of artisan bakers. ❋ BREAD CELEBRATES the richest and simplest pleasures of daily living. It is an expression of earthy culture and is fundamental to our everyday eating habits. Bread is the staff of life, part of our historical development and a mainstay of our modern diet – offering roughage, providing energy, acting as a carrier for other foods. The making of bread is comforting, tactile and empowering, a response to some primal urge and a skill too often overlooked and ignored in our acceptance of the instant and the immediate. Bread-making offers a physical sensuality – and with the addition of the zestiness of spices, it opens up a whole new world of food discovery. ❋ WHATEVER BREAD you choose to bake or buy, the breaking of bread at the table symbolises a bond of friendship, giving and generosity.

1 Combine all ingredients except vegetable oil and ghee in a food processor until a ball of dough forms. Knead dough by hand for 15 minutes until pliable, shiny and elastic. Divide dough into 12 pieces and roll each into a ball. Rest dough, covered with a tea towel, for 1 hour at room temperature.

2 Roll each ball of dough into a round on a lightly oiled bench, then stretch dough with your hands to make it as elastic as possible without tearing it (or try flinging it into the air as for pizza dough!).

3 Dust bench with a little flour, then pleat each round of dough and fold it into a curled ball shape. Rest pleated dough balls, covered with a tea towel, for 30 minutes at room temperature.

4 Pat each ball with a rolling pin to flatten and roll until dough is about 1 cm thick and 12 cm in diameter.

5 Heat a roti pan or a similar flat pan, then coat surface with ghee and fry a paratha at a time until golden on both sides.

6 Serve warm.

500 g plain flour	3 teaspoons castor sugar	vegetable oil
65 ml milk	175 ml warm water	ghee, melted
1 small (55 g) egg	$^1/_2$ teaspoon sea salt	

Parathas

A wonderfully rich and flaky Indian bread to serve with spicy foods. When I spent time in India recently, I observed and tried making parathas by several methods and have included two versions here. Traditionally, the dough is flung into the air, much like the dough for a pizza is, to ensure maximum elasticity and paper-thin sheets.

Try it when you feel more confident with the dough and procedure!

1 Dry-roast cumin seeds over gentle heat until fragrant. Cool, then grind to a fine powder.

2 Sift both flours into a food processor and add salt.

3 Melt half the ghee, then, with the motor running, pour ghee and water into food processor and blend until dough forms a ball. Rest dough in a greased bowl for 1 hour, covered with a tea towel, at room temperature.

4 Divide dough into 12 pieces. Melt remaining ghee. Roll each piece of dough into a round 15 cm in diameter, then brush with melted ghee and sprinkle with ground cumin. Make an incision from the edge to the centre of each round.

5 Roll dough into a spiral or cone on a floured bench, beginning at the cut edge and working around, keeping the dough tightly rolled. It should look like an inverted cone with the point facing you when you hold it. Press down on cone to flatten it slightly, then use a rolling pin to flatten dough completely.

6 Roll dough into a round about 1 cm thick.

7 Heat a roti pan or a similar flat pan, then smear with ghee and cook a paratha at a time on both sides until golden and puffy.

1 teaspoon cumin seeds	300 g plain flour	200 g ghee, melted
100 g stoneground wholemeal flour	2 teaspoons sea salt	250 ml warm water

Parathas – another version

This version of making parathas involves rolling the dough into a cone shape before the final rolling out,

which helps achieve a light, flaky pastry.

1 Blend flour, salt and oil in a food processor. Add water and blend until dough forms a ball.

2 Knead dough by hand for 5 minutes. (The longer you knead the dough, the softer and more pliable it becomes and the better the texture.)

3 Divide dough into 12 pieces, then roll each piece into a ball with your hands. Flatten each ball, then roll into a thin round on a lightly floured surface.

4 Heat a chappati or roti pan or a similar flat pan and add a drizzle of melted ghee. Cook chappatis on both sides until golden and surface is bubbling.

5 Remove from pan and brush with melted ghee and sprinkle with garam masala. Cover with a tea towel to keep warm as you continue cooking. Wipe out pan between each chappati so any burnt ghee isn't cooked into the next.

6 Serve immediately.

500 g stoneground wholemeal flour
1/2 teaspoon sea salt
25 ml vegetable oil

300 ml warm water
75 g ghee, melted

2 teaspoons Paramount's Garam Masala
(page 34)

Chappatis with garam masala

Chappati is the flatbread typical to India, Pakistan and Malaysia, where it is known as roti. It is often made and cooked

by streetside vendors and at market stalls and is a staple and essential part of the daily diet. You can buy

the large, flat cast-iron pan used to cook this bread from Indian kitchenware shops.

1 Warm caramelised onion gently in a saucepan.

2 Mix flour, salt and nigella seeds in bowl of an electric mixer fitted with a dough hook.

3 Dissolve yeast and castor sugar in warm water. Stir warm onion and yoghurt into yeast mixture, then immediately pour into flour and knead with dough hook on medium speed for 15 minutes.

4 Cover bowl with plastic film and a tea towel and allow to rise at room temperature until dough has doubled in volume, about 1 hour.

5 Punch down dough, then knead by hand for a few minutes until smooth and elastic. Divide dough in two and roll each piece into a round loaf and transfer to a baking tray. Dust lightly with rice flour.

6 Glaze dough with egg yolk and allow to rise at room temperature until doubled in volume a second time, about 20 minutes.

7 Meanwhile, preheat oven to 200°C. Bake loaves for 15 minutes until bread sounds hollow when tapped on its base. Cool on a wire rack. Best eaten warm and fresh.

1 cup Caramelised Onion (page 342)
500 g bread flour
1 teaspoon sea salt
2 teaspoons nigella seeds

20 g fresh yeast
1 teaspoon castor sugar
150 ml warm water

$^{1}/_{2}$ cup thick plain yoghurt
 (at room temperature)
fine rice flour
1 egg yolk

Onion nigella bread

This bread is fabulous with spicy food, pickles and chutneys. The yoghurt keeps the bread moist and soft-textured

and the spice gives a kickstart of heat. The bread can also be baked as thin breadsticks to use as

a base for a spicy canapé.

1 Dry-roast cumin, coriander and fennel seeds, separately, over gentle heat until fragrant. Cool, then grind separately to a fine powder.

2 Melt ghee in a saucepan and fry garlic and ginger over gentle heat until fragrant, about 2 minutes. Do not let aromatics colour. Stir in ground spices and cook for 30 seconds, then remove from heat.

3 Blend flour, baking soda, salt and spiced ghee in a food processor until mixture resembles breadcrumbs. Add water and blend until dough forms a ball.

4 Rest dough in a plastic bag for 30 minutes at room temperature.

5 Preheat oven to 170°C.

6 Roll dough into a long sausage and cut into 6 pieces. Roll out each piece on a lightly floured surface until about 3 mm thick. Cut dough into desired shapes and arrange on a baking tray lined with baking paper.

7 Bake for 15 minutes until crackers are crisp and golden. Cool on a wire rack.

8 Store in an airtight container for up to 2 days – the crackers can be reheated in a gentle oven to warm before serving, if desired.

1 teaspoon cumin seeds	4 cloves garlic, minced	250 g plain flour
1 teaspoon coriander seeds	1 teaspoon minced ginger	$\frac{1}{2}$ teaspoon baking soda
$\frac{1}{2}$ teaspoon fennel seeds	1 teaspoon ground turmeric	1 teaspoon sea salt
75 g ghee	$\frac{1}{2}$ teaspoon chilli powder	125 ml water

Curry crackers

These are great little bite-sized crackers to serve with snacks, drinks and yoghurt-based relishes or sauces.

1 To make the starter, blend flours and water in bowl of an electric mixer fitted with a dough hook (or mix by hand). Knead with dough hook on low speed for 15 minutes until soft and sticky. Transfer starter dough to a large bowl and cover with a damp tea towel. Leave dough in a draught-free place at room temperature for 2 days if you live in a warm climate and 3 days if you live in a colder climate – keep tea towel slightly damp throughout this time. The dough should rise only slightly but will give off a mildly acidic, yeasty aroma.

2 To make the bread dough, put flours, salt and pepper into bowl of an electric mixer fitted with a dough hook and stir to combine. Add starter dough and water and knead with dough hook on low speed for 30 minutes.

3 Cut a piece of dough (about a quarter of the whole) and set it aside in a bowl, covered. (This is the starter for the next loaf – you must feed it with flour and water, as you did to make the original starter dough, every second day. Set bowl aside at room temperature for 2 days or refrigerate for 5 days. If you refrigerate starter, allow it to come back to room temperature completely before kneading. This will take about 5 hours.)

4 The remaining dough will be quite wet, soft and sticky, more so than regular bread dough. Do not be alarmed by how difficult it is to handle.

5 Line a buttered bread tin with baking paper, then position remaining dough in tin and slash top a couple of times with a razor blade or sharp knife to allow bread to expand during proving and baking. Cover with a damp tea towel and allow dough to rise at room temperature until doubled in volume for anything up to 24 hours, depending on air temperature and humidity.

6 Preheat oven to 175°C. Bake loaf for 45–50 minutes until golden brown and bread sounds hollow when tapped on its base. Cool on a wire rack. The bread should have a perceptible acidic aroma, a firm chewy crust and irregular air holes in the centre.

Starter dough
300 g stoneground unbleached flour
100 g rye flour
250 ml warm water

Bread dough
400 g stoneground unbleached flour
200 g rye flour
1 teaspoon sea salt

1 teaspoon freshly ground black pepper
350 ml warm water

Pepper sourdough

Making sourdough is a time-consuming, unpredictable art form. Made from a starter culture that ferments slowly and gives a slightly sour flavour, it is the most difficult bread to master. It's like having a child: the starter needs constant nurturing, feeding, patience and handling. If you ignore or mistreat it, it will die. But the feeling of success when you master the process is worth any amount of angst. This recipe has been adapted from the methods used by France's most prominent baker, Lionel Poilâne. I add pepper to the dough to spice it up as I like to serve the bread with cheese. You can experiment with different types and grades of flour, but I suggest you try a good-quality stoneground unbleached flour first.

1 Mix dry ingredients, then blend in a food processor with liquids to make a crumbly dough. Work dough on a bench until it comes together in one mass.

2 Roll in plastic film and rest at room temperature for 1 hour.

3 Preheat oven to 160°C.

4 Cut dough into 6 pieces, then roll each piece through the rollers of a pasta machine, starting at the widest setting and rolling until each sheet has passed through the finest setting. Sprinkle dough with a little extra flour as you go to prevent sticking.

5 Cut sheets into desired shapes and arrange carefully on a baking tray without overlapping.

6 Bake crackers for 8–10 minutes until crisp and slightly coloured.

7 Cool on a wire rack, then store in an airtight container.

220 g plain flour
1 teaspoon freshly ground black pepper, sifted

½ teaspoon sea salt
1 teaspoon castor sugar
50 ml strained lemon juice

100 ml water
50 ml olive oil

Pepper crackers

We make these wafer-thin biscuits at the Restaurant to serve with cheese. They are wonderful with aged cheddar, gruyère, washed rind and blue cheeses. Quince paste completes the taste sensation. (See photograph opposite.)

1 Mix flour, polenta, chilli flakes and salt in bowl of an electric mixer fitted with a dough hook. Dissolve yeast and castor sugar in warm water. Whisk eggs and add to yeast mixture.

2 Add yeast mixture to flour and knead with dough hook on medium speed for 15 minutes.

3 Cover bowl with plastic film and a tea towel and allow dough to rise at room temperature until doubled in volume.

4 Punch down dough and knead by hand for a few minutes.

5 Divide dough in half, then roll each piece into a ball and flatten the top. Glaze with egg yolk, then sprinkle lightly with extra polenta and slash top twice diagonally with a sharp knife or razor.

6 Preheat oven to 220°C.

7 Transfer loaves to a baking tray and allow to rise at room temperature until doubled in volume a second time.

8 Bake loaves for 20 minutes until bread sounds hollow when tapped on its base. Cool on a wire rack.

500 g bread flour	2 teaspoons sea salt	275 ml warm water
250 g fine polenta	30 g fresh yeast	2 large (61 g) eggs (at room temperature)
2 teaspoons chilli flakes	1 teaspoon castor sugar	1 egg yolk

Chilli cornbread

This bread has a denser texture than regular bread and keeps well for a few days. Even when this bread is a few days old, you can brush it with oil and grill it on the barbecue or chargrill. Spread it with a mild chilli jam or relish, add your favourite topping and away you go! Use fine ground polenta in the dough or the bread will feel quite gritty in the mouth.

(See at top left of photograph on page 278.)

1 Mix water, yeast and honey in a bowl.

2 Mix flour and salt in bowl of an electric mixer fitted with a dough hook. Add yeast mixture to flour, then knead with dough hook on low speed for 15 minutes until dough is firm, shiny and elastic.

3 Cover bowl with plastic film and a tea towel and allow dough to rise at room temperature until doubled in volume, 45 minutes–1 hour.

4 Punch down dough, then knead by hand briefly and divide into 12 pieces. Form each piece into a ball, then roll out into 5 mm thick rounds.

5 Transfer rounds to a lightly floured baking tray and allow dough to rise slightly a second time, about 10 minutes.

6 Preheat oven to 225°C.

7 Press your fingers into dough to make a few indentations and brush dough with olive oil. Bake for 10 minutes until bread is pale brown.

8 Remove from oven and sprinkle with za'atar while still hot. Best eaten warm and fresh.

600 ml lukewarm water
50 g fresh yeast
50 ml honey, warmed

750 g stoneground unbleached flour
$^1/_2$ teaspoon sea salt
extra-virgin olive oil

2 tablespoons Za'atar (page 37)

Flatbread with za'atar

This is a type of pita bread, the flatbread popular in the Middle East and Mediterranean. An alternative way of serving the bread is to bake it without brushing it with oil and to serve it with a dish of extra-virgin olive oil and another dish of za'atar for dipping, so people season the bread themselves as they go. You can also serve hot Turkish bread, Lebanese lavash or Italian focaccia the same way. *Flatbread and Flavours: A Baker's Atlas* by Jeffrey Alford and Naomi Duguid is well worth consulting if you want to explore the art of flatbread-making more thoroughly. (See at bottom of photograph on page 278.)

1 Mix flour, salt and spices in bowl of an electric mixer fitted with a dough hook.

2 Gently warm milk and water together to blood temperature, then remove from heat and mix in yeast and castor sugar. Add yeast mixture to flour, then mix in beaten eggs and knead with dough hook on medium speed for 15 minutes until dough is elastic and shiny.

3 Cover bowl with plastic film and a tea towel, then let dough rise at room temperature until doubled in volume, about 40 minutes.

4 Meanwhile, make the caramel sauce by bringing all ingredients to a boil in a saucepan. Remove from heat and pour into a 30 cm square buttered tin.

5 Punch down dough, then knead by hand for a few minutes. Divide dough into 4 pieces and roll each one out to make a 24 cm square. Brush surface with a little melted butter and sprinkle with some brown sugar. Roll dough into a log and cut into 4 pieces.

6 Sit dough rolls on top of caramel in tin with cut edge facing up. Continue until you have rolled all the pieces of dough and they have been positioned in the tin. Be sure there are slight gaps between each roll so that they can expand while proving. Brush tops with melted butter.

7 Preheat oven to 200°C. Cover tin with a tea towel and let buns rise at room temperature for 15 minutes.

8 Bake for 20 minutes, then check the centre of a roll with a skewer. If it is a little sticky, cover tin with foil and bake a few extra minutes.

9 Turn cooked buns out of their tin onto a plate and let the caramel sauce soak through the hot buns. Best eaten while still warm – if you can wait that long!

500 g plain flour	125 ml water	*Caramel sauce*
pinch of sea salt	30 g fresh yeast	500 g brown sugar
1 teaspoon freshly ground cinnamon	25 g castor sugar	500 ml golden syrup
2 cloves, freshly ground	2 large (61 g) eggs, beaten	125 g unsalted butter
1/2 teaspoon freshly ground allspice	butter, melted	
125 ml milk	brown sugar	

Spiced sticky buns

These finger-lickin' good treats, an old American classic, were baked every day at our Paramount Store during its brief assault on Sydney life. That is another story, but we used to bake a double batch so that the morning staff could have their share before the buns made their appearance centre stage. All were usually sold within a couple of hours – the regulars knew the routine. Our waistlines are probably better off these days without such indulgences, but the memories linger.

1 Slice figs, dates and apricots into a bowl, then add raisins. Pour in boiling water to cover fruit and leave for 5 minutes. Strain fruit, discarding water.

2 Mix flour, salt, spices and reconstituted fruit in bowl of an electric mixer fitted with a dough hook.

3 Dissolve yeast and brown sugar in warm milk, then stir in beaten egg. Add yeast mixture to flour, then knead with dough hook on medium speed for 20 minutes until dough is firm, shiny and elastic.

4 Cover bowl with plastic film and a tea towel and allow dough to rise at room temperature until doubled in volume.

5 Punch down dough, then knead by hand for a couple of minutes. Divide dough in half and roll each piece into a rectangle. Put loaves into buttered bread tins and glaze with egg yolk, then allow to rise at room temperature until doubled in volume a second time.

6 Meanwhile, preheat oven to 200°C. Bake loaves for 20 minutes until bread sounds hollow when tapped on its base. Cool on a wire rack.

50 g dried figs	500 g bread flour	25 g fresh yeast
50 g pitted dates	1 teaspoon sea salt	100 g brown sugar
100 g dried apricots	$\frac{1}{2}$ teaspoon freshly ground cinnamon	250 ml warm milk
100 g seedless raisins	$\frac{1}{4}$ teaspoon freshly grated nutmeg	1 large (61 g) egg, beaten
boiling water	$\frac{1}{2}$ teaspoon freshly ground allspice	1 egg yolk

Spiced fruit bread

This is a bread you either make for breakfast to have with lashings of pure butter or to have with poached fruits and lots of

clotted cream for dessert, whatever your preference. Either way, it tastes fantastic and is very straightforward to make.

1 Infuse saffron in the boiling water for 5 minutes for colour to develop. Meanwhile, mix yeast and castor sugar into the warm water and allow to stand for a few minutes.

2 Mix saffron water, milk, eggs and melted butter until combined.

3 Mix flour and salt in bowl of an electric mixer fitted with a dough hook. With the dough hook turning slowly, add yeast mixture first and then pour in saffron mixture.

4 Knead dough for 25 minutes until shiny, firm and elastic.

5 Cover bowl with plastic film and a tea towel and allow dough to rise at room temperature until doubled in volume, about 1 hour.

6 Turn dough onto a lightly floured bench and knead by hand for 5 minutes, working the excess flour from bench into dough thoroughly.

7 Divide dough in half and roll each piece into an oval shape, then transfer to an oiled baking tray and brush with egg wash. Allow loaves to rise at room temperature a second time until doubled in volume, about 30 minutes.

8 Meanwhile, preheat oven to 200°C.

9 Bake loaves for 25–30 minutes until bread sounds hollow when tapped on its base. Cool on a wire rack.

1 teaspoon saffron threads	200 ml warm water	600 g bread flour
50 ml boiling water	100 ml warm milk	2 teaspoons sea salt
30 g fresh yeast	2 eggs, beaten	egg wash
2 teaspoons castor sugar	60 g unsalted butter, melted	

Saffron bread

Saffron gives this rich loaf, somewhere between bread and brioche, a wonderful colour and an even better flavour.

It can be made into loaves or small buns, whichever you prefer.

(See at top right and centre of photograph opposite.)

1 Combine flour, ground almonds, salt and half the castor sugar in bowl of an electric food mixer fitted with a dough hook.

2 In another bowl, dissolve yeast in warm milk with remaining sugar and ground cardamom. Whisk eggs.

3 Add yeast mixture to flour with dough hook on low speed, then add eggs and knead on high for 5 minutes or until dough appears elastic.

4 Continue kneading on high and add butter in small chunks until thoroughly combined and dough is smooth and shiny.

5 Transfer dough to a lightly greased bowl, then cover with plastic film and allow to rise at room temperature until doubled in volume, about 45 minutes.

6 Punch down dough, then roll or knead by hand for a few minutes.

7 Butter and sugar your chosen moulds (either one loaf tin or 6 small brioche moulds), then shape dough accordingly and place in tin(s). Allow dough to rise again at room temperature until doubled in volume.

8 Meanwhile, preheat oven to 190°C.

9 Bake small brioches for 12 minutes and a large loaf for 20–25 minutes. If serving immediately, turn hot brioches straight onto plates. Otherwise, allow brioches to cool slightly in their tins, then turn out onto a wire rack to cool.

200 g plain flour	15 g fresh yeast	3 large (61 g) eggs
50 g ground almonds	50 ml warm milk	250 g unsalted butter, softened
pinch of sea salt	seeds from 2 green cardamom pods,	
60 g castor sugar	ground	

Spiced almond brioche

I make this brioche when apricots, nectarines and yellow peaches are in season. I poach the fruit in a light sugar syrup with

a hint of cardamom and vanilla and serve it with the brioche and pure thick cream for an ethereal taste combination.

I'm sure it's on the menu in heaven!

1 To make the brioche, combine flour, 1 tablespoon of the castor sugar, ground cardamom and salt in bowl of an electric mixer fitted with a dough hook.

2 Mix yeast into warm milk with remaining sugar in another bowl. Whisk eggs in another bowl again. Add yeast mixture to flour with dough hook on low speed, then add eggs and turn speed to high. Knead for 5 minutes or until dough appears elastic.

3 Continue kneading on high and add butter in small chunks until thoroughly combined and dough is smooth and shiny. Transfer dough to a greased bowl and cover with plastic film.

4 Allow dough to rise at room temperature until doubled in volume, about 45 minutes.

5 Punch down dough, then knead by hand briefly and roll out into a rectangle about 32 cm × 24 cm.

6 Spread marmalade over dough, then roll up into a roulade and transfer to a buttered 24 cm bread tin. Cover tin with a tea towel and allow brioche to rise again at room temperature until doubled in volume, about 30 minutes.

7 Preheat oven to 180°C.

8 Bake brioche for 20–25 minutes until golden and cooked through – it should sound hollow when base is tapped. Turn brioche out of tin and cool on a wire rack. If serving warm, allow brioche to sit for a few minutes before slicing.

1 cup good-quality cumquat
  marmalade

Cardamom brioche
250 g plain flour
2 tablespoons castor sugar
seeds from 8 green cardamom pods,
  ground

pinch of sea salt
10 g *or* 2 teaspoons fresh yeast
50 ml warm milk
2 large (61 g) eggs
150 g unsalted butter, softened

Cardamom brioche with cumquat marmalade

This brioche is baked with the cumquat marmalade inside it. You can, however, make the cardamom brioche as a loaf,

then slice and toast it and spread it with the marmalade. Serve the cardamom brioche with

Pickled Cumquats (see page 54) for yet another taste sensation.

DESSERTS

DESSERTS   Sugar and spice are natural partners in the food world, coming together to perfection in the refined, silky textures of desserts. Sugar and spice are as old as time itself and are synonymous with edible luxury.   SUGAR AND SPICE are agents of preservation and enhance the intensity of the perfume and flavour of fruits. Sugar and spice bring a sensuality to food, conjure up exotic images and provoke a sense of awe and mystery.   SUGAR AND SPICE unite a symphony of flavours, unleashing in their very finest state the same emotions as beautiful music. Sugar and spice incite passion and excite the palate.

1 Scrape seeds from vanilla bean into milk in a saucepan, then add bean and bring to a simmer over very low heat. The slower the infusion, the better the flavour.

2 Whisk egg yolks and castor sugar in a bowl until pale and creamy, then whisk in hot milk mixture.

3 Stand bowl over a saucepan of gently simmering water and cook, stirring, until mixture coats back of a spoon.

4 Strain custard through a fine-meshed sieve into a clean bowl and discard vanilla bean. Allow to cool. The custard should be speckled with the minute vanilla seeds.

5 Stir cream into cooled custard, then churn in an ice-cream machine according to manufacturer's instructions until firm. Freeze in a sealed container.

2 vanilla beans, split	6 large (61 g) egg yolks	500 ml pouring (35%) cream
500 ml full-cream milk	150 g castor sugar	

Vanilla ice-cream

Vanilla ice-cream is perhaps the definitive ice-cream of all time, so please don't get cheap and use vanilla essence or the imitation variety. This ice-cream demands the flavouring only available from the spectacular little seeds of the vanilla bean.

1 Bring milk to a simmer in a saucepan over very low heat.

2 Whisk egg yolks and castor sugar in a bowl until pale and creamy, then whisk in ginger juice followed by the hot milk.

3 Stand bowl over a saucepan of gently simmering water and cook, stirring, until mixture coats back of a spoon. Strain custard through a fine-meshed sieve into a clean bowl. Allow to cool.

4 Stir cream and candied ginger into cooled custard, then churn in an ice-cream machine according to manufacturer's instructions until firm.

5 Freeze in a sealed container.

450 ml full-cream milk
6 large (61 g) egg yolks

150 g castor sugar
50 ml Ginger Juice (page 342)

500 ml pouring (35%) cream
75 g candied ginger, minced

Candied ginger ice-cream

Wonderful with tropical fruits such as mango, pineapple, custard apple, lychees and rambutans to name a few.

Try it, too, with freshly baked gingerbread (see page 307) or waffles and golden syrup.

1 Heat tangelo juice in a stainless steel saucepan over low heat until reduced by half.

2 In another saucepan, bring sugar syrup and tangelo zest to a simmer.

3 Remove from heat and strain out zest.

4 Whisk eggs until light and creamy in an electric mixer, then slowly pour in hot sugar syrup mixture with beaters operating. Whisk in reduced tangelo juice, ground cardamom and orange-flower water.

5 Allow to cool.

6 Whisk cream into cooled tangelo custard, then churn in an ice-cream machine according to manufacturer's instructions until firm.

7 Freeze in a sealed container.

500 ml strained tangelo juice
400 ml Sugar Syrup (page 343)
zest of 2 tangelos

5 large (61 g) eggs
seeds from 4 green cardamom pods,
    ground

50 ml orange-flower water
500 ml pouring (35%) cream

Tangelo cardamom ice-cream

This is a variation of the orange cardamom ice-cream included in *Paramount Desserts*. The pungent, sweet spiciness of the cardamom combines beautifully with the tangelo. Make this during the winter months when tangelos are in season, or substitute blood-orange or mandarin juice for a slightly different flavour.

1 Bring milk and star anise to a simmer in a saucepan over very low heat. The slower the infusion, the better the flavour.

2 Whisk egg yolks and castor sugar in a bowl until pale and creamy, then whisk in hot milk mixture.

3 Stand bowl over a saucepan of gently simmering water and cook, stirring, until mixture coats back of a spoon. Strain custard through a fine-meshed sieve into a clean bowl and discard star anise.

4 Allow to cool.

5 Stir cream into cooled custard, then churn in an ice-cream machine according to manufacturer's instructions until firm.

6 Freeze in a sealed container.

500 ml full-cream milk
3 star anise, broken

6 large (61 g) egg yolks
150 g castor sugar

500 ml pouring (35%) cream

Star anise ice-cream

My time spent working with Phillip Searle taught me, among other things, how to incorporate the delicate flavour of spices into dessert work. This ice-cream forms part of his sensational, definitive chequerboard ice-cream. I make it to serve with caramelised oranges, Spiced Pineapple (see page 313), toffeed apples or young coconut flesh.

1 Bring milk and cassia bark to a simmer in a saucepan over very low heat. The slower the infusion, the better the flavour.

2 Whisk egg yolks and castor sugar in a bowl until pale and creamy.

3 Whisk in hot milk mixture.

4 Stand bowl over a saucepan of gently simmering water and cook, stirring, until mixture coats back of a spoon. Strain custard through a fine-meshed sieve into a clean bowl and discard cassia bark.

5 Allow to cool.

6 Stir cream into cooled custard, then churn in an ice-cream machine according to manufacturer's instructions until firm.

7 Freeze in a sealed container.

500 ml full-cream milk
1 tablespoon cassia bark, broken into
    small pieces

6 egg yolks
150 g castor sugar

500 ml pouring (35%) cream

Cassia ice-cream

Perfect with Cinnamon-baked Apples (see page 292) or any other apple preparation that incorporates

the warmth of cinnamon.

1 To make the sambuca ice-cream, bring milk and anise seeds to a simmer in a saucepan over very low heat. The slower the infusion, the better the flavour. Whisk egg yolks and castor sugar in a bowl until pale and creamy, then whisk in hot milk mixture.

2 Stand bowl over a saucepan of gently simmering water and cook, stirring, until mixture coats back of a spoon. Strain custard through a fine-meshed sieve into a clean bowl and discard anise seeds. Allow to cool.

3 Stir sambuca and cream into cooled custard, then churn in an ice-cream machine according to manufacturer's instructions until firm. Half-fill your chosen mould or moulds with ice-cream, then freeze.

4 Melt chopped liquorice in water over gentle heat in a saucepan to make a wet paste. It may be necessary to add a little extra water as you go to achieve a paste. Allow to cool slightly.

5 Brush liquorice paste over surface of sambuca ice-cream in mould(s), then freeze. Reserve remaining liquorice paste.

6 To make the mace ice-cream, bring milk and mace to a simmer in a saucepan over very low heat. The slower the infusion, the better the flavour. Continue making ice-cream following instructions for sambuca ice-cream.

7 Spoon mace ice-cream over sambuca layer until mould(s) are full, then freeze for 30 minutes.

8 Brush liquorice paste over surface of ice-cream and freeze again.

9 To serve, dip mould(s) into hot water to loosen, then carefully turn out ice-cream.

100 g liquorice sticks, diced
200 ml water

Sambuca ice-cream
500 ml full-cream milk
$^{1}/_{2}$ teaspoon anise seeds
6 egg yolks
25 g castor sugar
100 ml sambuca
400 ml pouring (35%) cream

Mace ice-cream
500 ml full-cream milk
2 teaspoons crushed mace blades
6 large (61 g) egg yolks
175 g castor sugar
500 ml pouring (35%) cream

Mace and sambuca ice-creams with liquorice

I layer these ice-creams with liquorice paste to give the dessert definition and for a more formal presentation, paying homage to the masterly skill of Phillip Searle's famous chequerboard ice-cream once again. Any shaped mould, large or small, can be used. In fact, the quantities given make more than enough for half-a-dozen small moulds as well as a large log, if that's the way you'd like to go. The moulded ice-cream is wonderful to eat in its own right but is also spectacular with Pears Poached in Spiced Red Wine (page 301) or spiced blood plums.

Choose good-quality liquorice from a gourmet food store, if possible.

1 Cook milk and cardamom seeds in a wide-based saucepan on a heat mat over extremely low heat, stirring regularly to prevent sticking and a skin from forming, until milk has reduced to 750 ml. This will take about 3 hours. The milk must not boil but should simmer very gently. If you try and speed up the process the result will not be the same.

2 Pass thickened milk mixture through a fine-meshed sieve and discard cardamom pods.

3 Stir palm sugar and nuts into hot milk and blend in a food processor.

4 Allow to cool.

5 Pour cooled mixture into kulfi moulds and freeze until firm.

6 To serve, dip moulds into hot water to loosen, then carefully turn out ice-cream. Serve with extra freshly chopped pistachio nuts when in season and, if desired, wrap ice-cream in edible silver leaf.

2 litres full-cream milk	75 g palm sugar, shaved	edible silver leaf (optional)
seeds from 8 green cardamom pods, cracked	25 g shelled pistachio nuts, chopped	

Kulfi ice-cream

An Indian iced confection, kulfi is eaten as a snack or served as a dessert with a garnish of edible silver leaf. It is made without eggs or cream and gets its creamy texture from reduced milk that is then flavoured with nuts, spices or saffron. Traditionally, small silver or aluminium conical moulds with a lid or cap are used. In *Harvest of the Cold Months*, Elizabeth David writes: 'The kulfi mould is in fact almost identical with the tall conical ice-cream mould which in Europe became known as a bombe mould. Did European confectioners take it as a pattern from the Persians and Indians? Or was it the seventeenth-century Indian imitation of the European ice mould?' Whichever, we are the beneficiaries of these inventions.

(See photograph opposite.)

1 Preheat oven to 180°C. Very finely dice 3 of the apples and dice half the butter. Mix diced apple and butter with candied citron, ground cinnamon and half the brown sugar and stuff remaining apples.

2 Arrange stuffed apples in a buttered ovenproof dish and add cinnamon sticks. Cut remaining butter into 6 slices and put a piece on top of each apple. Sprinkle remaining brown sugar over apples, then pour on golden syrup.

3 Bake apples, covered with foil, for 30 minutes, basting with sauce from dish every 10 minutes to keep moist and glazed. Test apples with a skewer – they are cooked when golden and softened but still holding their shape.

4 Remove cinnamon sticks from caramelised cinnamon sauce in dish. Put an apple on each plate, then pour over sauce and serve with cassia ice-cream.

9 braeburn apples, peeled and cored
90 g cold unsalted butter
6 teaspoons minced candied citron

1 teaspoon freshly ground cinnamon
60 g brown sugar
3 sticks cinnamon

200 ml golden syrup
1 quantity Cassia Ice-cream (page 288)

Cinnamon-baked apples with cassia ice-cream

Perfect in early winter when the apples are crisp and full of flavour and showing no signs of having been in cold storage.

The spices heighten the flavour of the apples even further.

1 Bring all ingredients except pears to a boil in a wide, heavy-based saucepan over moderate heat. Reduce to a simmer and cook over low heat for 15 minutes.

2 Peel, halve and core pears and add to cooking liquid.

3 Cover pears with a sheet of baking paper to keep submerged for even cooking and to avoid discoloration. Poach for 20 minutes or until soft.

4 Remove pears carefully from pan and set aside.

5 Increase heat and reduce saffron liquid to a syrup. Strain syrup through a fine-meshed sieve, discarding whole spices. Scrape vanilla seeds into syrup, then pour syrup over pears.

6 Serve pears warm or at room temperature.

1 litre Sugar Syrup (page 343)	50 ml Poire William eau-de-vie	1 teaspoon saffron threads
375 ml Sauternes *or* other dessert wine	3 mace blades	zest of 2 oranges
50 ml orange-flower water	1 vanilla bean, split	6 William *or* Josephine pears

Saffron pears

The intoxicating fragrance and flavour of saffron works wonderfully with pears. Saffron pears can be served just as they are or complemented by a fragrant ice-cream or sorbet, a moist almond cake or brioche. This recipe comes from *Paramount Desserts*, where the pears were teamed with orange cardamom ice-cream. They go equally well with Tangelo Cardamom Ice-cream (see page 286).

1 Bring all ingredients to a boil in a large stainless steel stockpot. Reduce heat to a simmer and cook for 1 hour or until plums lose their shape and become mushy.

2 Press contents of pot through a conical sieve, extracting as much juice as possible and discarding solids.

3 Pour sauce into hot, sterilised jars and seal.

4 Cool, then refrigerate.

2 kg blood plums, halved and stoned
1 litre water
1 kg castor sugar

100 ml brandy
150 ml cassis
1 vanilla bean, split

1 stick cinnamon
3 cloves
2 mace blades

Spiced blood plum sauce

Make this sauce in late summer when blood plums are plentiful and at their peak, then refrigerate it in sealed jars and use it to spice up desserts through the winter months. I like it with fruit tarts, baked brioche or cake, waffles and Vanilla Ice-cream (see page 284), fruit crumbles and so on. It is equally delicious served warm or cold.

1 Remove stems from cherries. Bring all ingredients except cherries to a boil in a wide, heavy-based saucepan, then simmer for 30 minutes.

2 Strain liquid, discarding spices.

3 Return liquid to rinsed-out pan, then bring to a boil and reduce to a simmer. Add cherries and simmer gently for 15 minutes, stirring occasionally to keep fruit covered with liquid.

4 Spoon cherries and their syrup into hot, sterilised jars and seal. Refrigerate for up to a few months.

5 To serve, remove stones from cherries. Reduce liquid over heat to a syrup and pour over fruit.

2 kg sweet black cherries
1 litre Sugar Syrup (page 343)
2 pieces lemon zest

1 stick cinnamon
1 vanilla bean, split
3 mace blades

300 ml cherry brandy
75 ml brandy
75 ml kirsch

Brandied cherries

Cherries are one of summer's most longed-for fruits, and their flavour lends an incomparable versatility and vitality

to desserts. I cook the cherries whole to retain their shape and juices, then pit them as needed

after they are removed from the syrup.

1 To make the tokay pepper syrup, bring all ingredients to a boil in a stainless steel saucepan, then simmer for 15 minutes until liquid has reduced by a quarter to become a light syrup.

2 Strain syrup through a fine-meshed sieve, then discard spices.

3 Cut peaches, nectarines and plums in half, then remove stones.

4 Arrange fruit on a baking tray, cut-side up. Add cherries to tray and sprinkle fruit with demerara sugar. Grill fruit for 5 minutes until it starts to caramelise.

5 Spoon some tokay pepper syrup over fruit and cook for a further 3–4 minutes.

6 Arrange fruit on plates, then spoon over syrup and serve with slices of brioche toast or little meringues and thick cream.

3 yellow peaches
3 nectarines
6 blood plums
250 g cherries, pitted
1/4 cup golden demerara sugar

Tokay pepper syrup
1 litre liqueur tokay
300 ml Sugar Syrup (page 343)
2 tablespoons coarsely cracked black
    peppercorns

2 teaspoons freshly cracked
    allspice
1 stick cinnamon
1 vanilla bean, split

Peaches, nectarines, plums and cherries with tokay pepper syrup

A bowl of summer stone fruit is one of the most divine desserts imaginable, in my mind. Choose perfectly ripe fruit and a good-quality liqueur tokay for the best results. (When I'm being really decadent, I use Campbell's Liquid Gold thirty-year-old tokay from Rutherglen in Victoria's North-East.) (See photograph opposite.)

1 Zest and juice lemon and orange. Bring all ingredients except peaches to a boil in a wide, heavy-based pan, then simmer gently for 30 minutes.

2 Add peaches and poach very gently for 10 minutes, turning fruit regularly with a spoon to prevent discoloration. When soft, remove peaches from syrup with a slotted spoon.

3 Allow to cool enough to handle, then peel.

4 Bring poaching liquid back to a boil and reduce to a syrup over moderate heat.

5 Remove pan from heat and pass syrup through a fine-meshed sieve, discarding solids.

6 To serve, cut peaches in half and remove stones, then pour over Sauternes syrup.

1 lemon	1 litre Sugar Syrup (page 343)	1 stick cinnamon
1 orange	200 ml Grand Marnier	12 white peaches, washed
1 litre Sauternes *or* other dessert wine	2 vanilla beans, split	

Sauternes peaches

Use the perfect white peaches of mid-summer for this sublime dish – and take it to even greater heights by adding lychees
and raspberries to the syrup when serving. To be extravagant, cook the peaches in the French wine of
the Rhône region – perhaps Muscat de Beaumes de Venise – and drink the wine with the dessert.
Your tastebuds will be in a state of nirvana!

1 Bring all ingredients except pears to a boil in a wide, heavy-based saucepan, then simmer for 15 minutes to allow flavour to intensify and liquid to reduce slightly.

2 Peel, halve and core pears, then arrange carefully in liquid. Cover pears with baking paper and simmer gently until cooked and softened, about 30 minutes.

3 Remove pears from poaching liquid, cut in half again and set aside.

4 Reduce poaching liquid over medium heat to a syrup. Strain syrup through a fine-meshed sieve, discarding solids. Allow to cool, then pour over poached pear quarters and refrigerate.

750 ml Sugar Syrup (page 343)
1 tablespoon minced ginger
1 stick cinnamon

1 teaspoon freshly ground
  allspice
150 ml Stone's Green Ginger Wine

250 ml Poire William eau-de-vie
6 beurre bosc pears

Spiced ginger pears

This is one of my preferred methods of preparing pears during winter, and one of my favourite flavour combinations.

Serve the pears unadorned or with warm gingerbread (see page 307), brioche or crème brulée.

1 Preheat oven to 150°C.

2 Bring all ingredients except quinces to a boil in a wide, heavy-based pan, then reduce heat to a mere simmer.

3 Peel quinces, then cut them in half lengthwise, leaving their cores and seeds intact.

4 Put quinces into simmering liquid, then press a sheet of baking paper over fruit and cover with a lid. Transfer pan to oven and poach gently for 7–8 hours until fruit is soft and red.

5 Carefully remove fruit from syrup with a slotted spoon and transfer to hot, sterilised jars. Strain syrup, then pour over fruit until covered.

6 Seal jars and refrigerate for up to 3–4 months.

7 As you need to use the fruit, remove it from its syrup and cut away core and seeds. The poaching liquid can be reduced over heat until thick and syrupy and served as a sauce.

2 kg castor sugar	1 stick cinnamon	6 quinces
3 litres water	2 cloves	
2 star anise	1 lemon, thickly sliced	

Spiced quinces

Cooking quinces has become a necessary ritual of mine in early autumn when this fruit is ripe and plentiful. Quinces make

a wonderful partner for many of the sweet spices – they seem to belong so naturally together – yet the fruit is often eyed

with suspicion. Perhaps it is because the quince is perceived as being an old-fashioned, inhospitable fruit

as it cannot be eaten in its raw state. The secret lies in perseverance and patience: cook quinces slowly

and their character, flavour and texture change completely to reveal a hidden beauty.

1 Bring all ingredients except pears to a boil in a stainless steel saucepan, then simmer for 5 minutes.

2 Peel pears, then arrange in a saucepan in an upright position so that wine just covers them.

3 Reduce heat, then cover pan with a lid and simmer for 25 minutes or until pears are soft. Remove cooked pears with a slotted spoon and set aside.

4 Reduce spiced wine over heat by half until the consistency of syrup. Strain syrup through a fine-meshed sieve, then pour over pears and serve.

750 ml shiraz
200 ml crème de cassis
250 g castor sugar
4 mace blades

2 sticks cinnamon
$1/4$ teaspoon freshly grated nutmeg
5 cloves
5 allspice

1 vanilla bean, split
zest of 1 lemon
zest of 1 orange *or* tangerine
6 firm beurre bosc *or* Josephine pears

Pears poached in spiced red wine

When prepared in this manner, the pears take on an ethereal, translucent glow and have the appearance of beautiful ruby

jewels. They can stand on the plate alone and unadorned or be served with a spiced ice-cream such as Mace (see page 289)

or Cassia (page 288), or with Cinnamon Clotted Cream (page 306).

1 Cut pomegranates in half and remove seeds.

2 Reserve half the seeds for serving, then press remaining seeds through a sieve to make pomegranate juice. Stir pomegranate juice into rosewater syrup.

3 Hull strawberries and cut in half lengthwise.

4 Toss strawberries and reserved pomegranate seeds in a bowl, then stir through rosewater syrup and serve.

3 pomegranates   90 ml Rosewater Syrup (page 263)   750 g strawberries

Strawberries and pomegranate seeds with rosewater syrup

This is a very simple and light fruit salad to have at the completion of a rich, spice-laden dinner.

The flavours are sweet and sour; the textures are soft yet crunchy – very refreshing.

1 Roughly chop apples, including peels and cores. Bring chopped apple and apple juice to a boil in a large saucepan over gentle heat, stirring regularly to prevent sticking.

2 Pour contents of pan into a conical sieve positioned over another pan, then press as much apple and juice as possible through sieve, using a large wooden spoon.

3 Discard any solids that remain in sieve.

4 Add brown sugar, spices and lemon zest to apple purée and cook over gentle heat for 45 minutes until thickened.

5 Ladle apple butter into sterilised jars, then seal and refrigerate.

2 kg Granny Smith apples
350 ml sparkling apple juice
250 g dark brown sugar

seeds from 6 green cardamom pods, ground
1 teaspoon freshly ground cinnamon

$^{1}/_{2}$ teaspoon freshly grated nutmeg
1 teaspoon minced lemon zest

Apple cardamom butter

Make this versatile fruit butter to have on hand to add to a tart or baked pastry, to spread on brioche or toast,

or to flavour a winter pudding. Try making the butter with apricots, the flavour of which

is also wonderfully enhanced by cardamom.

1 To prepare the spiced plums, quarter plums, removing stones. Melt butter with brown sugar in a frying pan, then stir in spices and cook for 1 minute. Add plums and cook for 5 minutes over moderate heat, tossing to coat with spiced butter, until fruit has softened but is still holding its shape. Remove pan from heat and allow plums to cool completely.

2 To make the frangipane, cream butter and castor sugar, then add egg and mix well. Stir in ground almonds and flour, then refrigerate for 1 hour.

3 Position 2 sheets of filo pastry, one on top of the other, on a bench, longest side facing you. Brush edges with melted butter, then fold edge closest to you over by 5 cm. Spread 2 teaspoons frangipane down centre of folded pastry and sit 6 plum slices on top. Sprinkle with 1 teaspoon pistachio spice mixture.

4 Fold pastry over to enclose plums, then tuck in edges about 2 cm. Brush with more butter and continue to roll pastry until cigar shaped, then brush with butter again. Continue making pastries (leave some pistachio spice mixture for decorating later on). Put finished pastries, perfect-side up, onto a buttered baking tray and refrigerate.

5 Preheat oven to 175°C and bake pastries for 10–12 minutes until golden. Remove tray from oven, then brush pastries generously with rosewater syrup and sprinkle with remaining pistachio spice mixture. Warm spiced plum sauce gently, then spoon some onto each plate. Position a pastry on sauce and serve immediately.

12 sheets filo pastry	*Spiced plums*	*Frangipane*
125 g butter, melted	9 blood plums, peeled	60 g unsalted butter
1 quantity Pistachio Spice Mixture	25 g unsalted butter	60 g castor sugar
(page 263)	1 tablespoon brown sugar	1 egg
100 ml Rosewater Syrup (page 263)	2 cloves, freshly ground	60 g ground almonds
250 ml Spiced Blood Plum Sauce	2 allspice, freshly ground	2 teaspoons plain flour
(page 294)	pinch of freshly ground cinnamon	
	pinch of freshly grated nutmeg	

Baked plum and pistachio pastries with spiced plum sauce

These cigar-shaped pastries are hot favourites of mine, and, like most things, are easy to assemble once the base

components have been prepared. The spices work to lift and lighten the whole taste sensation.

(See photograph opposite.)

1 Preheat oven to 180°C.

2 To make the crumble mixture, combine all dry ingredients, then rub in butter.

3 Combine ground cinnamon and castor sugar and fold carefully through clotted cream, then refrigerate.

4 Halve and peel plums, then remove stones and slice fruit.

5 Arrange sliced plums in individual (or one large) buttered gratin dishes, then spoon over some plum sauce and top with crumble mixture.

6 Stand gratin dishes on a baking tray and bake for 7–8 minutes only, just enough to warm plums (a large dish will need a little longer).

7 Transfer gratin dishes to a hot griller and cook for 5–6 minutes until crumble softens and colours under the heat. Serve immediately with cinnamon clotted cream.

1 teaspoon freshly ground cinnamon
2 teaspoons castor sugar
$^1/_2$ cup clotted cream
18 blood plums
120 ml Spiced Blood Plum Sauce
   (page 294)

Crumble mixture
50 g fresh brioche crumbs
50 g plain flour
50 g roasted hazelnuts, ground
60 g brown sugar
$^1/_2$ teaspoon freshly ground cinnamon

$^1/_4$ teaspoon freshly grated nutmeg
minced zest of 1 lemon
75 g unsalted butter, softened

Spiced plum crumble with cinnamon clotted cream

This dessert is full of warming flavours and textures. It's a feel-good, down-home dish, and ever so easy to prepare!

1 To make the gingerbread, preheat oven to 160°C and grease and line a 15 cm square cake tin. Sift flour, baking powder, ground ginger and ground cinnamon into a bowl.

2 Melt butter with golden syrup and brown sugar in a saucepan over moderate heat. Whisk eggs with milk, crème fraîche and candied ginger in a bowl, then stir in melted butter mixture.

3 Stir egg mixture into spiced flour until combined.

4 Pour batter into prepared tin and bake for 35 minutes or until cooked through – test centre with a skewer. Leave cake in tin for 5 minutes, then turn out onto a wire rack to cool.

5 To make the caramel sauce, cook brown sugar in a saucepan over high heat until it starts to caramelise. Stir in cream and cook for about 5 minutes over moderate heat, then whisk in butter, a little at a time, until sauce has thickened. Remove sauce from heat and keep warm.

6 To serve, cut 6 × 8 cm squares of gingerbread. Warm pears gently in some of their syrup, then sit 2 pear halves on top of each square of gingerbread and spoon over caramel sauce.

7 Serve immediately.

1 quantity Spiced Ginger Pear halves
  (page 299)

Gingerbread
175 g self-raising flour
$^1/_2$ teaspoon baking powder
2 teaspoons ground ginger
1 teaspoon freshly ground cinnamon

100 g unsalted butter
70 ml golden syrup
125 g dark-brown sugar
2 large (61 g) eggs, beaten
125 ml full-cream milk
2 tablespoons crème fraîche
2 teaspoons minced candied ginger

Caramel sauce
300 g dark-brown sugar
250 ml pouring (35%) cream
200 g cold unsalted butter, diced

Gingerbread with pears and caramel sauce

This is the epitome of comfort food; it combines childhood textures with grown-up flavours.

1   To prepare the apricots, bring all ingredients except apricots to a boil in a wide-based saucepan. Add apricots to syrup and simmer over gentle heat for 20 minutes until fruit has softened, stirring regularly. Remove 12 apricots, leaving remaining fruit in syrup for colour and flavour. Allow the 12 apricots to cool, then halve fruit and remove stones. Set aside until ready to serve.

2   Cook apricot syrup over high heat until reduced by a third to a thicker syrup. Strain syrup through a fine-meshed sieve, discarding solids, and allow to cool.

3   To make the cardamom cream, bring cream and cardamom pods to a simmer in a saucepan over low heat. Whisk egg yolks and castor sugar in a bowl until pale and creamy, then whisk in hot cream. Stand bowl over a saucepan of gently simmering water and cook, stirring, until cream is thick and coats back of a spoon.

4   Soak gelatine in a little cold water until softened, then squeeze out excess water and stir into hot cream. Strain cream through a fine-meshed sieve into a bowl, then stir ground cardamom into cream. Press plastic film down onto cream to stop a skin forming. Sit bowl of cream over a bowl of ice-cubes and refrigerate until set.

5   Preheat oven to 160°C. Line a rectangular tin 32 cm long × 24 cm wide × 4 cm deep with baking paper and lightly grease paper with hazelnut oil.

6   To make the meringue, beat egg whites until stiff peaks form, then gradually beat in castor sugar until meringue is thick and glossy. Fold in vanilla, vinegar and cornflour. Spread meringue into prepared tin with a spatula and bake for 20 minutes. Allow to cool in tin for a few minutes, then turn out onto a sheet of baking paper dusted with icing sugar. Allow to cool for 10 minutes.

7   Spread cardamom cream over meringue and add a few poached apricots. Roll meringue carefully into a roulade using baking paper to keep it firm. Wrap with plastic film and refrigerate on a tray for 3 hours before serving.

8   To serve, cut meringue into thick slices, then top with remaining apricots and drizzle around some apricot syrup.

hazelnut oil
icing sugar, sifted

Poached apricots
1 litre Sugar Syrup (page 343)
10 green cardamom pods, cracked
1 vanilla bean, split
375 ml Sauternes *or* other dessert wine
125 ml brandy
20 apricots

Cardamom cream
400 ml thick (45%) cream
12 green cardamom pods, cracked
6 large (61 g) egg yolks
50 g castor sugar
1 gelatine leaf
seeds from 2 green cardamom pods,
   ground

Soft meringue
250 g *or* 10 egg whites
375 g castor sugar
2 teaspoons pure vanilla essence
2 teaspoons white vinegar
2 teaspoons cornflour

Apricot meringue with cardamom cream

This version of the soft meringue roulade I love so much uses apricots when they are at their peak in summer.

You can also use the same flavours with a traditional pavlova.

(See photograph opposite.)

1 Whisk eggs and castor sugar until pale and creamy. Stir in orange zest, orange juice, ground cardamom and cream, then refrigerate overnight.

2 Make pastry as instructed, then line a 24 cm flan tin and blind bake as instructed.

3 Strain egg mixture through a fine-meshed sieve and discard solids.

4 Preheat oven to 160°C.

5 Put cooked tart shell on a baking tray, then arrange halved dates over base of tart and gently pour in egg mixture. Bake for 30 minutes or until custard has set.

6 Remove cooked tart from oven and allow to cool for 3 hours before removing it from its tin.

7 Slice tart into wedges to serve.

4 large (61 g) eggs
180 g castor sugar
zest of 2 oranges

120 ml strained orange juice
seeds from 4 green cardamom pods,
    ground

150 ml pouring (35%) cream
1 quantity Sweet Pastry (page 345)
18 fresh dates, halved and pitted

Orange, date and cardamom tart

This dessert, with its Middle Eastern flavours, first appeared in *Paramount Desserts* but begs for a place in this chapter because of its obvious spice content. Oranges and cardamom are natural and easy partners in the flavour spectrum, which is why they are often combined in sweet confections. You could substitute tangelos, blood oranges, mandarins or clementines for the oranges.

1 Preheat oven to 180°C.

2 Cut quinces into thin slices lengthwise.

3 Starting from the centre of each pastry round, arrange quince slices around pastry, slightly overlapping them as you go. Mix sugar and cinnamon, then dust fruit.

4 Bake galettes for 15 minutes until pastry is puffed and golden.

5 Warm 200 ml syrup from spiced quinces and serve with hot pastries.

1 quantity Spiced Quinces (page 300)
6 × 15 cm rounds puff pastry

1 tablespoon golden demerara sugar

2 teaspoons freshly ground cinnamon

Baked quince and cinnamon galettes

A galette is a fine tart with ethereal light layers of pastry and fruit. For a special spice treat, add a scoop of Mace Ice-cream (see page 289) to the centre of each tart as you serve them.

1 Melt ghee in a frying pan and cook pineapple, vanilla bean and star anise over moderate heat until caramelised slightly. Stir in rum, sugar and honey and cook for another 5 minutes.

2 Remove pan from heat and discard vanilla bean and star anise.

3 Strain pineapple and serve warm. (If making the pina colada mousse on page 319, reserve juices for making the accompanying syrup. Allow juices to cool completely, then remove layer of fat – it will cloud syrup if left.)

4 If using pineapple in another preparation, allow to cool completely.

50 g ghee
600 g diced fresh pineapple
1 vanilla bean, split

2 star anise
40 ml dark rum
2 tablespoons brown sugar

2 tablespoons honey

Spiced pineapple

Pineapple and star anise make a heady combination, especially when teamed with the warm flavours of rum and honey.

This versatile concoction (see photograph opposite) can be enjoyed with Star Anise Ice-cream (see page 287), used in tarts

(see Glazed Pineapple and Star Anise Tarts on page 314) or can become part of a more elaborate preparation,

such as Pina Colada Mousse with Spiced Pineapple and Coconut Wafers (page 319). Look for the fabulous

Bethonga pineapples from southern Queensland for a truly exquisite result.

1 Make pastry as instructed, then line 6 × 12 cm flan tins and blind bake as instructed.

2 To make the star anise cream, bring cream and star anise to a simmer in a saucepan over low heat.

3 Whisk egg yolks and castor sugar in a bowl until pale and creamy, then whisk in hot cream. Stand bowl over a saucepan of gently simmering water and cook, stirring, until cream is thick and coats back of a spoon.

4 Soak gelatine in a little cold water until softened, then squeeze out excess water and stir into hot cream.

5 Strain cream through a fine-meshed sieve into a bowl, then press plastic film down onto cream to stop a skin forming. Sit bowl of cream over a bowl of ice-cubes and refrigerate until set.

6 To assemble, half-fill tart shells with spiced pineapple, then fill with star anise cream. Smooth surface of cream, then sprinkle with demerara sugar and glaze with a blow torch or brulée iron until sugar caramelises. Remove tarts carefully from their tins and serve immediately.

1 quantity Sweet Pastry (page 345)	*Star anise cream*	6 large (61 g) egg yolks
½ quantity Spiced Pineapple (page 313)	400 ml thick (45%) cream	50 g castor sugar
2 tablespoons golden demerara sugar	2 star anise, broken	1 gelatine leaf

Glazed pineapple and star anise tarts

The success of this tart relies on the flavour of the fantastic Bethonga pineapples that are grown in southern Queensland. They are extremely sweet and juicy and respond well to being cooked briefly with spices. Roughie pineapples work just as well for flavour. You need a blow torch or brulée iron to caramelise these tarts – both are available from good kitchenware suppliers.

1 Bring cream and ginger to a simmer in a saucepan over low heat.

2 Whisk egg yolks and castor sugar in a bowl until pale and creamy, then whisk in hot ginger cream. Stand bowl over a saucepan of gently simmering water and cook, stirring, until custard thickens and coats back of a spoon.

3 Stand bowl over a bowl of ice-cubes and whisk until cool.

4 Pour cream into 6 × 100 ml deep pots and refrigerate until set, about 2 hours.

5 To serve, sprinkle cream with a fine layer of demerara sugar and caramelise with a blow torch or hot brulée iron. Peel lychees, then halve fruit and remove seeds.

6 Stand brulées on plates and serve with lychees alongside.

350 ml thick (45%) cream	6 large (61 g) egg yolks	6 teaspoons golden demerara sugar
40 g minced ginger	50 g castor sugar	18 fresh lychees

Ginger crème brulées with lychees

A classic dessert given a hint of spiciness with ginger. I sometimes partner this rich cream with crisp shortbread studded with candied ginger – similar flavours but a contrasting texture. Fortune cookies, available from Asian food stores, make an easy accompaniment, too. Small baked madeleine cakes flavoured with candied ginger are another alternative.

1 Juice and zest orange.

2 Bring sugar syrup, spices and orange zest to a boil in a saucepan, then reduce heat and simmer for 15 minutes. Add orange juice and liqueur and simmer for a further 10 minutes.

3 Allow syrup to cool completely to allow flavour of spices to infuse – overnight, if you have the time.

4 Strain syrup through a fine-meshed sieve, discarding solids. Bring strained syrup to a boil, then add figs and poach gently for 7–8 minutes until figs have softened but are still holding their shape. Stir regularly during cooking to ensure figs are covered with liquid.

5 Remove pan from heat and allow figs to cool to room temperature in syrup.

6 To serve, remove figs from cooled syrup, then cut in half.

7 Arrange figs on plates with raspberries and spoon syrup over fruit.

1 orange	1 stick cinnamon	75 ml Grand Marnier *or* Cointreau
400 ml Sugar Syrup (page 343)	1 vanilla bean, split	12 large black figs
2 star anise, broken	5 allspice, freshly cracked	400 g raspberries

Fig and raspberry compote

A simple summer treat which features two fruits that harmonise beautifully.

1 To make the cake, preheat oven to 160°C and line a 24 cm springform tin (10 cm high) with baking paper. Shave chocolate into a bowl, then add butter and melt gently over a saucepan of gently simmering water. Allow to cool.

2 Whisk egg yolks and half the castor sugar in a bowl until pale and creamy. Whip egg whites in another bowl until stiff peaks form, then slowly beat in cinnamon and remaining sugar.

3 Stir melted chocolate butter into egg yolk mixture with flour until combined, then gently fold in egg whites. Pour batter into prepared tin and bake with a water bath on the shelf below for 30 minutes or until cake has set. Test with a skewer – if it comes out clean, the cake is cooked. Remove cake from oven and allow to cool completely in tin.

4 When cake is cool, press cake to edges of tin to make sure the surface is even and cake is hugging sides ready for the mousse layer to be added.

5 To make the chocolate mousse, melt chocolate in a bowl over a saucepan of gently simmering water, then allow to cool. Whisk egg yolks and castor sugar in a bowl until pale and creamy, then whisk in cooled melted chocolate. Whip cream, then gently fold in cinnamon and fold this in turn into chocolate base.

6 Whisk egg whites until stiff peaks form, then fold into chocolate base carefully. Do not overbeat or mousse will lose its volume and become dense. Spoon mousse on top of cake in tin and spread evenly. Refrigerate for 3 hours until set and firm.

7 To make the cinnamon cream, whip cream with castor sugar and cinnamon until stiff. Spread a thin layer of cinnamon cream on top of chocolate mousse. Remove tin and baking paper and smooth edges of mousse and cream with a palette knife. Cut cake into wedges with a hot, sharp knife to serve.

Chocolate cake
200 g dark couverture chocolate
200 g unsalted butter, diced
6 large (61 g) eggs, separated
300 g castor sugar
1 teaspoon freshly ground cinnamon
25 g plain flour

Chocolate mousse
120 g dark couverture chocolate
3 large (61 g) eggs, separated
30 g castor sugar
100 ml thick (45%) cream
1 teaspoon freshly ground cinnamon

Cinnamon cream
200 ml thick (45%) cream
1 tablespoon castor sugar
1 teaspoon freshly ground cinnamon

Cinnamon chocolate mousse cake

Many spices are masked by the cloying, fatty nature of chocolate, which is why you don't often find chocolate recipes that use them. But this elegant chocolate cake lends itself beautifully to gentle spicing. If you want a more elaborate dessert, top the cake with chocolate curls or flakes. Remember to use the best-quality couverture chocolate – it makes all the difference to the final flavour.

1 Preheat oven to 180°C and butter and sugar 6 × 150 ml (5 cm deep × 8 cm wide) dariole or pudding moulds. Sit moulds in a deep-sided baking dish. Slice dates and arrange with candied ginger over bases of moulds.

2 Bring golden syrup, ginger wine and liquid glucose to a boil in a saucepan and simmer for 5 minutes. Allow syrup to cool, then pour over fruit in moulds to cover.

3 To make the puddings, beat egg yolks and castor sugar in an electric mixer until pale and creamy. With beaters on medium speed, add melted butter, then pour in ginger juice and milk. Sift flour and baking powder, then fold into egg mixture. Whisk egg whites until stiff, then fold into batter. Spoon pudding mixture into prepared moulds until full.

4 Pour hot water into baking dish until it comes halfway up sides of moulds, then cover dish with foil. Bake for 15 minutes, then rotate dish to ensure even cooking, and bake another 15 minutes. Remove moulds from their water bath and allow to cool for a few minutes before turning out.

5 While the puddings are cooking, make the ginger custard. Bring cream, milk, ginger and ginger wine to a simmer in a saucepan over low heat. Whisk egg yolks and castor sugar until pale and creamy, then whisk in hot ginger cream. Stand bowl over a saucepan of gently simmering water and cook, stirring, until custard coats back of a spoon. Strain custard through a fine-meshed sieve into a clean bowl, discarding ginger.

6 To serve, run a small knife around edges of puddings to loosen them, then turn out onto serving plates.

7 Spoon hot ginger custard around puddings and serve immediately.

9 fresh dates, halved and pitted
6 teaspoons minced candied ginger
65 ml golden syrup
30 ml Stone's Green Ginger Wine
30 ml liquid glucose

Sponge puddings
3 large (61 g) eggs, separated
100 g castor sugar
25 g butter, melted
2 teaspoons Ginger Juice (page 342)
160 ml full-cream milk
200 g self-raising flour
1 teaspoon baking powder

Ginger custard
500 ml pouring (35%) cream
200 ml full-cream milk
1 tablespoon chopped ginger
50 ml Stone's Green Ginger Wine
8 egg yolks
150 g castor sugar

Steamed date and candied ginger sponge puddings with ginger custard

Little sponge puddings to serve during winter – a time when we yearn for rich, warm and filling treats.

Serve these puddings as soon as they are made for the best results.

1 To make the coconut bavarois, bring milk and shredded coconut to a simmer over low heat. The slower the infusion, the better the flavour. Whisk egg yolks and castor sugar until pale and creamy, then slowly whisk in hot milk and coconut. Stand bowl over a saucepan of gently simmering water and cook over medium heat, whisking continuously, until custard coats back of a spoon.

2 Soften gelatine in cold water, then squeeze out excess water and stir gelatine into custard until dissolved. Strain custard through a fine-meshed sieve into another bowl and discard coconut. Stand bowl over another bowl of ice-cubes and whisk until cool. Whisk whipped cream into cooled custard. Spoon bavarois into 6 × 150 ml dariole moulds until half-full, then refrigerate until set.

3 Make the spiced pineapple as instructed, reserving 1 tablespoon pineapple and cooking juices for pineapple syrup. Spoon cooled pineapple over bavarois and refrigerate.

4 To make the star anise bavarois, follow instructions for making coconut bavarois, then spoon into moulds over pineapple to fill. Refrigerate for at least 3 hours.

5 To make the pineapple rum syrup, bring all ingredients except reserved pineapple to a boil in a saucepan, then simmer over moderate heat until reduced to a syrup. Remove from heat and stir in reserved pineapple. Allow to cool completely.

6 Make the coconut wafers as instructed.

7 To serve, dip moulds into hot water for 20 seconds, just enough to loosen each bavarois, then turn out onto plates and spoon pineapple syrup around. Sit a wafer over each bavarois to conceal it. Push freshly shaved coconut into top of wafers, leaving some protruding. Serve immediately.

$^1/_2$ quantity Spiced Pineapple (page 313)
$^1/_4$ cup freshly shaved coconut, shredded
6 Coconut Wafers (page 345)

Coconut bavarois
110 ml full-cream milk
25 g shredded coconut
2 egg yolks
75 g castor sugar
$^3/_4$ gelatine leaf
125 ml thick (45%) cream, whipped

Star anise bavarois
100 ml full-cream milk
2 star anise, broken
2 egg yolks
50 g castor sugar
1 gelatine leaf
125 ml thick (45%) cream, whipped

Pineapple rum syrup
250 ml dark rum
150 ml strained fresh pineapple juice
375 ml Sugar Syrup (made with
  brown sugar) (page 343)
200 g castor sugar
reserved juices from $^1/_2$ quantity Spiced
  Pineapple (page 313)
1 tablespoon Spiced Pineapple (page 313)

Pina colada mousse with spiced pineapple and coconut wafers

This dessert comes from the early summer menu at Paramount and epitomises the fresh flavours of that time of year,

while also being a parody of the popular Caribbean cocktail. I admit it has quite a few components,

but with the preparation undertaken in advance, it takes only seconds to serve.

WINE AND SPICE

THERE HAS BEEN quite a lot of noise made in the past that there can be no relationship between wine and spiced food. I find this a lazy response to a challenge, and operate on the premise that the two form a perfect partnership when considered with care, intelligence, a good palate and an open mind. How often have you read that beer is the only alcohol to drink with spicy food? There have been recent, ground-breaking advances made by cooks and vintners alike to dispel this myth. The starting point is determining the character and flavour of the food and/or wine, how they feel on the palate, how they interact together. One should taste to understand the layers of flavours; the fullness of the palate; the acid, sweet, sour components; the complexity. ❖ WINES ARE MADE to enhance the flavour of food, and your palate should be seduced equally by the taste of the food and the wine. While there can be guidelines and suggestions, there are no prescribed hard and fast rules. Taste is a subjective pleasure, a response to personal preference. When I am looking for a perfect match between wine and food, I taste the food first to get a feel for the flavours, balance and structure of the dish. Then I look for a wine that completes the palate, that carries the flavours through and doesn't fall short, that is harmonious with the specific ingredients in the dish. I choose a few different wines and then taste each one with the food to see which adds to the length of palate, works in harmony with the flavours and best highlights the character of the wine. GETTING THE PERFECT MATCH In the past, there has been a tendency to adopt a certain set of prescribed rules, the primary one being that white wine goes with fish, seafood and chicken, and red wine goes with red meat. This axiom, however, is too broad and inflexible to apply in every case, as the protein in a dish is only one aspect of that dish. There must be room for variance. For example, how many times have you read on a wine label or in a wine review that the wine is 'best drunk with chicken'? Chicken in cream sauce? Chicken satay? Chicken with tamarind? Chicken curry? Chicken chasseur? There are a million and one recipes for chicken and they all taste different. It would be almost impossible to find a wine that matched every chicken dish in existence. What must be considered is the richness, the acidity, the tannic structure and the length of palate of the wine, and how it will enhance or detract from what you are eating. Just as a full-bodied wine can over-power a subtle or delicately flavoured dish, fresh, pungent, acidic food with chilli heat can overshadow and reduce to inconsequence a soft, mellow or buttery wine. ❊ AUSTRALIAN FOOD TODAY draws on many different influences, styles and tastes and the food I like to cook – in particular, the food contained in this book – relies on balance and harmony. It is essential that the wine chosen to accompany the food has the ability to be drawn to the elements in the food, not to overpower or be overpowered by them. When tasting wine with food, it is vital that the wine flavours be allowed to 'weave in and out'. It often helps to think of wine as another ingredient in a recipe. A curry paste is a combination of spices and aromatics that complement and balance each other, one ingredient not overriding another. Likewise, wine is a further ingredient, added afterwards in the mouth, that balances with all the other elements. ❊ AN OBVIOUS EXAMPLE of incorrect matching in an Australian context is the successfully marketed love affair with chardonnay. Big, rich, buttery and wood-driven, this wine variety tastes bitter, unpleasant and merely alcoholic when paired with heav-ily spiced food or food with clean acidic flavours or sour and salty flavours. A nasty chemical reaction occurs in the mouth, with a full-on war between zesty fresh flavours and the buttery richness of the wine. I would suggest that in most instances, the food found in this book is better suited to any other wine variety than chardonnay. (The scenario is quite different when you consider the lighter, 'drink-now' varieties of chardonnay that respond more sympathetically to complex spicy flavours.) MORE THAN ONE MATCH? Winemaking in Australia has gained as much global attention as our food and cooking, if not more. Our innovative approaches show that we have adopted the principles of the old world and adapted them to a unique, intrinsically Australian style that many practitioners around the world are now trying to emulate. On the whole, vintners in Australia are responding positively to their market and to food trends, which is why we are seeing a return in popularity of lesser-utilised wine varieties. ❊ SEVERAL FACTORS need to be taken into consideration when choosing wine to go with food. Regional variations for particular varietals mean that we need to consider style as much as basic characteristic flavour and place of origin. For example, an aged, barrel-fermented semillon from the Barossa Valley has a rich, toasty palate – very different to a lively, lemony, fresh young unwooded semillon from the Hunter Valley. It is important to consider how a wine has been cellared and for how long, and to realise that two totally different wines can be matched to the same dish. There have been many times at the Restaurant when we have matched particular food equally well with both a rich white wine and a light, fruitier red wine. Crab and Coconut Salad with Chilli and Pickled Green Mango (see page 85) has been paired equally well with a sparkling rosé, a viognier and a floral-style riesling. Similarly, Seared Beef Fillet with Lemongrass (see page 81) has been perfectly matched with a floral riesling, a grenache and a sparkling rosé, and quail pastries (see page 252) have worked beautifully with both a South Australian grenache rosé and a rich Barossa semillon. ❊ SUCH ARE THE VAGARIES of taste that a wine tasted with food often alters the perception of the wine. Sometimes the best wine in a line-up is not the best match with the food; similarly, a wine which may not be entirely desirable to sit back and quaff is often transformed into a perfect match with a particular dish. The most important considerations are the flavour and weight of the food and finding a wine with qualities that match those elements. SOME BASIC RULES In her *Oxford Companion to Wine*, Jancis Robinson suggests some basic rules for food and wine matching: 'White wines generally (although not universally) taste more acid than red wines, so it makes sense to serve them with simple fish dishes which would normally call for the sort of acidity in lemon juice or vinegar.' This principle extends to flavours such as lemongrass, lime, tamarind and acidic spices. Robinson continues: 'All dry wines taste horrible with sweet foods which seem to emphasise their acidity.' This applies to sweet or richly spiced food where the acid element in the wine would be emphasised. For example, the Spicy Masala Sauce (see page 64) that accompanies Lamb with Roasted Cumin Crust (see page 186) has a rich, sweet, complex flavour which would not sit comfortably with a fresh young sauvignon blanc; a shiraz with sweet ripe fruit and underlying spiciness would be better suited. ❋ IN HIS BOOK *Red and White*, Australian wine writer Max Allen supports my theory by saying: 'I'm going to throw the vinous cat among the gastronomic pigeons and say that when it comes to putting food and wine together, everything really depends on how the food has been cooked.' In fact, he goes on to say that most spicy foods are wine-friendly, giving many specific suggestions and combinations. We certainly need more of this kind of thinking, discourse and power of suggestion to the public palate, for the benefit of both our food and wine industries.

AS A GENERAL GUIDE, I have briefly outlined some Australian varietals – by no means an exhaustive list – with regional variations and ageing characteristics, and suggested flavours that could be matched with them. Experiment, have faith and trust in yourself, and find the food and wine combination that suits your palate, remembering that they enhance each other. ✳

THE WORLD OF FOOD AND WINE is an exciting, never-ending journey of discovery: explore it, learn and listen, taste – but most of all, enjoy it.

chardonnay

This is currently the most widely consumed and grown white grape variety in the country. It is very important to the Australian wine industry for both domestic consumption and the export market. It is a most likeable wine, achieving good ripeness and rich levels, and the ability to be manipulated by vintners to achieve many different results. However, it is not the only wine on the market – a surprise to some people – and it can be very difficult to match well with some foods, especially foods with hot, spicy, pungent flavours. Using chardonnay as the example of a 'food wine' (a wine best consumed with food, as opposed to a wine best quaffed or drunk by itself), many wine critics and writers have stated that 'spicy food and wine simply do not go'. Hopefully, by the time you have read this section I will have proved that theory wrong, but I guess the test is in the tasting, so try for yourself. Remember, I am giving you my personal preferences – not a blueprint for what is absolutely correct or not!

Here is not the place to go into all the different treatments of this grape – such as malolactic fermentation, lees contact and different barrel treatment. It is sufficient to say that chardonnay appears in many different guises. While they held a presence in earlier decades, unoaked or unwooded chardonnays developed a strong trend during the early 1990s. They were initiated onto the recent market by Australia's first Master of Wine, Michael Hill Smith, in partnership with Martin Shaw, and madly copied by many other vintners. These are wines made to drink now, easy to quaff and relatively easy to match with food. It is interesting that Michael Hill Smith should now comment that unoaked chardonnay may prove to have one of the shortest product life cycles in marketing history!

I like the chardonnays produced in Victoria and Tasmania and some specific examples from Western Australia. These are the ones I seek out to match with the more mellow elements of my food, as they seem to show more versatility. The big, rich, buttery chardonnays with generous oak and high viscosity do not sit well with fresh, lively, spicy flavours, as the fruit in the wine is masked and altered by the oak treatment. However, I have found many dishes I cook to be compatible with lighter-style chardonnays. Sichuan-spiced Duck and Seared Scallops (see page 74) works equally well with either a cooler-climate chardonnay or a big, buttery, full-bodied Hunter Valley chardonnay with its warmer-climate fruit; Tea-smoked Tasmanian Salmon (page 128) sits beautifully with a richer-style chardonnay; and a ripe younger variety works well with Saffron-braised Scallops with Spiced Tomato Chilli Pickle (page 134), where the spicy oak elements in the wine are picked up and extended by the food flavours. Some varieties of chardonnay also come alive with the toasty, nutty flavours of sesame, which feature in Soy-braised Chicken with Sesame Noodles (page 238), for example.

gewürztraminer

This white wine variety is instantly recognisable for its extremely aromatic nose and palate. Known for its heavy scent of lychees and roses, it is a full-bodied wine with a pungent quality – an ideal match for chilli and the stronger, pungent spices. It is not widely grown in Australia, since warmer areas like the Hunter Valley can produce overly fat and oily wines or, if picked too early, wines which do not have the full aromatic pungency gewürztraminer should achieve. Some cooler areas of Victoria, the Clare Valley and Tasmania are now showing what can be done with this variety in Australia, with some dry styles in evidence.

Gewürztraminer is very much a food wine: it is a little too overpowering to drink on its own due to its full-bodied and highly aromatic nature. The more aromatic and sweeter styles work well with tropical, intense food flavours because of the wine's exotic fruitiness, while the drier-style gewürztraminer is a more delicate wine with a good structure that can withstand many headily pungent and aromatic dishes, such as Chilli Mudcrab (see page 116), Fremantle Sardine Fillets Stuffed with Pancetta, Capers and Burghul with Salsa Verde (page 115) and Masala Lobster (page 118).

pinot gris

This is a relatively new white grape variety in Australia, transplanted from Alsace in France. It produces a rich, ripe style of wine with good length of palate. A popular variety in northern Italy as well, it is known there as 'pinot grigio' and has a lighter, drier style than its French cousin. To date, there are only a few vintners in Australia – in Victoria and Tasmania – producing either of these varieties. However, given our interest in producing wines to match our food, it is only a matter of time before we see this wine fully realise its potential. You can determine the style of the wine by the name ('gris' or 'grigio') and information given on the label.

I came across this variety a couple of years ago when visiting Washington State and Oregon in the USA, where the pinot gris in particular has a spicy fruit character and is received with great popularity. It seemed a natural and equal partner to many of the spicy seafood and fish dishes I ate at restaurants there, so on my return home I endeavoured to source it in Australia and feature it at Paramount because of its compatibility with my particular style of food. The grape produces a crisp, rich style with melon flavours and a dry, full-bodied spiciness that lends itself to a diverse range of spicy and aromatic flavours. One of my favourite dishes to serve with this wine is Oxtail Consommé (see page 109). Others include Spiced Rock Lobster and Saffron Soup (page 106), Chicken Laksa (page 104) and Seaweed Noodles with Pacific Oysters and Coriander Pesto (page 236).

riesling

Riesling is an elegant wine which shows great versatility and harmony with food. It should be one of the most popular wines in Australia, whether drunk in its youth or with bottle age, but in some parts of the country there has been resistance to its virtues, due to past mismanagement and maybe also because of many people's obsession with chardonnay. Clare Valley and Eden Valley in South Australia and the Great Southern district of Western Australia have elevated this grape variety to a world-class standard. In many ways, riesling is the great unsung hero of the wine world, the cornerstone of our white-wine industry. Made mainly as a 'dry style' with long, almost searing acidity in its youth, it is a wine that gives outstanding structure to a wide range of food preparations. It can be drunk as a fresh, youthful, limey-style wine with good fruit character, but as the Clare Valley producers have shown, it develops some beautiful characteristics as it ages.

A fantastic partner to various spicy and aromatic foods, youthful rieslings are characterised by a dry citrus-fruit and aromatic nose, and a tight structure with a good clean acidity on a long finish. Light salads using fish, seafood, chicken or vegetables with a lime-juice dressing belong with such a wine. Try Grilled Moreton Bay Bug Tails (see page 91), the Paramount classic Crab and Coconut Salad (page 85), Deep-fried Spanner Crab Cakes (page 125) or Grilled Tasmanian Ocean Trout with Roasted Chilli, Shallot and Mint Salad (page 82). The clean, uncomplicated taste of Steamed Chicken with Green Garlic Ginger Relish (page 162) is another favourite.

An aged riesling produces a totally different flavour and nose. It smells of toast and kerosene, with well-rounded acid fruit balance on the palate and a viscosity that performs well with rich spicy flavours. I have served Tasmanian Salmon Escabèche Salad (see page 92), Spiced Scallops (page 86) and Coconut Chicken Salad (page 77) with an aged riesling, to name a few. Be careful, though: once the wine is over a decade old, its character changes again and the flavour will be lost on spicy food it may have accompanied at an earlier age.

sauvignon blanc

Sauvignon blanc is a highly acidic wine best drunk in its youth, within the first two or three years of being bottled. This wine variety has proven itself more successful in the cooler climates of Australia, like Victoria and Tasmania, with distinctive styles coming from the Adelaide Hills in South Australia. It would be inappropriate to overlook the great sauvignon blancs produced by our neighbours in Marlborough in the south of New Zealand. They have established a worldwide reputation for their wine's concentration and fruit-driven characteristics.

A wine that reflects its origins (its *terroir*) and the way it is made by individual vintners, sauvignon blanc is generally produced in the simpler and purer form without oak maturation; however, a few producers allow some oak input. The unoaked variety is known for its pungent and piercing fruit flavours, ranging from grassy passionfruit to gooseberry, and herbaceous characteristics.

As with a young riesling, the acidity of sauvignon blanc has to be considered seriously when matching the wine with spicy food. The opulent fruitiness of the wine lends itself extremely well to crisp, zippy flavours like Salt-and-pepper Oyster Fritters (see page 141), freshly shucked oysters, Chicken and Scallop Consommé (page 107) and Satay Prawn Sugarcane Sticks (page 119).

semillon

Semillon made in Australia has come to be regarded as a first-rate wine, and our vintners are claiming recognition for establishing points of difference from the same varieties grown elsewhere. According to the 1996 *Australian and New Zealand Wine Industry Journal*, 'Semillon is vying for a position as an "Australian" style. In just the same way that Australia has embraced Shiraz as its own, it is now realising that Semillon could also be adopted as a national icon, distinguishing Australian wines from the multiple contenders on the world market.' The article goes on to say that semillon wine has been given a raw deal in the past, often being used as a stock wine for white burgundy and incorrectly labelled as 'Hunter riesling'.

The characteristics of this wine variety vary greatly according to the region and the style the winemaker wants to achieve. Where the grapes have been botrytised (sweetened on the vine) before picking, they have also proven to be highly successful and shown great potential in the making of dessert wine. I find semillon quite a versatile wine and it accompanies with a gracious elegance many dishes I cook.

The Hunter Valley has established great status for its unwooded aged style of semillon. The wine from this region is usually fermented dry, with very little residual sugar. As a young wine, the crisp, lemon fruit and herbaceous nature of the grape are very much in evidence. These elements work beautifully with dishes such as Stuffed Squid with Black Ink Noodles and Ponzu Dressing (see page 114) and Crab and Lemongrass Broth (page 96), where the lemon flavours in the food enhance the same elements in the wine. A classic trait of Hunter Valley semillons is their ability to age uniquely, maintaining their fresh lemon acidity and developing into quite a full wine with lychee and lanolin properties and a capability to stand up to richer food, like Sichuan-smoked Duck with Duck Livers and Smoked Eggplant (page 161) and Tuna Pepper Steak with Spinach and Anchovy Sauce (page 133).

The Margaret River region in Western Australia also produces a very distinctive style, which is altogether different from the Hunter style. Margaret River semillon is generally made in the same unoaked fashion, but some producers use oak influence to achieve a richer style. The wines differ from other regions because of a more fruity and herbaceous presence in their youth, with sauvignon blanc properties sometimes seeming to be evident. Try Grilled Quail with Chermoula (see page 148) with this variety.

There are also the big, full-blown styles from the Barossa Valley in South Australia, where a much riper style of wine is often produced. It is frequently given generous oak treatment, resulting in lemony, buttery and nutty oak flavours. Semillon generally doesn't have a powerful fruity palate and this style of wine would not be suitable to use with strongly spiced or flavoured food. However, soft and gentle spicing can work extremely well, like with Quail Breasts Deep-fried in Beancurd Skins (see page 252).

semillon/sauvignon blanc blends

Winemaking is just like cooking. In both, the better the ingredients, the better the end result; in both, the idea is to capture the flavour of the raw materials and let that flavour shine; and in both, the art of blending is central. Max Allen says: 'Blending two or more different white varieties is quite common with unwooded wines, because the characters of each grape can combine in a way that increases the complexity of the end result.'

One criticism of semillon is that it can be a little bland on the nose and the palate, and for this reason it is often blended with sauvignon blanc. The lively acidity and pungent fruitiness of sauvignon blanc make up for the shortcomings of the richer but blander semillon grape. This blend can cope with slightly richer, spicier foods because of the wine's structural richness, and seems to match many spicy tastes and textures with a natural ease. Try Chilli Salt Squid with Sweet Grilled Eel, Black Ink Noodles and Pimiento (see page 135), Chilli Salt Beancurd with Steamed Vegetables and Blackbean Sauce (page 200) or Grilled Tasmanian Ocean Trout with Fish Crackling (page 82).

verdelho

This white variety can be characterised by its burst of passionfruit with traces of sweetness on the mid-palate, and its clean, acidic finish. It seems to be better suited to the warmer climates of the Hunter Valley in New South Wales, McLaren Vale in South Australia and Margaret River in Western Australia.

A food wine, verdelho's combined sweetness and acidity allow it to work with food elements which help to bring its overt fruitiness into line, such as lemongrass, mild chilli, kaffir lime, galangal and fennel. Try it with Salt-and-pepper Oyster Fritters with Shaved Fennel and Blackbean Dressing (see page 141), Chicken Livers with Pickled Lamb's Tongue, Mustard Spaghetti and Garlic Sauce (page 146) or Chargrilled Octopus with Saffron Rouille and Roasted Onion and Pimiento Salad (page 84).

viognier

A dry-style white wine with a good fruit acid balance, this is a grape variety originating near Lyon in the Rhône Valley in France. There are limited plantings and production in Australia to date, but the best examples come from the Barossa Valley and Eden Valley in South Australia, with a small amount being produced in Victoria and the Canberra region. Viognier has the potential to become very popular because of its flexible nature. Its recent increased presence on the market is the winemakers' response to demand for a wine that works in perfect harmony with the assertive flavours we seek in the food we cook and eat today.

At their best, these wines are rich, heady and full-bodied with apricot and musk fruit flavours and bold, spicy characteristics. They are best when young and have proven to be a highly successful match with many spicy foods, particularly ginger and chilli-based dishes. The full-bodied richness of spicy food gives the wine a fullness of palate, making it an attractive choice to serve with Crab and Coconut Salad (see page 85), Saffron-braised Scallops with Spiced Tomato Chilli Pickle (page 134), Wild Barramundi with Green Masala Sauce (page 136) and Reef Fish and Bug Tails in Spiced Coconut Milk (page 131).

cabernet sauvignon and cabernet blends

Perhaps the most extraordinary aspect of cabernet sauvignon is its ability to travel, to set down roots in distant lands and still produce something that is recognisably 'cabernet' whatever the circumstances. What makes cabernet sauvignon remarkable to taste is not primarily its flavour and aroma – the former often likened to black-currants, the latter to green capsicum – but its structure and ability to provide the perfect vehicle for individual vintage

characteristics, winemaking and elevage techniques, and local physical attributes, or *terroir*. Jancis Robinson observes: 'It is a wine variety that is extremely popular, commonly regarded as the world's most renowned grape variety, grown in every country, and in just about every region in Australia, some with more success than others, and is seen as a very attractive and approachable wine because of its ability to age well in the bottle. It is a wine that requires intelligent, careful thought when matching it with appropriate food to bring out the best characteristics of the wine.'

Cabernet sauvignon in its pure, unblended form has proven itself extremely well in South Australia's Coonawarra district, which produces a very concentrated and 'complete' wine from its terra rosa soil. These wines are robust and rich with strong tannic structure in their youth that require equally rich, strong flavours and textures in accompanying food. Gentle, warm spicing can work with these wines, like Slow-braised Beef Brisket with Spiced Potato, Preserved Lemon and Saffron Cous Cous (see page 176) or Seared Venison with Celeriac Gratin and Mushroom Mustard Sauce (page 189). Complex and overtly spicy food is lost on these wines, the combination leaving a metallic tanginess on the palate and doing both food and wine a disservice.

Some cabernet sauvignon producers are playing down the oak content and allowing softer tannins in the wines to make them more approachable to drink when young, which makes them more food-friendly as well. There is, however, a tendency to blend cabernet sauvignon with other varieties of the cabernet family such as merlot, cabernet franc and malbec. This

practice emulates what is known as the 'Bordeaux blend', often labelled as 'cabernets'. Jancis Robinson points out in the *Australian and New Zealand Wine Industry Journal* that 'the Australian Cabernet experience has been typically independent of European tradition. Rather than slavishly following the French, like the Californians did with their top château imitations, Australian winemakers showed a much less reverential policy towards blending their Cabernet.'

This process of blending serves the purpose of filling the holes left by pure cabernet sauvignon by adding more fruit roundness to the palate, softening the tannins, reducing the astringency in the taste and making the wine more complex. In this form, the cabernet blend is produced widely all over Australia. Victorian cabernet sauvignon and cabernet blends tend to be more elegant, softer and not as full-bodied as their Coonawarra cousins. Their flavour can fall away too easily when paired with much of the spicy food I cook, although they can match well with slight pepper used with rich textures in food, like Milk-fed Veal with Sweetbreads and Foie Gras (see page 180) and Seared Venison with Celeriac Gratin and Mushroom Mustard Sauce (page 189).

The Margaret River area is also renowned for good, richly concentrated cabernet sauvignon and blends. This climate seems ideal for producing cabernets of outstanding quality, with some producers using the seductive powers of the merlot grape in the blending, making very drinkable wines that are among the best in Australia. Try Cassia Beef Noodles with Spinach and Garlic Chives (see page 230), Roasted Rib of Beef with Chilli Cumin Dal (page 177) or Slow-braised Beef

Brisket with Spiced Potato (page 176) with a cabernet from this region.

Cabernet shiraz, a blend that dates back to nineteenth-century practices in France, was one of the first cabernet blends made and popularised in Australia. It established itself as a precursor to what has euphemistically become known as an 'Australian style'. More recently, as consumer demand for French-style wines with Australian characteristics has taken precedence, we have moved away from this style and vintners have concentrated their efforts on producing the classic Bordeaux blend of cabernet merlot franc.

grenache

Grenache is a widely planted grape variety throughout the world, but until quite recently was used only as a blending variety and as such was a mainstay of red-wine production in Australia. It has had a resurgence of interest, particularly in warmer, dryer climates like the Barossa Valley and McLaren Vale in South Australia.

A Barossa grenache is generally pale in colour, but this is not an indication of its flavour. Grenaches are generous, full-flavoured wines with sweet cherry fruit and liquorice hints and generally high alcohol levels. They are not the most elegant wines on the market, but their spicy character lends itself to some elements of the food spice world, such as star anise, liquorice and cassia, the classic flavours of northern Chinese food. Grenache's low tannin levels make it a good wine to match with food that has chilli and spices cooked into it. I have matched this wine with Tea-smoked Tasmanian Salmon with Star Anise Broth (see page 128), Sichuan-smoked Duck with Smoked Eggplant

(page 161), Twice-cooked Chicken with Chilli and Garlic Eggplant Salad (page 154) and Fragrant Beef Tartare (page 79).

Grenache grapes have also been used to produce a rosé style in some parts of South Australia. In this instance the skins are removed after a short maceration with the juice and before fermentation, to give faint colour. According to Jancis Robinson, the length of contact time depends on the darkness of the grape: 'While the rosé style retains the spicy character of the grape and the cherry fruit, it has a more delicate structure that cannot stand up as well as its big sister to spicy food, its palate becomes overwhelmed by the full flavours.' This wine is usually served chilled, and has more subtlety than a true grenache. I have found it to be a great partner to quail pastries (see page 252).

pinot noir

The best examples of this wonderful wine come from cooler Australian climates – warmer climates tend to make it overly sweet and jammy. Tasmania, southern Victoria, the Adelaide Hills in South Australia and, more recently, Pemberton, Western Australia, have all had great success with this grape variety due to long, slow ripening in their more gentle summer heat. Of course, the quality and taste of pinot noir depend on who makes the wine, where it is made, the vagaries of the vintage, the size of the crop, and so on, and it can be too easy to dismiss this wine if you have tasted one that is too thin and short on the palate. I think it is one of the most gorgeous, versatile, delectable and food-friendly red varieties available, so invest and experiment.

The appeal of pinot noir lies in its elusive subtlety. It is a light red wine with

sweet, cherry/strawberry fruit and soft tannins – a wine with soul. It is definitely a food wine, with its spicy, chocolate, smoky and rich characteristics, but needs to be considered carefully when matching with spicy and aromatic food. I find that pinot noir mixes terrifically with warmer, sweet spices if the wine has developed its characteristic earthy, pungent nose. I look for well-rounded, soft flavours with a gentle punch to bring out its best, such as Spiced Duck-neck Sausages with Celeriac (see page 157), Spiced Pigeon Pastries (page 244), Chicken Breasts Stuffed with Spinach, Water Chestnuts and Ginger Deep-fried in Beancurd Skins (page 262), Tea-smoked Tasmanian Salmon (page 128) and Sichuan-spiced Duck with Smoked Eggplant (page 74). Younger, fruitier-style pinot noirs are better able to withstand spicy elements in food, more so than the developed wines with more gamey and subtle characteristics. Try Braised Five-spice Duck with Shiitake Mushrooms, Garlic Chives and Rice Noodles (page 225), Stuffed Squid with Ponzu Dressing (page 114) or Tuna Pepper Steak with Spinach and Anchovy Sauce (page 133).

shiraz

Shiraz, a grape variety thought to have originated in an ancient Persian city of the same name in what is now southern Iran, has developed into one of Australia's individual styles of wine. Also known as 'hermitage' in France and 'syrah' in the United States and Spain, it is grown in most wine-growing areas of Australia and is the most planted red variety in the country. In the early days of our industry it was usually referred to by its French name, hermitage.

Shiraz gets better with age. It is usually tough and tannic when young, but can also be balanced with strong, assertive flavours to prevent that domination of the palate. The Barossa Valley has some of the oldest vines and produces a ripe, rich style of wine with a spicy backbone and good structure. This style of shiraz can be an ideal match for roasted chilli and warm, rich spices, because the sweet, blackberry-ripe fruit enhances the flavours without detracting from the wine or the food. The assertive characteristics in the wine match the bold flavours of the food. Victorian shiraz is grown in a colder climate and tends not to be as ripe or sweet, but it does have a strong black-pepper and spice element. The Hunter Valley also has an acclaimed reputation for shiraz, producing wines which tend to develop into much smoother and more leathery styles with age.

Some wine writers and critics argue about the feasibility of matching spicy food with a spicy wine. There is no decisive answer to this question: it is a concept of balance. The spices in the food must not clash with the spices in the wine – you must look for harmony on the palate. I find that by roasting and cooking spices for a long time in various preparations, they mellow and take on rich flavours and characteristics that perfectly suit the riper elements of shiraz. It is the easiest red wine to match with the spicy food I cook.

Some wonderful combinations I have had with shiraz wines include: Five-spice Duck and Shiitake Mushroom Pies (see page 260), Soy-braised Chicken with Sesame Noodles (page 238), Wild Barramundi Baked in Banana Leaf with Red Chilli Paste (page 138), Lamb with Roasted Cumin Crust, Smoked Eggplant Purée and Spicy Masala Sauce (page 186),

Duck Livers with Garam Masala Potato (page 152) and Spiced Lamb with Cardamom Rice Pilaf and Hot-and-sour Coconut Sauce (page 172). As you can see, I have a strong affinity with this wine variety – it partners much of what I cook perfectly because of its adaptability and generous flavour.

sparkling shiraz

The best examples of this wine variety come from South Australia, where many are made but only a few shine. It is made in the same way as a méthode champenoise, with producers using a mixture of older shiraz vintages. It is this blending of the older base-wine stock that separates the best from the ordinary. The blend is fermented in the bottle then left on its lees for a year, after which it is liqueured – a process that introduces a vintage port or brandy to give a touch of sweetness to what would otherwise be a bone-dry wine.

Sparkling shiraz can be a great quaffing wine, much like a champagne or a full-bodied meaty wine, consumed with food that stands up to the best the spice world can offer. I serve it with fried pastries and deep-fried crispy meat morsels like Fried Tamarind Chicken (see page 150) and Peppered Kangaroo Fillet with Nori Omelette (page 174).

zinfandel

This is a red wine just made to accompany spicy food. It is commonly regarded as an indigenous grape variety of North America, although it is related to the Italian primitivo grape. The *World Wine Encyclopedia* states: 'Whether or not this is the primitivo of southern Italy, the fact is that

in California it makes singularly unique wine and is regarded as a native grape. The style can vary from light and elegant, as in the white or rosé wines, to massive and tannic in the red wines, but the grape's intrinsic berry-like character always comes through.'

Little known as yet in Australia, a small amount of this black grape variety is being produced in the Margaret River region of Western Australia and in some parts of South Australia. It is a very popular wine in California, where I first tasted it and found it to be an exciting and natural partner to full-bodied spicy foods. Because it has not come from French stock it has never been taken seriously in the international wine arena, but its big, juicy, black-cherry flavours with spicy overtones make it well suited to rich, spicy foods. I hope we see more of this variety in our market in the future because of its great potential as a food wine. Watch this space!

Taste an Australian-made zinfandel next to an American one, pick your favourite and try matching either wine with Soy-braised Chicken with Sesame Noodles and Eggplant (see page 238), Five-spice Duck and Shiitake Mushroom Pies (page 260), Spiced Duck-neck Sausages with Celeriac, Mustard and Horseradish (page 157) or Wild Barramundi Baked in Banana Leaf with Red Chilli Paste (page 138). There are probably many other dishes that would also work magic on the tastebuds when paired with a zinfandel – it's up to you to find them out.

dessert wines

Like savoury dishes, desserts vary dramatically in flavour, texture, structure and spiciness and different desserts respond to particular wines. The unifying factor in all desserts is sugar, and it is important to remember when pairing wine with dessert that the wine should have a sweetness that withstands the sugar in the dish. Therefore, the sweeter the dessert, the sweeter the wine. We need to consider in this equation the array of dessert wines available – rich-tasting botrytis semillons ('Sauternes' in France); fruitier, more youthful, lighter-style and fresher-tasting botrytis rieslings; noble muscats; liqueur tokays and muscats made from fortified stock; light sparkling shiraz; and Champagne and Australian sparkling wines. At Paramount we match each dessert on the menu with a specific wine, so we taste various wines with each dish – just as we do for the rest of the menu – to determine which combination works the best on the palate. I can only suggest you do the same – it's a most rewarding exercise in which to indulge!

Fresh, tropical-fruit flavours such as passionfruit, pineapple, lemon and mango work well with young botrytis rieslings, while pineapple cooked with star anise can be matched with a botrytis semillon. Try Pina Colada Mousse (see page 319) or Glazed Pineapple and Star Anise Tarts (page 314). Stone fruits cooked in a sweet, spicy syrup also make wonderful companions for botrytis semillons, as do Gingerbread with Pears and Caramel Sauce (page 307), Ginger Crème Brulées (page 315) and rich coconut concoctions. Chocolate can mask the flavours of many dessert wines because of its fatty nature, but its taste comes alive when matched with the musky floral overtones of a liqueur muscat or noble muscat.

If a fruit has been cooked in a particular wine, it makes sense to drink the same style of wine with the food. For example, Peaches, Nectarines, Plums and Cherries with Tokay Pepper Syrup (page 296) would be matched with a liqueur tokay, while Pears Poached in Spiced Red Wine (page 301) would sit happily with a light sparkling shiraz.

THE BASICS

THE FOLLOWING PREPARATIONS are used numerous times throughout this book – most of them are standbys with which all good cooks should be familiar. ※ MAKING AND FREEZING stock when you can, preparing sauces from summer produce for winter use, keeping sugar syrup and tamarind liquid at the ready mean that, in conjunction with the preparations in Spice Mixes (see pages 31–47), your culinary repertoire can expand as if by magic. If you put the effort in when you have the time, you can reap the benefits when you don't – and enjoy the fruits of your labours.

Fish stock

A basic stock to have handy as it forms the basis for soups and sauces in many recipes. Use good-quality, fresh, cleaned fish heads and bones as they affect the flavour of the stock. Any deep-sea white-fleshed fish is suitable here.

heads and bones of 2 large fish
6 green onions, chopped
1 knob ginger, sliced
1 teaspoon white peppercorns
500 ml dry white wine
cold water

Wash fish heads thoroughly to remove all blood, then remove gills as they make stock bitter. Put all ingredients into a stockpot and cover with cold water. Bring to a boil, then simmer gently for 2 hours, skimming frequently to remove any scum. Strain stock through a conical sieve first, pressing to extract as much juice as possible, then discard solids. Strain stock again through a fine-meshed sieve to remove all sediment. Cool completely before refrigerating or freezing.

Crab, crayfish, rock lobster or marron stock

Make a shellfish stock following the instructions for Prawn Stock (at right), substituting other shells for the prawn shells.

Prawn stock

Use the heads and shells from fresh green prawns to make this rich, fragrant stock. Once cooled after cooking, it is best kept frozen unless used immediately.

6 tomatoes
1 kg prawn heads and shells
100 ml Chinese Shaoxing rice wine
50 ml vegetable oil
1 brown onion, chopped
6 cloves garlic, sliced
3 slices ginger
2 slices galangal
1 stalk lemongrass, finely sliced
2 red bird's-eye chillies, chopped
1 teaspoon Sichuan peppercorns
1 teaspoon fennel seeds
1 star anise
2 kaffir lime leaves, chopped
3 litres Fish Stock (at left)

Preheat oven to 200°C and roast tomatoes for 20 minutes until coloured and softened. Heat a large wok and add prawn heads and shells and toss over high heat until they start to colour, then deglaze wok with rice wine. Remove from heat.

Heat oil in a stockpot and sauté remaining ingredients except tomatoes, prawn heads and shells and stock over moderate heat until they start to colour and become aromatic. Add cooked prawn heads and shells and their juices, tomatoes and stock. Bring to a boil, then simmer gently for 2 hours, skimming frequently to remove any scum. Strain stock through a conical sieve first, pressing to extract as much juice as possible, then discard solids. Strain stock again through a fine-meshed sieve to remove all sediment. Allow to cool completely, then use or freeze immediately.

Dashi stock

A useful stock for Japanese-inspired preparations.

1 × 5 cm piece kombu (dried kelp)
3 litres cold water
1 snapper head
$1/4$ cup dried bonito flakes
1 teaspoon sea salt

Soak kombu in cold water for 1 hour, then drain. Wash snapper head thoroughly to remove all blood, then remove gills as they will make stock bitter. Put fish head into a stockpot with softened kombu, then add water and bring to a boil. Reduce heat and simmer gently for 30 minutes. Add bonito flakes and salt and simmer gently for 10 minutes. Strain stock through a fine-meshed sieve to remove all sediment, then discard solids. Taste stock and adjust seasoning if necessary. Allow to cool completely before refrigerating or freezing.

White chicken stock

1 chicken carcass
1 free-range, corn-fed chicken
several slices ginger
handful of green onion tops
several white peppercorns,
   freshly cracked
500 ml dry white wine
cold water

Wash chicken carcass in cold water to remove all blood. Put all ingredients into a stockpot and cover with water. Bring to a boil over gentle heat and simmer slowly for 2 hours, skimming frequently to remove any scum. Remove solids carefully (strip meat from chicken and keep for another use) and discard. Strain stock through a fine-meshed sieve to remove all sediment. Allow to cool completely before refrigerating or freezing.

Brown chicken stock

This is a richer stock than its white counterpart, the roasted bones and vegetables lending more colour and flavour to the stock.

3 kg chicken carcasses
250 ml red wine
12 tomatoes
2 brown onions, chopped
3 large carrots, chopped
2 heads garlic, cut in half
5 green onions, chopped
1 knob ginger, sliced
2 bay leaves
1 teaspoon black peppercorns
handful of flat-leaf parsley
5 litres White Chicken Stock (page 337)

Preheat oven to 200°C and brown chicken carcasses in a baking dish to render them of some of their fat. Deglaze pan with red wine. In another pan, roast tomatoes while bones are browning for 20 minutes until coloured and softened.

Sauté onion, carrot, garlic, green onion and ginger in a little oil in a large stockpot until fragrant. Stir in bay leaves, peppercorns and parsley, then add browned bones and deglazed juices, tomatoes and stock. Bring to a boil, then simmer gently for 3–4 hours, uncovered, skimming frequently to remove fat and scum.

Strain stock through a conical sieve, pressing firmly to extract as much juice as possible, then discard solids. Strain stock again through a fine-meshed sieve to remove all sediment. Allow stock to settle, removing any fat that rises as stock cools. Return stock to rinsed-out pot, then bring to a boil and reduce slightly for a thicker consistency and richer flavour, if required. Allow to cool completely before refrigerating or freezing.

Duck stock

Make duck stock when you have used the meat for another purpose – the bones have far too much flavour to throw out after one use only! A good stock to have on hand for making soups or a sauce, and necessary when making Five-spice Duck and Shiitake Mushroom Pies (see page 260).

4 duck carcasses
200 ml Chinese Shaoxing rice wine
2 brown onions, chopped
1 head garlic, cut in half
5 green onions, chopped
1 knob ginger, sliced
vegetable oil
2 bay leaves
1 teaspoon black peppercorns
handful of flat-leaf parsley
5 litres White Chicken Stock (page 337)

Preheat oven to 200°C and brown duck carcasses to render them of some of their fat, then deglaze pan with rice wine.

Sauté onion, garlic, green onion and ginger in a little oil in a stockpot until fragrant. Stir in bay leaves, peppercorns and parsley, then add browned bones and cover with stock. Bring to a boil, then simmer gently for 3 hours, uncovered, skimming frequently to remove fat and scum.

Strain stock through a conical sieve, pressing firmly to extract as much juice as possible, then discard solids. Strain stock again through a fine-meshed sieve to remove all sediment. Allow to cool, then remove any fat that rises as stock cools before refrigerating or freezing.

Squab stock

Make this stock when you have a supply of carcasses, perhaps after making Crispy-skinned Squab with Chinese Spice Salt (see page 149). Like duck carcasses, these bones contain lots of flavour worth capturing in stock.

10 squab *or* quail *or* pigeon carcasses
2 brown onions, chopped
2 leeks, sliced
6 large garlic cloves, sliced
1 carrot, sliced
vegetable oil
2 sprigs thyme
2 bay leaves
handful of flat-leaf parsley
2 teaspoons black peppercorns
300 ml red wine
2 litres White Chicken Stock (page 337)

Preheat oven to 200°C and brown carcasses. Sauté onion, leek, garlic and carrot in a little oil in a stockpot until softened. Add thyme, bay leaves, parsley and peppercorns and stir for a minute or two, then add wine and allow to boil for a few minutes.

Add browned bones and stock to stockpot, then bring to a boil. Reduce heat and simmer for 3 hours, skimming frequently to remove fat and scum. Strain stock through a conical sieve, pressing to extract as much juice as possible, then discard solids. Strain stock again through a fine-meshed sieve to remove all sediment. Skim any excess fat from surface with a ladle. Allow to cool before refrigerating or freezing.

Chinese master stock

A master stock for red-braising is a mandatory preparation in the kitchens of northern China. This stock should never be thrown out – as long as it is brought to a boil every week, and is kept refrigerated in a sealed container, it will grow better and richer with age and can be kept topped up. Every time you cook meat in it, just make sure you strain the stock through a fine-meshed sieve before refrigerating it to keep it free of any particles that may cause bacteria to grow. The Paramount master stock is now eight years old and is used constantly as I am addicted to the food cooked in it!

This master stock gives a rich, reddish-brown, lacquered appearance and a wonderfully penetrating flavour and aroma to meat and poultry. As Ken Hom says in the *Encyclopedia of Chinese Cookery Technique*, it is a stock 'that is at once salty from the two types of soy sauces; sweet from the sugar; spicy on account of the peppercorns, anise and fennel seeds; and mellow from the rice wine'. As the process of red-braising is a very gentle one, it also gives anything cooked in it a tender, velvety texture.

3 litres White Chicken Stock (page 337)
300 ml dark soy sauce
250 ml soy sauce
100 ml Chinese Shaoxing rice wine
40 g Chinese yellow rock sugar
2 star anise, broken
2 pieces cassia bark
1 teaspoon fennel seeds
1 teaspoon Sichuan peppercorns
1 black cardamom pod, cracked
2 pieces dried orange peel
2 red bird's-eye chillies, split
4 slices ginger
2 slices galangal
3 pieces liquorice root

Bring all ingredients to a boil in a large stockpot. Simmer gently for 1 hour, then strain through a fine-meshed sieve and discard solids. Allow stock to cool completely before refrigerating in a sealed container.

Beef/veal stock

A rich stock made from roasted beef bones, shanks and veal knuckles that forms the basis of good sauces and soups with a great depth of flavour.

2 kg beef bones
2 kg split shanks
2 kg veal knuckles
1 litre red wine
10 tomatoes
4 brown onions, chopped
2 large carrots
handful of flat-leaf parsley
1 tablespoon black peppercorns
2 sprigs thyme
cold water

Preheat oven to 200°C and brown bones in a baking dish for 30 minutes. Put bones into a large stockpot – there should be room to spare. Remove any fat from baking dish and deglaze with red wine, then tip wine and juices into stock. Roast tomatoes, onion and carrot in baking dish until softened, then add to stockpot with remaining ingredients and cover with cold water. Bring to a boil, then reduce heat and simmer gently for 6 hours, skimming regularly to remove scum.

Carefully remove bones, then strain stock through a conical sieve and discard solids. Strain stock again through a fine-meshed sieve to remove all sediment. Skim off any excess fat from surface with a ladle. Allow to cool completely before refrigerating or storing.

If your recipe calls for reduced stock or a demi-glace, simply cook stock until its volume decreases (reduces) and it becomes thicker and more unctuous so that it coats the back of a spoon.

Oxtail stock

Although this stock is prepared in the classic western method, I have incorporated the fresh flavours, aromatics and textures found in the wonderful Vietnamese pho soup to cut through and lighten its inherent richness. Ask your butcher to chop the oxtails into pieces for you. Oxtail stock is required to make Oxtail Consommé with Dumplings, Bean Sprouts, Mint and Chilli (see page 109).

2 grain-fed oxtails, cut into pieces
1 brown onion, quartered
4 cloves garlic
1 large carrot, quartered
100 ml port
2 teaspoons black peppercorns
4 sprigs thyme
3 sprigs flat-leaf parsley
4 litres White Chicken Stock (page 337)

Preheat oven to 200°C and roast oxtail, onion, garlic and carrot in an oiled baking dish for 30 minutes or until brown and crisp, then transfer to a large stockpot. Deglaze baking dish with port, then add port and juices to stockpot with peppercorns, herbs and stock. Bring to a simmer over gentle heat and continue simmering, very slowly, for 5 hours, skimming occasionally to remove fat and scum. Carefully remove oxtail and transfer to a tray to cool.

Strain stock through a conical sieve, pressing to extract as much juice as possible, then discard solids. Strain stock again through a fine-meshed sieve to remove all sediment. Allow stock to cool completely. Refrigerate overnight to settle, then remove any fat or sediment that may have risen to the surface and refrigerate or freeze.

White pork stock

This fragrant, Asian-inspired stock is required for Steamed Pork Belly with Star Anise Consommé (see page 185). It can also be used as a base for a soup such as Oxtail Consommé (page 109) – the fresh aromatic ingredients lift the flavour.

cold water
2 kg pork bones
1 pig's trotter
75 ml Chinese Shaoxing rice wine
handful of green onion tops
100 g chopped fennel
2 tablespoons sliced ginger
1 teaspoon white peppercorns,
    freshly cracked
2 bay leaves

Bring a stockpot of water to a boil and blanch pork bones and trotter for 2 minutes, then remove from pot and plunge into cold water and drain.

Return blanched bones to rinsed-out pot with remaining ingredients and pour in 5 litres cold water. Bring to a boil slowly, then reduce heat and simmer gently for 2 hours, skimming frequently to remove scum. Strain stock through a fine-meshed sieve to remove all sediment, then discard solids. Allow stock to cool completely, then skim surface of any excess fat before refrigerating or freezing.

Spiced vegetable stock

This versatile vegetable stock can be made ahead of time – it can be used as a base for a vegetable curry, added to a stir-fry or enriched with coconut milk to make a sauce.

1 head garlic
6 dried Chinese black mushrooms
2 cups warm water
25 ml vegetable oil
1 brown onion, chopped
2 carrots, peeled and finely sliced
1 stalk celery (with leaves), chopped
1 tablespoon minced ginger
5 green onions, sliced
3 red bird's-eye chillies, sliced
2 teaspoons black peppercorns
2 teaspoons Sichuan peppercorns
1 tablespoon minced turmeric
2 litres water
1 lemongrass stalk, finely sliced
50 ml fish sauce

Preheat oven to 180°C and roast garlic wrapped in foil for 30 minutes until softened. Unwrap and separate cloves. Meanwhile, soak dried mushrooms in warm water for 15 minutes until softened.

Heat oil in a stockpot and sweat onion, carrot, celery, ginger, green onion, chilli and roasted garlic over low heat until softened, about 15 minutes. Add mushrooms and their soaking liquid, both peppercorns, turmeric and water and bring to a boil. Simmer for 30 minutes, then add lemongrass and fish sauce and simmer for a further 15 minutes. Strain stock through a fine-meshed sieve, then discard solids. Allow to cool before refrigerating or freezing.

Egg noodles

The following quantities are sufficient for the dishes in this book that include egg noodles. However, if you want to make the noodles the feature of a meal, you will need to increase the quantities – simply multiply the ingredients as required. The following will feed three or four people as a main course.

250 g bread flour
3 large (61 g) eggs
20 ml olive oil
pinch of sea salt
rice flour

Blend all ingredients except rice flour in a food processor until dough forms a ball. Wrap dough in plastic film and refrigerate for 1 hour.

Cut dough into 4 pieces, then flatten each piece by hand or with a rolling pin. Pass each piece of dough through the rollers of a pasta machine, starting on the widest setting and working your way through each setting until you reach the finest. Dust dough with rice flour before moving onto next setting to prevent sticking (rice flour is used as it is free of glutens, which could toughen the dough at this stage).

Hang sheets of dough over a broom handle or back of a chair to dry for 10 minutes – this makes the dough easier to cut. Pass dough through spaghetti cutters on your pasta machine, then hang noodles over a broom handle or back of a chair for 30 minutes or until ready to cook.

Bring a large saucepan of water to a rolling boil, then add noodles and allow water to return to a boil. Cook for 2 minutes, then remove noodles from heat with a sieve and drain. If not eating immediately, refresh noodles under cold running water to stop cooking, then drain and toss lightly with a little oil to prevent sticking. To reheat, immerse noodles in boiling water for 10 seconds, then drain.

Black ink noodles

The following quantities are sufficient for the dishes in this book that include these noodles. However, if you want to make the noodles the feature of a meal, you will need to increase the quantities – simply multiply the ingredients as required. The following will feed three or four people as a main course.

3 large (61 g) eggs
2 teaspoons squid ink
2 teaspoons olive oil
320 g bread flour
pinch of sea salt

Blend eggs, squid ink and oil in a food processor, then add flour and salt and blend until dough forms a ball. Wrap dough in plastic film and refrigerate for 1 hour. Pass dough through pasta machine as instructed for Egg Noodles (see page 340), then cut and cook as instructed.

Pepper noodles

The following quantities are sufficient for the dishes in this book that include these noodles. However, if you want to make the noodles the feature of a meal, you will need to increase the quantities – simply multiply the ingredients as required. The following will feed three or four people as a main course.

250 g bread flour
3 large (61 g) eggs
20 ml olive oil
pinch of sea salt
2 teaspoons freshly ground black pepper

Blend all ingredients in a food processor until dough forms a ball. Wrap in plastic film and refrigerate for 1 hour. Pass dough through pasta machine as instructed for Egg Noodles (see page 340), then cut and cook as instructed.

Mustard spaghetti

The following quantities are sufficient for the dishes in this book that include this spaghetti. However, if you want to make the spaghetti the feature of a meal, you will need to increase the quantities – simply multiply the ingredients as required. The following will feed four people as a main course.

3 eggs
2 teaspoons grain mustard
$1/2$ teaspoon sea salt
30 ml olive oil
350 g plain flour

Blend eggs, mustard, salt and oil in a food processor, then add flour and blend until dough forms a ball. Wrap dough in plastic film and refrigerate for 1 hour. Pass dough through pasta machine as instructed for Egg Noodles (see page 340), then cut and cook as instructed.

Saffron noodles

The following quantities are sufficient for the dishes in this book that include these noodles. However, if you want to make the noodles the feature of a meal, you will need to increase the quantities – simply multiply the ingredients as required. The following will feed three or four people as a main course.

25 ml reduced Tomato Essence (page 342)
$1/2$ teaspoon saffron threads
225 g plain flour
50 g gluten flour
$1/2$ teaspoon sea salt
1 teaspoon white pepper, freshly ground
3 large (61 g) eggs

Slowly bring reduced tomato essence and saffron to a simmer to infuse, then allow to cool. Blend all ingredients in a food processor until dough forms a ball. Wrap dough in plastic film and refrigerate for 1 hour. Pass dough through pasta machine as instructed for Egg Noodles (see page 340), then cut and cook as instructed.

Seaweed noodles

The following quantities are sufficient for the dishes in this book that include these noodles. However, if you want to make the noodles the feature of a meal, you will need to increase the quantities – simply multiply the ingredients as required. The following will feed three or four people as a main course.

2 nori seaweed sheets
250 g bread flour
$1/2$ teaspoon sea salt
3 large (61 g) eggs
2 teaspoons extra-virgin olive oil

Toast nori sheets over direct flame for a few seconds until crisp and colour changes to a darker green. Chop sheets and grind to a powder. Blend flour, salt and ground nori, then add eggs and oil and blend until dough forms a ball. Wrap in plastic film and refrigerate for 1 hour. Pass dough through pasta machine as instructed for Egg Noodles (see page 340), then cut and cook as instructed.

Tamarind liquid

The most refined way to use tamarind is to make tamarind liquid, getting maximum flavour without the coarse, fibrous texture of the pulp.

tamarind pulp
water

Simmer 1 part tamarind pulp to 4 parts water for 30 minutes or so, then pass pulp and water through a coarse-meshed or conical sieve. Discard fibre and seeds. Refrigerate tamarind liquid for up to 1 month.

Tomato essence

An exquisite way of adding the intense flavour of summer's best tomatoes to sauces and the like, and a great way of extending, via freezing, the season.

5 kg tomatoes

Pulp tomatoes, then drain in a jelly bag or double layer of muslin suspended over a bucket for 24 hours to yield 1 litre essence. To keep essence clear, do not push or force pulp through bag. To make reduced tomato essence, bring essence to a boil and reduce by half. This increases the sweetness slightly and intensifies the flavour. Freeze in ice-cube trays for later use.

Saffron butter

Use as a flavouring for enriching sauces and stir in at the last minute.

50 ml Tomato Essence (at left)
$^{1}/_{2}$ teaspoon *or* 2 g saffron threads
250 unsalted butter, softened

Bring tomato essence to a boil in a small saucepan, then add saffron and infuse for a few minutes only. Whip butter in a food processor, then blend in saffron liquid gradually until incorporated. Refrigerate in a sealed container.

Caramelised onion

Serve as a condiment, use as a tart filling or even add it to bread dough – see Onion Nigella Bread on page 269. Caramelised onion is especially good made with the sweet, golden Kununurra onions from the Kimberley region of Western Australia, which appear in spring.

brown onions, finely sliced
olive oil

Cook onion in a good quantity of olive oil in a wide, heavy-based pan over moderate heat until onion caramelises and tastes sweet. Strain, reserving flavoured oil for other cooking. Refrigerate for up to 2 weeks.

Fried shallots

Made from Asian shallots, these crisp, wafery slices can be sprinkled over stir-fries, noodle dishes, curries and so on for a richly flavoured texture contrast. They can be bought from Asian food stores, but are easy to make at home.

red shallots
vegetable oil

Slice shallots finely lengthwise, then fry over moderate heat in a good quantity of oil until golden brown – the shallots should float freely in the oil as they cook. Remove pan from heat immediately and pour hot oil through a sieve into a stainless steel bowl. Spread fried shallots on paper towel to drain and cool. Reserve flavoured oil for other cooking. Store fried shallots in a sealed container to keep crisp.

Fried garlic

Garlic cloves can be sliced finely and cooked in the same manner as Fried Shallots (at left).

Ginger juice

2 ginger roots, minced
cold water

Put ginger into a food processor with just enough cold water to wet it. Blend for a minute or two, then press through a fine-meshed sieve to extract as much juice as possible. Reserve ginger pulp for flavouring a stock or sauce. Refrigerate juice in a jar.

Cucumber juice

This green juice imparts a mild cucumber flavour and is useful for adding flavour to salad dressings.

1 cucumber
water

Peel cucumber, then chop flesh roughly. Blend flesh with a little water in a food processor. Pass juice through a fine-meshed sieve and discard pulp. Refrigerate cucumber juice for up to 3 days.

Horseradish cream

Great with grilled meat or sausages and particularly good with kangaroo (see pages 174 and 188). Try it spooned into scrambled eggs with smoked salmon, too.

$^1/_4$ cup crème fraîche *or* sour cream
1 tablespoon finely grated horseradish
$^1/_2$ teaspoon freshly ground white pepper
2 teaspoons finely chopped chives

Mix all ingredients gently. Refrigerate in a sealed jar for up to 2 days.

Roasted garlic aïoli

This rich mayonnaise, heady with the mellow flavour of roasted garlic, is wonderful with other robustly flavoured preparations, such as the pancetta-stuffed sardine fillets on page 115.

2 heads garlic
$^1/_2$ teaspoon sea salt
25 ml strained lemon juice
2 egg yolks
40 ml white-wine vinegar
$^1/_4$ teaspoon freshly ground white pepper
250 ml extra-virgin olive oil
250 ml vegetable oil

Preheat oven to 180°C and roast garlic wrapped in foil for 30 minutes or until soft. Squeeze garlic from cloves and mix to a paste with sea salt in a mortar and pestle. Blend garlic mixture with lemon juice, egg yolks, vinegar and pepper in a food processor. With the motor running, slowly drizzle in combined oils in a thin, steady stream until sauce emulsifies and thickens. Refrigerate in a sealed container for up to 1 week.

Sugar syrup

castor sugar
water

Bring an equal quantity of castor sugar and water to a boil and cook until sugar has dissolved, about 5 minutes. Allow to cool before refrigerating. One litre water and 1 kg sugar yields about 1.5 litres sugar syrup. Keeps indefinitely. Sugar syrup can also be made with brown sugar.

Coriander peanut pesto

An Asian version of the Mediterranean pesto – spoon it over hot noodles, serve it with won tons or stir it into soups.

200 ml peanut oil
40 g raw blanched peanuts
2 green bird's-eye chillies, minced
1 tablespoon minced ginger
8 cloves garlic, minced
100 g *or* 2 firmly packed cup Thai *or* holy basil leaves
25 g *or* $^1/_2$ firmly packed cup laksa (Vietnamese mint) leaves
100 g *or* 2 firmly packed cups coriander leaves
1 teaspoon shaved palm sugar
2 teaspoons fish sauce
20 ml strained lime juice

Heat oil in a frying pan and fry peanuts over moderate heat until golden. Strain peanuts from oil and allow to cool. Reserve oil. Blend cooled peanuts in a food processor with chilli, ginger and garlic. Add herbs and half the reserved oil, then blend to a smooth paste. Blend in palm sugar, fish sauce and lime juice until herbs are finely minced. Gradually pour in enough remaining oil with motor running to make a smooth paste. Spoon into a container, then cover with a film of oil and seal. Refrigerate for up to 2 months, but best used soon after it has been made.

Saffron rouille

Another rich mayonnaise, this time spiced with the luxurious saffron. Great with fish and shellfish soups, and required for the chargrilled octopus salad on page 84. Look for roasted pimiento strips in Spanish food stores.

2 heads garlic
1 soft-boiled egg
2 egg yolks
$1/4$ teaspoon saffron threads
1 tablespoon roasted pimiento strips
$1/2$ teaspoon Dijon mustard
$1/2$ teaspoon sweet paprika
20 ml strained lemon juice
few drops of Tabasco
$1/2$ teaspoon sea salt
$1/2$ teaspoon freshly ground white pepper
200 ml fruity extra-virgin olive oil

Preheat oven to 180°C and roast garlic wrapped in foil for 30 minutes or until soft. Squeeze garlic from cloves into a food processor and blend to a smooth paste with soft-boiled egg, egg yolks, saffron and pimiento. Add remaining ingredients except oil and pulse to blend. With the motor running, slowly drizzle in oil until sauce emulsifies and thickens. Refrigerate for at least 2 hours to allow colour and flavour to develop. Before serving, stir to incorporate saffron. Refrigerate in a sealed container for up to 1 week.

Crème fraîche pastry

I use this short, flaky pastry to make the Five-Spice Duck and Shiitake Mushroom Pies (see page 260) and other pies with dry fillings. I don't recommend it for tart cases as it is too short and will fall apart. This quantity will yield enough pastry for 6 individual pies.

125 g cold unsalted butter
200 g plain flour
$1/2$ teaspoon sea salt
125 g crème fraîche

Chill bowl and blade of a food processor in refrigerator. Chop butter into chunks and, while still cold, blend with flour and salt in food processor until mixture resembles breadcrumbs. Add crème fraîche and pulse until just incorporated. Don't overwork dough at this stage or pastry will be difficult to handle when rolling. Form pastry into a ball by hand, then wrap in plastic film and refrigerate for 2 hours.

Roll and cut pastry as required. Keep pastry as cool as possible when working with it – you may need to return it to the refrigerator as you roll and cut. Refrigerate assembled pies for at least 1 hour before baking. Preheat oven to 220°C and bake pies for 16 minutes until golden.

Chickpea batter

This batter is used to make Prawn Fritters with Pickled Eggplant Yoghurt Salad (see page 88) and Vegetable Pakoras with Eggplant Pickle (page 202). Try your hand at making your own fritter combinations using this batter.

2 teaspoons minced garlic
vegetable oil
2 teaspoons sea salt
$1/2$ teaspoon chilli powder
$1/2$ teaspoon ground turmeric
1 teaspoon Paramount's Garam Masala (page 34)
$1/2$ teaspoon freshly ground black pepper
100 g chickpea flour
1 teaspoon baking powder
100 ml warm water

Blend garlic, 40 ml vegetable oil, salt and spices in a food processor. Blend in flour and baking powder, then add water and blend to a smooth batter. Refrigerate for 2 hours before using.

Heat vegetable oil in a deep-fryer to 180°C. Coat your chosen ingredients with batter and cook as instructed – for example, prawns need only 2 minutes, and vegetable fritters take about 4 minutes. Drain on paper towel.

Samosa pastry

I give two recipes for samosas in this book (see pages 246 and 248), but you may also like to try your own filling combinations.

200 g plain flour
50 g chickpea flour
1 teaspoon sea salt
100 g ghee, melted
75 ml warm water
vegetable oil for deep-frying

Blend all ingredients except vegetable oil in a food processor until dough forms a ball. Wrap dough in plastic film and rest at room temperature for 2 hours.

Roll pastry into a long sausage. Cut pastry into 18 pieces, then roll pieces out thinly into rounds. Spoon your chosen filling into centre of each round, then fold in half and then in half again to make a triangle, pressing edges together firmly with fingertips to seal.

Heat oil in a deep-fryer to 180°C and fry a few samosas at a time for 5 minutes until golden and crisp – keep samosas submerged in hot oil with a slotted spoon to ensure even cooking. Drain on paper towel.

Sweet pastry

A versatile sweet pastry for dessert work – the addition of sugar ensures a crisp and delicate result. This quantity is sufficient for six 12 cm tarts or a 24 cm one.

80 g icing sugar
125 g plain flour
75 g unsalted butter, diced
2 egg yolks
$^1/_2$ vanilla bean, split

Chill bowl and blade of a food processor in refrigerator. Sift icing sugar and flour, then blend with butter in food processor until mixture resembles breadcrumbs. Add egg yolks and scrape in seeds from vanilla bean, then blend until dough just comes together. Wrap dough in plastic film and refrigerate for 2 hours.

Roll dough out on a cold, floured surface until 5 mm thick, then cut it into the required shape(s). Grease your chosen tin(s) with butter if it is not non-stick, then line. Refrigerate pastry for 30 minutes before baking. Preheat oven to 160°C. Blind bake pastry until crisp and pale golden. Small tart shells will take 11 minutes; a larger one will take about 18 minutes.

Coconut wafers

These delicious wafers accompany Pina Colada Mousse with Spiced Pineapple (see page 319). This quantity is sufficient for six wafers to accompany six 150 ml bavarois.

50 g unsalted butter
50 g castor sugar
2 egg whites
50 g plain flour
25 g shredded coconut

Cream butter and castor sugar in an electric mixer until pale and creamy, about 10 minutes. Fold in unbeaten egg whites a little at a time. Mix in flour until smooth. Refrigerate dough for 30 minutes.

Using a palette knife, spread a thin layer of wafer mixture over a buttered and floured 30 cm × 24 cm baking tray, then sprinkle evenly with shredded coconut. Refrigerate until firm, about 1 hour – this prevents wafer from fracturing during cooking.

Preheat oven to 160°C. Make a template by moulding cardboard around a 150 ml dariole mould and cut to same shape. The template should look like a semi-circular collar and will bend so as to cover outside surface of mould.

Bake chilled wafer mixture for 4 minutes until set but not coloured. Cut around template on hot wafer with a sharp knife to make 6 biscuits. Lift off extraneous mixture. Return wafers to oven and cook for another 3–4 minutes until pale golden brown. Mould hot wafers quickly around empty moulds the same size as those containing bavarois. Hold briefly until wafers begin to cool and set. The wafers should resemble volcanoes!

GLOSSARY

anchovies, dried Chinese

The Chinese excel at the art of drying fish and seafood, and these ingredients are a feature in much of their cooking, where they add strength of flavour. Dried anchovies impart an intense flavour when used in stocks and soups. Available in packets from Asian food stores, they should be stored in an airtight container once opened.

belacan

The Malaysian version of fermented, compressed prawn (shrimp) paste, known as kapi in Thailand, trasi in Indonesia and mam ruoc in Vietnam. It is made by salting small shrimps, fermenting them in the sun and then mashing them to a paste. Belacan is dark brown in colour and is usually sold in block form. When dry-roasted and crumbled and added to a dish, it gives a complexity of flavour. Belacan has a pungent aroma and should be stored in a plastic bag in an airtight container in the refrigerator.

betel leaves

Dark-green leaves of Indian origin that grow on a creeper vine in hot, humid climates. They are used in Indian and Thai cooking, and are highly regarded for their stimulant and antiseptic properties. Betel leaves are available at some Asian food stores (sold in bunches). They are not related to the betel nut (see Spice Index).

dal

Three groups make up this legume family: lentils (toor dal and masoor dal), peas (chana dal) and beans (urad dal). All varieties of dal can be purchased from Indian food stores and some of the more common ones are also available at health-food shops and supermarkets. An important source of protein and fibre, dal is a versatile ingredient that offers a panorama of textures and flavours. Dals cook more quickly when they have been soaked in cold water for 1 hour beforehand. Never add salt to dal preparations while they are cooking or they will remain hard; add it at the end of the cooking process, after you have taken the pan off the heat.

chana dal

Also referred to as gram lentils or Bengal gram, this yellow dal is a small, split chick pea, larger and firmer in texture than other varieties of dal, with a strong, nutty taste. Chana dal stands up well to longer cooking. It can be ground to make flour (also known as besan or gram flour).

toor dal

Small, pale-yellow lentils that can be purchased oily, with a glossy surface, or non-oily, where the lentil has a matte appearance. The oily ones need to be soaked before cooking. Quick to cook and soft in texture with a subtle nutty flavour, cooked toor dal can also be puréed to make a batter.

masoor dal

Small, red lentils with a musky flavour. Masoor dal is the ideal dal to use with strong flavours such as onion, ginger, garlic, tamarind and red meat. The colour fades to a pale yellow when cooked.

urad dal

These beans, sometimes referred to as black gram, are black when whole and white when husked and split. Small and oblong in shape, they have a rich, heavy taste and are glutinous and develop a thick, creamy texture when cooked. Used with potatoes and other root vegetables, they are also great teamed with mustard. Urad dal is an essential ingredient for making the famous idli (steamed rice cakes), a south Indian speciality.

kapi

The Thai version of fermented, compressed prawn (shrimp) paste, known as belacan in Malaysia, trasi in Indonesia and mam ruoc in Vietnam. Kapi is slightly pink to purple in colour (not dark like its southern relatives) with a strong, pungent aroma. A rich source of protein and vitamins, it is essential for authentic flavouring in Thai dishes. Available in small plastic containers at Asian food stores.

mitzuba leaves

Small, green leaves of Japanese origin, used in salads. Also known as trefoil, mitzuba is a type of wild chervil. It is sold at Japanese food stores and by some fruit and vegetable suppliers. Other small green leaves can be substituted if mitzuba is not available.

mizuna leaves

Delicate, green, feathery salad leaves, related to herb mustard, available loose or in bunches from better greengrocers.

mushrooms

black wood fungus

An edible tree fungus, sometimes referred to as the cloud ear mushroom, which has a subtle mushroom flavour and a crunchy texture that absorbs the flavours with which it is cooked. Black wood fungus is available fresh in small punnets from some greengrocers and supermarkets, or in its dried form from Asian food stores.

dried Chinese black

These fragrant black mushrooms, related to the Japanese shiitake, impart a gentle mushroom flavour and also take on the flavours with which they are cooked. Available at Asian food stores, they are a staple in Chinese cooking. Reconstitute in warm water for 30 minutes before using.

shiitake

A mushroom of Japanese origin with a black cap, fine stem and distinct meaty, fleshy flavour and aroma. Now grown fresh in Australia, shiitake are also available in dried form at Asian food stores.

shimeji

Delicate, small, pale-coloured mushrooms that grow in clusters, shimeji mushrooms are grown hydroponically and are similar to oyster mushrooms. They are available in small punnets at discerning fruit and vegetable providores and Japanese food stores.

nori seaweed sheets

Paper-thin nori sheets are made from laver, a highly nutritious seaweed. Used predominantly for making sushi, they are available already toasted (greenish in colour) or untoasted (black) from Asian and Japanese food stores. Toasted nori sheets have improved flavour and texture. To toast, hold a black nori sheet with a pair of tongs over a direct flame for a few seconds. Once a packet of nori sheets has been opened, the sheets should be kept in a sealed, dry container as they deteriorate when exposed to moisture.

onions

golden shallot

The European variety of shallot, larger than its Asian cousin. These shallots are golden brown in colour with thicker skins than red shallots. They are very easy to peel and have pale, creamy flesh with a raw sweetness and a mild, subtle flavour without the usual 'bite' of an onion.

green onion (scallion)

These onions have a firm white base (with no onion bulb) and green leaves that are of uniform size throughout, and a very mild flavour. They are sometimes referred to as spring onions or shallots, highlighting the need for vegetable providores to take responsibility for correct labelling. Green onions can be used raw or cooked.

Kununurra onion

A medium-sized, golden sweet onion grown in the Kimberley region of northern Western Australia. Kununurra onions are available in spring and early summer and have less acidity and bite than brown onions.

red onion

A mild, sweet-tasting onion that can be used raw in salads and does not have the usual bite of a brown onion. Also known as Spanish onions, red onions are available all year.

red shallot

The Asian variety of shallot, smaller than the golden shallot and similar in size to garlic. Red shallots have fine skin, a reddish tinge to the flesh and a sweet, strong taste and perfume.

spring onion
see green onion

pork sausage, Thai

Pork that has been soured with tamarind and has a slightly fermented flavour. It is made locally and is available fresh in small packets from Asian food stores. You can substitute Chinese pork sausage, but it has a different, saltier taste and texture.

scallops, dried

Round and golden, with the appearance of butterscotch toffee (but not the flavour!), these are sea scallops that have been sundried. They are used to flavour soups, stocks and sauces. Sometimes referred to as conpoy on Chinese menus, they are available from Chinese herbalists or medicine shops. Dried scallops are expensive to buy and have a full-bodied, intense flavour and aroma – so use sparingly.

shallots
see **onions**

shiso leaves

Leaves from the perilla plant, sometimes also referred to as the beefsteak plant, related to the mint family and Japanese in origin. The leaves can be either green or red and are small, delicate and aromatic. They are used to flavour salads, rice and sashimi. Available at Japanese food stores (usually sold in small bunches).

A COOK'S CONVERSION TABLE

Liquid measurements

metric	imperial	
5 ml	⅙ fl oz	1 teaspoon
10 ml	⅓ fl oz	2 teaspoons
20 ml	½ fl oz	1 tablespoon
40 ml	1 fl oz	1 tablespoon + 2 teaspoons
60 ml	2 fl oz	¼ cup
125 ml	4 fl oz	½ cup
250 ml	8 fl oz	1 cup

Linear measurements

metric	imperial
3 mm	⅛ inch
5 mm	¼ inch
10 mm (1 cm)	½ inch
2 cm	¾ inch
2.5 cm	1 inch
5 cm	2 inches

Dry measurements

metric	imperial
15 g	½ oz
28 g (25–30 g)	1 oz
40 g	1½ oz
50 g	2 oz
125 g	4 oz (¼ lb)
150 g	5 oz
200 g	7 oz
225 g	8 oz (½ lb)
450 g	1 lb
500 g	1 lb 1 oz
1 kg	2 lb 2 oz

Oven temperatures

Celsius	Fahrenheit
100°C	210°F
125°C	240°F
150°C	300°F
180°C	350°F
200°C	400°F
220°C	450°F
250°C	500°F

SPICE SUPPLIERS

Some spice shops and suppliers with which I am familiar in Australia and abroad are listed below. (This list is by no means exhaustive; add your favourites for an even better repertoire.)

Sydney

BKK Food Centre – 53 Park Road, Cabramatta 2166 (02) 9726 8088

Burlington Centre – Thomas Street, Haymarket 2000 (02) 9281 2777

The Essential Ingredient – 4 Australia Street, Camperdown 2050
(02) 9550 5477

Fiji Market – 59 King Street, Newtown 2042 (02) 9517 2054

Herbie's Spices – 745 Darling Street, Rozelle 2039 (02) 9555 6035

Hong Lee Trading – 21 Campbell Street, Haymarket 2000
(02) 9212 6793

Moses Spices – 108 Brighton Boulevard, North Bondi 2026
(02) 9130 3234

Shiu On Tong – 22 Campbell Street, Haymarket 2000 (02) 9211 1719

Simon Johnson Purveyor of Quality Foods – 181 Harris Street,
Pyrmont 2009 (02) 9552 2522
also at 55 Queen Street, Woollahra 2025 (02) 9328 6888

Tokyo Mart – Shop 27, Northbridge Plaza, Sailors Bay Road,
Northbridge 2063 (02) 9958 6860

Melbourne

Bombay Bazaar – 197 Brunswick Street, Fitzroy 3065 (03) 9417 2123

Casa Iberica – 25 Johnson Street, Fitzroy 3065 (03) 9419 4420

Curry Creations – Shop 712, Prahran Market, 177 Commercial Road,
South Yarra 3141 (03) 9827 1344

Great Eastern Grocery – 185 Russell Street, Melbourne 3000
(03) 9663 3716

Let's Eat – Elizabeth Street, Prahran 3141 (next to market)
(03) 9520 3287

Maison de Tunisie – 24 Smith Street, Collingwood 3066
(03) 9416 1385

Simon Johnson Purveyor of Quality Foods – 12–14 St David Street,
Fitzroy 3065 (03) 9486 9456

The Vital Ingredient – 206 Clarendon Street, South Melbourne 3205
(03) 9696 3511

Adelaide

Asian Bazaar – 11 Market Street, Adelaide 5000 (08) 8231 4242

Asian Kitchen – 40 Gouger Street, Adelaide 5000 (08) 8231 2021

Athens Gourmet Foods – 3 Western Mall, Central Market, Adelaide 5000
(08) 8231 2260

Bottega Rotolo – 43 The Parade West, Kent Town 5067 (08) 8362 0455

Kuo Chi Grocery – Shop 2, 88 Gouger Street, Adelaide 5000
(08) 8212 7130

Lien Heng – 7 Western Mall, Central Market, Adelaide 5000
(08) 8212 5373

Brisbane

Rock'n Roll Fruit'n Deli – 500 Logan Road, Greenslopes 4120
(07) 3394 3522

Perth

Kakulas Bros – 183 William Street, Northbridge 6003 (08) 9328 5285

Kong's Trading – 425 William Street, Northbridge 6003 (08) 9328 2943

Lucky Import & Export – 112 Brisbane Street, Highgate 6003
(08) 9328 9262

Paris

Fauchon – 26 Place de la Madeleine, 8th arrondissement (1) 4742 6011

Hediard – 126 rue du Bac, 6th (1) 4544 0198
also at 21 Place de la Madeleine, 8th (1) 4266 4436

Izrael – 30 rue François-Miron, 4th (1) 4272 6623

General streets of interest:

Belleville, in the 19th arrondissement – for Vietnamese, Thai and
Moroccan food

Menilmontant, in the 20th – for African food; street food market on
Saturday mornings for many exotic ingredients

rue Faubourg St Denis, in the 10th – for various shops with Tunisian
food products and spices

rue Montorgueil, near rue Rambuteau, in the 1st – a fabulous food street,
the only remnant of Les Halles

rue Mouffetard, in the 5th – a popular food-merchant street which winds
up the hill

London

Bluebird Foodmarket – 350 Kings Road, Chelsea SW3 5UU
(0171) 559 1222

Harvey Nichols Food Emporium – 5th Floor, 109–125 Knightsbridge
SW1X 75J (0171) 235 5000

The Spice Shop – 1 Blenheim Crescent, Notting Hill W11 2EE
(0171) 221 4448

Talad Thai – 320 Upper Richmond Road SW15 6TL (0181) 789 8084

Waitrose Supermarkets – throughout London

Hamburg

Hot Spice Museum – Paap & Vierk Verlag, Am Sandtorkai 32, 20457
  (40) 367989

Tokyo

The Asian Market – Shokuan Dori, Shinjuku-ku

Honma Shoten (Chinese Grocery Store) – 2-6-5 Nisui Asakusa, Taito-ku,
  Kappabashi-dori

Isetan Food Hall – Basement, Isetan department store, 3-14-1 Shinjuku,
  Shinjuku-ku (3) 3352 1111

Matsuya Food Hall – Basement, Matsuya department store, 3-6-1 Ginza,
  Chuo-ku (3) 3567 1211

New York City

Angelica Herb & Spice – 147 1st Avenue 10003 (212) 677 1549

Balducci's – 424 Avenue of the Americas 10011 (212) 673 2600

Dean and Deluca – 560 Broadway (cnr Prince Street) 10012
  (212) 226 6800

Gourmet Garage – 453 Broome Street 10013 (212) 941 5850

Zabar's Gourmet Foods – 249 West 80th Street 10024 (212) 787 2000

San Francisco

Harvest Ranch Market – 2285 Market Street 94114 (415) 626 0805

La Palma Mexicatessen – 2884 24th Street 94110 (415) 647 1500

Seattle

World Spice Merchants – Pike Place Market, 1509 Western Ave
  98101-1521 (206) 682 7274

Other cities in the USA

Baltimore, Maryland – Vanns Spices, 1238 Joppa Road 21286
  (410) 583 1643

Pittsburgh, Pennsylvania – Bachri's, 3821 Willow Avenue 15234
  (412) 343 2213

Santa Fe, New Mexico – Coyote Cafe General Store, 132 West
  Water Street 87501-2137 (505) 982 2454

Vancouver

Meinhardt Fine Foods – 3002 Granville Street V6H 3J8 (604) 732 4405

Singapore

Jason's Gourmet Supermarket – 1 Claymore Drive, #01-01 Orchard
  Towers, 229594 (65) 235 4355

Rasool Shop – Block 664, Buffalo Road #01-03, 210664 (65) 298 8786

Hong Kong

E-SARN – 19 Stone Nullah Street, Johnson Road, Wan Chai
  (65) 2591 9768

Indian Provision Stores – Ground floor, 34 Bowrington Road, Wan Chai
  (952) 2891 8324

The Oriental Store – 49 Sharp Street East, Wan Chai (852) 2891 8442

Shing Fat Coconut & Spices – Ground floor, 18 Spring Garden Lane,
  Wan Chai (65) 2572 7725

Jakarta

P.D. Jaya Abadi – Jalan Medan, Glodok Selatan No. 39–41, 11120
  (21) 629 7888

Sekali Coba Pasti Terasa – Pasar Mayestik wet markets, South Jakarta
  12120 (21) 7279 3831

BIBLIOGRAPHY

Here are some books that you will find invaluable if you are as addicted to spice as I am. I use many of them as constant references.

Al Hashimi, Miriam. *Traditional Arabic Cooking*. Garnet Publishing, UK, 1993.

Alexander, Stephanie. *The Cook's Companion*. Viking, Ringwood, 1996.

Alford, Jeffrey and Duguid, Naomi. *Flatbread and Flavours: A Baker's Atlas*. Morrow, USA, 1995.

Bharadwaj, Monisha. *The Indian Pantry*. Kyle Cathie, UK, 1996.

Boxer, Arabella. *The Hamlyn Spice Book*. Hamlyn, UK, 1997.

Cost, Bruce. *Ginger East to West*. Aris, Berkeley, 1984.

—— *Asian Ingredients*. Morrow, USA, 1988.

David, Elizabeth. *Spices, Salt and Aromatics in the English Kitchen*. Penguin, Harmondsworth, 1970.

—— *Harvest of the Cold Months*. Penguin, Harmondsworth, 1994.

Hom, Ken. *Encyclopedia of Chinese Cooking Techniques*. Ebury Press, UK, 1984.

Hutton, Wendy. *Singapore Food*. Ure Smith, Australia, 1984.

Jaffrey, Madhur. *A Taste of India*. Pavilion, UK, 1985.

Lambert Ortiz, Elisabeth. *The Encyclopedia of Herbs, Spices and Flavourings*. Dorling Kindersley, UK, 1993.

Lin, Hsiang Ju and Lin, Tsuifeng. *Chinese Gastronomy*. Jove Publications Inc., New York, 1977.

Miller, Mark. *The Great Chile Book*. Ten Speed Press, Berkeley, 1991.

Morris, Sally and Mackley, Lesley. *The Spice Ingredients Cookbook*. Lorenz Books, London, 1997.

Norman, Jill. *The Complete Book of Spices*. Dorling Kindersley, UK, 1990.

Owen, Sri. *Indonesian Regional Food and Cookery*. Transworld, UK, 1994.

Patnaik, Naveen. *The Garden of Life: An Introduction to the Healing Plants of India*. HarperCollins, New Delhi, 1993.

Pruthi, J.S. *Spices and Condiments*. National Book Trust, India, 1976.

Quintana, Patricia. *The Taste of Mexico*. Stewart, Tabori & Chang, USA, 1986.

Roden, Claudia. *A New Book of Middle Eastern Food*. Penguin, Harmondsworth, 1986.

—— *Mediterranean Cooking*. BBC Books, London, 1987.

Sahni, Julie. *Savouring Spices and Herbs*. William Morrow, New York, 1996.

Santich, Barbara. *Looking for Flavour*. Wakefield Press, Adelaide, 1996.

So, Yan-kit. *Classic Food of China*. Macmillan, London, 1992.

Solomon, Charmaine. *The Complete Asian Cookbook* (rev. edn). Lansdowne, Sydney, 1992.

—— *Encyclopedia of Asian Food*. William Heinemann, Melbourne, 1996.

Stobart, Tom. *The Cook's Encyclopedia*. Macmillan, UK, 1982.

Tannahill, Reay. *Food in History*. Penguin, Harmondsworth, 1973.

Thompson, David. *Classic Thai Cuisine*. Simon & Schuster Australia, Sydney, 1993.

Trager, James. *The Food Chronology*. Henry Holt, USA, 1995.

Tropp, Barbara. *The Modern Art of Chinese Cooking*. William Morrow, New York, 1982.

Wine

Some resources we use at Paramount that you may find helpful as a general guide include the following.

Allen, Max. *Red and White*. Hamlyn/Reed, Sydney, 1997.

Australian and New Zealand Wine Industry Journal Varietal Report (published monthly).

Australian Gourmet Traveller's *Wine* magazine (published bi-monthly).

Halliday, James. *Wine Atlas of Australia and New Zealand*. Angus & Robertson/HarperCollins, Sydney, 1991.

Robinson, Jancis, ed. *Oxford Companion to Wine*. Oxford University Press, Oxford, 1994.

Robinson, Jancis. *Confessions of a Wine Lover*. Penguin, Harmondsworth, 1997.

Shield, Mark and Hooke, Huon. *The Penguin Good Australian Wine Guide*. Penguin, Ringwood (published annually).

Stevenson, Tom. *The World Wine Encyclopedia*. Dorling Kindersley, UK, 1988.

INDEX

Numbers in **bold** indicate photographs.